Matchsticks Contemplating Eternity

Matchsticks Contemplating Eternity

Life, Death, and Faith in What Is

GREGORY W. BROWN

WIPF & STOCK · Eugene, Oregon

MATCHSTICKS CONTEMPLATING ETERNITY
Life, Death, and Faith in What Is

Copyright © 2022 Gregory W. Brown. All rights reserved. Except for brief quotations in critical publications or reviews, no part of this book may be reproduced in any manner without prior written permission from the publisher. Write: Permissions, Wipf and Stock Publishers, 199 W. 8th Ave., Suite 3, Eugene, OR 97401.

Resource Publications
An Imprint of Wipf and Stock Publishers
199 W. 8th Ave., Suite 3
Eugene, OR 97401

www.wipfandstock.com

PAPERBACK ISBN: 978-1-6667-3408-9
HARDCOVER ISBN: 978-1-6667-2956-6
EBOOK ISBN: 978-1-6667-2957-3

.   JANUARY 7, 2022 10:33 AM

All Scripture quotations, unless otherwise indicated, are taken from the Holy Bible, New International Version®, NIV®. Copyright ©1973, 1978, 1984, 2011 by Biblica, Inc.™ Used by permission of Zondervan. All rights reserved worldwide. www.zondervan.comThe "NIV" and "New International Version" are trademarks registered in the United States Patent and Trademark Office by Biblica, Inc.™

This book is dedicated to Dr. Donald E. Pitzer and Dr. Egon Guba who taught me to value beliefs and worldviews beyond my own, and to my father who taught me that ideas and theology without love are empty.

Contents

Preface | xiii

Acknowledgments | xvii

Introduction | xix

    A Sermon I've Never Heard | 1

    Single Prayer Saints? | 5

    Water Images for Crossing Over | 11

    No Pattern Is the Pattern | 14

    Is Dirt Better Than a Primate? | 16

    The Disruptive Power of a Real God | 22

    Achieving the Heights | 26

    An Unorthodox Contemplation of Paul | 27

    Impossible Images | 34

    The Church of the American Commercials | 37

    Three Years on the Journey | 40

    Bangs, Gods, and Freedom | 43

    Elders in a Self-Contained World | 46

    God Is Love | 50

    Experiencing God | 55

    The Tower of Babel | 59

    The Example of Jesus's Life | 63

    Pushing Water | 68

    Consumption Reigns | 72

    Is the Arc of the Universe Good? | 76

A Threefold Approach | 80
Everybody Knows—Or Do We? | 84
An Attempt at Brevity | 86
We Worship a God We Do Not Know | 88
The Inadequacy of Equations | 91
Why Theology? | 93
If You Kick a Bear | 96
The Continuing Evolution of Consciousness | 100
How does UFT Deal with Forgiveness of Sin? | 105
Was Jesus God? | 110
Unbelief and UFT | 114
God in Schrödinger's Box | 118
The Second Commandment | 121
When Life Won't Stop | 124
Why Is There Something Rather Than Nothing? | 127
Is Eternal Life a Dangerous Error? | 132
The Universal Power to Be | 136
$E = MC^2$ in World Religions | 140
Space and Time | 143
Is US Christianity the Religion of Paul? | 145
Things from Math that Do Not Exist in Nature | 149
The Present as a Koan | 153
The Observable Works of God Are the Powers of Nature | 156
Free Will | 160
The Probability of Specific Humans | 163
What I Miss about Church | 167
Song Lyrics and Copyrights | 169

A Matter of Names and Perspectives | 172
Connections Across Space-Time | 175
When the Right Answer Is the Wrong Argument | 179
Something Was Conceived | 185
Waiting on the Light | 189
The Advent of Snow | 191
Advent as Solidarity | 192
Advent as Practice for Democracy | 196
Waiting to Be | 199
What God Would Not Do | 201
A New Year | 204
I Know Why Old Men Stop Talking | 207
Gratitude | 211
The Location of Consciousness | 214
Death | 217
Expanding Universe | 220
What I Would Tell My Younger Self | 222
Greed and Eternal Life | 227
Further Thoughts on Death | 232
Humans as Particles | 237
Proposing a Human Uncertainty Principle | 240
Human Particles and Thermodynamics | 244
Particles that Think | 248
This World Is a Scary Place | 251
Why Does Religion Emphasize Sex? | 254
Accepting the Impossible as a Sign of Faith | 258
Corona Capitalism | 264

The Plague | 267
Human Strength in a Scary World | 268
Is There a Fall in UFT? | 273
Humans Being | 278
Falling Short of the Glory | 283
Growing Up with a Christian Witch | 287
Religion Abhors a Vacuum | 290
Normal | 295
"It Is Finished?" | 303
Life in Prism | 307
Antisemitism and the "Old Testament" | 310
A Different Reading of Genesis 3 | 316
Quantum Reality of All Things | 320
The Blood | 321
Why I Write About Hope | 325
Life After Life | 329
The Trinity and Unified Field Theology | 331
Predicting What God Will Do | 334
For a Twelve-Year-Old Granddaughter | 338
A Momentary Vision | 341
It Is the Living Who Die | 345
Approaching the Bible | 348
Unexamined Relativism Devalues Factual Research | 353
My 2020 Declaration | 358
Rocks of Fire | 359
Sympathy for the One | 362
Movement in a Field | 365

Fall as Revelation | 367

When Science Is Wrong | 370

Approaching the Bible as Music | 374

Crimson and Gold | 377

Who Fears the Deep State? | 378

Weep | 383

Just War | 384

Infinity Plus One | 388

Intolerable Dark and a Lack of Advent | 391

Places Too Holy | 395

What We Think We See | 399

Life | 401

When Humans Choose Destruction | 402

The Denial of Death and Pascal's Wager | 407

The Final Illusion | 409

The Universe Knows | 411

Death and the Circle of Life | 416

Matchsticks Contemplating Eternity | 419

Bibliography | 421

Preface

WHEN I FINISHED *UNIFIED FIELD Theology* in 2018, I thought my next essays would become lighter—not flippant or comedic, but free from the weight of my earlier journey away from beliefs of my youth. I expected to explore the experiences of living in a world where God is known to be the real power of the physical universe. I would include essays on various passages of the Christian Bible freed of the demand to be literal histories to share with us whatever wisdom ancient writers have to give. And I would also contemplate the significance of new discoveries and changes in scientific understanding of the nature of the universe.

Some of that has happened, and there is life and joy in much of my thinking. As the book found its audience, I made new friends in places I did not expect. Even though I published *UFT* thinking of young people who cannot accept all the things still taught at churches like the one of my youth, I found new relationships with people my own age and older who appreciated the honest questioning and pursuit of truth. But I had no idea how many dark events were on the horizon.

Politically, my country seemed to turn its back on our progress towards greater rights and inclusion—substituting instead division, distrust, and disdain for anyone with differing views. Despite many warnings from scientists that such an event could happen, we were caught unprepared for the first global pandemic since the advent of twentieth-century medicine.

The world continued to act as it always has. Life included times of death, some expected at the end of long years and others sudden and disorienting. Many of my contemplations turned toward these experiences and my desire to understand these heavier life events. Living in the unified field of twenty-first-century science included more darkness than I expected.

Through it all, living in truth with hope and love continues to be my focus. When unexpected events bring grief to those we care about, it is time to offer comfort without resorting to discarded truisms. Expecting to use my ordination to help celebrate life's joys, I have found myself performing funerals. And there is celebration during grief and partings. One unexpected death led to celebrating the life of their common friend with a group of people including farmers, bikers, conventional midwestern church members, and Amish families. At the family's request the service was done within the framework of UFT, and everyone there received it kindly and expressed appreciation. Other funerals have been for family members reaching the normal end of life with peace and dignity. Bringing comfort and encouragement for family and friends with more traditional beliefs included familiar passages and hymns presented as honestly as possible. Future funerals are already being planned for friends who wish to be remembered with truth as well as love and gratitude. These are darker times than I expected.

While collecting my writings since *UFT* for editing and placement within this new volume reminded me of the number that deal with dark topics, I am also encouraged that this does not equal a view of life itself as dark or lacking in hope. Now providing an education for two of my grandchildren during the pandemic, we often go outside for gym and recess in the midday sun. We bike around my peaceful neighborhood, collect nature samples, and watch in wonder as red-tailed hawks and bald eagles join us overhead. We enjoy it and we learn together immersed in Earth's display of nature's more gentle powers. But when I want to take them into consideration of the greater powers of the universe we come inside and turn to texts and videos to explore things beyond our power to observe in the beauty of the midday.

Direct experience of the vastness of the universe, the seeming endlessness of its expanse, and the awe of realizing one is viewing objects as they were in the far distant past require waiting. To see the light that has traveled to us across lightyears of space-time, we need the dark. When our own star dominates the sky, warms our bodies, and lights our adventures, the rest of the universe remains hidden from our eyes. It is night when the universe becomes observable from our spinning orbiting platform. The further one can escape from artificial lights, the grander the display becomes. The Milky Way becomes truly magnificent when city lights are far away. Observing from the dark, the light of the universe is far more spectacular than in the pleasant glow of the sun.

Preface

So, my life and contemplations since releasing *UFT* include more dark events than I expected. Essays from those experiences are included in the order they were written to allow the approaching changes of the pandemic to have their effect in the same order they were experienced. Living in the truth of the universe controlled and sustained by the unified field has not been all sunshine and daydreams. And I am glad. For in the dark, the true grandeur of both the universe and our own existence becomes more evident. I invite readers to join me in this field. Comforted by each other and unencumbered by dogmas that do not truly answers life's questions, we are free to look up and out. Together we can share the wonder of a universe that exceeds our imaginations and provides light traveling to us from out of the ancient past while we both bask in the light of day and marvel at the wonders revealed only in the dark. The light is good and allows us to comfortably enjoy the simple things of life. Let us also learn to treasure the dark as we are reminded that the universe always exists in all its grandeur and reveals itself most clearly to us when we dance together in the dark.

As in *UFT*, I have tried to stay away from academic terminology and use language familiar to a broader audience so that technical expertise in neither theology nor physics is required. I have included footnotes to sources which will take the reader deeper into the areas of study mentioned in the essays. Within the essays the reader will find re-examinations of Bible passages and interpretations, responses to life events since the release of my first book, and reflections on the significance of new discoveries in science. Those familiar with religious naturalism will find many parallels while the major assertion of UFT remains that God, the omnipotent, omnipresent creator and sustainer of the universe, is real and known to twenty-first-century readers as the natural forces studied by physicists.

While the essays are arranged in the order they were written providing a timeline of the ideas included, they may be read in any order. As I am editing this introductory essay, I am also texting with a person who is using specific essays from *UFT* as they seek to deal with the sudden death of a friend. I share these essays with the thought that readers can turn to them as they see fit for deeper understanding of evolving understandings of the world and our place within it, as comforting pieces in time of sorrow, or as suggested explanations when questions about faith or meaning need answers. It is my hope that the essays will enrich the lives of those who take this journey with me through the medium of this book.

Acknowledgments

THIS VOLUME WAS PRODUCED WITH the help and support of friends also on the journey of seeking increased understanding and meaning. Roger and Ranelle Hubele, Don Janzen, Morris McCall, Sam Melchior, and Don Pitzer patiently read each essay, often sent before decent editing, with understanding and support. Each also gave me feedback on my thinking in correspondence and face to face discussions.

Jennifer Neyhart's Progressive Theology Book Club on Facebook provided a forum to share ideas and more importantly to read about the thoughts and questions of others, including the issues most on people's hearts alongside descriptions of the work of authors who speak to those issues.

Brian McLaren gave time and encouragement to read my manuscript and offer both suggestions and encouragement as I prepared to publish this set of essays.

I am also grateful for the patience of my wife, Jennifer, who sat beside me many evenings as I stared into the computer screen and typed my attempts to record these thoughts in a way that would make sense to others.

Introduction

A BRIEF INTRODUCTION OF MYSELF may help the reader understand my comfort with unknowns, opposites, and paradox. My journey began in a world of absolutes and continued through a period of US history marked by controversy and change to bring me to today's convictions that we can humbly accept that there is much we do not know and that it is OK.

I was born into the mid-50s world of Southern Indiana. Sundays and often Wednesday evenings were spent in church where we learned exactly what the Bible taught about any life question worth asking. The accounts of the ancients were literal histories and the teachings recorded in the Bible meant exactly what they said and were true for all time. The United States had helped to win World War II. We were global heroes and the protectors of human freedom. The government was to be trusted and obeyed. My father went to work and earned enough to meet our needs and provide occasional new cars and yearly family vacations. We knew who we were, what was right and wrong, and the world made sense.

But the seeds of change were already beginning to quietly break through life's soil. The church we attended as fundamentalist, literalist, evangelicals was part of Presbytery USA which was moving in far more progressive directions. The armed forces that had defeated the power of Hitler were bogged down first in Korea and then Vietnam as our country tried to exert its will in other countries. And while I never truly agreed that public education included a secular humanist agenda, teachers attempted to present subject matter according to the best research in each discipline in ways that were neutral to religion. It did not take long for those lessons, especially in science, to directly contradict the world I was taught in church.

As I reached high school years, I found many of the answers I was looking for in the writings of Francis and Edith Schaeffer. Instead of ignoring other post-Enlightenment ideas, Schaeffer confronted them and gave the conservative Christian responses I wanted to be true. At the same time, I loved rock music and hated the waste of life in the Vietnam conflict. I had entered a world of paradox. By the time I finished high school I was a long haired, anti-war, Christian present and applauding at the conferences when Francis Schaeffer and others launched the pro-life religious right.

After high school I tested out of my freshman year at the local state university and prepared to do a degree in elementary education as that school's closest thing to a general liberal arts degree. I planned to sample widely across the disciplines, focusing on math and science. Then I would go to work for the evangelical organization, Young Life, to do my studies in theology, and bring unchurched high school students into saving relationships with Jesus Christ. But plans changed first as the school required all students in my major to take nine hours of basic math instead of the calculus I was looking forward to learning and again when I walked into the history courses of Dr. Donald Pitzer. Don became the first in a series of academic mentors who would guide me into a more open view of reality and the human condition.

I continued to work as a volunteer leader in Young Life teaching high school students a basic message of love and salvation available through Jesus Christ and spent a short time on staff starting Young Life in St. Joseph and Benton Harbor, Michigan after college. But a subtle change had begun. One of the most addictive and life-changing things I gained as I did a minor in US history focused on both religious and secular communal groups, was the awareness that every discipline has a history. Everything we know, or think we know, today has a history of ideas, discovery, and evolution over time. In many areas I was able to blend that with my previous assumptions of fact. However, it was revolutionary when applied to my understanding of Christianity. The version I knew and had been led to believe came to us unchanged from the birth of the church also had a history that included both great diversity in belief and practice and many changes over time.

My tenure with Young Life was brief as I experienced the difference between being a participant and a staff member in US Christian organizations, and I fell back on my teaching degree. Working as a classroom teacher, I completed a traditional master's in education, served on both administrative and union committees, and published texts in state history. I also married a church friend I had known since childhood, and

Introduction

we started a family. But church became a place of arguments and division after the death of our long-serving and much-loved pastor. The presbyterian format of decision-making by congregational meeting became a setting of controversy, insult, and bitter feelings. One of my greatest lessons from that time came from the most successful businessman in the church. After one particularly heated exchange at church he called me, still a long-haired kid, to his office to let me know that I would always matter more to him than any issue that might cause us to disagree. I have tried to maintain that attitude of grace towards others for the rest of my life.

Then an administrator from the school system's central office who had used me on many committees called me in and told me I was going to get my doctorate, refused to take no for an answer, and called Indiana University making my appointment to go and enroll. The coursework in IU's doctorate in school administration was one of joyful discovery. I had the privilege of studying research methods with Egon Guba, a guru of naturalistic evaluation. Dr. Guba is the first true constructivist I ever met, believing that the world we perceive with our minds is the only reality that matters. I was still well within the traditions of church and beginning to serve in Christian missions hoping I might still move to fulltime Christian work at some point in my career. So, I did not fully accept Dr. Guba's worldview. I did learn to appreciate that the way each person sees the world is the only world that matters to them, a lesson which would serve me very well in working with the children my city expelled from middle school. Over time I would continue to grow in appreciation of the beauty of views other than my own.

During the time that I was doing literature reviews, I constantly came across the work of Schwartz and Ogilvy detailing how paradigms were changing across all disciplines. The problem was that while many authors in administration and organizational theory were citing the work of these two pioneers in the evolution of twenty-first-century thought, the original was unavailable due to publication by a think tank for corporate members. Through a series of frustrations and errors, I was lucky enough to speak with one of the authors who sent a copy to my home without my awareness that I had given him my address. I was back to the revelation of intellectual history. Worldviews are not permanent. They change and evolve. And at the end of the twentieth century both the general worldviews of the disciplines and my own understanding of the world were undergoing rapid change even while I continued to frame everything within my Christian upbringing and service.

Each mission trip changed me as I learned from the people I met in Mexico, Haiti, Africa, China, and on the reservation at Wounded Knee. Their kind hospitality and acceptance of me despite complicated histories between the church and their own people helped my own views to continue to broaden and become more appreciative of views and experiences different from my own. And I still planned to move from public school teaching to full-time service when I could retire. I became ordained through the Christian Church congregation at the school in Haiti I often visited. And I served as both board member and president during my tenure with them.

Through it all, I continued to study history, science, and theology. As I prepared for ordination, I asked seminary professors to tell me the most important books they required students to read as well as sources that would give a different view. In history I remained active in the study of communal societies in the United States with their wide variety of views regarding religious and secular reasons for the pursuit of greater human community. In science, I continued to read books and articles on the search for the grand unified theory. All these areas brought evolution in my own thinking which I often shared with Don Pitzer who has remained a lifelong friend and mentor. Eventually he suggested that it was time for me to commit my journey and ideas to writing and I began to produce the essays which I published as *Unified Field Theology*. That first collection of essays documents my journey away from literalist interpretations of the Bible to a broader faith in the universe that is. In brief, *UFT* asserts that the combined forces of nature studied in the search for the unified field fulfill all the ancient omni characteristics of God making God real within the physical universe rather than isolated in a separate spiritual realm or confined to the hopeful imaginations of humans seeking meaning.

For that work, I summarized my journey with the following passage which appears on the back cover.

Introduction xxiii

I USED TO KNOW IT ALL

I was sure I knew it all;
who was bound for heaven and who would be in hell,
how the contradictions in the Bible all fit together when read with guidance from the Spirit and in keeping with our church's exact teaching,
how to fix the US government, end war, and balance capitalism with community,
how to reach every child and teach them anything,
what was true and what was false,
how the world made sense and why it was fair.

Then I heard myself spewing foolishness as wisdom and others doing the same. And I was repulsed. Such hubris! Each of us know-it-alls living on one small planet on an obscure arm of an unremarkable galaxy but claiming to know all things. Each of multiple branches of my religion claiming to have the correct meaning that everyone else still missed. And I saw myself in the garden with fruit juice staining my face claiming to know it all, daring to declare myself a god.

Now I know mostly little things;
the love of family,
the importance of children,
the need to live in the circle of a tribe,
the freedom of unknowing,
the joy of being in trees and on rock under birds in flight,
the comfort of not being responsible for all things and all people,
the power each moment to choose behavior that will add to the heaven or hell experienced in the present by real people,
the beauty of the dance of atoms and stars bracketing the grand diversity and mysteries of life.

And I know One Universe which walks with me, creates, knows, sustains, and is.
And that is all I need to know.
One is enough.

What follows here are the essays of my continued journey since the publication of *UFT* in 2018. Through both good and bad times, including the emergence of the first global pandemic, I continue to assert that the all-present, all-powerful force which sustains all things and continues to inspire us to awe and wonder is real. This God continues to be revealed to us in new ways as we study and gratefully enjoy the world that is.

A Sermon I've Never Heard

10/24/2018

MATT 25:31–46; 16:18

THERE ARE CERTAIN FAMILIAR TEXTS that match the theology taught by denominations and local congregations and they get repeated often enough to turn a preacher gray trying to say anything in a new way. Many conservative congregations do not want something new. A preacher can get in trouble teaching a new thing. Familiarity brings comfort and a sense of order to the world. Still, those who stand in the pulpit must find ways to say old things in fresh ways. Sometimes, you can do that by combining two already familiar passages. I have never heard that done with these two selections.

In Matt 25, Jesus is quoted as saying that the people who belong to him are those who have cared for the least—the hungry, and the prisoner—without realizing they are caring for him. Those who fail to care for those in need are the ones left outside the kingdom in their own suffering. Matthew 16:18 is about Peter being established as head of the church, so some protestant churches stay away from what might sound like a Catholic topic. But it also includes the statement that the gates of hell, or hades, shall not stand against the church, which I have often heard proclaimed in sermons.

An interesting thing happens if the two are considered together that may provide the answer to a question I have about the passage from chapter 16. When is the church going to storm the gates of hell? Gates don't advance for us to need assurance that they will not get us. People advance on gates and may need assurance that they can break them down. But when is this assault on the gates of the dead?

I have heard sermons that say it is done through preaching and missions. That we overcome the gates by preventing people from ever passing through them. It feels like a semantic stretch to me even granting that we are considering interpretations of translated words. I want to think of it as an occurrence in an actual story. Those who belong to the Christ at some time, in some way, are depicted as launching actual assault on the gates of hell.

It is a story that I do not see happening in much of church practice. In fact, I have heard too much that sounds like rejoicing that certain undesirable groups will be locked behind those gates. We hear spoken condemnation to eternal punishment for terrorists from other religions, for those who are not birth-sex-identifying heterosexuals, for those who side with an opposite political party, and with less joy for even those who simply never hear of the religion which would save them. Much of the rhetoric of today sounds more like a church that would simply rejoice in its own safety from both the horrors behind those gates and from the people who will be confined there.

So how could it be different? In this passage where Jesus describes separating the sheep who are his own from the goats that he rejects. He does not say the division is based on proclaimed beliefs or loyalties. In fact, in Matt 7:21 Jesus is quoted as saying that many who have called him "Lord, Lord" will be among the rejected. In this story of sheep and goats the distinction is not membership in a tradition, adherence to a dogma, or saying a special prayer. It is simply a separation of those who care for those who are suffering from those who fail to meaningfully care for others.

Now we have a mental picture of the people on the two sides of those gates. In the place of death are those who fail to care for others in need. In the place of life we have those who care enough to actively eliminate suffering. Those who are outside the gates are identified as the ones who care enough to take action about the suffering of those inside the gates! Is that not the point where the collective force of their caring would call for an assault on the gates to free those who have been condemned? Jesus specifically includes those who have been condemned to earthly imprisonment among those who need care. Why not those behind these gates that will not prevail against his collective followers? Those who thought they knew it all, had it all, and deserved it all, are now suffering. And all of those who care about all others are looking at those gates. I believe their very nature would mandate an assault on the barrier of separation.

And I want to take it a step further. If we avoid the trap of predicting a literal future event and a magic set of physical gates, we may place ourselves in the story. And we can ask which position we occupy. Which side of the gates are we on now?

Following the images of the passage, those who actively care about others are on one side and those who do not take care of others are on the suffering side. And, already my mind hears some who believe they are sheep celebrating their good fortune and approving of the suffering of those who fail to live as they live. Until we combine passages! Then those who truly are sheep are those who feel deeply the suffering of those in need.

It took me many years to realize how true this latter description is. Trying to understand the thinking and behavior of people in power who did not actively care for those they were supposed to serve included puzzling over how they could fail to understand the actions of those who did. Slowly it dawned on me. Not possessing hearts that cried out to help others, neither did they see others as having those hearts. They live in an uncaring world. They look out for themselves first, middle, and end because they do not imagine that anyone else will care for them. Engaging in psychological projection of their own personalities onto others, they see themselves fighting to survive in an uncaring world. Beyond bound for an existence of hellish suffering and death at some point in a future phase of life, *they are in it now.*

How will those of us who see ourselves as the caring sheep respond? If we say, "Good, they are where justice requires them to be!" have we not joined them?

Can we do anything about their condition? The second passage says that if we dare to broach the gates we will prevail—not the gates. In caring for those who fail to care, these two passages suggest at least the possibility that we will disrupt the worldview of those who fail to care. They believe in a world of living for yourself, and we arrive in contradiction of everything they expect to view. I cannot claim it is magic. What we believe determines in deep ways what we can see and experience. I have history with people who saw my caring only as manipulation to gain something for myself, a reflection of their own motives. But sometimes the lights go on. Some realize that it is possible to live in a way that demonstrates in real ways that others matter. If their heart awakens to caring for others, have they not escaped the gates of their own self-serving existence?

I know we can cross the gates and rescue those who are controlled by the power of indifference. I have seen it over and over as caring teachers dare to create places of safety and growth for children who have experienced hellish existence under the educational leadership of people who do not care about them. I have seen church people who care become centers of caring for other members who were in deep need of affirmation but receiving only pronouncements of organizationally approved dogma. I have not observed that the actions of those who care can rescue all of those who choose to live in selfish ways. I have seen many counterexamples. So, I have trouble running a mental movie of this passage where the gates are blown down and everyone is free to move to the side of love and belonging.

However, I know that rescue raids across the gates often succeed. I have watched others do it. I have been honored to be involved in work where people who had been taught that no one else cared learned that there are loving people in the world who invited them to leave the prisons of their hardened hearts and join us. I have seen them change.

This is a sermon I long to hear or deliver!

Are we among those that Jesus called the sheep?

Where do we see the walls that imprison others in suffering through uncaring eyes?

Will we cross the gates and offer them love and the possibility of escape?

Or do we face the painful realization that we have been living as goats?

If this last is true, the moment or realization can become the moment of transformation and liberation!

And it is not about dogma or arguments of grand designs and belief systems.

The bottom line is, "What will we do for others?"

Is it hopeless?

Matthew 16 says that if we have the hearts to act in love, the gates will not prevail.

Single Prayer Saints?

11/18/2018

WHAT COULD POSSIBLY BE WRONG with a human being confessing their need to a loving God and accepting the gift of salvation? Growing up as an active evangelical, I led many people in this very ritual. I never could accept doctrines of strict predestination where God decided everything and those not chosen were powerless to change their fate. So, it seemed to make sense that those drawn to faith would have a simple method of expressing their commitment. In fact, over time I came to appreciate even more Meister Eckhart's quote, "If the only prayer you ever say in your entire life is thank you, it will be enough."[1] Of course, those with strict adherence to the sinner's prayer would require adding exactly who one prays to and what they say thank you for.

I discussed my problem with this way of human salvation as a strict requirement when most of humanity has lived and died with no knowledge of it in *UFT*. What I am considering here is something else—hypocrisy. Christians love to complain about being accused of it. They love to trade what seem like convincing arguments that the person pointing it out from outside the circle of faith is worse than they are. But I have seldom heard a pastor with the guts to stand in the pulpit and tell the congregation to fix it.

Driving my thoughts on this are several observations that greatly disturb me. I had to personally deal with a man working with the declared goal of bringing people into this relationship with God, who chose to bring some number of them into sexual relationships with himself

---

1. Eckhart, "If the Only Prayer."

instead. That behavior caused serious damage to his organization, and the effects on the women involved remain a family secret. Then, I read public anniversary brags about how wonderful his marriage is which included his wife saying she would not change anything about their lives. I find it deeply disturbing that she still does not care enough about the women, or the pain of others who trusted her and her husband, to believe it never should have happened. Perhaps I attach too much meaning to the glib things people post on social media for special occasions.

I have also grown weary of businesspeople who conveniently separate the way they operate at work from the teachings they claim to believe on Sundays. I am told there is no other choice than to tell customers what they want to hear, or that reports sent up the line to supervisors—I refuse to say superiors—must be positive even if the numbers have to be manipulated. School personnel tell me that they have no choice but to cheat on the state exams if they wish to continue in the occupation. Politicians have reached a level where nobody will believe one even if they tell the truth because nobody expects them to do so.

This brings me to the current President of the United States. Here we have a man who has bragged about being wealthy enough to get away with sexually assaulting women, who dates prostitutes and buys their silence, who imports nude models to marry, and who publicly announces that everyone who opposes him is guilty of treason, a crime punishable by death. And yet, when I open my social media accounts, I see church people praising him for his faith. It baffles me. But they have a video of him saying things about the saving power of God, so he is a leader standing up for their beliefs. Never mind how he lives. Some evangelical leaders say they were with him when he prayed the sinner's prayer and seemed sincere, so all is well and God's leader is in charge.

I have no problem if they like him because he is fiscally conservative, because they agree that too many immigrants are being allowed entry to the country, because they like his tough talk, because they believe he is a highly successful business man and that he will make better decisions for the country, or because they have been offended by years of being told they must accept people they do not accept and must not use terms for them that they grew up believing were acceptable. I do not agree with these things. But the US system is not based on having to agree on everything. It is designed to accommodate serious differences of opinion while maintaining a stable society. So please do not read this as a political attack. Neither do I have a problem if people believe that he is forgiven and accepted by a God of grace. What has caused me to spend time contemplating this issue is when a person with a self-indulgent unrepentant lifestyle is defended as an example and a leader based on faith.

How does that happen?

One answer is that religion and politics have been combined in this country for my entire life regardless of party. Voters want to believe that their choice is a good person. I understand that. But, at least at some point in the past, I believed that people based their decision on whether to support a potential leader partially on deciding first if they were a good person, however each voter defined good. Now it seems to have reversed. It looks like, if they are from the party that has my allegiance, I must believe they are a good person. Perhaps I just do not understand it because I have some immunity to it. I do not believe that all democrats are proven to be good people because they rise to power, or simply belong to, the party I usually favor. I will leave that alone and move on to my real issue.

I have also discussed in other essays the appearance in church practice that what a person says, or never says, is more important than their actions. Couples in many legalistic churches can have children, especially in the years before widespread birth control, in less than the required gestational period after marriage if nobody counts, comments, or says that such behavior is acceptable. Deacons can smoke behind the church. A gay music leader is a great gift to worship as long as nobody admits what they know or says that they approve. The leader who engages in extramarital relationships or misuses the church's funds is OK if it never causes a disruption in the organization, and if they move quietly along to the next city if things become too well known.

Now the two begin to combine in my thinking.

US Christianity has gradually become an institution where saying the right thing is how people measure a person's status within the faith. If I claim to be a Christian, especially if somebody heard me say the correct script of the sinner's prayer, then I am saved. The days of having to prove one's salvation to the church are in the distant past before the Great Awakenings. The person is what their own words say they are. And just like we cherrypick what the Bible says, we pick which words a person utters to fit our desired outcome. Find one or two pieces of evidence where a person you want to be right says the right thing and they are OK. One or two where a person you oppose says the wrong things, and if they are saved, they are at least not living within the faith.

It is about words.

The worst of sinners can be adopted into the family of faith by saying the right words. I was raised on that teaching as part of understanding the grace extended by a loving God. I wanted it to be true dealing with specific cases even while beginning to question its fairness to those who never knew the correct incantation.

But it was about words spoken at one precise moment in time mattering for all of eternity.

Now, I see the outcome of not also watching for a change in behavior. My childhood church did. We had that verse from Matt 7 which says you will know people "by their fruits."[2] Never mind that the same chapter says, don't judge, here is how to judge, ask and you will receive like a father gives to a child, but very few will ever make it—confusing stuff indeed if taken all together. But as more and more adjustments were made for the simple humanity of church members who acted like humans, it became more and more about what you say. Say you trust Jesus and you trust Jesus.

Let me try to bring it all together. When we are speaking about a family member, friend, church associate, or neighbor there is a grace in trusting what they say about their own relationship with God. There is a freedom from authoritarianism in not allowing a hierarchy of church officials to claim to hold the keys to communion here or to heaven someday. Applied as a specific grace, there is great attraction to the simplicity of a sinner's prayer—if we believe it is available to all and ignore evidence to the contrary.

However, when religion becomes a marker for political leadership and support of a person who matches a certain type of faith becomes a requirement, it is very problematic. A man or woman says they love Jesus; some self-selected leader of evangelical Christianity says they heard them pray the required prayer; they speak correct words at a photo op; and they are God's representative who should not be questioned? I know Christians who go even further and use Rom 13:1 to say that no authority is to be challenged. The very act of rising to power means that God chose them for some purpose. But I cannot go even the first step.

Hypocrisy is easy for me to forgive in the people who sit beside me as humans as frail as I am. Accepting their word that they know right from wrong is a refusal to play God. But a far different thing happens when life does not change. I do not believe that the man who cheats on his family is

2. Matt 7:16.

in good relationship with the universe and that I should not question his acceptability to leadership just because he says everything is OK. Neither do I see in him a moral authority to stand up and tell me how to live my life. I certainly do not consider such a person to be marked as God's choice for unquestioned loyalty locally or nationally simply because they said the right prayer at some point in the past, occasionally give a speech with the right content, or say that they feel called to lead.

Bonhoeffer called it cheap grace when applied only to an individual life. Jesus said that those who loved him were those who kept his commands to love those in need, and that many who said the right things would learn they were not his. It was Paul, not Jesus, who gave qualifications for church leadership and even he said the person's life must show the effects of their faith. I once read an article where Arlo Guthrie was asked how he defined being a Christian in terms of the people who came to work at the Guthrie Center. His answer as I remember it was that he accepted anyone who was willing to come and care for those in need.

So, I now have several reservations about the little prayer that used to give me great comfort:

1. I do not believe in magic formulas known to some and not others as the determiner of correct life here or as a ticket to eternity.
2. I look for change of heart by watching for a matching change of action, even while recognizing that we are all humans and will do human things.
3. I believe that the right to govern comes from the governed, not an external player, not even if people claim that player is God. Divine right of kings is a doctrine rejected long ago.
4. I respond to truth and evidence and honor those who care for those who most need care.
5. I believe the church would be well served to pay less attention to how many people say certain words or go through the baptism ceremony and instead paid more attention to equipping people to care for the world.
6. I do not believe the church has any higher standing, moral authority, or accuracy of measure for who will rule a country wisely than any other organization. I certainly do not recognize any church leader's proclamation of having heard the sinner's prayer to mean

that I should ignore the personal and political behavior of a national leader.

The leader who matters to me, is the one who guides their country, organization, or church to behave in ways which allow everyone, especially "the least of these,"[3] to know that they matter as fellow humans on this journey through cosmic wonder. Life is lived by being. It is not lived more correctly by voicing any incantation. This is the time for us to be—better.

---

3. Matt 25:40.

Water Images for Crossing Over

11/24/2018

I HAVE RECENTLY BEEN PONDERING why images and metaphors for death so often involve crossing over water. And I had a short-lived thought that I might find some common meaning across many expressions. So, I started a list and quickly came up with the following from my own memory of beliefs and observations.

JUDAISM:

Earth formed from the formless face of the deep. Lifeless dirt became human when filled with the breath of God. Life remains after the Earth is cleansed by flood due to the sailing of the ark bringing the living through the waters of death. Leaving the bondage of slavery involved miraculously crossing the Red Sea. Moving into the promised land included miraculously crossing the Jordan River.

CHRISTIANITY:

Birth is by water. Jesus is baptized in water, walks on water, controls the storm, changes water to wine—dies in the air and is buried in stone—but ascends into the clouds. Salvation is expressed through baptism in water.

HINDUISM:

Water, the Ganges, comes from heaven and has the power to free the soul from the fire of curses for rebirth.

BUDDHISM:

Water returns to its source and returns to *live* again.

NATIVE AMERICAN TRADITIONS:

Living human beings are of Earth, but the Red Path leads one beyond the clouds while maintaining the possibility of being invisibly present like water in the air.

SCIENCE:

Water revives the dying. Water is our most required external form of sustenance. The moist breath of the living ceases at death. Things dissolve in water. When water evaporates, the dissolved matter, especially life-giving salt, remains. Water can be present as visible moving liquid, stationary solid, or invisible gas. Water in rivers appears always to be leaving and yet eternally present. Water continuously moves through the cycle, returning pure for another trip on Earth.

LITERATURE:

The sea appears endless to the ancients, and even to us despite our maps and knowledge. Solid forms appear to dissolve and vanish when mist and fog fill the air. Both the joy of birth and the sorrow of death bring water to family eyes. Those on the shore cannot follow those who sail.

    I do not believe there is a universal pattern of belief. Various faiths have different stories for the significance of the water. Many people need no more than the images from stories and songs they have heard since their youth. Water is a major factor in all human life both directly and indirectly in all our other forms of sustenance. And each culture gives its own expression to the significance of it.

But maybe, I have simply come to understand why it remains powerful to me within UFT. As changeable and persistent as water is on Earth, light might first seem to be a better choice for quantum explanations of existence and the continuation of the universe. But most of us observe the effects of light as the illumination and shadow of other objects more than we notice light itself. Rare is the mind and soul invited to join Dr. Einstein on the beam and enjoy the very nature of light. It is water we easily observe appearing, changing forms, moving away and yet always here. Unobserved, the quanta do the same. They surround us, form us, light our world, and sustain us but we do not see them. However, our bodies are better equipped to observe similar patterns in water.

For me the pervasive images of water in human expressions of hope beyond current existence are both beautiful and logical. Like time where the moment is always vanishing but forever here, water does the dance before our eyes. The water we observe is always moving or disappearing back into the sky, and yet it is forever here surrounding and sustaining us. We know the world existed before anyone here imagined our individual existence. We know time will continue and others will continue to live as we gradually become part of the past remembered by few, or for most of us, none. And we want to believe there is a permanence to our existence and importance.[1] But where is the visible evidence of things not seen?

The quanta are beyond our vision and remain too abstract to comfort us in times of need.

Water is here.

We watch the streams and rivers flowing ever onward, carrying with them the debris from the life that surrounds them.

Onward they move.

Yet in front of us they remain.

Summer rain gives way to winter snow, but nonetheless the water continues to return and surround us. Even as we watch it change and depart, we know it is here.

And we hope the same is true for those we love.

For me water has become the most beautiful symbol of our hope for permanence in the face of obvious change.

Water is the visible ever-changing constant.

---

1. Tillich, *Eternal Now*.

No Pattern Is the Pattern

12/3/2018

ENTROPY IS ALWAYS INCREASING IN total—solid to liquid to gas, less concentration, more possible states, less order, and less energy available for work. No solid weight to hang on our machine and make the gears turn. We value work and we see arrangements that make energy available for our use as positive. But there is a lack of uniformity or oneness in the concentrated forms. One space contains matter and potential for work and more space is empty of potential. In a room, if the solid melts we say that entropy has increased and increases again in the transition to gas. But the uniformity of atoms throughout the room increases as the pattern becomes more all-inclusive.[1]

The most even pattern considering the entire space is when the gas is totally dispersed in what we usually consider the highest disorder. Once the molecules are completely evenly spread, movement towards each other results in a greater concentration and greater potential for work, but a less consistent pattern. Still, we have molecules of gas surrounded by space without molecules. What if we break up the molecules and allow the atoms to spread evenly? Thermodynamics says they will. They will move to greater entropy and less potential for work, but our pattern is becoming more uniform. Perhaps my next step already gives itself away—instead of stopping at evenly spaced atoms, we break them into the neutrons, protons, and electrons we were all taught in elementary school. The dispersion is becoming more and more complete and the

---

1. This must be understood as a mental experiment. If we had the capacity to be present and do these things, our bodies would constitute a major disruption to the patterns.

potential for work in our usual terms is decreasing as nothing is concentrated in any one place to be moved by a force. Now, let us divide those parts all the way into quanta.

We are no longer sure if we are talking about very small units of matter or energy as they can be shown to behave as either according to the external conditions we impose. But we will not impose. We will leave them to simply be. Our traditional definitions of potential to work are based on our constructions of manipulating force and matter to do things. In our room now, everything is evenly spread, and the pattern is completely uniform. Now there is an even distribution of the potential of all things. A pure pattern of universal source energy and material without disruption.

If we go two steps further as the discovery of the Higgs boson confirms that we may, we are at a pattern with no disruption whatsoever because there is of yet nothing to disrupt the pattern. There is no spot of matter or ray of energy. There is simply the everywhere consistent potential of what we grew up believing was nothing. And we will have dissolved the walls of our room so that these conditions exist without boundaries.

If we reach that perfect state after all things or before the explosive appearance of all things from one unimaginably small location in the Big Bang our pattern is completely even and beyond our experience or expression based on human observation or thought. Everything and everywhere is now One. The pattern is perfect because nowhere is there any interruption to it. There we find no-thing which exists apart from our pattern of potential and no other energy or power because there is no-thing to emit or be manipulated by it.

We are in the presence of God.

Is Dirt Better Than a Primate?

12/4/2018

FOR MY WHOLE LIFE I have listened to evangelical Christians ridicule the theory of evolution with rather basic humor about not being monkeys. I have watched the aversion to Darwin's theory and the more advanced work based on it that few evangelicals ever study lead to a tendency to dismiss any truth from science that challenges their interpretation of the Bible. Now, if one's pastor and one's political party says increasing world temperatures are not happening, they are not. Or, if they finally admit it is happening and maintain that it is normal and that scientists are just part of some conspiracy to provoke panic, the faithful believe them. Evidence and data need not be consulted because faith and science have separated with each side claiming to hold truth while the other teaches falsehoods.

However, I was recently contemplating the book Christians call Genesis and something else struck me. To be drawn to the story of Genesis as literally true and reject the claims of science seems to imply that some people would rather believe that they come from dirt than from another intelligent species. The more we learn about the lives of primates, the more we see them caring for one another, making tools to decrease the work needed for life tasks, and at times showing the same violent tendencies as man. They are far more like us than what I was taught as a youth, even by science teachers who believed in evolution. Why is it so insulting to consider that a species like us is our ancestor? Why would people prefer to believe we come from dirt? My mind sees several possibilities.

Many people do not analyze data and think scientifically at all. They believe what they have been told by people they trust. Growing up being told an explanation of the world is correct by both family and church, they simply continue in those beliefs without critical reflection. This is especially true when they are taught that abandonment of any of their fundamental beliefs might destroy their faith, their status with God, or at a minimum their acceptability in the local church community. So, I turn to possibilities that might occur without intentional consideration.

We know that the body decays after death and returns to the earth which supplied its building blocks during life. And it makes better poetry to say that from dust we come and to dust we return rather than from primate we come and to dust we go. There is a balance to the idea of being made of and returning to dirt when we look at individual lives rather than all of life over long periods of time.

We observe that canines have canine offspring and felines produce felines, etc. When different animals are produced through crossbreeding, we see the mule with its inability to reproduce. How could it begin a new line of evolution even coming from similar animals? The logic of observation during a single lifetime seems obvious. What is a fish today is not a land creature tomorrow or a bird next week. Things remain themselves and they have offspring like themselves. I encountered such observations often growing up among biblical literalists who wished to maintain young Earth beliefs.

If we try to point out that evolution does not happen within the lifetime of one bear, we may hear, "So if the bear somehow does not die and swims a hundred years, a thousand, a hundred thousand, you believe he will become anything besides an old, tired bear?" The entire science of gradual change in offspring over time is simply ignored in order to believe that what can be directly observed in brief periods remains true regardless of how much time is involved. I suspect it also avoids the need to study and understand more complex scientific concepts such as DNA structure and change.

I recently learned of a twist in this from one of the very places defending the literal Bible—Kentucky's Ark Museum. This huge recreation of Noah's ark is used to confirm in the minds of the faithful that the story of the flood is literally true. And they have dinosaurs on board to maintain their consistency that everything lived well within the previous 10,000 year period. But they have a problem. Even if we ignore the animals that were to be collected in groups of more than two and simply calculate the space needed for every known species to be on one vessel, their huge boat is too small. If they are questioned about this, they will point out accurately enough that the term "species" is from a time long after the famous flood and that the biblical language is best translated as *kinds* of animals. So, Noah only needed animals of the feline kind, the canine kind, etc. And all the diversity within that grouping could occur naturally after the flood through adaptation.[1] Still not accepting full change from one kind of animal to another, they have suddenly introduced post-flood evolution within *kinds* all occurring in perhaps five thousand years. Some people would rather believe this unlikely argument rather than the timetable and progression that scientific observations and interpretations indicate.

My own comparison using what I know of tribal beliefs suggests other possibilities. If we come from the same natural process, then we are relatives to all other life. And, while I have heard sermons saying that humanity came last in creation and is the pinnacle of creation, evolving last makes all other living things our elders. This theme appears from several different angles when I look at the history of man and the stories in the Bible. Man wants to be a god. We want to be more than the animals and certainly not the youngest child in the family of life. There is pride involved in believing we are the ultimate of creation, and there is freedom to see ourselves as separate, different, apart, and independent of what we cause or allow to happen to the rest of life.

I believe there is another even less attractive reason. For centuries the non-Europeans of the world were considered less than human. The answer to my own questioning of how a loving and just God can leave most of humanity out of the plan for eternal life, was for centuries that the inhabitants of those other continents must be sub-human. Natives in what we call the Americas could be wiped out because they were not human beings, or at least were not human beings God had chosen for his purposes. Once thought changed to say that the inhabitants of these continents had souls, the exploitation turned to Africa. We could capture Africans to own and work them like animals because they were seen as less than human. Colonizers were not colonizers of other humans; they were described as great explorers opening whole new areas of the earth for settlement and cultivation by white humans. As late as the 1950s and 60s of my youth, terms like porch-monkeys and yard-apes were often used to describe black children. Everyone who used those terms knew that they were not compliments! I know some people who still use them and still believe other races are inferior to whites. The irony of some US

---

1. "How Many," lines 5–7.

hate groups now referring to other races as *mud-people* does not escape me. Racism does not need to be logical, only to have perceived benefits for the adherent.

Racism works very well without careful thought or analysis. That is part of what allows widespread racism. The beliefs, attitudes, and responses to others just seem part of the pattern of what is and are not consciously chosen in a manner that leaves the racist feeling responsible for their bigoted beliefs. But I never thought about the connection of these ideas until recently. If I declare that I am standing firm in the defense of the truth that God revealed, I can continue to feel religious and superior to others. If I accept the evidence that we not only evolved like other animals, but that we did so and emerged as human beings in Africa, a very different result appears. Not only do I have to admit to being like other animals, but I must also admit to being the same as, not better than, other races. In fact, the evidence shows that I am a descendent of Africans, making them my elders.

This also brings me to Derek Bell's theory on the permanence of racism. Dr. Bell argues that racism is permanent because it keeps the large mass of white workers pacified and not rebelling against the wealthy few who reap nearly all the rewards. In books like *Faces at the Bottom of the Well*, Bell argues that if the workers of the world believe they have somebody to look down at, they do not turn and look up at the real oppressors. Racism serves to maintain the stability of the status quo.

US religious organizations with their tax-exempt properties and financial collections also have a vested interest in the stability of the current system. This is the insidious nature of societal racism. There does not have to be a conscious conspiracy for different parts of the society to work together to maintain the current system. Although, given the history of the US church in directly working to support US capitalism and democracy from perceived threats during the cold war years, some level of cooperation with the side in power during the upheaval of the civil rights movement would be worthy of research.

Nevertheless, the possibility remains that evidence which would disrupt racist attitudes would disrupt the status quo with its benefits to business, the state, and the church. Some parts of the US church still cling to ideas of US exceptionalism and special divine rights as the new Israel. Dropping what has now been taught for decades about the status and origin of human beings and openly accepting facts that would show the adherents have the same common ancestors as all other people would be disruptive to these teachings and the leadership which perpetuates and benefits from them.

Maintaining the status quo does not have to be done deliberately. There does not have to be a smoking gun of conspiracy. When the same things benefit different human organizations, they will continue doing them without any central planning. In fact, such practices will continue without the need for conscious consideration. They work, so they continue to be done. Racism continues without anyone having to recognize bigoted thoughts in their own practice. The ideas, concepts, and practices grow during an early period when people have not developed sensitivity to the included hatred or sophistication of understanding of the others in question. After generations of practice, they simply become the way things are and do not seem to require examination of the racist practices of the past behind current reality.

It is entirely possible that part of the power of creationism over evolution is that white Christians would rather be dirt selected, animated, and favored by God than animals descended from the same ancestors as black- and brown-skinned people. It would not require intentional effort to perpetuate such a system. It would require very deliberate, as well as painful and disruptive, study to bring about change instead of stasis. It would require individuals willing to assume great personal risk to tease out areas where churches which believe they teach that "Jesus loves the little children, all the little children of the world," actually maintain harmful teachings and practices from the past with no memory of the racial underpinning.

On the face of it, it would not seem to make any difference whether we all come from dirt or earlier primates. If it is all common ancestry, why should it matter whether that ancestor was born to primate parents or assembled from dirt if we accept our common background and membership in one human family? Simple examination would indicate that they are equal. But a deeper look at the history of our cultures and our ideas reveals patterns that are easily hidden in what seems harmless. Change would be difficult, but what would be the reward? Do we dare to hope that the difference could be growth towards a more inclusive humanity or religion?

Most people in the majority culture do not think about such things. They accept what they are taught. They do not wish to alter from what seems to be the safe pattern of their beliefs. Presenting alternative views is often seen as blaming the person spoken to for somehow causing the system that is—resulting in angry denials. The burden of exposing the truth and working for change is the blessing and the curse of those who awaken to the connections in our beliefs and behaviors both now and in our cultural past. Some have paid a heavy price for trying to teach new things about old patterns. Some simply walk away from it all. In the US atmosphere of consumer Christianity, it is easy enough to simply change to another denomination where one feels more comfortable. I am only thinking through the possibilities behind an observable oddity in twenty-first-century thought. If true, we will each decide what impact we will allow it to have on ourselves and those around us.

The Disruptive Power of a Real God

12/5/2018

SURPRISING SOME OF HIS CRITICS by informing them that he believes Jesus to be a real human being who existed in the first century, Bart Ehrman asserts that the greatest challenge to current views and teachings about Jesus is that they do not match who the real Jesus was. Dr. Ehrman asserts that the first-century Jewish apocalyptic prophet is a more serious problem for current beliefs than an imaginary one because that very real person does not match most of the teachings associated with his name today, and knowledge of a real person is harder to twist to new meanings than a mythical one.[1]

It occurs to me that something very similar exists with Unified Field Theology. If God is only seen as a human construction, that image can be changed. If the many images and behaviors of the God of the Christian Bible are seen as expressions of changing human understandings of God over time, those understandings are free to continue to mature. Faced with challenges that God is dead, merely an archaic superstition, or one human construction among all possible constructions, many of us have hoped for a way to prove that what we call God is real.

But if the omnipresent, omni-powerful, eternal source and destinations of all things is real, then any valid attempt at understanding will need to match that reality rather than images we wish to be true. And this is precisely what I am claiming in UFT. There is a background potential revealed in the scientific search for the unified theory that precedes our universe, is the source and power of our universe, remains present now,

---

1. Ehrman, *Did Jesus Exist?*

and would continue even if all the matter and energy we know as our universe somehow ended. This reality beyond the matter and energy we know meets the criteria of being the eternal source of all things, present everywhere those things exist, and logically beyond them, as well as representing the apparent condition to which all things would return if the universe ceased its current existence. From our vantage point as part of the universe, we observe the power as the natural forces scientists are studying in the search for the unified theory.

The Christian student of the attributes of God will already notice some omissions from my list. I did not say the scientific source of the universe is omniscient. We could if we wish. If the source is present everywhere and nothing exists apart from it, then the opposite statement would seem false. There would not be anything beyond, or unknown, to it. I have chosen to leave omniscience off my list because this characteristic immediately steers our thinking towards knowing in the way a human mind perceives things to be known. I do not think we have any reasonable evidence to assert that the source of all things functions in any way that requires the biochemistry of human thinking. I also have not said that it is good, loving, or just. If I use the word "just" in this context, I do not mean prone to justice. I mean "only." The background potential of the universe is just what it is. It simply is. The application of terms that imply thinking or qualitative characteristics like goodness or leaning toward justice are human attempts to explain the world that is. I would propose that we would do better to reflect on whether they apply in positive ways to our individual and collective lives.

Which brings me back to Ehrman's thoughts about the Jesus of history. In the same way that history attempts to approximate what really happened without forcing the past into the patterns of our favored myths, science looks for what is without agreeing that it must fit with our images of the divine or our favorite Sunday School stories. There is no reason the forces that control the universe would choose—again the danger of terms for human perception—our planet over any other, one tribe or nation over any other, or some people for eternal salvation and others for hell. That force gives us no reason from scientific reasoning to assign it human traits at all and will not agree to fit the patterns of our religious convictions.

And this is where it becomes more disruptive to current constructions than older arguments about whether a God exists in a magic or spiritual realm outside of the natural world. If the atheist says that they refuse to believe in a God without proof, the believer in a spiritual God can categorize them as unwilling to accept spiritual proofs and perhaps too defiant to subject themselves to understandings of right and wrong revealed from that spirit realm. Once we make the leap from observable evidence and logical reasoning to faith, we can justify any religion which makes sense to us, seems to lead people to what we believe are good lives, or maintains the stability of our culture. Acceptance or rejection will be based on each person's perceptions of experiences with physical, mental, and emotional events. Many things in our experience still evade our best attempts at logical explanation and the person who accepts a separate spiritual realm can attribute things they experience as positive or negative to forces within that realm which can only be defined by faith in what one perceives or is taught.

However, if God is real, if the attributes which have traditionally been labeled God are part of the universe which can be observed and studied through the methods of science and mathematics, then that power has defined characteristics which are observed within the natural world, and we lose the ability to escape into the magical or spiritual. I have already recorded my thoughts on how we see the power of the universe as good, bad, positive, or negative in relationship to human existence in *UFT*. My sole purpose here is to consider just how disruptive to existing systems acceptance of such a theory as true may be. We are left with the fact that what is, is. What is has no need to comply with any of our wishes for control over life and death, promises of future rewards, or assurances of safety beyond the laws of nature.

But then, good theology—choose any religion you like—never claimed that God was a puppet to be manipulated by our desires in the first place. Whether spiritual or natural, it has always been a defining characteristic that we are subject to God, never that God is subject to us. I find possibilities for unity and peace in the idea that we are now realizing the ultimate power which is beyond the limits of time and space is real. And that natural power leaves us to decide who and what we are and will be. The atheist looks at this evidence and rejecting magical constructions of the ultimate, existing in some separate spiritual realm, says that there is no God. I look at the evidence and conclude that we now know there is something real beyond all material things—not in a separate spiritual realm known only to the enlightened, but inside the realm of observable and researchable phenomena. And I conclude yet again that God is real. God is simply under no obligations to please us by fitting into the patterns we find individually comforting or socially controlling as our perceptions, needs, or desires dictate.

Achieving the Heights

12/30/2018

Achieving the Heights,
Of Wealth and Power
By the Accumulation and Avarice,
Ambition and Determination,
Of Their Ancestors,
They set the Price of Credential,
The Barrier to Ascension,
That No Future Interlopers,
Might Displace,
Their Descendants.

An Unorthodox Contemplation of Paul

2/4/2019

THE CHURCH PERSECUTED AND SCATTERED (Acts 8): "And Saul approved of their killing him. On that day a great persecution broke out against the church in Jerusalem, and all except the apostles were scattered throughout Judea and Samaria. 2 Godly men buried Stephen and mourned deeply for him. 3 But Saul began to destroy the church. Going from house to house, he dragged off both men and women and put them in prison."

Saul's Conversion (Acts 9): "Meanwhile, Saul was still breathing out murderous threats against the Lord's disciples. He went to the high priest 2 and asked him for letters to the synagogues in Damascus, so that if he found any there who belonged to the Way, whether men or women, he might take them as prisoners to Jerusalem. 3 As he neared Damascus on his journey, suddenly a light from heaven flashed around him. 4 He fell to the ground and heard a voice say to him, "Saul, Saul, why do you persecute me?" 5 "Who are you, Lord?" Saul asked. "I am Jesus, whom you are persecuting," he replied."

Paul's Suffering (2 Cor 11): "23 Are they servants of Christ? (I am out of my mind to talk like this.) I am more. I have worked much harder, been in prison more frequently, been flogged more severely, and been exposed to death again and again. 24 Five times I received from the Jews the forty lashes minus one. 25 Three times I was beaten with rods, once I was pelted with stones, three times I was shipwrecked, I spent a night and a day in the open sea, 26 I have been constantly on the move. I have been in danger from rivers, in danger from bandits, in danger from my fellow Jews, in danger from Gentiles; in danger in the city, in danger in the country, in danger at sea; and in danger from false believers. 27 I have labored and toiled and have often gone without sleep; I have known hunger and thirst and have often gone without food; I have been cold and naked. 28 Besides everything else, I face daily the pressure of my concern for all the churches. 29 Who is weak, and I do not feel weak? Who is led into sin, and I do not inwardly burn?"

Paul's Trial (Acts 26:24): "At this point Festus interrupted Paul's defense. 'You are out of your mind, Paul!' he shouted. 'Your great learning is driving you insane.'

> 25 'I am not insane, most excellent Festus,' Paul replied. 'What I am saying is true and reasonable. 26 The king is familiar with these things, and I can speak freely to him. I am convinced that none of this has escaped his notice, because it was not done in a corner. 27 King Agrippa, do you believe the prophets? I know you do.' 28 Then Agrippa said to Paul, 'Do you think that in such a short time you can persuade me to be a Christian?' 29 Paul replied, 'Short time or long—I pray to God that not only you but all who are listening to me today may become what I am, except for these chains.' 30 The king rose, and with him the governor and Bernice and those sitting with them. 31 After they left the room, they began saying to one another, 'This man is not doing anything that deserves death or imprisonment.' 32 Agrippa said to Festus, 'This man could have been set free if he had not appealed to Caesar.'"

My thinking about Paul, the founder of Christianity as a religion among the gentiles, causes me to connect these passages. First, we have Saul, a man willing to imprison and seek the death of those he believes to be heretics. Second, Saul experiences a vision and becomes Paul the missionary. Third, he suffers life-threatening abuse on many occasions. And fourth, he demands to be tried before Caesar.

The traditional interpretation of these events is that they happened as reported by Paul and that his representation of his own motives is accurate. Having seen Jesus, he is transformed completely from an abuser of those whose beliefs differ from his own to a servant willing to suffer so that the same message of Jesus may spread across the known world. Going to Rome, the center of the empire, is just a logical step in visiting a gentile church and in spreading the gospel of Jesus in the most effective way possible.

My early experiences with Christianity as a child often included similar testimonies of those who experienced complete changes of personality and temperament. The addict to alcohol, drugs, or earthly pleasures was suddenly and completely transformed as they accepted Jesus and left their old selves and lives behind. It was not unusual to hear the personal testimony of one or more such people at events intended to win new converts to the faith.

But there was a problem. These miraculously changed people had a pattern of relapsing to their former weaknesses. After being held up as examples of the instantaneous change available through belief and baptism in Jesus, they would fall back into old habits or replace them with new addictions. I watched the church slowly stop using these stars of transformation. The explanation which seemed to make sense to everyone within the faith was that these new converts had been placed too quickly into the spotlight, making them easy targets for temptation. Their failure was our fault because we did not allow them time to mature and become discipled in the faith before holding them up as examples. The change that had been presented as instantaneous became a matter of learning and practicing Christian life and beliefs.

All of this brings me back to Paul. During the time the disciples of Jesus were traveling with Jesus, watching his example, listening to his teaching, getting it wrong over and over and receiving further instruction, Saul was not there. The Gospel accounts are filled with examples of how many times the future apostles had to be corrected, retaught, and dissuaded from seeking who would be the greatest among them. We have only Paul's word that he received his own instruction directly from the risen Jesus qualifying him to be an apostle. Strangely, he seems to name others as apostles but makes no claim that they received direct instruction from the risen Christ.[1] In Paul's accounts that honor is reserved to Paul alone. Paul has been elevated to become the one who gives God's teaching.

My question is as simple as it is unorthodox, perhaps even heretical.

What evidence do we have that Paul was exempt from the temptations of his previous life?

The traditional answer is that we have his accounts, now part of the official canon, and therefore established by God as the word without error in all that it affirms. Since the Bible says that he suffered all this

---

1. Rom 16:7.

persecution at the hands of those who refused to believe as a gentle servant sharing in the suffering of Christ, then that is what happened. But history does not include any point where God or the apostles officially declared exactly what writings were and were not worthy of inclusion as God's infallible word. That process took place over time through the practices and decisions of men, respected men of faith to be sure, but men rather than God. And that gives me pause to consider Paul's accounts through the lenses of a student of history as well as of the Bible and the church.

One of the most basic lessons of historical research is to maintain a healthy skepticism of what people claim about themselves. Most psychologically healthy people make themselves the heroes of the stories they tell. Those with an agenda of establishing themselves as authorities, leaders, or significant historical figures are even more suspect to include this bias in favor of the self. Historians know that the founding of Jamestown did not happen exactly as John Smith wrote it. His accounts make wonderful Disney movies. But they do not match the rest of the historical record. It seems to me that a similar critical read of Paul might cause us to pause and contemplate the likely accuracy of his self-recorded history. Is it likely that a man with experience as the oppressor would change so completely to a man willing to repeatedly be the victim of the worst non-lethal punishments available with no temptation to reclaim his former power?

In the book of Romans, Paul confesses that while he trusts Jesus to free him, he is not yet free of his former self. Many people are familiar with his confession that he does what he wishes he would not do and fails to do what he should.[2] Paul does not claim to have become superhuman in his ability to live a perfect life free of error. While he continues to speak of the great changing power of God through Christ, he also admits that the human struggle continues. My own life and my observation of those examples of supposedly miraculous change from my youth affirm that this is true even for the sincerest of believers.

How strong would the temptation be to regain his old power when he was constantly in danger from those who rejected his teaching? How badly would a man beaten to within one lash of death desire to have back his old power and authority? Paul says he received these beatings five times plus three with rods. He was stoned and had to flee out a window

---

2. Rom 7.

in the city walls during the night to protect his life.[3] He remains true to his new faith. But what if there was a way to reclaim his old position of safety and power as he proclaimed these new beliefs? He cannot go back to Jerusalem for authorization. His new teaching is hateful to those who used to be his associates. The power now to rule over other citizens is in Rome. The power to authorize traveling the Mediterranean unchallenged and unharmed resides in Rome. And Paul sets off to go there.

Perhaps I am being unfair. He was taken prisoner, accused of causing civic unrest, and exercised his rights as a citizen to appeal his case. It would appear unfair and biased to claim that a prisoner being transported against their will to probable torture or execution was doing so with a personal agenda positive or negative. Here it is Luke, the author of Acts, who tells us that two different Roman authorities would have set Paul free if he had been willing to accept their decision instead of demanding to go to Rome.

Paul claims for himself that he remains a prisoner in order that the good news of the risen Christ might be shared at the center of world power in his day. His letter to those in Rome says,

> [11] I long to see you so that I may impart to you some spiritual gift to make you strong— [12] that is, that you and I may be mutually encouraged by each other's faith. [13] I do not want you to be unaware, brothers and sisters,[d] that I planned many times to come to you (but have been prevented from doing so until now) in order that I might have a harvest among you, just as I have had among the other Gentiles. [14] I am obligated both to Greeks and non-Greeks, both to the wise and the foolish. [15] That is why I am so eager to preach the gospel also to you who are in Rome.[4]

By his own words, he is traveling to Rome for the same grace filled reasons that have taken him to many other cities. He is coming because God is sending him to reveal the truth.

But I see something interesting even in his account. No sooner has he given this friendly introduction of his purpose, than he introduces a new idea. Only a couple of sentences later he begins to talk about the wrath of God being unleashed on those who refuse to believe. This discussion of God's wrath is repeated often in the letter when referring to

---

3. I should note that his account of these death-defying moments is just as subject to challenge as the brags of any other self-reporting adventurer under the rules of historical study.

4. Rom 1.

those who do not believe. Then in chapter 13, he goes further in the name of urging civil obedience,

> Let everyone be subject to the governing authorities, for there is no authority except that which God has established. The authorities that exist have been established by God. ² Consequently, whoever rebels against the authority is rebelling against what God has instituted, and those who do so will bring judgment on themselves. ³ For rulers hold no terror for those who do right, but for those who do wrong. Do you want to be free from fear of the one in authority? Then do what is right and you will be commended. *For the one in authority is God's servant for your good. But if you do wrong, be afraid, for rulers do not bear the sword for no reason. They are God's servants, agents of wrath to bring punishment on the wrongdoer.* [emphasis added]

I have heard verses such as this one quoted more than once in defense of US leaders who I believed were abusing their power—the one in authority is there by God's hand and may not be challenged. It appears far more threatening to me in the context of this contemplation of Paul and his actions. The authority to punish and even kill those who oppose the message because the killer is carrying out the will of God is precisely the authority wielded by Saul before his conversion to Christianity. He has barely begun this letter of hope and salvation to those in Rome before he begins talking about the wrath of God toward those who will not believe. Then, he includes this section which conventional interpretations present as a friendly warning to remain safe through civil obedience.

I am raising the unsettling possibility that this man who fell from prestige and authority to a refugee and a target of torture because of his conversion to a new faith may have had his old power very much in mind. Within the context of his times, his experience, the behavior of other believers for centuries after, I consider it likely that he would consider gaining such power as beneficial to those who would be forced to hear the truth of his words.

I am contemplating nothing less than the possibility that Paul insisted on going to Rome in the hope of winning back his own power and authority. It did not happen for him or in his lifetime. Christianity did not become the official religion of Rome until the fourth century. And once it came to power, how did the religion travel the rest of our planet? To be sure, examples abound of gentle and loving missionaries going out at great personal cost to share the truth as they saw it out of love for those in other places. But even then, the soldiers were often close behind. In addition, we have the Crusades, the Inquisition, the Divine Right of Kings, Holy War, the Age of Discovery, and Conquest all carried out under authority of the church. History reveals the genocide and/or enslavement of the aboriginal peoples of the continents of Africa, Australia, North America, and South America in the belief that God chose the Europeans to spread around the globe as his beloved. And Western society continues to live within the context of military prowess and just war.

The religion of love has a dark side including the destruction of others. Once Christianity became aligned with power, it used that power, or that power used Christianity, for the domination and destruction of others. The church, after all, only acted on behalf of the will of God and the eventual salvation of the world.

I no longer find it beyond belief that the founder of the gentile church, a man well acquainted with wielding brutal power before becoming its victim, would seek audience with Caesar to regain his authority to carry forth his message empowered by the sword.

Impossible Images

2/10/2019

RECENTLY MY MIND HAS BEEN engaged in several musings about the relative movement of objects in space-time. The first difficulty with this is seeing space-time as one thing. We think we understand because we are familiar with thinking about space and time, as well as space or time. It is easy to picture two objects occupying the same space if they are there at different times, or existing at the same time if they occupy different spaces. That is space or time. We are also used to common thinking that two objects trying to occupy the same space at the same time will collide with predictable results on a macro scale. That is space and time. Seeing space-time as one inseparable thing makes things feel more complex rather than easier to understand.

I started my recent contemplations considering situations of acceleration in space-time. Space-time is usually depicted as a two-dimensional grid, sometimes with waves or depressions to indicate being pulled in a third direction. It is not difficult to visualize traveling at a steady rate across that grid. When I introduce the idea of acceleration, it becomes more complicated. If I accelerate, I am now covering more distance through space in less time. If the grid represents only space as on a simple map, there is no problem. I am moving across the physical grid more rapidly and cover more squares in less time. But if the grid is a unified composite of space-time, my acceleration appears to make me cover more of one and less of the other. If the grid was an XY axis with each representing one factor of space or time, the situation would be easy. I would be covering more distance on the space axis and moving to a

Impossible Images

smaller amount on the time coordinate. But it is not a simple grid of two factors it is a common field of one unified thing called space-time.

Those who are fluent in the math and imaging of this phenomenon tells us that acceleration causes our flat grid to warp or curve to allow for the accelerated movement. This warping is very similar to the bending of space-time by gravity as explained by Einstein. This also tells me that we are not dealing with grids like those we used in arithmetic. There is no dimension to allow raising or lowering of part of my grid in the flatland of two-dimensional space. But the temptation to convert to a basic XYZ coordinate system simply reintroduces the old problem of seeing time and space as separate things designated by separate axes. It is not, it is all one thing.

Relative motion (is there definitionally any other?) is even more curious. How do I visualize acceleration that is a turning to one side or the other relative to another point? If I am riding in or on that object, I physically feel the acceleration of changing direction, but my speed may remain the same. It is difficult to visualize what this does in the singular reality of space-time. Now moving at the same pace, I may be making negative progress in terms of another object. I am covering the same amount of space and time but moving further from the original target. Even worse, if my acceleration is in a straight line but negative, I am still decreasing space but increasing time between myself and my destination. On top of this the entire universe is rapidly expanding, so the other object and myself are also traveling in a direction away from the center of the universe. Space-time must bend in ways beyond what my mind pictures in two or three dimensions.

I then began to wonder about the measured speed of an object observed in motion relative to myself. It seems that if another object is moving the same direction I am, its apparent speed would be its speed minus my own. If we are traveling toward each other it seems that perceived speed would be the two velocities combined. This raises the question of whether two objects traveling toward each other could have a perceived speed greater than the speed of light. If both are traveling at greater than half the speed of light, would the combined numbers equal a perceived speed greater than that of light? Simple arithmetic would seem to make the answer yes. But at least two phenomena would be at play. Relative speed includes relative time, and by now those of us who are fascinated by such phenomena know the example of two observers passing each other at high speeds each thinking the other's actions take twice as long as their own. It does not seem that this would change if the two were on a collision course rather than simply able to pass each other.

Then, I realize something else. In what seems a logical redundancy, perceiving anything requires the ability to perceive phenomenon. Now I have a problem filling in the blanks for my simple computation. To measure the oncoming velocity of the other object, light, or some other perceivable signal has to reach me to be measured. No such signal travels faster than light. If our combined approach speed exceeds the ability of light to reach me, we will collide before I know the other object exists. By the time we could perceive each other, we would no longer exist to be perceived. And this phenomenon would occur well below the speed of light when a human being is involved. Our ability to see and make sense of the situation also takes time which would further reduce the relative speed required to annihilate each other before knowing the other existed.

So far, no practical, philosophic, or religious meaning of these rambling thoughts has occurred to me. But I think I am beginning to understand why it is necessary to use more than our three or four perceived dimensions in order to describe the universe and the behavior of matter and energy within it!

It brings me new appreciation of Robert Graves's poem, "In Broken Images."[1]

Sometimes our best thinking simply reminds us that there is reality beyond our grasp, confirming our ability to reason even while reality exceeds our current understanding. It calls me always forward to continued research and contemplation.

---

1. Weick, *Social Psychology*, 224.

The Church of the American Commercials

2/10/2019

WITH TONGUE AT LEAST A little in cheek, I am thinking of church as the place people turn for hope.

As I read and watch news, it appears that the United States has abandoned trust in the science that warns us about what we are doing to the planet and its possible implications in a very short period of time. Years ago, the church split from science over Darwin's evolution and findings in geology and astronomy indicating a very old universe.

When I listen to our president and his followers or see the stories of people in trouble for expressing how they really feel about people different from themselves, it seems like our society has admitted that we hate more than we accept or love. The stories flooding the news would make it appear that we are splintered into groups based on race, LGBTQ+ status, wealth, ethnicity, immigration, and geographic region. Having accepted a leader who refuses to be muzzled by political correctness, other citizens are also speaking their minds and telling the truth about how much they despise those who are *other*.

It looks like we have abandoned all progress toward being one civil society made up of a widely diverse population while also replacing confidence in facts with each person's perception of the world. In this new world the view of the person who can yell the loudest prevails regardless of fact or fairness. There would appear to be little hope for those of us who have placed our confidence in a nation of people seeking always to move forward in understanding of the world and each other. Where do we turn?

While I have rejected most predictions of human behavior based on the generalizations of experimental statistics, I have been thoroughly trained to see observations based on data as superior to opinions based on personal ideas or anecdotal evidence. And strangely, that causes me to look to the much-maligned territory of the television commercial for hope. This realm of loud car salesmen, carefully worded deceptions, and overpriced bargains would seem to be the last place to turn. But I see something there that is different from what the supposedly trustworthy news platforms are telling us.

My hypothesis is based on these assumptions of fact. National advertising on television costs in the millions for a single advertisement. Large corporation do not become and remain successful by wasting millions of dollars. National advertising campaigns present a society which accepts diversity in all its forms. Even companies involved in profit directly from fossil fuels often include environmental awareness as one of the emotional elements to make their company and their product attractive. And my conclusion is that their research data on public attitudes and advertising effectiveness tells them that their customer base still values the images portrayed in their ads.

However, survey research and polling data is often wrong. Projections on the most recent presidential election proved unreliable. So why should there be any hope in data which appears to guide national advertising? These companies also measure advertising effectiveness. A single advertisement might badly miss the mark. Some must be pulled immediately when any content thought to be entertaining turns out to offend a segment of the society. They can be wrong. But companies pull ads that do not work. They do not continue to pay for airtime to show commercials that turn away customers, and they do not buy new advertising that has been shown to harm their profit margin. Successful companies put their money where it makes them more money.

So, I believe there is hope in the very part of television that often irritates me. A constant stream of advertisements showing mixed groups and families, same-sex parents, friendliness to immigrants, and love of the environment tells me that people with the most invested know these things are attractive to people who purchase their products. It has become an aphorism, usually a negative aphorism, in understanding political actions and alignments to advise interested persons to follow the money.

As someone who values diversity, inclusion, and environmental action based on research, following the money leads me to believe those who invest enormous sums in media promotions know that most US customers also find these ideas attractive.

So, when the news and the politics of the day cause my soul to despair, when the policies of the current administration cause me to question whether our society values wise action based on science, when my heart aches from the animosity voiced towards the immigrant, the different, the other—I wait for the commercials. And I go to church!

Three Years on the Journey

2/23/2019

In 1962 I was six years old. I had encountered school for the first time at two very different schools, one that considered kindergartners hungry minds that enjoyed learning conversational French and the second that saw us as babies who should take naps on our rugs. My sister had been born and we had moved to my parent's first house that would be our permanent home.

We were at church in the original sanctuary of the small white frame building where my grandparents were founding members. The preacher who would be the pastor of my entire childhood was preaching about the love of God exhibited through Jesus Christ. And a delicious golden warmth enveloped me. When the pastor gave an invitation at the end of the service, I felt sure it was time for me to go forward and make my faith official. However, the church did not see children of my age as capable of making lifelong decisions with eternal consequences. So, I was treated kindly and sent along home.

In 1968 I turned twelve in a country enveloped by chaos. My country was in the middle of a war opposed by the young who were being forced to go to fight its battles and die. Campuses across the country were erupting in protests. The country in turn was shooting protestors. Both Martin Luther King Jr. and Bobby Kennedy stood forth to say there could be a positive future, and they were both killed. Inner cities across the country were burning with riots and the Black Panthers were in full power. The country responded to them with violence as well. At the same time, rock music was reaching out from every radio screaming that our generation had a voice that would be heard!

Three Years on the Journey

Amid all of that I was at church again. This time we were in the fellowship hall of the same family church. This room was where we held youth nights and family potluck dinners. Where the sanctuary was focused on God, this room was focused on us and the community of people who made this place their spiritual home. On this evening we were listening to some missionaries report on their work in Africa. As recent as 1968 seems to me now, it was a separated by a lifetime of change from the mission trips I would later take. The possibilities for dying in the field were real. And these people appeared to be focused only on the fact that their lives were invested in bringing life changing love to people in Africa. I wanted to live like they were living. In a world of chaos, they were leaving the insanity of my home culture and sharing the possibilities of God's kingdom with others. I went forward again and this time my parents and the church agreed that I understood what I was doing, could be saved, and officially join the church. I would remain part of that church into my adult years. During a period of their own turmoil and reorganization, I would help to write their new constitution and bylaws. On my first evangelical venture, moving to SW Michigan to start an outreach to unchurched high school students, they would support me financially.

As I am writing this reflection, I am watching a documentary on the creation of the Who's rock opera, *Tommy*, which was released as a movie in 1975. Music had already become the language of my soul and to this day everything I do is accompanied by an internal soundtrack. When I went to see this movie, I would not have been surprised in any way if my inner elation had been accompanied by physical levitation. Here was everything—rock, lyrics of freedom, the desire for somebody—anybody—to understand me on a deep level. I was transported by the ending with its glorious celebration of freedom with Tommy physically climbing up to the sun realizing that we are free to leave the temple. I went back as often as my parents would allow me to buy another ticket and every single viewing, I came out of the theater dancing in the streets of Evansville not caring who saw or what they thought. There was celebration on the other side of chaos.

Even though I continued for many years in the church and mission work, the significant event that made of all this different did not happen in my family's church or any other. In the fall of 1974 I enrolled at Indiana State University Evansville on a full-ride scholarship after testing out of my freshman year. I had an excellent high school experience in US history, but really did not intend to continue in that field beyond what was required. Like too many students, I had been conditioned to see it as a dead subject—the past happened, it was recorded, we could study as much of it as we cared about and try to be informed in the present. But it was not a field that inspired me to future deep involvement. I was going to use the freedom of extra course choices from my banked year of credits to go as far as possible in science and math while majoring in elementary education as the university's best liberal arts option at the time. Then, I walked into the auditorium and sat down in US History 101 with Dr. Don Pitzer. I found a fellow traveler and mentor on the journey to learn everything possible about what it means to be human together.

Tonight, after sitting with Don at a book signing for *Unified Field Theology*, I think back about these three out of many important years. And I am grateful. I am free. I am blessed. There is meaning, life, music, and dancing even in the midst of the chaos of humans being.

Bangs, Gods, and Freedom

2/23/2019

My mind travels backward in time and space to a location probably overplayed by Hollywood. Villagers gather looking up at the terror of a volcano coming to life. Smoke and rocks shoot up into the air while the percussion of explosions assaults the ears. And they turn to their shaman. Why is this god angry? What offense has been committed? What can be done before liquid fire begins to flow down to destroy their lives? And the shaman performs rituals, perhaps partakes of local herbs, and goes into a trance. Then she tells the people what to do. As long as they do not live at the foot of a frequent flow, most of the time the shaman's lessons seem true and the volcano does not unleash its full wrath on the people.

We might picture the same at the sudden confusion of an earthquake. Or out on the plains of any continent the priest may be consulted if the god of thunder appears too angry—threatening to unleash destructive hail and wind—or if rain is too long in appearing, bringing drought and shortage. The forces of the earth are larger than the powers of the people. So, a logical assumption is made that a larger power is at work. Once those beliefs are codified, the representatives of the powers, or of the people before the powers, are seen as critical guides to survival and wellbeing. If they demand, no price is too large for peace and safety. Modern entertainment loves to portray sacrificing the group's own children or neighbors to appease the unseen powers behind the acts of nature.

Then the age of science spreads around the globe. Perhaps after a period of convincing and even double practice—both learning scientific explanations and hedging one's bets with old practices—the god of the volcano becomes a character of historic folklore rather than a present reality. Now, it is the scientists we turn to for explanation of what is happening. And they are correct often enough to reassure us that their observations and theories are true explanations of what is happening or may happen in the future. And the religious orders must turn to new roles. It is not enough to claim magic knowledge of the storm. A larger more encompassing religion must be taught that explains things beyond simple observed facts and interpretations. The God of religion becomes a universal power. The pattern is well known and has been thoroughly documented by anthropologists.

What I assert in Unified Field Theology is that while we scoff at practices of the prescientific past, we are on the precipice of the final move away from ignorance, superstition, and magic. We have moved from terror and worship of local gods for large local events. We nod our heads in affirmation of logical understanding when the bangs of nature startle us and bring our focus to things larger than ourselves. But one bang remains for many well-educated and sophisticated people—The Big Bang. Surely an event of such magnitude as the formation of the universe itself requires a power beyond understanding as the author of what we observe. And many people continue to turn to their local preacher, priest, or guru to explain what that power is and how humans can relate to it in acceptable ways.

What happens when the current knowledge of quantum and macro physics spreads to common understanding? How do human minds and emotions respond to realization that the biggest bang of all is another act of the natural world with no magic puppeteer?

If there is no God beyond the physical world, the religious leaders will not be able to claim power based on leading people into proper relationship to that power. Old systems of building explanations of the meaning of life in the context of pleasing the God of Creation, become meaningless if there is no such God. Sacred texts and stories, maintained for millennia by various cultures, will no longer be useful in the same ways they were used in the past. And leaders of those various sects will proclaim that they are under attack. Science will be attacked as a false religion requiring the same faith in unseen things that animates the traditional religions. And those who are not fully educated in the methods and realities of science will for a time cling to old beliefs. I believe this is exactly the age we are currently observing.

Giving up the gods behind the phenomena along with beliefs that we can establish relationships with them and control forces large enough to destroy us is terrifying. This is true for the god presumed to be behind the Big Bang as it has been for the gods assumed to be behind the local bangs. The illusion of control must be surrendered. Science searches for ways to predict natural events more successfully to give warnings. In some cases, such as the flooding of rivers, it brought us knowledge of hydrology and systems of dams and levees[1] to control the power of water. But the volcano, the earthquake, and even the wind and thunder elude human ability to exert control. Correctly understanding their power, we are humbled by our size and vulnerability. Accepting that the cosmos does what it does because that is what it does, with no intervening external god choosing sides or granting miracles or divine protection—this is the final terrifying step into understanding our tiny status on our beautiful little watery rock of a planet.

I have already asserted in *UFT*, that we will have to turn to each other, our need for each other, and our treatment of other humans and the rest of life for meaning. It is also time to consider what that implies for the various forms of human priesthood. We will have to define the role, if any, that the shaman/rabbi/priest/pastor/imam/elder will play in a post-magic world. It seems to me that some of the leaders from the East will be at an advantage due to already teaching that the correct path is one of aligning with, rather than changing or controlling, what is. Yet even there, some cling to practices honoring local gods or spirits for blessings or curses.

I will explore the possible direction of these roles in my next essay.

---

1. Which also have negative impacts that are currently becoming more obvious.

Elders in a Self-Contained World

2/28/2019

FROM A POINT FAR IN antiquity, now thought possibly to precede agriculture and extending to the present, humans have turned to various assortments of intermediaries to explain and help them to deal with forces attributed to the divine or local spirits. It is time to consider what happens to those roles and relationships in a self-contained universe. If everything that is, including the grand characteristics traditionally assigned to God, is part of the natural world unaffected by ritual and magic, then these interceding roles will need to be examined.

I strongly suspect that a significant number of people will simply refuse to do so. With the discomfort and uncertainty of living in a world which simply does what it does, I predict that many will cling to religious explanations of natural phenomena regardless of any factual evidence presented by science. It is an easy prediction. It is already happening among educated people in response to evolution, the age of the universe, and the negative effects of the Anthropocene era. Human beliefs and practices are based on complex combinations of thought and emotion. Change seldom occurs by simply being presented a set of facts and adjusting one's worldview. So, I expect there will continue to be traditional roles for rabbis, preachers, and imams even as knowledge of new science becomes widespread across the globe.

However, some of us are already moving beyond traditional acceptance of the teachings and the authority of these professions. As I write this, scandals in both the Catholic and Baptist churches, as well as a major school of Buddhism, are revealing the extent to which those who have been exalted as holy emissaries are subject to the same aberrations of behavior and socially condemned behaviors as any other group. The math may even show that those granted great power are more likely to engage in actions abhorrent to those they presume to lead. The inflated status and praise as representatives of God may in fact be variables which make humans more susceptible to assuming for themselves the right to engage in behaviors forbidden to others. In response, I suspect significant numbers of people will continue to walk away from anything considered religious and attempt to negotiate life on their own without guidance from any of these traditional sources. This is also about as difficult to predict as whether the earth will keep turning because it is already happening and easily observable as people increasingly turn to beliefs and practices labeled spiritual rather than religious.

Optimistically, I believe it is time for a new version of ancient practice to emerge. Many varied societies of the past and present have placed great emphasis on the role of the elder. The protestant churches of my own past and ordination use the term for a leadership role, usually male, filled by lay members of the religious community. In other societies as well, elders were revered as those who have had more time to learn the ways of both the natural and spiritual worlds. There has also been respect based on the natural wisdom gained through years of experience. These foreshadow the future role I am anticipating.

People who accept the observations, theories, and facts presented by science will still live in a world with many forces far beyond their control. Volcanoes will still erupt. Storms in increasing size and severity will still threaten life and property. Looking up at the night sky understanding that one is looking into an expanse of unimaginable size will still tell us that we are very small. And the behavior of other humans from those labeled as criminals to those who rise to recognized positions of authority will continue to include selfish, misguided, and often dangerous acts making people long for some reassurance that we are safe within a world we cannot control. Being able to accurately label that which is powerful enough to harm us, does not remove fear of those phenomena or cause us to live with less need for assurance that we and our offspring will be all right.

I believe people will need elders. They will need people who can explain to them what is happening, to help them build small circles of relative safety and comfort within the larger society, to rejoice with them when life is good and to grieve with them in times of loss, and to help them find meaning in a world which will often make them feel insignificant.

Quality religious leaders of the past and present fill those roles. Elders of both sexes also have a long tradition of doing so in families, communities, and collections of people small enough for personal interaction. If the dimension of external magic is removed, I believe the role of the elder will remain and increase in value. There will be individuals with the personal qualities which cause others to turn to them for assurance amid apparent chaos. This role may be based on knowledge of the world, skill in counseling methods, age, gender, perceived wisdom, charism, or other characteristics of both the leader and the person seeking guidance.

It does not have to be defined by traditional categories. If we stop speaking of the forces at work in the cosmos solely as the God of Western religious texts—overwhelmingly identified by male pronouns regardless of theology in many examples of past and present practice—there will be less reason to assume that leadership should also be male. We can reach the point where we acknowledge what is already present in ancient languages which uses feminine word forms for wisdom such as *sophia*. In family settings it is often the mother or grandmother figure that people turn to in times of distress. Even in the antebellum United States, where blacks were still portrayed as incapable of participating successfully in white society, southern families entrusting the raising of their children to black women is well documented. There is no reason larger social groups should not approach leadership in fully inclusive ways as the idea that God resembles a certain type of person diminishes.

There is also no reason to assume that elder must imply older as it often has in the past. Eastern traditions have often included recognition of the gifts of a new leader, or a current reincarnation of an old leader, at a very young age. The Christian Gospel of Luke claims that others were able to recognize Jesus as their expected divine leader soon after birth and includes assertions that he possessed impressive spiritual knowledge and insight as a child. Two terms in current use are old souls and empaths describing people who possess wisdom, insight, and empathy formerly identified with traits developed through years of experience. There appear to be people who have the needed traits from a very young age. Some people are even using them to describe awareness and ability to comfort which they find present in their pets. Those who emerge as able to comfort and lead others through life in the world that is should be a very diverse group.

I see these elders as people who will provide individual mentoring and counsel, help to celebrate markers of life journeys such as births, formation of families, and the death of loved ones. Many reformed rabbis act in a very similar fashion already—helping people live without demanding a specific dogma about reality or promising anything about eternity. Some leaders of Eastern thought might also continue in much the same pattern of helping people find their oneness with reality through centering, meditation, detachment, and service.

I suspect that some groups would continue to choose elders through formal training and selection as in current practices for clergy. But I see reasons why others might suspend requirements for such formal arrangements. Elders may be those who arise naturally within groups to fill the desired roles, and there is no reason to assume that all roles should be concentrated in one person.

Above all an elder in UFT would offer others the gift of themselves. An often-stated teaching of Christianity is that God dwells inside the believer rather than exclusively out in a separate spiritual realm. The seed is there. Meaning and significance of individual lives will come from within and through the acknowledgement of each other and the way we treat each other. Safety in times of uncertainty will come from the strength of the individual and the collective spirit of the group. Reassurance of help in times of need will be strengthened by involving learners in serving others in times of need. Realizing that the planet we live on is the context of our own journeys and the journeys of all our descendants,[1] a good elder will help people to live in wise sustainable ways that do not destroy our only known habitat in the universe.

An elder should be a person who can give voice to the joys and pains, accomplishments and insecurities, and the significance and loneliness of life in ways that empower others to live more fully within the wonderment of a cosmos that is inspiring and frightening, certain and uncertain, strange and foreign, and most of all home. Elders should walk beside us and help us to constantly improve the practice of living as humans being.

---

1. While many believe and promote the idea that humanity will escape to other planets, current experiments in space indicate that any successful inhabitants would change physically and genetically to match the new planet and might cease to be what we consider "human." Regardless, they would have to show the same care of environment, even more so in attempts to occupy the environment of a new planet.

God Is Love

3/4/2019

ONE OF THE SHORTEST, MOST widely used, and most universal statements about the nature of God is found in the final phrase of 1 John 4:8. In *UFT*, I critiqued many of the ways the church has presented God as anything but loving in its interactions with others. Now, I want to reflect on what such a simple statement could mean when applied to a universe that contains God within the natural forces observable by science. In what ways can the forces of the universe be said to "be love?"

An obvious application would be in the attractive force of love and the pervasive presence of gravity in the universe. This would seem to correlate to the Greek word *philia*, as the objects studied in astronomy tend to gather into relatively local systems. We see this in the orbital patterns of solar systems and galaxies. Much like the dynamics of families or close social groups, the individual members follow their own paths, closeness or distance from the center, and speed of travel. And still, the total forms an orderly dance with each acting in coordination with the others. The gravitational pull of each affects all other members in varying degrees based on size and distance, forming a balanced whole.

Other metaphors for this ancient term for love are easily constructed. In earthly life forms, we also observe the herding instinct or group dynamic across many species from the very large to the insect world considered too small to have brains capable of conscious decisions to love. It is simply the nature of many forms of life to participate in this familial type of arrangement which improves life through the protection and benefits of group behavior. In fact, it is so pervasive that terms like lone wolf or rogue elephant are used to denote unusual behavior rather than the expected.

With twentieth-century emphasis on the erotic side, the Greek *eros*, this aspect of love might seem harder to translate to the general scope of the universe. But this is the creative and reproductive aspect of love. When we look at the universe as a self-contained whole, we see that it does in fact demonstrate a ubiquitous characteristic of generating new forms. Stars and planets are still forming. The descent of matter into the black hole of a collapsed star which at first seems only an act of destruction, has already been found to be the creative ground of the unparalleled brightness and power of the Quasar. Theories under consideration, but not yet proven, suggest that black holes might also emit matter as whole new universes or into new areas of the existing cosmos, creating new realities from the seeds of the old. We know that complex combinations of chemicals over time can reach the ability to self-replicate resulting in what we know as life.

Once that process of life begins, evolution begins and the simple begets the complex as newer forms emerge. When that complexity reaches the level of male and female varieties within a species, we have the emergence of sexual reproduction and *eros* is easily observed. Members of the two sexes are attracted to each other, ensuring the arrival of the next generation and the continuation of the process of DNA recombination leading to species adaptation and change over time. And, while previous religious explanations of the emergence and significance of life emphasized Earth as unique and focused on humanity as the zenith and purpose of creation, scientific observation gives no reason to assume the processes are limited to one planet out of all possible environments in the universe. The standard assumptions of science that the same natural forces and processes work in all settings within the boundaries of local conditions would indicate the opposite. This ability to bring forth life and then develop more and more complex forms is now expected to be ubiquitous in the universe. *Eros* also appears to be part of the basic nature of what Is.

By now those familiar with Christian teachings on this verse may be growing frustrated that I am neglecting the Greek form of love believed to be correct for "God is love," in 1 John, *agape*. This form of love emphasizing a self-sacrificing dedication to the well-being of others fits well with traditional Christian theology. The Christian God is one who loves humans enough to sacrifice his own Son to save humanity from evil. Or, in the interpretation I prefer, God is willing to suffer everything we endure to be united with us. This is seen as the ultimate in love which gives oneself for the benefit of the other. So, we must consider whether this form is observable in the natural order if I am to continue this game of comparing Christian texts to the known world. We could perhaps more easily abandon the ancient texts as outdated, but I prefer to reflect on how the wisdom of these long-preserved traditions and teachings match our emerging understanding of the universe.

Starting with Earth as the only platform where we have been able to observe complex life forms at this point in our history, there are indeed examples. Animal parents often behave in self-sacrificing ways to care for their young. Mother animals will starve, freeze, or fight to death in order to protect their young. We could cite many examples from human behavior if we do not engage in the mind game of assuming that we are somehow different from other animals exhibiting traits developed in the natural evolution of our own species. Traditional religion applies these human examples to being created in the image of God. I am saying the same! I am however defining God as the all-present nature of *What Is*, not a spirit father from another realm pouring unique gifts into Earth and humans as the created forms of primary importance and meaning in the universe.

These reflections also cause me to look towards the sun, often seen as a god in ancient times including the Roman Empire at the time of the rise of Christianity. While some warmth on Earth comes from its hot center, most of life on Earth depends on the constant supply of new energy each day from the star at the center of our solar system. It is the light from this star that allows for the photosynthesis of plant life and the natural food chain from herbivores to omnivores and carnivores. The sun continuously provides to Earth the energy to sustain life and growth. After periods of clouds and precipitation we long to simply be in its light. What has this to do with *agape*? While the process takes place over amounts of time measured in astronomical units rather than human generations, stars do this by nuclear consumption of the star's substance leading to eventually burning out—described in scientific texts as death.

The energy which provides life here comes from the nature of the sun which causes it to continue consuming itself in ways that release the energy on which we live. The problem I see is when we try to anthropomorphize the sun or the process. If we fall into the temptation of assigning thought, intention, or emotion to a star to fit our preconceptions of a term like love, we will have taken a side path into error. The sun is not one of us doing things helpful or harmful out of the type of processes to which we attribute our own behaviors. But it is happening nonetheless by the nature of *What Is*. Both sun and Earth are doing what stars and planets do. And while we have not yet traveled or seen far enough to observe it in other places, we have every reason to believe it happens in many locations across the universe once we abandon the idea that we are the center of all things.

Philosophers will point out that I am playing fast and loose with assigning vocabulary associated with human behaviors—behaviors we struggle to define in conclusive ways even in humans—to inanimate objects. They are correct. That is the nature of the game if we want to see how these classic texts with their anthropomorphic language make sense as we seek meaning in a self-contained universe.

To briefly consider the other alternatives, the universe would seem at worst to be neutral. There is little evidence to conclude that the universe is in anyway malevolent. Neither planets nor atoms pursue each other to destruction. The gravity of most objects pulls others into the dance of orbits, not the destruction of collision. Animals normally do not slaughter others for the mere joy of killing. As mentioned above, they are more often found in family groups, herds, and mixed species habitats.

When we look for the opposite of what we label love, it appears to be most common in our own species, not the general rules of the universe. And even when humanity is at its worst, we find the desire for order rather than chaos, the protection of one's own, and concern for the well-being of innocents among our enemies as well as our own side. Jesus of Nazareth went so far as to teach the love of enemies.

We could conclude that the universe is neutral or ambivalent. That might seem to be a concept more congruent with Eastern thought which teaches one to give up entanglements in the process of learning to live at peace with *What Is*. But I do not believe this is a contradiction without resolution. Entanglements come from clinging to our own constructions of what should or should not be, what should continue, usually pleasure, and what should end, usually pain, rather than allowing the cosmos to simply unfold according to its own laws. The enlightened person comes to full nonjudgmental acceptance of the world without demanding anything in return—a sentiment which we might easily equate with unconditional love of a world that could exist without us.

The universe could certainly continue with no life on Earth. There is no observable reason to conclude that the rest of the universe would be different if we disappear or had never existed. And yet, here we are. The reality of the cosmos is that its laws, forces, and conditions all combine in a way that results in our thinking, caring, searching, and creative existence.

It appears that the observable universe does in fact exhibit the traits of collective motion and mutually beneficial group behavior, the physical attraction of mates in the continuation of species survival and evolution, and the passing of life-giving energy at the expense of one body to another by the laws of physics and biology. *Philia*, *Eros* and *Agape*—constructions of the concept contained in the English word love—do appear present in the forces that function to create and maintain *What Is* as long as we do not impose thoughts and emotions anywhere except in life forms evolved to a level of observable conscious behavior.

God is love?

Yes, the power of the universe is bent toward continuation and growth rather than destruction. *What Is* supports and nurtures what comes to be.

Experiencing God

3/18/2019

> The Lord said, "Go out and stand on the mountain in the presence of the Lord, for the Lord is about to pass by." Then a great and powerful wind tore the mountains apart and shattered the rocks before the Lord, but the Lord was not in the wind. After the wind there was an earthquake, but the Lord was not in the earthquake. [12] After the earthquake came a fire, but the Lord was not in the fire. And after the fire came a gentle whisper. [13] When Elijah heard it, he pulled his cloak over his face and went out and stood at the mouth of the cave.[1]

IN UFT I ASSERT THAT God is in the natural processes that produce and sustain the universe. All things come from and return to that universal source, and nothing is unknown, or separate from, it. This accepts the traditional characteristics of the divine without ignoring the facts of science. But humans, as far back as we know, have sought to understand this God, this power that affects every aspect of our lives. Since the physics and math involved in the search for the unified field are beyond what most people are taught, or even wish to understand, I want to look at how we experience this definition of God. And this ancient text is a very nice sample to consider.

In my essay on how humans react to the large "Bangs" of nature, I have discussed how these have often been considered gods until scientific understanding of the phenomena caused humans to stop worshiping and

---

1. 1 Kgs 19:11.

even sacrificing to these dramatic natural places and events. But we must consider where that leaves us as we live out our lives in a universe, or just on our own planet, which often behaves in ways which leave us feeling powerless and alone. I believe this ancient text has great wisdom to share.

This ancient story takes place as Elijah is about to call Elisha to succeed him as a prophet. Just before this, Elijah is said to have miraculously displayed the superior power of Israel's God over Baal, the local god that people have turned to in a time of famine and rule by an evil government. Then when he hears that the queen now intends to kill him, he is terrified and runs for his life. This passage follows as God reassures Elijah of his presence and power.

We might expect the story to include a grand display of a very large "Bang." It does but dares to say that God was not in the great wind, the earthquake, or the fire. God is finally made known to this ancient prophet in a still small voice. Obviously, we know that the powers of the universe would be involved in everything that happened. Even a traditional religious explanation would not make sense if it claimed God had nothing to do with those large events and they just happened by chance as the day unfolded. Claiming that God is not involved in the large dramatic signs of power is not the point of the story. The point is found in placing the emphasis on the still small voice.

When we picture the large dramatic natural events as God or the manifestation of God's presence there are two problems. The God who appears is terrifying when present, absent, or unavailable for long periods of time between events. This story is amazing in its contrast to many people's understanding of the God of the ancients. God is not revealed until Elijah can hear the still small voice. This resonates deeply with me and my understanding of the universe, of human experience, and our attempts to make peace with what is.

The ancient traditions of the East tell us to silence our own bodies and minds to find oneness with reality. The wisdom literature of the ancient Jews teaches the superiority of quiet. Jesus of Nazareth is described as frequently withdrawing to quiet places. Christian contemplative tradition teaches the seeker to stop all the noise and quietly seek the presence of God. Spaces considered sacred across multiple world belief systems inspire those who enter to display quiet reverence. And here, we have the God which Christians have often considered violent and warlike in ancient times showing his representative that the presence is found in the "gentle whisper."

There is humility in silence. In silence we stop our endless talk of what we think we know about things which exceed our thoughts and language. In silence we stop proclaiming the superiority of our views and condemning those we see as others. In true silence, we stop condemning ourselves as well.

It is contrary to much that is found in US society. We talk, post, and tweet constantly to promote our views or to make sure others know we are here. When the big events of nature happen, we both praise and criticize our government for what is done and the extra we believe could have been done. Religious leaders speak out to declare God's wrath with those who do not accept and live by their doctrines or God's favor and protection over those who do. When it is all too much, we frequently turn on more noise—music, television, or movies to distract us from what we fear we cannot endure. And we know little of the power of the universe, whether we speak in religious or secular language.

Here we are invited to do something different. In fact, the advice is to stop all our doing and be still. In this story the man who experiences God doesn't *do* anything! He stands silently as the power and the quietness of the world happen. He has stopped his doing to *be* in the presence of the greatest power. When we investigate the universe honestly, there is very little of consequence that we can change. The planet, solar system, galaxy, and cosmos all continue doing what they do in apparent indifference to our individual actions or speeches. It remains to be seen if we will learn soon enough that much of our doing causes the planet to become toxic to our own and other species. The age of modernity has given way to acknowledgement of the Anthropocene Era as we realize that all the doing of human progress has its equal and opposite reaction in the destructive effects of our inventions and activities. It now appears that for our species to survive we may need to collectively stop doing much of what was considered great achievement and progress. If we wish to continue to be, we must stop and be.

In *UFT*, I included an essay on why I rock climb. Many of us have found that there is healing in withdrawing from our manmade environments and going out to experience the healing presence of the planet in more natural settings. When we work at not working and begin the process of learning to quiet our minds and bodies, one of the first things we experience is the quantity of noise which surrounds us. Many of us hunger to be where those sounds are wind, water, birds, insects, and even the sounds of our own bodies and beating hearts. When we stop doing, to quiet ourselves and be, we begin to experience our nature as part of the world.

I love to study and to teach. I seek out voices whether audible or in print that can guide me further in my understanding. I long to share my experiences and visions of the universe with others by talking or recording these essays. But when I want to experience connection to all things. When I need to be in the presence of the beauty and power behind and in all things, I find that I must stop and become silent. We experience our oneness with everything else, with all others, with the power in all things, with God, when we stop and allow the stillness to speak to us and simply enfold and hold us as humans being.

The Tower of Babel

Evidence of the Changing Concept of God in the Bible

3/9/2019

I BRIEFLY MENTIONED THE GENESIS account of the Tower of Babel in *UFT*. It makes sense as an ancient story explaining why humans speak so many different languages and opens the possibility of an original common language of God before this event. It provides an answer beyond chaos and chance for why humans spread to all parts of the planet. And, I have heard it used in missions training to encourage completing the work of having the praise of the one true God come from every diverse culture on Earth.

Lately, I have been contemplating something else about it. Within scientific explanations of space as everything beyond our planet's atmosphere, an expanse which is constantly found to be larger than we previously knew, it makes no sense. Aside from the engineering difficulty of believing the ancients could build a tower from the plain of Shinar to heights exceeding the Himalaya, the tower would lead only to death. Any human who ascended such a tower would find themselves in an atmosphere continuously decreasing in available oxygen until they were unable to breathe. But the biblical account presents it as an actual event if read literally.

Something I think I already knew, came to my recent contemplations. The ancients as recorded in the Bible believed that there was an actual physical barrier between the earthly realm of men and the heavenly realm of God. Stars were not great nuclear balls of gas. They were light shining through holes in this physical barrier. The story of Noah and the flood says God opened that barrier and allowed water from the heavens to pour down onto the Earth. When all was flooded, the gates were closed. This places the barrier as close as the clouds of flooding rain.

The story only makes sense as a literal event if the hearer believes that there is this physical ceiling which could be reached. Then, an opening could be made, and man would have access to the realm of God. The story only makes sense as a spiritual writing if the author also believed in such a world. If not, it would be an intentional fiction to play on the ignorance of the reader, or more correctly to the time, the listener. This leads me to the conclusion that the story can only be seen as a literal account within a scientifically ignorant world.

If the story only required us to believe that those building the tower, and the person recording the story, believed in a naïve version of reality, we could still accept it as a literal account of what they tried to do and its aftermath. But God is in the story. God—who by definition is the all-knowing Creator of the heavens and the Earth—is described in this story as also believing that they *can succeed* at building their tower to heaven. Now there is a problem with the understanding of God. The God in this story knows no more about the reality of the universe than the ancient people of Babel. The God in this story is an upstairs neighbor to those who live upon the surface of the planet. What happens to that God when man discovers that the stars and planets are real things existing at great distances from the Earth with no ceiling separating the two?

If the story were only of the actions and explanations of humans, that would be the end of it. Read literally, a group of ancients try to do what makes sense within their worldview and fail with the rather problematic result that humans begin speaking different languages and disperse to live among those who can understand each other. However, the inclusion of God in the story leads to a more significant conclusion. The God described in a prescientific period must change as knowledge of the world increases. This is not the unchanging—same yesterday, today, and tomorrow—God of much religious dogma.

This is a God who knows no more about the actual universe than the people who worship and write about the actions of their God. This should cause serious pause to the literalist interpreters of ancient texts as should the account in Joshua 10 that claims God stopped the sun in the sky in order to allow the army he favored to more fully slaughter their enemies. I have actually heard intelligent and educated evangelicals claim there is evidence in NASA files that there is a matching anomaly in the apparent position of the sun. Basic knowledge of the movement of objects would tell us that unimaginable destruction would occur if the rotation of the Earth was to suddenly be stopped and then restarted. I suppose the true believer will simply say that the lack of such a result was all part of the miracle. If God could stop the earth from turning to help an army, then God could prevent other negative effects of that stoppage. It is logical within the presuppositions of faith. Within the rules of science and the uniform behavior of physical objects across time and space, it is not. If the descendants of the ancients to whom the story belonged believed everything in the accounts to be literally true, I would expect the great divide between science and religion to have occurred long before the publication of more recent theories on evolution and the age of the Earth.

We know that widespread belief in the literal truth of these accounts is as recent as the science that contradicts them. Much of those teachings are reactionary to the science which people within the religion found unacceptable. The Jewish owners of the texts allowed their definitions of God to evolve over time. Judaism, the religion which produced the story, is tolerant of multiple views about the nature of God and the interaction of God with ancient and modern man.

My conclusion is that an evolutionary understanding of God is as evident in the text as it is logical to believe. As humanity expanded its knowledge of the world, its explanations of the power behind reality changed as well. The same as those who used to worship the volcano change to a larger definition of their god or gods as they learn the true nature of a volcano, humanity in general has adjusted its understanding of God as our breadth and depth of understanding of the natural world has expanded. People's explanations of the characteristics of God change over time along with the increase of knowledge. As a result, the God in our recorded stories changes over time and that includes the God of the Bible. The biblical God is not static, but changes from a being that walks and visits with early man, to an all-powerful spirit that uses the miracle of a virgin birth to do the same thing in the Gospels.

UFT's change in belief from a spirit God who lives in some unknown separate realm to belief that the characteristics of God are discoverable within the physical universe is an enormous alteration in Western worldviews. Eastern teachings evolved millennia ago to methods for humans to experience oneness with the world rather than gaining favor with an external God. The change process is not unique to our present time. The change process has been going on as long as man has been recording stories about the interactions between humans and the divine. UFT is a new verse in a long and ancient song.

The Example of Jesus's Life

3/19/2019

OVER THE YEARS I HAVE heard different theories on who Jesus of Nazareth was and what his life teaches. The teaching of my youth was that he was God in human form who came to explain what was necessary for a right relationship with God, to die as payment for the sins of all people who would accept his salvation, to rise from the dead to show his victory, to ascend back to heaven to prepare a place for believers, and to return one day to bring all things to their proper end. Later, I learned of Christian teachings which still maintain that Jesus was God come to teach us how to live, but which say Jesus accepts people of many beliefs and at some future point may accept all of humanity into the presence of God for eternity.

Alongside these views are those who believe Jesus is an archetype of the good man, a human being who lived an exemplary life that others might emulate in order to live holier lives. Then, there is the historical view that he was a first-century rabbi in rural Galilee who taught revolt against the Roman oppressors in coded examples and stories, or the view of scholars like Bart Ehrman who believe he was an apocalyptic preacher who tried to prepare people for a cataclysmic change in history which he and his followers believed was going to happen within a generation.

There is some evidence for every one of these views. The first views that Jesus was God on Earth require the greatest reliance on faith in both Jesus as a person and in the written scriptures, as well as in the interpretation of those writings by a specific church or mentor. The later views are more tightly aligned with the search for the historical Jesus. While they do not require faith in a certain belief about a spiritual world, they also require faith in the academic work of scholars and the choices they make in evaluating the historic record.

Belief in Jesus as God and Savior from sin is based on faith and life experiences evaluated through the lens of that faith. There is simply no scientific or historical method that will prove to the nonbeliever that this crucified rabbi was in fact God. Faith in this interpretation of Jesus and his life requires faith in the scriptural record which has been passed down by the church and translated in a variety of ways that mostly resemble each other; faith in the correct interpretation of the texts, some of which contradict the Jewish interpretations of Jewish texts from before the lifetime of Jesus; and faith that conclusions about life events made by individuals, churches, and religious leaders as evidence of the hand of God are also valid. We cannot prove any of that by other means despite some best-selling books to the contrary. We cannot prove to anyone who does not accept the suppositions of faith that Jesus was God any more than we can scientifically prove that the current Dalai Lama is the reincarnation of all previous Dalai Lamas.

In my opinion, the view of Jesus of Nazareth as revolutionary is even harder to defend in spite of all I have heard and read over the years. Many of Jesus's teachings are ambiguous enough that different deeper meanings can be applied to them, and that includes revolutionary meanings. His reported execution under a sign mocking a claim to be the true King of the Jews can also be used in that argument. But I do not see any evidence in the Bible of his participation or sending out others to participate in violent revolutionary acts. There is no account of participating in the murder of authorities which a Zealot of the time might have committed. There are no recorded teachings of how to prepare for open confrontation and battle. I find Bart Ehrman's interpretation of Jesus as a rabbi teaching about a coming apocalyptic event far more in keeping with the written accounts of his life and actions interpreted without reliance on divine explanations.

With that background, I have been considering the recorded life of Jesus in terms of UFT. To do so I must leave faith-based explanations exactly there, within the realm of faith. I want to look at any evidence that he was a rabbi who taught things consistent with the emerging worldview of the twenty-first century. This is a risky game. The religious skeptic will surely object if I begin to imply that a person not proven to be divine already knew the scientific discoveries and theories of today. But

Christianity is my lifelong tradition and I believe there is territory here to be explored.

First, there are the many teachings of Jesus in the form we call parables. Using examples of life in the home or in occupations of the day, Jesus declares that positive outcomes are like the kingdom of heaven. Those who abuse others or behave in deceitful or unworthy ways are cast from the kingdom and into suffering. Readers who believe in the saving Jesus of faith sometimes find these stories confusing when combined with theologies of salvation, but they are generally seen as examples of the nature of heaven or exclusion from heaven, often interpreted as hell. I believe we may also look at these stories in another way consistent with UFT. We might read them as concrete examples of living each day in the universe as experiences of heaven or hell. The woman who finds her lost coin after searching all day is ecstatic. She is in heaven. The ungrateful servant not only makes another person's life one of suffering, he also ends up in misery. He is in hell.

These stories make sense within the conclusions of UFT that humans matter as we matter to each other in the present tense. The woman searching for her lost coin is acting within knowledge of the behavior of physical objects. She knows that misplaced items remain where they have been put until they are found and moved again. She knows that dropped round objects may roll into hidden corners or fall through cracks in ways that might tempt one to use language such as hiding or disappearing. But she works all day in confidence that what is lost in her home will be found in her home. And when her efforts are successful, she is full of joy, now, in her home, in the world that is. It can, and has been, used as an example of a future hope. But it also works perfectly well as a story of experiencing joy in the present. The same is true for the negative parables. They can be interpreted as examples of future punishment. But they do not have to be. They make perfect sense as stories of how human behavior leads to human suffering in current reality.

I also want to briefly consider the way Jesus of Nazareth is recorded to have lived. He left no written record of what people were to do or believe in order to be rewarded after death. Historians who do not assign any divinely acquired talents to him tell us that a first-century people from the rural area of Galilee were most likely illiterate. And yet there is an account that says Jesus read from the scroll of Isaiah. His reported gatherings were large enough, and his activities were funded by others who were wealthy enough, that I would expect there would be someone who could have served as his scribe if his purpose was to leave a precise dogma for achieving eternal happiness. Instead, we have records of the stories discussed above, his conversations, one prolonged teaching usually called The Sermon on the Mount, and details of what he did as he traveled around the countryside.

How did he behave in his daily interactions? He is described as constantly going out of his way to be with people considered to be sinners. He went to the homes of tax collectors, fishermen, and others considered unworthy of attention from the religious people of the day. He broke traditions by associating with, conversing with, and teaching women along with his male disciples. Although the version that has come down to us seems to indicate some initial reluctance on his part, he also went to the homes of and met the needs of non-Jews including Romans.

I believe the recorded life of Jesus is precisely what one would write to show that the presence of God is in the universe in the here and now. Not just because Jesus is that presence, but because that is how life works. The universe does not discriminate. We are all here, the people we like and approve of and those we do not. In the only life we know about through direct observation, we are here on this planet together. We can make life better or worse for each other, but we coexist. I see Jesus as recorded in the Christian Bible consistently going out of his way to include everyone, the forgotten, the despised, and even those others deemed deserving of death. In fact, as recorded in the Gospels, Jesus even includes the dead. He is never recorded as passing a funeral without bringing the person back to life and reuniting them with their loved ones. Whether one literally believes those stories through faith or not, they take inclusion about as far as it can go. Another of his parables does the same as he talks about the poor and the people of the street being brought into the banquet the wealthy are too busy to attend.

In a universe where we know we matter because we matter to each other, the life of Jesus as recorded and passed down seems to me to be an exemplar. In these accounts there is no sitting in a place of power and acceptance while condemning those who do not belong. This Jesus travels the countryside including the poor, the rejected, the ill—including lepers that others would not allow within feet of themselves—people given to fits of violence and rage, and even the Roman oppressors. Jesus of Nazareth comes to town and announces that the kingdom of God is here.

Other theologians can investigate, debate, and, I suspect, create, meanings to the teachings and life example of Jesus. Most of those constructions will require acceptance or rejection based on whether one has faith in the written sources and the current interpretations. Beginning with what we can know through scientific observation automatically makes UFT inclusive rather than exclusive. In a universe that contains everything, even the attributes traditionally attributed to God, everything is included. There is no list of who or what is in or out. Everything we know or have any expectation to learn is within the universe. There is no need for theological debate about who is here, who will remain beyond death, or who is leaving. The laws of physics make very clear that we are all compositions of matter and energy which remain while the universe remains even though they are no longer in a combination identifiable as us. The universe includes us all and excludes no one. There is no physical evidence of anything leaving to exist in another realm external to the universe. Those beliefs require faith in religious explanations which move outside the realm of observable facts. The facts we know say that everyone, even life from other planets if discovered, is part of the universe. We are all in. I believe the recorded life and teachings of Jesus make beautiful sense for living a heavenly life in the universe we know as we invite others to do the same.

Pushing Water

4/1/2019

Every day when he could escape from work at the family boat he would go to the beach and build. He built sandcastles, beautiful imaginative sandcastles. They were so delightful that after a time, tourists even began paying him to build castles with their children. But there was the tide. It too came every day, without fail, erasing his work. And he hated it. Each week his indignation grew that this water, this force, this other would come and take away his place, his joy, and his income. He was pushed aside every day and felt helpless, and he vowed that somehow, one day, he would fight back.

And then the day came. One day as he glared at the tide and cursed its damage to his work, it began to recede. Jumping up he spread his arms as wide as a great seabird and screamed. He screamed as he ran toward the tide that today was his and it must recede. And it did! Faster than he could run, it gave up its usual position and retreated further than he had ever seen it go. Today he was master of the world. Today he could push the water, and he pushed until he could not see it and raised both hands in ecstasy. Never fearing that something was amiss, and danger was near, he clasped his hands together over his head in victory. He had won. And then he died as the tsunami rolled ashore.

Today US evangelicals believe they have won an impossible battle. For years they have hated an unstoppable tide they fear will take their place in the world and their privilege. It is a tide of darker skinned people. It is a tide of women. It is a tide of people who do not accept their religious beliefs or accept their calls to choose faith in an ancient text over the findings of science. It is a flood of people in all walks of life telling them that they are by birth not CIS or heterosexual, that they are according to the religion's definitions an abomination to the evangelical God. It is a tide of court rulings and government actions favoring the people who want to replace them and destroy their castles. And they have been angry and waiting for a time when the tide would turn.

So, when a former liberal turned conservative candidate for president in 2016 and said he could turn the tide, they turned to him. They donned their red hats and raised their arms and they yelled. They cheered and watched in amazement as the campaign the experts said could not win gained momentum. And their candidate said they were right. The white male believers in God were the ones being persecuted by these others with their rights to behave in unnatural ways. Their candidate said he would stop the flood of darker skinned immigrants threatening to become the majority in their country. They could again build their nativities on courthouse lawns, hang the Ten Commandments in public places to tell others how to behave, and refuse to accept a world out to destroy the world they loved.

And now they are pushing back. They are ignoring all signs that something is wrong and that everything is not what it seems to be. A wall is going to be built to stem the dark-skinned tide. Their rights to act only according to their own beliefs and not have to serve those *others* in their stores or work beside them in their businesses are finally being promoted by the head of the free world. The impossible has happened and they do not care why. Their day has returned. And they are celebrating without looking out to sea.

But pushing water is a dangerous thing. When the world reverses itself, it is time to observe carefully. By an odd combination of symbols, in the United States the elephants are rushing out upon the beach. In Sri Lanka, those who knew to watch saw real elephants head for high ground while everyone else wondered at the strange turn of events. Every swimmer knows you can push against water. You can propel yourself through it by doing so, some swimmers can do so with great efficiency and speed. But the water returns to its place. If you move according to its nature, it works. But you cannot by any human means move all the water to one side of the pool. What is pushed returns in a rebound wave. And if you are as unfortunate as Sri Lanka was in 2004, no matter what you believe, no matter how innocent or pure, no matter if you take notice at all, the tsunami comes.

And this is an essay of great pain for me. While I no longer claim the label or attend the activities of US evangelicals, I was one of them. Many people I love still are. Unlike my suspicions of too many leaders, they are sincere. They really believe they are standing for what is right and that their own place in the world has been usurped. Now as I watch the danger of their position cheering the retreating tide, I cringe. There are church leaders speaking out for what is right, but others are cheering them on that now is the day to retake the beach. Finally, they can say things they have been told not to say. They can speak openly about what they truly believe is truth revealed by the one and only God. And I fear they will not see the water turn. Water can be pushed so far, then it returns.

I fear for my former colleagues in Christian ministry. I worry about friends believing it is now safe to express the views others find offensive in public and at work. While I disagree with their conclusions that they are being oppressed if they must bake someone a cake, grant them a state license, or let them use a public building, I see the possibility that real oppression of their views could be closer than they know. While I do not agree with their desire to express their views no matter who they offend, I understand it—having served as a public-school teacher reminded that I should not share my own beliefs with my students because the Constitution prohibits Congress from establishing a religion. As much as I have changed, I have not lost my loving concern for those who still occupy a space I decided to leave. And I see a possibility that in this time of apparent victory, they may finally be at true risk.

Politics are less predictable than water. But they do tend to shift in pendular swings. When things are pushed to one extreme, it is logical to expect the return swing to also move far past center. So, I am watching with great concern. Their chosen leader is a man who shows little or no constraint. While some may notice that things are being pushed too far as children die in chain-mesh desert cages, others are still cheering. The courts are becoming more conservative but so far that tide has not turned. The current status is mixed on whether it violates a person's rights to have to sell something their beliefs prohibit using. The current courts have not ruled that they can act as if the whole country shares their beliefs. And I am watching. It remains to be seen how far this tide will recede. And so, it is also too soon to predict how harshly it will return.

Twenty-nineteen is a strange year in the United States. Twenty-eighteen showed some sign that people felt the tide had been turned far enough. Twenty-twenty is up for grabs. I do not believe anyone on the night I am recording these reflections can predict what will happen. But if I could, I would warn my religious friends not to celebrate a turning of the tide too quickly and not to try to push water too far no matter how powerful they may feel now or in 2021. What unexpectedly travels one direction may come back the other with great force and destruction. Tsunamis kill. I am concerned that believing they are winning back lost ground for their faith, their lives, and yes, their selfish rights and profits, they will go too far and incubate the very hate they believe is already present. The tide that suddenly surrenders, will return. I hope that those who claim to follow the Prince of Peace will not push their advantage too far and provoke the very animosity they fear.

I would prefer that we follow the real elephants up the hill. Let's step away from danger. Let's take care of one another like the Christian faith has always claimed we should. Let's protect each other from the onslaught of all extreme agendas. And if there is destruction by the time we weather this phenomenon, may we all be here to rebuild together.[1]

---

1. Twenty-twenty held surprises for everyone.

Consumption Reigns

4/12/2019

MY RECENT CONTEMPLATIONS HAVE TURNED to the pervasiveness of consumerism as a decisive factor in US views on all areas of life.

I remember discussions decades ago about how our attitudes had shifted from ideas of duty and responsibility to a constant search for happiness. It was said that fathers in the 1950s who went to work and then came home to eat a TV dinner in front of their black-and-white TV would have described their life in terms of meeting their responsibilities to their family. They were earning needed money for the family. They were paying their bills and taxes. They kept their property in acceptable order. They watched the news to stay informed and they voted as a responsibility of citizenship. They sent their children to school so that they would be prepared to take up their duties as adults and live responsibly. They might not have even understood questions about whether they enjoyed their work and were happy with their packaged meal.

Then, somehow in the sixties and seventies, which I remember fondly, there was a shift to my generation which focused on what made us happy. Jobs were now supposed to be enjoyable, or at least fulfilling. Bosses were supposed to care about our feelings, not just our productivity. We want news presented in a way that does not offend us at a minimum and that ends with a happy story that leaves us feeling good. Eating is entertainment as well as nourishment and people often post pictures of the food they are enjoying so much that surely others want to see a picture of it. Any activity that we do not find enjoyable is discarded whether it is personal, community, religious, or civic. Many voters fail to achieve

Consumption Reigns

any sense of empowerment and significance in the act of voting, so it is abandoned as a responsibility of citizenship.

The shopping mall made even the act of consuming into a multi-sensory form of entertainment. Buying clothing was not just a matter of selecting suitable items. Now, the store had to be attractive and have the right music at the correct volume. Food and entertainments had to be easily available without having to go back outside or drive to a new location. Young people began to see the shopping area as a place to gather socially and older folks found a place to walk for exercise in the company of others and out of the weather. Churches that wanted to grow large congregations soon followed suit. A worship center, no longer called by old-fashioned names like a sanctuary, was not enough. Churches added coffee shops and gathering areas along with gymnasiums. Music had to match current style preferences and be played at a volume that matched the desires of the target audience. All these changes have been widely examined and discussed.

I am wondering if seeing the world as a consumer has now overtaken every aspect of our society.

Our candidates for office approach it as both entertainers seeking followers and as consumers of our votes. Enormous sums of money are collected and spent to market candidates as attractive brands. Position platforms are crafted and presented in ways that party experts say are most likely to command our attention and attract our votes which are a product the candidate needs to accumulate. Those elected now seem to me to consider many issues based not on some standard of right or wrong, benefit or harm for the community, state, or nation; but rather, in terms of what they will get in return for spending *their budgets* as opposed to the public's funds.

Education is no longer seen as a significant responsibility of society to prepare the next generation. Schooling is an expensive commodity bought with tax funds under the question of what will be produced in return. The responsibility to learn and achieve no longer lies with the student. Teachers are paid and are therefore expected to produce desired results. Accustomed in the twenty-first century to immediate consumption, waiting until students graduate to evaluate whether they are prepared for the next phase of life is too long. The government wants immediate evidence of return on investment. Being too far removed to evaluate the multiple facets of education directly, they have turned to another purchased product in the yearly exam. If the exam scores are not at the level the legislature and governor wish to see, there is no complex analysis of data to determine what improvements students need in order to learn more. The test has been purchased with promises of accuracy in determining the quality of education and teachers have been paid to prepare students for it. If the state as the customer does not get the results they wanted for their expenditures, then teachers have failed as service providers and are identified as the problem. It is reduced to an annual financial transaction.

However, the desired result is not simply a new crop of workers. Politicians want people who will be drawn to their political brand. They want people who will be productive and continue to pay higher taxes, but who will vote on perennial promises of reduced taxes. If fully educated people are too likely to see all sides of issues or identify contradictions in political promises, then quality education leading to abilities to think critically and make informed decisions becomes a great sales pitch, but an undesired product. So, the curriculum and school experiences are reduced to narrow lists of specific knowledge and test preparation.

It seems to me that a similar logic appears in the arguments for all government actions. What will the state be buying with its money? What will the politician get in return for their votes? Will their action attract big money donors for the next campaign? Will their votes be packageable as a brand the public will buy? Our votes are a product they want to buy with their actions. They are marketable brands that will need advertising dollars and a pleasing package for voters to buy in the next election.

Now we go to church if we enjoy it and leave feeling positive about life, not in obedience to a God or the requirements stated in texts we claim are holy commands. We participate in civic events if we enjoy them and feel rewarded by them. We expect education at all levels to please and never offend us. We expect vehicles to thrill and entertain us rather than simply transport us safely. The news is supposed to support the views we already hold, entertain us, and leave us feeling good. Everything we do has become focused on whether what we purchase through funds or effort will make us happy.

Which brings me finally to our current president. I have been baffled by continued support of him despite constant lies and hate speech, plus evidence of possible illegal, unethical, and unpatriotic activity. Then I considered the phenomenon through these lenses. People bought him and they are still buying him. They grew to like him in his television show. They liked watching him turn to people usually considered privileged or powerful and saying, "You're fired!" They like the created image of a man who has achieved great success and wealth. Reality does not matter as much as the image. Here is a plain-spoken man who says things they would like to say and appears to have become fabulously rich. They buy it.

It now makes sense to me as I sit and shake my head at the daily outrageous acts and statements. People consume them. They listen to him blame somebody else for their problems and they respond, "There! I knew it!" They hear his latest insult of anyone, and they holler, "Wow, did you hear how he just roasted [insert any name]!?" Feeling constrained and insulted for years by being told that things they want to say are offensive to others, they cheer when he says them. Whether they agree with what he says or does, or whether they even understand what is happening, he is entertaining to a significant percentage of US citizens, and they buy him. Another way to see it is in the contrast. His opponents are described as dull, judgmental, or evil. The abortion issue allows those who favor women's rights to be labeled as baby killers. People buy the insults and not the candidates. They are positioned as unattractive products.

I no longer believe that much of anything in our society is based on ideas of right or wrong, or valued as an ethical responsibility. I fear we have crossed into an age where everything is about buying what makes us feel good now.

Is the Arc of the Universe Good?

4/20/2019

MANY PEOPLE KNOW THE QUOTE attributed to Martin Luther King Jr.: "The arc of the moral universe is long, but it bends toward justice." The origin of the quote likely goes all the way back to transcendentalist, Theodore Parker in the 1800s in a somewhat longer form.[1] However; as I continue to explore the significance of living in a universe where the powers traditionally attributed to God by the monotheistic religions are found within the natural order, I am forced to look further into whether there is any logical way to assume that such a universe can be described as *good*.

It seems to me that justice is limited to the known realm of reasoning creatures, which as of this time remains the world of humans. I am drawn to the optimism of assuming that human history over time shows a pattern, even if gradual, to greater justice. It is attractive to see the history of humans as progressing toward any positive trait. But such optimism may be self-congratulating and based more on the hope for progress than the known facts. There are reportedly forty million people suffering various kinds of slavery today.[2] We apparently live in a time when endless war has become a socially accepted phenomenon. The United States has spent trillions of dollars on wars in Afghanistan and the Arabian Peninsula since 9/11. Within my own culture, minority citizens are more likely than whites to be killed by police. And there is compelling evidence that many white citizens believe this is justified because they believe that minorities are more likely to be involved in violent confrontations with other

---

1. Parker, "Of Justice and the Conscience," paras 4–7.
2. "Slavery Today," para. 1.

citizens and the police. The current president has a substantial base of support while actively promoting fear and hatred of immigrants, Muslims, and other minorities. Humanity continues to ignore warnings that we are exhausting the basic resources of our planet and raising the global temperature as long as we can have the lifestyles we currently enjoy at the expense of the two-thirds world and possibly all future generations. The bend towards justice may be hard to see from a nonprivileged perspective. But I believe whether the arc of justice among humans is positive, is a matter of human choice. I want to turn toward the totality of existence.

Where this intersects old ideas of a cosmos called into being by God, we also face the term *holy*. And we find that it is a peculiar word to transform into ordinary understanding. Rather than some ultimate standard of pure or unadulterated, things that are holy are things dedicated to the use by, or worship of, God. Holy things are God's things. In ancient times the various furnishings and utensils of the temple were considered holy because they were made and only used for religious purposes to honor God. One candlestick is not more holy than another because of its gold content or shape. The candlestick is considered holy when it is set aside for the purpose of worship rather than common use. The same is true for buildings and places. Early cultures considered places holy because people interpreted their feelings there as a special presence of the divine. The tent of the Tabernacle and the original temple were considered holy because Israel believed that God dwelt in the Holy of Holies. Now buildings are declared set apart through specific prayer rituals possibly including anointing with oil or water dedicated to worshipful acts. Some traditions honor only a few humans as holy, as totally set apart to the service of God, while protestant Christianity tends to label all within the faith as holy through divine adoption, and possibly all humans as containing a least some holiness due to creation in the image of God. Ps 24:1 says that the whole Earth is God's. "The earth is the Lord's, and everything in it, the world, and all who live in it."

But how do we apply such a word to a universe with no anthropomorphized God? What is holy in a world which exists according to the laws that caused it to come into being and which continue to determine its actions? I believe we could play the same circular game of word meaning. It is holy in the sense that everything came into being in keeping with universal laws, behaves according to them, and cannot be shown to be for any purpose outside of the known universe. But I doubt the helpfulness of that logic. Individuals confronted with a different view of reality want to know if that new way of seeing brings any assurance of their safety and well-being. If there is not a personality at the top of the powers, then the question of whether that cosmos acts in any intentional way towards itself is absurd. At this point in our knowledge, there is no solid evidence of cognition outside of what we observe in sentient beings on Earth.

It also seems to be a study in the absurdity of language to debate whether a black hole consuming everything in its vicinity is just, or good. Are the birth and death of stars with the effect on all surrounding space, just? It seems to be a ridiculous question. We have no categories of right and wrong for the non-human, natural bodies of the cosmos. They do what they do. Period. It is equally absurd on many levels for our one species on one watery rock to apply adjectives like good or bad to the totality of the universe without religious definitions based on acceptance of some ultimate designer and rule setter. The practices of the East would advise us to give up such games and focus on whether we are in tune with all that is instead of focused on our need for definitions, or for that matter our needs at all. We learn to accept what is, and our place in it. In Judeo-Christian terms, we quit trying to be gods.

Nevertheless, I think there is a way to play the game. We must first simply admit that we are using definitions of our own creation and preference. A quick search of online dictionaries will demonstrate a lack of agreement on such a simple term as good with some placing moral criteria as a first meaning, and others putting the original emphasis on meanings of being useful or beneficial. In a world dominated by belief in rules handed down from a ruling deity, the definitions of moral good require matching the rules of that deity. I assert that in the world of *what is* there is less distinction between these choices. Even among people who claim to follow a rule-giving deity, it seems to me that good often comes to mean what is beneficial or desirable to the person or group making the judgement. Good entertainment provides the emotion we desire—whether laughter, tears, or terror—when we pay the price of admission. A good neighbor may help us in times of trouble, but at a minimum causes us no problems. The practical definition of good applied to other humans seems to be largely an extension of the definitions we use for a neighbor. Good people outside of our own immediate group provide us desired products and services and do not leave us feeling threatened with harm. Most of the definition of good in actual human practice seems to be, that which is beneficial rather than harmful to ourselves and those within our circle of caring.

So, the turn to the universe is not as difficult as it might first appear. We are here. The laws of physics controlling the formation and arrangements of objects in space caused our particular rock to have water and a breathable atmosphere. It allows a temperature range that has supported a large variety of life over time which at the present includes human beings.

Is it good?

We are here.

If the universe was somehow capable of operating outside the rules set by a creator, I suppose we would label it as bad. Whether we start with beliefs based on an anthropomorphized version of the forces and laws that control reality, or accept them in their own right, there is no evidence that the cosmos is capable of violating the rules by which it exists. The entire discipline of science depends on this assumption that matter and energy anywhere in the universe obey the same rules we have observed in all currently known and documented situations. The universe behaves the way its rules of existence say that it functions. In human terms, it behaves. It does what it is *supposed to do.*

These are the definitions we have available to us. The universe acts according to the laws evident in human study of it. The universe that exists according to those rules results in our existence on a planet that provides ideal conditions for our existence. And, like the God of Genesis, we proclaim that it is good.

A Threefold Approach

4/20/2019

PART OF MY JOURNEY OF contemplation has required letting go of some tightly held former beliefs and ideas about the future that I would still like to be true. As I share my thoughts, questions, and conclusions, I am aware that many of my ideas ask others to consider doing the same. And while I have come to question many things I formerly believed to be true, I have not abandoned seeking the truth, nor would I ever ask others to do so. This tension causes me to propose a threefold approach to what we know, believe, and hope.

First there are things that can be known. We can test them through formal experimentation and daily experience. No matter what a person believes about the underlying nature of the universe, when I sit down my chair supports my weight and air alone will not. We know the boiling point of pure water at any given pressure. Watching the pot or discussing any theory about it will not change the observable fact. No matter how many people join the flat Earth movement, there are basic experiments, and photographic evidence that show we live on a round world.

But something happened. Scientific theory about things we know came into conflict with people's religious beliefs about the nature of the world. The variety of life on Earth and the suitability of various adaptations for the environments where animals live are observable facts. Fossils exist and can be compared to existing life forms. Then Darwin and the field of biology after his time combined those facts into the Theory of Evolution. But some Christians are taught by their religion that all life was created in a six-day period, destroyed by a flood except for the occupants of one large boat, and still resulted in the lifeforms we observe today. They find evolution distasteful and anti-religious. Their religiously based beliefs, including humans' difference from and superiority to other animals, cause them to reject the explanation of the observed facts held by almost all biologists. Now we have entered the second approach to knowledge—what we believe to be true.

Our beliefs about truth are based on our confidence in the people who present them to us, the sources they use, and our confidence in the correctness of the interpretation of the source. I accept the scientific method, the rigor of academic practice and theory, and the logic of the evolving theory of evolution. Therefore, I believe it. To do so, I also had to change my understanding of how the ancient scriptural text was recorded, transmitted, taught, and interpreted. This leaves me in an interesting place with intelligent religious friends, relatives, and acquaintances. Since we start with different suppositions about the interpretation of facts, neither the evolutionist nor the fundamentalist can prove their view to the other. The conclusions depend on our confidence in what we have been taught and the veracity of the interpretations. We can prove facts. We cannot force beliefs.

Lastly, there is a category of things we hope are true which overlaps in some ways the things we believe are true. We want to believe that our loved ones live on in some other realm. We hope that there is some continuing connection and/or some future reunion. As an example of the separation between belief and hope, there are many stories told of feeling that a person who has died is present or is now watching over the lives of those they loved. But the Bible upon which Christians who hold this hope base their beliefs, contains no such teaching. There are teachings about this life which appear to contain no promise of life after death, especially those that were written before the Christian era. There are teachings about a future judgement and reward for those have been faithful. There are apparent descriptions of heaven where souls live on in the presence of God. But there are no passages indicating that those we lose become guardian angels, or for that matter, angels at all. The text would seem rather to indicate the angels are a completely different type of eternal being from humans. But people hope their loved ones are still somehow close. And so, they believe things that are neither provable through direct observation, nor contained within the sources they believe by faith. They are views that are held based on hopes about the nature of the universe and eternity.

I believe our understanding of the world and our communication with each other can improve by understanding these three categories. It is good to know the difference between what we know, what we believe, and what we hope. What we claim to know should be demonstrable to another person regardless of whether they agree with our interpretations of it. A fact should not require pre-acceptance of any prior theory. A physical object is in the room, or it is not. However, once we cross into beliefs, something can be both present and not present. If we have a variety of Christian believers and nonbelievers in the room, there may be beliefs that the Holy Spirit is always present as a comforter and guide, is not present but able to be summoned by certain prayers and practices, or is a powerful myth created over time to explain events beyond our understanding. Each is real to the person who believes it, but none can be proven to the person who does not. Then there are hopes which we express as we communicate, especially when we comfort one another. When someone says that a deceased loved one is present and loving, I do not contradict their hope. It is not part of my beliefs that I should make the universe seem crueler and lonelier to them.

I would like to believe that various groups of humans could communicate more accurately and with greater kindness to each other by using this threefold approach. If a claim is made to know something, it should be demonstrable to others. Different beliefs can exist side by side when we acknowledge that they are beliefs. We can be prepared and willing to share why we believe what we do when others wish to know. But as beliefs, we can recognize that we all have different constructions of meaning without trying to force everyone to come to full consensus on every topic. And if we speak of our hopes as hopes, why should anyone wish to damage the dreams of another if the hopes are not destructive? For example, if another person claimed to hope for an all-white United States, I would consider it a misuse of the term I am using here. They believe, for whatever reason, that the US would be better without other races. I would reserve hopes for the positives they wish to see—perhaps a more stable country with less conflict. We can all hope for that without sharing their belief that nonwhites are the problem. Maybe I am separating things beyond what is critical. But I would propose that hopes be restricted to those positives we cannot provably predict, but which present a picture of a more positive universe both now and in the future.

I *know* that I typed these thoughts in the *belief* that they can benefit others as I *hope* for ways of being more fully human and caring as we interact with each other and the rest of the planet.

Everybody Knows—Or Do We?

6/1/2019

Today I was reading Amy-Jill Levine's *The Misunderstood Jew* with all the examples of things Christians think they know about Judaism in the first century or now. She discusses many things I have taught to others as true based on confidence in the people who taught them to me. And it suggested other things about the physical world. College science courses taught me three states of matter, leaving it to one of my fourth-grade students to teach me about the most common state of matter in the universe, plasma.

And somehow it hit me that what we are taught about even the North Pole is misleading. Of course, having been a scout and a backpacker, I knew that the magnetic and *true* north poles are different and must be accounted for to effectively use a map. Now the magnetic pole, which was never considered the true pole, is moving. If one wants to stand at the top of the planet, one must go to the true pole, or the south for the bottom. I even remember time-lapse sky photos of the stars appearing to circle when viewed from the pole.

But as the seasons are changing, I am reminded of another fact that everyone *knows*. We have seasons because the Earth is tilted on its axis. And it stopped me for a moment. If it is tilted, then the top is not where the pole is at all. To be on top one would have to be approximately at the article circle and move at the speed of Earth's rotation, about 1000 miles per hour. That would be an amazing job of log rolling on a planet!

But in space, everything is relative to something else. Up and down on Earth are determined by gravity. Up from gravity, makes every place we stand the top. Plus, Earth is tilted relative to the sun. The true poles were not just a mapmaker's whim. They are the ends of the axis of spin. If we do not make the sun the reference point, they are the top and bottom.

So, as I sit here and type, my mind is juggling images of this very chair as the top of the world, the North Pole as the top like I was taught in school, and a runner staying on top by constantly traveling the Arctic Circle at 1000 mph. The wall map in my classroom had the North Pole directly at top and the Atlantic Ocean as the center. The one I brought home from China still had the same orientation for North but placed China in the center. The one my friend has from Australia tilts the image so that Australia is centered, and North is no longer at the top of the map. And they're all true from some perspective, depending on the presuppositions and definitions we choose. Perhaps from one of our interplanetary probes, the top is whichever part of the solar system is currently closest.

Schrödinger's cat is alive, dead, and no longer in the box at all. Everything depends on the place we choose to begin and the meaning we choose. We know what we choose to know from our point of observation and the prior knowledge we bring from our own experience. Meanings based on the experiences of others often escape us entirely. Unless maybe, like a ten-year-old teaching me about plasma, another person can articulate for us a new view of reality.

May we have abundant opportunities to share views with any who are *other* to us and may we have ears to hear and minds and hearts to comprehend.

An Attempt at Brevity

6/6/2019

HUMANS HAVE OFTEN LOOKED AT nature and believed they saw gods. Living by rivers with power to sweep away everything and containing creatures that could suddenly appear to devour the strongest of land beasts, people believed in gods of the rivers. Living by mountains that sometimes exploded in fire and destruction, humans looked up and named mountain gods.

Then, the belief developed that there is one God over all. But people still looked up at the smoke and fire and said, "There he is." The wind destroys everything humans have built in an area and common speech and corporations today continue to declare the destruction as an act of God.

The science of the enlightenment grew and declared that rivers are just rivers, mountains are just mountains, the wind forms by natural causes, and that man only imagines supernatural beings and causes. Still, those who ride the rapid rivers, climb the peaks, or stand in the storm know. They know they are experiencing something much greater than themselves.

Now, science has investigated the smallest and largest realms. Humans have observed and recorded the realities of subatomic worlds and the vastness of the universe, and the results have been computed.

We have begun to comprehend the size and nature of the universe and the complexity of a single grain of sand. We have peeked behind it all and seen the field from which such things emerge. We have done the math.

And this time, this time unlike the others we have found the Eternal background, the particles and energy that are omnipresent in our universe, the omnipotent power of measurable energy throughout the cosmos, power which is everywhere and from which nothing is therefore hidden—in old language, the omniscient. And the possible combinations in this and perhaps many universes are Infinite. This time we have proven that the characteristics of God exist. And they are natural. They are found in the same quanta that compose each of us, our planet, and the vastness of the cosmos. God is real, but God is not supernatural. All the defining characteristics of God are present in the universe and the background field. Beyond the Deist, we can now declare that no external clock maker is required. All that man attributed to God is here and is part of what is.

But the magic persists. The way of the quark is not our way. The magnitude of the cosmos is beyond our mental capacity to grasp beyond recording numbers our minds have no ability to imagine. We do not know how one person can perceive the unspoken trouble of another across great distances or how particles know which way their counterpart spins. And so, we remain humble, in awe, perhaps reverent, as we contemplate the true nature of *God as natural* producing all things, sustaining all things, and reclaiming all things to the universal background we now know is as natural as the volcano, the river, and the wind.

We Worship a God We Do Not Know

6/15/2019

"For as I passed by, and beheld your devotions, I found an altar with this inscription, To The Unknown God. Whom therefore ye ignorantly worship, him declare I unto you."[1]

Paul, in the passage following this verse, argues that God is the Creator and not an object made by man and housed in any temple. But, while he can point to actions attributed to God and false perceptions of God, he is not able to show them this invisible One greater than their idols.

During the two thousand years from Paul's time to ours, the situation has not changed. When believers speak of the Creator, we have not been able to define the One we worship in terms beyond a vocabulary restricted to faith. Therefore, what I am asserting in UFT is not a new God, or a new definition of God. I am asserting that the quest for the unified theory in physics is approaching an original way of identifying the creative and sustaining power of all things in terms that can be defined without dependence on what Paul tells the Athenians is ignorant faith—faith in something we cannot see or define directly.

Instead, Christian authors like Tozer have correctly pointed out that some things can be known by reason and others only by faith. God is transcendent and we are finite. As one of my favorite verses says, "For now we see through a glass darkly; but then face to face: now I know in part; but then I shall know even as I am known."[2] It is no heresy to say that God has always exceeded our observations, our vocabulary, our

1. Acts 17:23 (KJV).
2. 1 Cor 13:12 (KJV).

interpretations, and our full understanding. It is Bible. And it is a problem. What the person of faith accepts, the person of another or no faith may easily reject.

In faith the preacher may assert that God could be visibly present inside a burning furnace with faithful followers who emerged unharmed, and at the same time be present everywhere else in invisible formless reality. The unbeliever responds with all sincerity that this makes no sense to them. We say that God is a Spirit, the Spirit, and can be both present in a place and present everywhere. When pressed to define what this word "Spirit" means, we have no definition outside of accepting explanations which only have meaning by faith. Our glass is indeed dark to those who question and seek explanation.

Until now.

Now we are closer than ever in human history to defining the forces that can create a universe from nothing, that work in the specific case and universally at the same time because they are both behind and in all things. Within our lifetimes this unified reality may finally be expressed in a single mathematical equation and explained in paragraphs of prose—prose composed of words with definitions that can be demonstrated in a scientific way that does not require blind acceptance of unseen things beyond the glass. Some highly respected people will conclude like Stephen Hawking that the need for God has been eliminated as all things now fit in a form that requires no magic. UFT asserts that we are approaching a definition of God—the creative, sustaining, all present power of the universe—that will not require blind acceptance by anyone with the capacity to study and understand the science and math.

We will reach a new plateau on the journey recorded in stories, poetry, and teachings from the ancients down to our own time. This new expression does not need to be seen as contradiction or refutation of all that came before. It is more accurately the glorious product of an evolution of understanding that has been unfolding through millennia of faith and experience. The collected wisdom of the ages, across multiple traditions, says very clearly that man has long stood in proper awe of a power greater than our species. With the ability to see, reflect, and build explanations we are creatures with a long history of crafting images of a unified reality that is beyond our grasp. The unified theory will be the culmination of this most epic of journeys.

But a problem will remain. That equation, or set of equations, will not fulfill our desire to know how those forces are involved in our joys and our tragedies. They will not carry the same level of comfort and reassurance that we find in the stories we create to explain the mystery of our existence and experience. We will continue to seek expression for our interaction with a reality greater than ourselves, whether that reality is shown to exist in the physical realm or described as part of a separate spiritual realm. Knowing that greatest *Other* to be real will not erase our desire for the meaning of life and life's events. We will still be creatures who ponder our relationship to the cause of our wonder.

The Inadequacy of Equations

6/20/2019

WHEN, OR IF, THE THEORY of everything is finally expressed in a single equation, academics and students of math and science will celebrate. It will be the culmination of millennia of study. We already have sets of equations that work either in the study of the very small or the large. But these equations tend to become meaningless mathematically when the numbers disappear in answers of infinity. Math students may remember that this happens when the denominator of a fraction becomes zero, nobody knows how many nothings there are in something. I already find these sets of understanding to be excellent representations of the power theology calls God. Theologians tend to speak of power(s) while physicists speak of force(s), but they are often speaking of more similar things than the twentieth-century divide between theology or science leads us to believe.

Will understanding of the natural forces replace theology and concepts of God as some scientists and new atheists insist? With no final equation in hand, I will use the ubiquitous $E = mc^2$. This elegant equation has led to discoveries that were not yet imagined by most even in the world of physics when Albert Einstein published his famous theories. It has made its way into common knowledge and expression regardless of deep understanding of its implications. But it is not what comes to mind in times of deep trouble or joyous celebration.

When life and health are threatened, no normal person would cry out, "$E = mc^2$ have mercy and protect us!" When experiencing awe while observing the natural world or holding a newborn child, I know of no one who would declare, "Look what $E = mc^2$ has done!" I do not expect that situation to change with a new equation. The most beautiful and elegant of equations does not express the deepest feelings of the human mind and heart. Eastern disciplines and practice will continue to provide a path for practitioners to acknowledge and live in the experience. Likewise, I believe traditional expressions of faith will continue to be the clearest form of expression for many people. If new knowledge of the forces that control all things simply helps us to see the ultimate power as an actual combination of forces rather than an invisible cosmic person often depicted as one of our own race, if not also gender, I will be content.

Ancient poetry continues to express our joy and despair, our anguish and hope, alongside expressions of our own time. Ancient stories still give expression to our perceptions of reality if we allow them to be story, metaphor, or myth. We are creatures of story and song. Human beings will not change to emotionless computers merely by acquiring deeper knowledge of the ultimate workings of the universe.

There are problems that equations can help us solve, and ones which they cannot approach. If we wish to objectively examine how the amount of carbon we release into the atmosphere changes the temperature of the earth, we have the math. If we wish to predict the changes in large-scale weather patterns, we have the math. If we wish to predict the possibilities of severe weather in one selected location on a given day, we have simulations which will help us with probabilities. However, if we must bury a child killed by one of the storms, math will not comfort the family, give hope to the grieving, or sustain our loving memories. For that we will need language that speaks to our core understanding of life. And for as long as we have records, that has been and remains the language of faith.

Why Theology?

6/22/2019

If the forces which can be studied through observation of the physical universe are shown to be self-sufficient, why continue to speak of God? Why bother with theology?

First the word "God" and various other names for God have always stood for the ultimate unity beyond all things and a power which is bigger than man. If that unified power is finally understood in ways that allow us to write equations and study its nature and interactions, the name need not arbitrarily be something other than God. Fire is still fire and lava is still lava after we have discovered their nature and behaviors. Although I suspect some religious people would object if the unified theory implied that we could manipulate the unified forces—that man could now manipulate God. However, religious practices have always had some of this characteristic. Despite theological assertions to the contrary, people engage in various religious activities often believing that God will honor their acts by doing what they desire instead of what appeared likely to happen naturally.

This brings me to the question of why continue theology if physics can explain the universe. Even if science provides explanations of the ultimate creative and sustaining power of the universe, I doubt that it will provide comfort or solace to most people. If people continue to refer to that power as God in their attempts to explain our relationship to it, theology will be indispensable. It is the theologians who confront the connections and disparities in our explanations of our place in the universe. It is the historians of theology who are positioned to explore the many misuses of religious teachings in the past.

The forces currently under consideration in seeking the unified theory have never been considered to have genders or gender preferences—not so the study of God. Millenia of study and practice implying that God is male and chooses males for leadership and extra favor are already under serious debate among theologians. Any continued use of the word God must deal with that heritage along with teachings that any one group of people is favored above all others, has the right to dominate others, or even—as a continued legacy of the twentieth century—has the right to commit genocide in the name of that power. Gravity, the nuclear forces, electromagnetism, light, thermodynamics, quantum forces and strangeness—none of these have any traits that indicate any justification for promoting the power of any group of humans over others. In a secular setting, philosophy—and in theology for those who continue to find the strongest expression of meaning in religion—humans will continue to confront these issues in the search for meaning and guidance for more evolved human behavior.

If we accept a unified theory of everything, it will imply a far more impartial universe than previous theologies, philosophies, and social theories have implied or stated outright. It reminds me of the anecdote that Lincoln was asked whether God was on the side of the Union and is said to have replied, "Sir, my concern is not whether God is on our side; my greatest concern is to be on God's side, for God is always right."[1] Arguably, this is the question in dealing with a universe controlled by value neutral forces. This will be straightforward enough in questions where physics and other sciences apply such as, "Is this the best way to build a bridge, power our machines, or travel through space?" It will be far more problematic for questions about the correct way to live, to respond to those not considered part of our own group, or how to use or conserve natural resources.

If we do not abandon every individual to their own whims and choices, no matter how ignorant, we will continue to look to philosophers, theologians, and ethicists for guidance. My own preference for continued use of the concept of God in considering the ultimate springs from both theology's long history of seeking to understand the greater power and the recorded life of Jesus as an example of the highest level of living a life that is fully human. I believe many Jewish scholars would find the new reality very similar to what they have studied and debated for

---

1. "Abraham Lincoln Quotes," para 52.

hundreds of years minus the example of Jesus as an exemplar. I already find friends who pursue Eastern practices of meditation and mindfulness very comfortable with the concept of aligning oneself with what is. While many of them do not use the language of God or religion, I believe that their practices will continue to be meaningful to many people.

Whether identified by various names of the higher power, accepted in a mystical form as reality, or recorded in an elegant equation, the power that controls the universe will always be larger than us. Humans will continue to turn to those who spend their lives in study of our relationships to each other, the planet, and the universe for guidance in our responses to life's joys and hardships. We will continue to need those whose daily work is to examine, question, and reexamine these issues of behavior, belonging, and social behavior.

If You Kick a Bear

6/30/2019

IF YOU KICK A BEAR, there is no punch line. The results are predictable. You are probably going to get hurt or die. Things like that are reasonably predictable in an interaction between a human and a bear. And there is a point. Nobody should blame the bear. It is not evil, overreacting, or exhibiting any other aberration of bear behavior. It is just being a bear. And your grieving friends and relatives will find no profound deep sounding answers when they cry out, "Why!?" to the universe. The answer is simple; you kicked a bear.

If you choose instead to take a ride in your car, your odds are better. On any given day almost 3300 people in the USA die in their cars. But since there are approximately 330,000,000 of us, your odds have improved. Your chances for the worst of luck in your car are only something like 1 in 100,000 assuming you do not add factors like driving under the influence, using excessive speed, or texting all your friends while eating your lunch. But any of us who choose to be on the road could be one of the 3300 without doing anything wrong. Another person ignoring the procedures for safe driving could be the bear without us kicking them at all. And others will grieve and ask why. We will look for deeper meaning. But the facts are that we know driving is a dangerous game as well. The odds are in our favor. But we are only able to figure those odds because there is a number. If death was not a predictable result for a known number of people, we would not be able to compare numbers and determine the odds. Of course, we see driving as less optional than kicking a bear. We have constructed cities and neighborhoods on a scale of miles which prohibits many people from meeting their needs without a motor vehicle.

If I continue to pursue my hobby of climbing, I increase my risk of being one of the 1 in 127 people who die from falling. The odds for those of us who choose to travel vertical surfaces are of course higher than for those who choose to live life on solid ground. It is a known risk associated with an activity that brings my friends and I much joy. My odds are good staying on the ground, something like 1 in 330,000,000. However, just by going into the woods I increase my risk to be one of the approximately 100 people per year killed by falling trees. This statistic inspired this reflection because the number of 100 per year in the country could be divided to two per state, and I have already been involved in dealing with two deaths by tree in my home state in the first half of this year. One was cutting down the tree; the other was just a young girl walking a gravel road in the woods with friends. We all want a reason. But the most defensible answer is that trees fall, especially if you cut through them, and humans who choose to be near the trees are more likely to be among the 100.

Or we could sit at home and do as close as humans are capable of to nothing. And still there are odds that we will then be one of those who die of coronary disease or some other factor we typically label as natural causes. To my mind it is a false distinction. An automobile is not a naturally found object; we know it is assembled by humans and their machines. Still, the human body has a tolerance for absorbing forces and when we get in our machines and accelerate across our section of the planet, we know we are increasing our risk. The cars themselves do nothing willful to us. When there is an accident, the body's ability to absorb collision forces or withstand being crushed by a collapsing metal container is a factor of our nature and the physics of our bodies.

Why does it happen?

We are mortal; a sentence which for some implies that there are other things which are immortal. There is no such automatic dualism. Even stars die. They simply live much longer than us. We are born. Most of us are lucky enough to grow and learn and make choices. Then, no matter what choices we have made, we die. It is the reality hiding behind all our doing, self-care, and risk taking. It is part of the nature of our being. We are creatures of a predictable *average* number of years of existence. Then our form ceases to exist as a recognizable whole although our essential building blocks continue. We want a deeper explanation. It seems cruel to say to those stricken by grief, "Well, they chose an activity with smaller odds of survival." Somehow people find it more comforting to speak of a controlling invisible being who needed them or will use their death to accomplish some greater good. I do not have evidence that the forces of the universe agree to meet that need for us.

It is the nature of averages that some of us will depart this fellowship of the living sooner and others will go later. We hate to say good-bye to most of them, and it seems especially hard for those whose journeys end early in their years. And we grieve. That too is as much a part of life as breath itself. But death also is natural. It is normal. It is not abnormal simply because it is painful to us. It is unavoidable. If we give up everything that brings joy and adventure to our lives, our day will still come. And disease may come upon us sooner the less we choose to be active, even though each type of activity has a known risk.

How do we respond?

I choose to live.

I am most alive when I go to the woods. I am most aware of being a part of everything that surrounds me when, assessing the risk and then using what safety measures are available, I choose to use the facility of my mind and the strength of my body to move up a rock wall. Not living in an area where big hill skiing is easily available, I enjoy the thrill of dancing with the planet when my car is running well and a curving road through interesting surroundings beckons me to accelerate to a point where I feel the shifting of forces and the clinging of my tires to the surface. All of it increases my odds of being one of those who leave early. But I choose the dance. I choose the joy. I choose the peace of belonging in the natural order.

I also choose not to kick the bear. Wisdom and an instinct for self-preservation tell each of us where our chosen limits are. We each assess and decide. Some make choices which seem excessive to me, even as my choices seem ridiculous to others. But we all make our choices for how to spend our hours among the humans who continue being. And the odds of us all ceasing to be at some point in time are one to one.

Some choose to participate in activities that seem as silly to others as kicking the bear. Some of us choose to walk in the woods and to introduce children to the simple exhilaration of feeling life's embrace as one walks in the woods. It is much safer than ascending a high-altitude peak or crossing a multi-lane highway on foot. But days come when trees fall at the very place we walk. We wish it was more subject to our prediction and control; but it is natural, and it is part of the reality we enter when we go there. For most of us the living is worth the dying; being fully here is worth the exit when we are no longer here. That end eventually comes to us all regardless of our choices.

My mind goes back to the ancient literature and the proclamation of the rules by which the ancient Hebrews were called to live. And even though the conclusion of the speech attributed to Moses is in the context of obeying those social codes, it sings to me as I consider the choices we make each day: "This day I call the heavens and the earth as witnesses against you that I have set before you life and death, blessings and curses. Now choose life."[1]

Sometimes the choices we make to live fully will place us among those who die. That is the risk. That is the gamble. It is the final reality regardless. We still stand before the two trees of Eden and choose to stretch out our hand to life or death. So, we look around, examine the world and ourselves, make our choices, and go forth to live.

1. Deut 30:19.

The Continuing Evolution of Consciousness

7/15/2019

As I grew up in the second half of the twentieth century, I learned two different views of man's place in the order of living things. The US evangelical worldview said that life came into existence very quickly in all its complexity with humanity intentionally placed above and distinct from the rest of the animal kingdom. Humans alone were capable of and in direct relationship with, or rebellion against, the Creator of all things. In the other dominant worldview, science had already adopted the theory of evolution with humans evolving from other life forms by the same process as all other living things. However, humans were still considered different from and superior to all other animals. Because of the opposable thumb, the discovery of tools, the ability to control fire, or some other factor such as learning to walk upright, humanity had evolved to a level of brain development that exceeded all other animals in both levels and forms of thinking. Both worldviews presented humans as the only animals that thought, reflected, experienced awe, or worshiped.

Since I was raised very deeply involved in the religious worldview, I may be remembering the scientific view as it was filtered by my mind to fit more closely what I believed was true. But I believe I am presenting what I was taught fairly. We were taught that only man made tools, took action after a process of thinking that surpassed instinct, or experienced emotions. Humans alone practiced altruism, or experienced patriotism at a level leading to war. Worship of a higher power was considered by science as part of social evolution occurring as people developed

The Continuing Evolution of Consciousness

agriculture and began living together in large groups. But it was still an activity unique to our species. Those distinctions seemed to be established, fixed, and stable.

The distinction no longer seems clear or stable. We have observed animals display grief, learn and use language, protect others including members of other species, make and use tools, and even mount organized attacks on other groups of the same species. Juvenile gorillas have been observed disassembling traps after the death of an infant gorilla in one of the snares.[1]

Research is also suggesting that even plants reach out to care for others through root structures in ways never imagined in the worldview I learned in school.[2] It causes me to contemplate whether these behaviors are new or were missed by earlier scientific observers.

Paradigm research raises the possibility that these behaviors were simply missed. Researchers firmly trained to expect only certain types of behaviors will tend to find the behaviors they are trained to find, fail to see contradictory evidence at all, or discount counterexamples as mere coincidence or human projection of our own characteristics onto other beings. Pet owners who have long maintained that their animals display emotions know well the response that they are making false assumptions of the animals exhibiting the emotions or thoughts of the owners. Indigenous people living closer to nature claim that four-legged and winged creatures are more like cousins to humans and tell stories of their intentional acts. But these views are often considered primitive by science and possibly demonic by the religious. I also recognize that Jane Goodall's revolutionary work in the study of animal behavior has caused a significant shift in how animals are studied and the results that are obtained. So, I recognize a real possibility that recent observations are recording realities that were already present but not yet observed.

However, I do not believe this is the only possibility. While caution is appropriate given the protracted periods of time involved in previous evolution, I now realize that continuing evolution is another potential explanation of the differences being recorded in the twenty-first century. I find it possible as described above, but improbable, that all earlier behavioral scientists missed these behaviors. I believe that primates making tools for hunting or moving from trap to trap and taking them apart

---

1. Than, "Gorilla Youngsters."
2. Grant, "Whispering Trees," 48; Wohlleben, *Hidden Life*.

would have stood out to a trained observer as extreme counterexamples to previous models of animal behaviors.

The possibility then exists that we are witnessing increasing consciousness in other species as evolution continues in our time. While pessimistic observation of human behavior tempts us to conclude that humans are becoming less aware or responsive to the needs of others, we may be witnessing the growth of mental awareness and emotional response in other species as an unpredicted but completely normal part of the evolutionary process.

Realizing that all animals, human or otherwise, are mobile and reproducing pieces of the universe, it is possible that there is something about the nature of the universe that leads to the development of self-observation and reflection. Perhaps the nature of the universe develops an awareness of itself through living beings. The pure secularists would, I expect, require an explanation of biological advantage consistent with the process of natural selection. The religious or post-religious might see a strong parallel to teachings of creation drawn to relationship with the Creator.

I believe ongoing work at sites such as Göbekli Tepe and the interpretations of this site and others fits within the discussion of evolving consciousness in both humans and other species. Before Göbekli Tepe, the traditional model of human cultural development proceeded from developing agriculture and more permanent and concentrated settlement patterns to growth of social patterns such as religion and government. In the traditional model, changes in settlement predate cognitive and social changes. Göbekli Tepe seems to fit a new model suggesting that cognitive and social changes may have evolved first with gathering around religious sites being a cause for improved food production rather than a result of it.[3] The physical evidence seems to contradict a logical order of progression in skills and cognition. Such a model would have at least some early humans developing a sense of self and concepts of something bigger than self very early in the development of human thought.

Göbekli Tepe makes far more sense if we are seeing the development of emotion and rational planning in other species, also prior to these life forms developing any significant scale of intentional agriculture. We may simply have been wrong about how early consciousness develops in the evolution of the brain. If this development of awareness is

---

3. Dietrich et al., "Cult as a Driving Force," 13.

the cause rather than the effect of human settlement in large groups and the development of agriculture, I believe it fits both the evolutionary enhancement of continued survival and the traditions of religion. Human beings developed greater safety and isolation from their environment as they settled in groups able to support each other in times of need and protect each other from danger including human competitors. Without returning to any literal interpretation of the Genesis account, I find it interesting that its account of early humanity places awareness of and interaction with the divine before any form of agriculture.

At the edge of current theory, we find panpsychism, the idea that the universe is self-aware.[4] This theory expands the concept to the physical features of the cosmos and entertains the idea that stars may think and choose the order we observe in their positions and movement. There is much study yet to be done in this area and the science involved is as complicated as it is new and controversial. The theory may develop in interesting ways or further research may cause it to be rejected as readily as we would dismiss the idea that a volcano decides when to rest and when to vent energy.

But it is not absurd. We are self-aware and we are bits of the universe no matter what other constructions we choose to form about our existence. If we are observing the growth of similar awareness and responses in other parts of the animal and even plant kingdoms, our evidence that the universe is self-aware is growing through observation.

Serious theologians abandoned concepts of a human like God sitting somewhere above the clouds centuries ago. Science has never relied on such a concept, although individual scientists may have entertained similar personal beliefs. As I discussed in the essay "We Worship a God We Do Not Know," the world's major religions have resorted to vocabulary indicating a force or being that is somehow outside of the natural realm even while interacting with it. This force or being is defined with words that have only religious meanings because only a small number of people continue to believe that it has any physical form that can be named. And both religion and science continue to give explanations and interpretations of the universe which exceed our imaginations. But the evidence is growing that living beings do evolve toward awareness of both themselves, others in the environment, and some sense of awe in response to the universe—perhaps at earlier stages than we imagined. If

---

4. Matloff, "Can Panpsychism Become," 524.

researchers of panpsychism continue to produce evidence that what we consider nonliving in the universe is also aware, ancient texts describing an interactive Creator will become less absurd when viewed as prescientific expressions of our relationship to the universe.

At a bare minimum we can interpret evidence currently in hand to say that part of the universe is conscious in the form of humans, and the evidence is growing that other forms we can observe are also aware, thinking, and proactive in behavior. Science provides no basis for assuming that the evolution of this trait stopped with man. It is entirely possible that we are observing a natural process of the universe giving greater and greater expression to its ability to perceive, understand, and respond in awe.

How does UFT Deal with Forgiveness of Sin?

7/29/2019

FOR MANY PEOPLE RAISED WITHIN theologies based on a human fall from grace, a condition of separation from God from birth or some age of accountability, salvation through the sacrificial death of Jesus of Nazareth, and eternal consequences of either eternal bliss or torment, this is far from an idle question. Many who give up various teachings from their youth as they learn more of both the world and the nature of the Bible itself, cling to all or part of this theological framework. If the attributes of God exist within the forces observable by science and explained in theories of the origin and functioning of the universe, how do we escape the debt of the wrong we do? Is the sacrificial blood of Jesus thrown out as superstition? If so, how does a human being know when or if they are right with the universe?

Unless a person makes an existential leap into some religion as the most acceptable way of expressing the relationship of humans to the grandeur of the universe, the question becomes absurd without definitions. If there is no supreme being who communicates to us what is right and wrong in a way which resembles human thinking and speech, what is sin? Before I move to any attempt at a concise answer, I wish to make a parenthetical statement about the fuzziness of the definition of sin under the current system. Many Christians have lists of things they believe people should and should not do based largely on the rules recorded as belonging to ancient Israel for an orderly society and a right relationship with the Creator. But the dos and do nots are cherrypicked from the ancient lists. I know many Christians who claim that homosexuality is a sin but have no problem with consuming shrimp or pork barbecue for lunch after church and would be offended by the idea that they are simply choosing the rules that please them. But choosing which ancient laws to observe is exactly what they are doing. Others convinced that science reveals sexual orientation and gender as factors determined by biology, find the idea that a Creator would make LGBTQ+ people and then condemn them for what they are to be absurd and cruel. Denominations such as the Seventh Day Adventists and Nazarenes follow very strict rules of personal conduct while progressive Christianity places far less emphasis on lists of rules. So, I begin by setting aside the idea that there is a universally agreed-upon definition of sin under the grand variety of current theology. What seems to be universal is the idea that sin is real and must be resolved before death to enter a blissful eternity.

But even the consensus on the existence of sin with consequences fades if we expand our list of religions. Many Jews pay attention to the ancient rules or *mitzvot* as guidelines for a positive life and healthy human relationships but entertain no specific beliefs about an afterlife. Islam contains a wide variety of beliefs about acceptable or condemned human behavior but usually places the fate of eternity completely in the hands of Allah, believed to be too far beyond the realm and influence of man to be manipulated into guaranteeing any given eternal outcome to the believer. Eastern religions take the discussion into other realms of repeated existence and progress towards awareness of universal truth and unity with the rest of existence.

Please forgive me if you are from one of those traditions of sin and salvation and expect me to force the reality of a universe created and governed by very real natural forces into a specific mold in order to fit with previous theology. I am not fond of explanations of existence which begin with humans as fallen, evil, or lost and then claim the problem is resolved only within the teachings of a specific group existing within a specific branch of a certain religion. Within the Christian traditions, I have always preferred beginning with humanity created in the image of the divine and seeking to live up to that heritage. Perhaps that is a personal existential choice, but I believe we see other people very differently based on whether we begin with an evil or a divine image. And while UFT eliminates the construction of a God who ultimately reflects our image in favor of seeing ourselves as a natural part of the universe, I believe something closer to this second option makes sense. We do reflect the universe. We consist of the same basic elements as the rest of life, the planets, and the stars. Our bodies exist, move, reproduce, interact with other parts of our world, and die all in accordance with the same natural properties as everything else we observe. We are not so different after all.

Sin is a word with such a negative universal history of condemning, rejecting, harming, and even killing others that I would not mind if it fell out of common use completely. I like the idea of the *mitzvah*. There are behaviors we know through tradition and practice make life more positive for ourselves and others. Whenever it is within our power, we seek to perform them. When we fail, we make amends if possible and we turn to the opportunities present in our next moment of now. This is similar to the idea of choosing between the trees of life or death in each moment which resulted in the cover art for *UFT*. This is how I and some others who have accepted the ideas of UFT are trying to live. In each moment I choose to be aware of whether I am acting in a way that enhances the life of everyone present or setting myself up as a god with the right to express my condemnation of people or circumstances that displease me. When I have reflected on my acts, and improved any situations I may have handled badly and am able to correct, I turn to see the two trees—the power in the next moment to choose or life or death— always before me.

As I now see the world, behaving in a negative way affects myself and those around me as an observable consequence. It does not change the forces which control the universe. Those combined forces may slam me to the floor if I unwisely try to ride my granddaughter's hoverboard. Physics works, whether for us or against us. But those forces do not become angry at my hubris. They do not pronounce judgement and punish me. There is no human emotion or will in them. All such assumptions are projections of our own emotions and thinking where we cannot demonstrate that they exist. On issues larger than an ill-fated ride on a toy, the consequences will also be more severe. I believe that humanity has the power to destroy ourselves by acting in ways counter to the forces of nature and thus changing the conditions which gave rise to mammal life on this planet. I do not believe any metaphysical being will re-emerge as visible in the physical world and rescue us all from our own destruction. Neither do I believe that the natural forces or any metaphysical being will be punishing us with our demise if we continue to ignore the warning signs of damage to our environment. Judgement and punishments are projections of our views of life onto natural forces or imaginary beings.

At this point, I have said enough to cause relatives, friends, and associates from my past to believe that I have chosen atheism and may be at risk for eternity. I discuss the relationship of UFT to atheism elsewhere. What I am saying, I find remarkably like the religious teachings of my past having realized that the attributes previously known as God are physical rather than metaphysical reality. Behaving in ways which align with the known effects of those forces is more likely to produce results we find positive. Behaving in ways we know contradict the natural functioning of the world will usually result in a painful or damaging outcome. Behaving in ways which hurt others physically, mentally, or emotionally makes life worse. Behaving in ways which comfort, enlighten, and empower others makes life better. All that I see missing from my previous beliefs is religious jargon.

But what about the crucifixion of Jesus? I continue to believe it is one of the most beautiful stories ever recorded by humans if it is taken as recognition of our desire to know we are not alone in the cosmos, especially when we suffer. It is even more beautiful to me as an example of the power of one person to absorb the suffering of others. I believe the quotation of Jesus, "My God, My God, why have you forsaken me?"[1] is perhaps the penultimate expression of our feelings of fear and abandonment which often multiply as we realize how large the universe is and how small we all are by comparison. As a piece of literature wherein the power of the universe will do anything to be one of us, it is among the best ever recorded. As a literal story of God orchestrating the murder of his son as punishment for the sins of man which Jesus did not commit and did not inherit by conception from an earthly father, it is absurd to me. Outside of religious indoctrination, most people would reject any work of fiction with similar characteristics.

If Jesus's blood did not reunite us with God, where is our hope? Very simply our hope for unity with the universe including the forces that control it is this, we have never been separated. We have no way to separate from *what is* except in science fiction by leaping to another universe with different properties. We are in it. We are made of it. We are it. We are not more, and we are also not less. We are combinations of the same particles as all other things in the universe although we have developed an ability to reflect on our existence. The forces which animate and order the entire universe are the same ones in which we live. Reality has no emotions or

---

1. Matt 27:46; Mark 15:34.

grudges against us which must be overcome. If we seek to be at one with what is, all that needs to change is our delusion of separation.

Was Jesus God?

8/1/2019

THERE ARE DIFFERENT ANSWERS TO this question within twenty-first century Christianity ranging from those who believe Jesus was by nature both fully God and fully human, to those who believe he gave up parts of his Godly power in becoming human, to those who believe he was the foremost example of a human life lived in synchronization with the divine. I begin with this partially out of concern for those who may consider what follows a further step into heresy. I want to clarify first that there is not one single view of the divinity of Jesus held by all who self-identify as Christians. I will briefly consider Gospel sources for this variety of opinion and then turn to considering the issue solely within the assumptions of UFT.

The poetic beginning of the Gospel of John states clearly that the Word has always existed, is God, and created everything that is. Accepting the apparent meaning of "the Word" as Jesus, the answer seems clear. Then in chapter 5, immediately after performing a healing, Jesus defends himself against accusations of breaking the Sabbath by saying that the Father is always at work and so is he. He is then quoted further as saying that he can do nothing by his own power and only does what the Father is already doing. Now, we have the possibility that in his time as a human he claims that he only has the power to do what he sees God doing. Then in chapter 6 the author of this Gospel and the author of Mark chapter 6 say that Jesus was able to walk on water to catch up with the disciples' boat. The author of Mathew takes things even further and states that Peter can walk on water as long as his eyes are fixed on Jesus. However, when he looks around at physical reality, gravity regains its natural power over him, and he begins to sink.

A more puzzling account can be found in the Gospels of Matthew and Luke during a series of challenges, presented in differing order by the two authors, from Satan to Jesus. Both accounts claim that Satan somehow took or led Jesus to the highest point of the temple in Jerusalem and then challenged him to prove that he was the Son of God by throwing himself off. And while neither account specifically states it, there is usually an assumption of some sort of supernatural power allowing them to suddenly arrive on top of the temple, attributed either to Jesus or Satan. What I find interesting for our purposes here is that Satan is not quoted as saying that Jesus should walk on air, or simply fly or float down by some supernatural power of his own. In both accounts Satan seems to imply that Jesus will in fact be subject to the law of gravity and will fall but quotes from Ps 91 to assert that angels will catch Jesus so that he is not harmed. Jesus rebuffs the challenge and so the story does not show him exhibiting any divine physical power. At the end of both accounts, the tempter simply leaves him with no word on how either came down from the temple. The book of Matthew ends the encounter in the mountains rather than on top of the temple and states that angels then came and tended to Jesus.

In an account with similar wording, the Gospel of Mark quotes Jesus as saying anyone with faith can perform what others would consider miraculous acts. In chapter 11, Jesus is quoted as claiming that anyone could tell a mountain to jump in the sea and it would happen seeming to imply that all humans possess the ability to order the physical world to disobey the laws of nature. If one takes this passage as a literal quote, then Jesus is either saying he is not more powerful than other humans, or that all humans possess divine power.

Those who continue to read this sampling and many other events in the Gospels with a metaphysical worldview will come to different conclusions about the nature and power of the earthly Jesus based on which portions they believe to be literal events and quotations as opposed to those seen as metaphor, hyperbole, events which might be explained by natural actions and effects, or even apocryphal accounts added by later believers.

Turning to the assertion of UFT that the omni-powerful, omnipresent, creative, and sustaining reality which has traditionally been called God is now known to exist within the natural forces of the universe will,

I believe, lead to a different answer. According to twenty-first-century physics every quantum of matter and energy that exists now came into being during the Big Bang—granting that at the quantum level individual particles disappear and reappear in manners which maintain a constant quantity of total matter and energy in the universe. Within this worldview we are temporary arrangements of those quanta in a form we see as our physical being. I have previously considered that this means all the building blocks which are currently us continue after death and do in fact return to *God* if we interpret that word as meaning the unified field of the forces that control the universe.

Considering the assertion beginning the Gospel of John that Jesus has always been, every bit of his human form would have consisted of quanta that have been in existence since the universe began. Whether Jesus contained, controlled, or was in some way also those forces in physical form is in some degree a metaphysical question. Staying within the framework of science, every part of the universe which we consider to be physically present, behaves in harmony with those forces. If anything, anywhere in the cosmos is found to behave outside the action of those forces, physics will be forced to alter theory and identify and reconcile the force affecting that body with all others. Jesus would therefore have been a composite of quanta that have always existed, and which behaved in total agreement with the known forces that control all things. For me this matches quite nicely with the quote attributed to him in John 5 that he could only do what he saw the power of the universe doing. But does that make him *God?*

If it does, then it elevates all of us to the same status. We are all made of quanta of matter and energy which are part of the universe that has existed since the Big Bang. We all act within the forces that created and control the universe. We are not capable of doing anything else. More discussion of this is found in the essay above exploring what happens to the idea of sin within the UFT worldview.

Jesus of Nazareth was not present before the physical universe came into being. The Christian New Testament contains the stories accepted by believers of how the physical body of Jesus of Nazareth came into being—either naturally like others, or half naturally! But all the building blocks of that body were there at the beginning. And nothing was made that is not composed of those building blocks controlled by the forces of nature. In a quantum permanence and rearrangement sense, he was there at the beginning, and nothing was made apart from the same building blocks and forces as him. Jesus was a full expression of that grand design and dance,

So are you, and so am I.

Unbelief and UFT

8/4/2019

I AM NOW READY TO consider what acceptance of UFT would mean in relation to both atheism and agnosticism. I will start with the most simplistic definitions of those two positions and then move forward to consider a more complex interaction of worldviews.

It is now possible that science has identified all the forces involved in the creation and maintenance of the universe even though the quest to unite them in one explanatory equation has not yet been completed. It is possible that some new force or factor will emerge, but the nature and existence of the universe as a result of physical forces is well established. If, and only if, those combined forces are accepted as the real omnipresent, omnipotent power that has traditionally been called God and we use the simplest definitions of atheism and agnosticism, then those two positions are now untenable. One could continue to deny that those forces exist, but science shows that they do. To continue to claim that they do not exist would, in my opinion, be as willfully ignorant as those who continue to insist that Earth is flat.

Claiming that one does not have enough evidence to decide if those forces are real would be a position of laziness. Taking a course in physics or reading established authors from science should provide all the evidence needed to form a conclusion. Those forces are or they are not. To deny or doubt them would require doubting the evidence much as is now done by religious circles that continue to insist on a young Earth or an actual global flood survived by a single boatload of land dwellers. One can easily claim anything. But the evidence for what is real is available.

But the atheist does not deny those forces. The atheist position is often more friendly to the evidence of early twenty-first-century science than is the religious. The atheist objection would more likely be to any effort to equate those forces with the religious concept of God. Absent any insistence on proof of some immaterial realm or supernatural beings based on evidence observable in the material world, the argument would be semantic. If I had grown up being told that I was fated for eternal suffering because of who I am or my desire to follow the truth wherever it leads, I would be reluctant to agree to such a use of the term as well. Much harm to others has been done by those who claim special relationship to God. Many examples are recorded in the Bible itself. To deny past abuse of the term would also be to ignore clear facts in evidence.

I will approach it from a different angle and return to the volcano example I have used before. A village facing the possibility of destruction by fire and molten stone from above might well believe for centuries that a god who must be kept happy lives in the high places. Learning the science and physics of a volcano would eliminate the need to explain reality by claiming there was some metaphysical being involved. But it would not require abandoning belief in the existence of the volcano, that it represents extreme danger in eruption events, or has potential to provide needed power through heat. The reality of the source of fire above the village does not change. Our knowledge of what that source is does change and decisions would be made about what to call it. Very possibly the former name of the being believed to live at the top would become the name of what we now know to be a natural geologic feature.

The person beginning with a naturalist position and the one coming from a religious one might not agree on the best name for the forces under discussion. But they would now have common ground for discussion and understanding if both accept the reality of the forces. This brings me to my point of agreement with the atheist. I prefer to call the universe, the universe; the forces involved by their names; and the unified theory, if and when it is finished, the unified theory. In this way we are dealing with demonstrable realities and leaving behind connection to significant amounts of horrific human behavior in the past done in the name of various proclaimed deities. It does not in any way diminish my awe at the grandeur and beauty of either the universe or the human mind which seeks to understand it. It does not diminish my gratitude for existence and the many beneficial aspects of my planet and the energy from the sun. It does not decrease my desire to live in peace with other people and the Earth. For me it increases our importance to each other. It simply calls a volcano a volcano rather than Vulcan.

I also see potential for a more complex relationship with agnosticism. In common usage at the time of this writing, the term is used to mean a deliberate neutral position on the matter of whether there is any metaphysical being known as God. I do not find that it implies refusal to believe scientific evidence about the world and I would not expect current agnostics to deny the natural forces, even if we demonstrate that they fulfill the role formally attributed to various gods. Convincing the agnostic to accept labeling those forces as God would likely remain difficult for the same reasons as the atheist.

Something different happens if I separate the root and prefix of the term. Gnostic beliefs claim privileged knowledge which gives the insiders special place or favor in this world and often in a separate metaphysical realm as well. The prefix *a* simply means *not*. At the root agnostic means not a gnostic and would imply rejection of the idea that there is special knowledge available to some. I agree. This is one of the attractions of a unified field explanation of the universe. The math of advanced physics is daunting for many people, but we also have authors who explain the realities expressed in the equations in prose available to anyone who wishes to know. The knowledge is there for anyone to study and understand without depending on revelation from any being inhabiting a separate nonmaterial realm. This seems far more defensible as a valid expression of reality than special revelations to small groups of people, leaving most of humanity in the dark. I also reject the existence of any special gnostic revelation of truth. Instead, UFT expands the *gnostic* group to all humans. For all we know, it may include in some way other life forms on this planet. We do not currently know how to communicate with other life forms well enough to clearly determine if they have beliefs. Knowledge of the universe that *is* could easily include intelligent life on other planets circling other stars but not currently known to us. The focus on known facts and best theories definitely includes all individuals with the intelligence and willingness to study the working of the universe.

So why theology at all? The term is probably too toxic for some coming from backgrounds of disbelief or those who have suffered actual harm at the hands of religious people. For now, I believe it continues to hold value as a term for our pursuit of meaning as reflective creatures bound together by a common life on Earth and growing in our observations of the universe. The forces of nature need not come from a metaphysical source to inspire awe and wonder for things greater than our selves.

God in Schrödinger's Box

8/7/2019

IN 1966 THE COVER OF *TIME* Magazine famously asked, "Is God Dead?" It seems to me that for most of my life, God has been ensconced in Schrödinger's box. Like the poor imaginary cat, God might be considered both dead and alive within the unknown conditions inside the box.

The world's monotheistic religions continued to insist that God was bigger than any box and that the evidence of continued existence was available to those who believe. Some of their evidence was acceptance of ancient texts which immediately forms a logic loop. If you accept the sources as true for all times, you come to one conclusion. Anyone who does not accept that the texts as valid proof of current reality remains unconvinced that God can be shown to exist based on those sources. The religions themselves contain a great variety of interpretations of what the texts mean, the nature of God, and God's role in the natural world. God is in the box.

Others pointed to what they accept as evidence of miracles or personal experience to assert that God is real and active. But miracles are as unconvincing to the skeptic as the texts. Quantitative research does not bear out the claim that prayer changes the prognosis of patients. I would not expect it to prove miracles. If the cures were common enough to show significance in quantitative research, they would be commonplace and no longer miracles by definition. Personal experience also fails to translate to others. Many atheists will allow the believer their personal experience which may be a powerful force within their own lives. They will not, however, accept that another person's claim of divine experience proves anything which can be transferred to others or expanded as general proof of God. Each is left very much with their own opinion of the reality within the box.

Many scientists have tried to proclaim that finding out if there is a god inside an imaginary box is separate from the realm of science. Their focus is on the empirical evidence of mass and energy in the universe and the theories which seem to best describe and predict objective observations. Any interpretation of those phenomena as having a cause from beyond the physical realm, is outside the aim and power of scientific methods.

Others approaching the unified theory have used religious sounding language. The Higgs boson was frequently called the God Particle. Many popular explanations of the quest for a theory of everything as science describes conditions nearer and nearer to the original singularity call the research a search for God. It is a logical use of language given the attribution of creation to God by the monotheistic religions. But it is also confusing. Such descriptions do not mean that science expects to reveal Allah or Yahweh. Only that research has taken human understanding closer and closer to understanding how the universe came into being—the forces and mechanisms of creation.

Atheists have been clear that they do not find the research to have anything to do with a non-physical being existing under the generic title of God. Stephen Hawking in his final book made it clear that the advances in science provide an explanation complete enough to eliminate the need for any idea of an external God to explain the universe. He concluded that there is no God. Despite many quotes misused and misrepresented by various religious publications, Einstein also did not believe in any personal God when he used such language to discuss exploring the secrets of the universe. God is still in the unknown condition of Schrödinger's box.

What I am suggesting in UFT is extreme if fully understood and will strike many people as outrageous. I believe that the origin of the universe, the current functioning of the universe, and the forces involved have now been revealed so completely that the box has been opened with strange results. The universe inflated very rapidly from what we normally would call nothing—no matter, no energy, no space, no time—and the forces that caused it and controlled how it happened and what form the universe took are real. The forces are real in the world which can be known through scientific research without depending on revelation from beyond the universe. This means that the creator of the universe is real and known; God is alive! But nothing in those forces implies a favorite-choosing, grace-granting, punishment-declaring reflection of humanity in a supernatural being. God is dead.

The open box does not resolve our ancient arguments any better than the mystery did. If we acknowledge reality as it is and are in awe of the power behind a universe which expanded and organized in a way that produced us to look out from our precious planet in wonder, we have found God. If we insist on a reflection of ourselves revealed to specific groups of people who passed the knowledge along to us as the favored ones, God is not just dead. There is no empirical evidence that there ever was such a being to die. There is no final scientific evidence of such a God. Many of the religious will turn back to their ancient traditions. Science will continue to explore the physical mysteries of the very first moments of the universe and mathematicians will continue to try to find an equation which can express it all.

With or without the box, God is just as alive and dead as Schrödinger's famous cat! In UFT I am asserting that the forces revealed by science fill the omni-roles the ancients attributed to their gods. I believe that God is real, not as a metaphysical mystery, but as part of what is. I believe we now know the omnipotent, omnipresent power and that it is our task to continue to reflect and examine history, philosophy, physics, anthropology, and psychology as well as cosmology to determine our proper relationship to this universe and each other.

The Second Commandment

8/9/2019

As I continue to contemplate how *UFT* relates to traditional beliefs and practices, I see common ground in the second of the ten commandments which forbids the making and worshiping of "any graven image."[1]

Growing up in the church, the emphasis I remember on this commandment was the jealousy of God, God as the only one who could be both jealous and holy, and the reality or lack of existence of any other god. Our entire focus was on God's demand for all human worship. It was logical within the assumptions of faith. As the Creator and Sustainer of all things, God deserved all worship and adoration—especially if the other gods were mere human imaginings. We were warned about the fine line between worshiping God and worshiping images or icons of God, Jesus, or the holy family. This of course gave us reason to assume that our practices were superior and more holy than those of the Catholic, Orthodox, and Coptic churches even though we had decided by then that displaying pictures of Jesus in the church was somehow an exception to this command.

Displays and images of the cross were also exceptions if the Catholic practice of depicting the risen Jesus still miserably attached to the cross was avoided. Doves were also acceptable as images of either peace or the Holy Spirit. After the much-loved lifelong pastor of our congregation died, a painting of him was also deemed appropriate and not considered an object of worship even though I suspect many looked at it with fond memory and praise for his work and character as often as they did

---

1. Exodus 20:4.

the picture of Jesus on the opposite wall that everyone had become accustomed to seeing. While claiming to be literalists, we made exceptions for whatever felt acceptable to us and did not match the practices of any tradition we believed to be in error. The biggest discussions I personally remember in protestant circles came later as people began to debate whether the traditional lamb-carrying pictures of Jesus as The Good Shepherd were too effeminate or too serious. New images appeared with a shorter-haired, often laughing, Jesus. But any debate was about which image was preferred, not whether we should have them at all.

Now to turn back to what any of this has to do with UFT. I believe our new knowledge of how the universe began and works gives a new explanation of the second commandment that does not contradict traditional theology. If God is the unified forces that govern the universe and which may soon find expression in the unified theory, there is nothing to carve, mold, paint, or draw. Gravity, the strong and weak nuclear forces, thermodynamics, or quantum strangeness, etc., are not any form of matter that can be made into an image. While I love art, including religious art and recognize the genius with which artists over the centuries have sought to give expression to that which is beyond depiction, there is no person or object to draw when talking about the Creator as the combined forces at work in the universe.

I find this observation parallel to traditional theology which has always held that the Creator and the Holy Spirit are both non-material. Theology has always maintained that the God of the Torah is a spirit and not a person or being in the physical world. Art has long sought ways to depict their presence using light or images like the dove based on the scene of Jesus's baptism.[2] We like representations of abstract things that cannot be seen. We like to feel that the intangible has been made visible. For the scientists and mathematicians, I might even argue that such expression is found in the beauty of the equations. And if the theory of everything results in a single elegant equation, I suspect the scientific and mathematic faithful will express admiration of it close to worship. But nether traditional theology nor UFT asserts that there is a physical, material something that is the Creator or the Spirit. Even the equation will not be the reality it expresses.

There are of course the complicated arguments about how Jesus is both distinct from the other two-thirds of the Trinity and a full expression

---

2. Matt 3:16.

of all three. The early church wrestled with those concepts for some time before developing the statements that were codified as creeds. And still our attempts to explain how one person can also be two other distinct entities is mind-numbing. I suspect many who are not clinging too tightly to past beliefs and practices will agree with me that those arguments are more likely to produce a migraine than appreciation for the greatness of the power that makes the universe possible. The Trinity makes sense to those who choose by faith to believe it. Even for those who believe in the Trinity, depicting the wholeness of God is only achieved by using abstract expressions.

So, my thoughts on the second commandment boil down to a simple fact. From the time of the ancients, the people of the monotheistic religions have been told not to make images of what is no-thing. Narrowing the great forces of the universe down to an image that can be contained in a painting or sculpture is an act of deception, no matter how well intended or how beautiful, in order to reduce universal power to a form we find comfortable. Perhaps we have known all along that it is wiser to stand in awe than to try to reduce the power of the universe to human scale.

When Life Won't Stop

8/18/2019

I SUPPOSE EVERYONE EVENTUALLY FACES times when shocking news rolls in faster than our minds and emotions can process. This year has been like that for my wife and me. A relative in the prime of life and a hero in the change we need in farming and ecology died in a moment due to a freak accident. A young child in my wife's favorite place on Earth died the same way despite my wife's efforts to care for her. My mother's sister and my father's brother-in-law both passed on this summer. One of my best friends makes it to the hospital in severe distress and then events at home prevented me from being able to go to him. Another freak accident and my wife's own car ran over her resulting in a week of trauma care and permanent injuries. As soon as she got home from the hospital—unable to drive or walk any distance—the message came in that her mother was struggling with congestive heart failure and headed to the hospital.

And I look to the sky and implore life, "Stop. Just stop!" Strange habit looking up to implore for help. Raise a child up with strange religious habits and when he is old, he will still be doing them![1] There is no reason that help should come from somewhere that is *up* from where I stand based on Earth's gravity any more than any other direction. I am surrounded by the physical universe from which, and in which, it all happens.

As I walk from the hospital, I meet an old friend from days in the evangelical megachurch. She asks what has happened and before I can finish telling her, she breaks into statements about the greatness and

---

1. Prov 22:6, reworded by me

goodness of God. She asks me, in a tone which implies that we both know, if I am not amazed by the goodness of God. And something deep inside me rebels, revolts, and feels as if my internal organs twist. No, I no longer find any comfort in a God who has the power to intervene in physical events and most often chooses not to save. An all-powerful loving God should prevent the accident and save the young people, not give us the strength to endure their death. Some metaphysical being gave my wife the strength to pull herself from under the wheel of a car? Then why would it not stop the car before it rolled on top of her in the first place? It seems either illogical nonsense or a celebration of cruelty to me.

I return to thoughts about life itself and it dawns on me that it is contrary to the basic nature of life to quit. From the very first molecular combination that refused to be dissolved or altered by the primordial soup and instead became self-replicating, life has refused to stop. At the mighty climax of the period of dinosaurs and at the moment of their destruction, life went on and small mammals scurried forth to become dominant on land. A single human life ends, but I turn and look at the children and grandchildren and there is the continuing likeness, the facial expressions, and the flash of a smile. I prepare to do a service of remembrance and look up the familiar words of comfort people long to hear. And there they are, the poetic expressions of authors who lived millennia ago, still speaking, still comforting, still affirming life today.

I realize that I have done a mental contortion as my original cry was for life to stop stopping in spite of my verbal shorthand. But life does neither. Life continues in the same cycles it has always traveled. DNA is passed from generation to generation and while one passes away the genetic blueprint guiding the next complex assembly of quanta goes on. Physical manifestations of the joy of life that have been dear to us lose animation, give back their energy and matter, and seem doomed to oblivion. But the living format of their being continues in new combinations in generation after generation. Life stops and refuses to be stopped.

I text my cousin who has experienced death this year as both the father and the son of those who ceased to live among us. And I tell him my conclusion—rather than trust to a God who could stop our pain and routinely chooses not to do so, I will dance with the universe that simply does what it does any day, every day, for the rest of my days. Life is. Even when it appears to end, it continues in ever-adapting forms. As I write this, my wife and her mother have returned home as has my friend. We continue to care about those who now live without family members who meant so much to them and to us.

It has been this way for billions of years and I expect the pattern to continue while the cosmos endures. When life refuses to stop? We dance. Sometimes with greater joy or sadness, but the choice remains to dance even when it hurts.

Why Is There Something Rather Than Nothing?

8/26/2019

GOTTFRIED LEIBNIZ, CREDITED WITH FORMULATING this bottom-line philosophical question more than 300 years ago, turned to religion and a metaphysical explanation. God wanted a universe, so God made one. Spinoza and Einstein agreed that there was something because there had to be. Kraus, whose work I have cited before, answers that gravity caused what appears to us as nothing to form into what is, while Bertrand Russel and others have suggested it is an unanswerable question trying to explain an obvious fact.[1]

Paul Tillich also found existence explained by accepting the reality of an eternal background expressed in current reality. Tillich stated, "Faith consists in being vitally concerned with that ultimate reality to which I give that symbolic name of God. Whoever reflects earnestly on the meaning of life is on the verge of an act of faith."[2] While Tillich remains within the context of theology, it is significant that he noted that the choice of the word "God" for the eternal background of the universe is symbolic rather than the name of a specific metaphysical being.

In his final book, Stephen Hawking stated that because gravity existed the universe was required to spring from nothing. He further asserts that no other explanation, including a personal God, is required. Nothing plus gravity will become something and form the universe. This

---

1. Strickland, "Answering the Biggest Question of All," paras. 10–11.
2. See "Paul Tillich Quotes."

has been popularized as a difficult to authenticate Hawking statement that nothing cannot exist forever.[3] I find layers of meaning possible in this elegant phrase. And believe that in the end it both supports Kraus over Leibniz and confirms the confidence in existence earlier attached to religious faith.

After encountering Hawking's statement, it occurred to me that in some ways it was taught to my generation from childhood. I remember many times being told that nature hates a vacuum. The actual wording I remember is Aristotle's "Nature abhors a vacuum."[4] In school, this was usually accompanied by lessons based on experiments to form a vacuum in a bell jar. And even though later instructors would inform us that the force at work was the pressure of the atmosphere on the outside of the jar rather than some magic draw from inside, the lesson remained that nature was not fond of emptiness.

The lesson held true in other scientific observations. Liquids and some solids with freeze points near room temperature gradually evaporate and their molecules move to fill the surrounding space. Where fire or some other disaster eliminates the previous lifeforms from an area, new species and offspring of the previous flora and fauna compete to refill the space. But emptiness does not prevail.

Of course, we were also taught the apparent opposite axiom that nothing lasts forever. Living things—plants and animals, including humans, exist for a season and then die. Their energy and eventually their material substance return to the universe from which they were taken. The changing pattern of existence is also true for geologic features including the largest of mountains, but their life cycle occurs over periods of time, requiring a knowledge of geologic processes and epochs. This natural order provides room for new generations and evolutionary change. The statement that all things pass was often used as a consoling idea in a time of loss, reminding the grieving person that it is in the nature of things to end. When the loss was a person we loved, we were assured that there was a metaphysical loophole and they continued on in a different realm where we will someday be reunited. I will look at that teaching again in another essay. For now, noting that the emptiness formed by the end of one earthly object is always filled with another is sufficient for our discussion.

3. Hawking, "Is There a God?," 23.
4. Wilson, "Nature Abhors a Vacuum," para 6.

Why Is There Something Rather Than Nothing?

In church the present-tense corollary was filling one's life with holiness rather than trying to simply remove sins. Where a spiritual vacuum was created, something would fill the void and what we believed ourselves to be primarily surrounded by was more temptation and evil. We even had a specific Bible passage where a demon cast out comes back with seven companions to take up residence in the life left empty.[5] We were also taught that humans were born with a physically unobservable hole, or emptiness, that only God could fill.[6]

In the secular instruction of public school and the religious instruction of the Midwestern church, the lesson applied to specific examples was that life would find a way to fill any space left empty. Now, here in the twenty-first century we find Stephen Hawking explaining a scientific issue from the far reaches of astrophysics and explaining that nothing cannot exist forever. I want to put it on a bumper sticker just to see the puzzled faces of those who read it expecting the opposite phrase, nothing lasts forever. Nothing lasts forever including any state of nothingness!

To move beyond word play, something much deeper is at stake here. As I read *Braiding Sweetgrass*, I am reminded that the indigenous people of my continent, far removed from the people of the Bible, also had their myths of the competition between the forces of creation and destruction. The people of the far East had theirs as well. Beyond questions of individual lives and ecosystems, humans have long pondered not just why we are here but whether order or disorder is the major force in the universe. Religion assured us that there was a master player in charge of everything who was greater than the destroyer who sought to end all things. The horrible destruction of Armageddon might come, but after that the final tranquility of victory of life and order over death and disorder would reign undisturbed.

When I was a child, the steady state theory of the universe was still taught in many science classes. The universe, in contradiction of creation stories, always was and always would be. Then came the theory of the Big Bang and disagreements about how our current expansive period would end. Would there be a point where gravity reversed the process and the universe caved in on itself? Would it expand forever eventually becoming too large for us to examine its far reaches? Learning that our sun is but one of the innumerable stars, we were faced with the knowledge that

---

5. Luke 11:24–25.
6. Martindale and Root, *Quotable*, 281–82.

a day will come when our star ends. This raised the specter again that the total of humanity, not just the individual life, might not last forever. Religions varied in their answers as to whether an eternal metaphysical home awaited the faithful. Some have looked to science and said that we can develop the capacity to move around the galaxy or universe and find new homes when life on Earth falters. However, recent results in space genetic studies and evolution tell us that any beings who continued in another part of the solar system or beyond would evolve to match that environment and would no longer be what we know as human.[7] Life would continue. Humanity might not.

This is a significant point of difference between the dominant interpretations of the Bible and UFT. When the ultimate source and control of existence is seen in the observable forces of the universe, there is no reason to consider humanity as either the pinnacle or focus of existence. Even the Genesis creation accounts can be read as indicating that we are the little brothers and sisters of all other life on Earth, a view more commonly found among aboriginal cultures living in closer proximity with nature. We are here and we have a reasonable self-interest in our continued existence. But whether we remain or cease to exist is a choice and a task of humans, not the universe or the power which sustains it. In a native story of the battle between existence and destruction as presented in *Braiding Sweetgrass*, Robin Wall Kimmerer relates that in the final roll of chance the deciding factor is all of creation calling out in favor of life.[8] I believe this may well be true for life on our planet as long as we do not claim that our hope for continued existence determines the fate of the entire universe.

For me, the largest question for contemplation as we determine the grand pattern of all things is the presence or absence of universal meaning.

In the end, does the natural world lead us to conclusions of a propensity for being over nonbeing?

Accepting time on an astronomical scale is our current world temporary and ultimately meaningless?

When we reach the limit of our equations is there something or nothing?

---

7. Leary, "After a Year Away."
8. Kimmerer, *Braiding Sweetgrass*.

Is the final backdrop of life one of orderly existence or one of chaos, randomness, and nothingness?

I find that I agree with Krauss and Hawking.

Nothing cannot last forever.

The nihil does not win.

We look around us and life is.

We look in the past and life was.

We investigate the very furthest past and what appears to be nothing birthed all that we see and know.

I look to the future and life is.

Whether that future includes humans we must decide.

But something wins over nothing.

The nihil does not win.

Existence exists.

Is Eternal Life a Dangerous Error?

8/30/2019

It seems like one of the greatest hopes of religion. A day will come when all of life's pain will cease and only what is good will remain. The faithful will find themselves in the presence of God and all of the loved ones who have gone on before. No longer will the divine be a mystery, we will know God as well as God now knows us.[1] Everything will be perfect and will last forever.

What could possibly be destructive about such a wonderful sounding hope?

The student of history might point out the use of reward in the next life for convincing slaves that they should accept their lot in this life. Eternal life is also used to threaten being sent early to an eternity of torture. The student of cultures might point out how Indian underclasses are taught to accept their lot in life in order to escape the cycle of rebirth and that they must have done something bad in their previous life to warrant this low status. But if they live perfectly in their current status, next time around they may be more in line with the Dharma. Like the slave, they also face the threat of being sent prematurely back into the cycle if they rise up against the higher classes. The critics of the religion of Islam point to a supposed promise of heaven accompanied by virgins for the one who willingly gives their life in jihad, including through suicide attacks. Never mind that the reward might be sweet raisins in paradise, I suspect things like sweet raisins in religious texts are often euphemisms for more carnal rewards.

---

1. 1 Cor 13:12.

But these things have existed for millennia and have not caused the faithful to question the effects that promising eternal bliss has on this life. This may be because few of the faithful have endured slavery, untouchable status, or the desperation that would drive one to self-destruction in the name of holy war. Never mind that the promises of this new world in what Christians call the New Testament were expected to occur within the lifetime of those who wrote them. Each new generation of Christians finds new evidence for why the arrival of Jesus to set all things right has not happened yet but may at any moment. This life is short, and the reward or punishment is eternal. Any hardship in life now is a small price to pay.

But is it?

There is now a significant attitude in the USA that we do not need to worry about our lifestyle overtaxing the Earth to the point of mass extinction of other species and possibly a large portion of humanity. Jesus will return and save the faithful. A new Earth will be provided and this one will no longer matter. The evidence of the damage to our world is real. The deaths are already occurring.[2] The hope that the one who created the planet for us will arrive with a new one is completely based on faith in interpretations of ancient texts. That is worth stating again. This faith in a divine rescue is not even based on clear agreed-upon statements from the prophets of the past. It is based on one of many interpretations of those ancient writings along with faith that those writings have not been changed over time to make them more promising after the failed arrival of the expected divine rescue.

I wrote about the callousness beliefs in heaven and hell cause towards those considered to be damned by God in *UFT*. It remains on full display now as those who are privileged enough to believe they will escape the worst ravages of climate change ignore the evidence of what is already beginning to happen to the poor of the world along with the plant and animal kingdoms.

And I grow concerned as I watch the effects in far less cataclysmic terms. A Christian friend posts a picture of a beautiful place, flower, bird, animal, or sky. Then others respond about how it points to the beauty that awaits in eternity. Friends gather for dinner and the talk turns to the time when everyone is together in the world to come. Something about the evening at hand, the food, and the friends is missed in anticipation

---

2. This essay was written with no idea of the pandemic coming in 2020.

of The Banquet instead of this night's companionship and flavors. Rather than focusing on the joy of moments like a kaleidoscopic sunset, their minds simply look forward to a world of beauty beyond our own. Instead of immersing themselves in the joyous wonder of now, they see only an imagined future when this life is over. If "imagined" seems harsh, I chose the word carefully. Much of what people express about heaven is based on their own imagining of the specific interpretation they have been taught. Too many of the things people are looking forward to are from their own mental images of the teachings they have heard, folk traditions, descriptions from fictional literature—sources other than the texts they believe are the word of God.

When I read the creation story in Genesis, I see God saying here is everything. Except for evil and death, you are free to enjoy it all. Nowhere in the story does God say, "Here is a pretty nice place. It will do until you join me in the real paradise." At the end of each day's creation, the story says God approves it. The text does not say that God looks and decides it will do until he makes the next one. It is a perfect place and humanity is placed there to enjoy it. Earth is supposed to be for now. Life is more than a preview of the real show to come. I am amazed at the view as I summit a mountain, turn a corner to see new colors of fall, observe the tiny insect that lands on my arm, or witness the power of a storm. I do not have to wait to see what the real ones look like on the other side. These are real and they are enough.

People hope to see loved ones again. So do I. People would like to fully understand the power that caused it all to happen. So would I. We have no proof that there is a world beyond this one. My contention that the powers controlling the universe are the very real forces studied in physics makes the possibility of a magic beyond seem less likely. But I do not want to steal the hopes and dreams people have about an end to the grief we feel as each new loved one ends their time on Earth.

However, I want us to see the heaven and heavens that surround us now in this universe. I want people to experience the miracles present in a single drop of water. I want people to bask in the full wonder of simple moments of being human together. And I want them to care about life and enjoyment of Earth's wonders continuing for their children and grandchildren, their neighbors with less resources, the poor in the two-thirds world, and the plant and animal kingdoms. All of those lives are interwoven with our own. I miss the assurance I used to have of a magic ending that would put everything right. At the same time, I am more aware of the beauty and the wonder of now.

The Universal Power to Be

8/30/2019

As I continue to contemplate the effect of the approaching theory of everything on faith and belief, I find power in the language of something versus nothing. It is there in the texts of the Western religions as the world is presented as pre-existing in chaos, darkness, or the void. It is observable in Native creation stories of a world pulled up from the mud under the formless water and made fertile by gifts that come from the sky.[1] And it is there in scientific discussions of the Big Bang. First there is nothing or chaos. Then there is something. By the end of his life, Stephen Hawking explained how science reveals the cause of this change in ways that have been transformed into the possibly apocryphal quote, "Nothing cannot exist forever."[2]

We have reached a point where science as well as religion maintains that the condition of nothing gave way to the power of something. The same forces that we observe in everyday life and scientific experiment form a situation where something is more probable than nothing. There is a power which makes existence dominant over nonexistence. This is

---

1. These descriptions of conditions before creation as water, mist, or darkness are more easily understood as the nothingness in light of Robert Kaplan's *The Nothing That Is: A Natural History of Zero* which points out the long periods of time involved in humanity's formation of the concept of nothing.

2. Dr. Hawking discussed the power of gravity on the pre-existent something which we see as nothing. This remains somewhat problematic to me having come to see gravity as the shaping of space-time. Before the moment of existence, space-time did not exist, so my mind struggles with gravity preexisting. Nevertheless, the laws of physics describe forces that caused a universe to spring forth from a tiny singularity emerging from what we know as nothing.

also where UFT differs from pantheism or panentheism. I am not asserting that we have shown all things to be or to contain God making the sky, my pet, and the soil in my yard equally worthy of worship. This is a crucial point of understanding. What science has now confirmed is that there is a power behind all things which favors existence over nothingness. The assertion of UFT is simply that this power is the power traditionally called God.

Religion, which tends to make truth accessible by anthropomorphizing things which are beyond simple explanation, says that God spoke. Science asserts that a concentration of the power to be produced a first particle.[3] Then gravity and the other physical forces still observable today cause the massive expansion of matter, energy, and space-time that we know as our universe. These two worldviews remain in conflict only when we insist on the existence of an all-powerful being from a separate nonmaterial world behaving in very human ways. If we allow ancient explanation of the very complex to be a description of that which remained beyond human understanding, the divide narrows considerably. There is a power (a combination of forces) that calls for something to exist instead of nothing. In the Bible that power declares to Moses that its name is "I am,"[4] the present tense first-person statement of to be.

Neither religion nor science agrees to call the things which come to exist, God. God is the power to be which brings everything into existence and provides the order of the cosmos. This is the fundamental assertion of UFT. After millennia of observation, study, reflection, theory, and experimentation we now know that the power to be is real. Knowing the forces which comprise that combined power by scientific names, many post-enlightenment thinkers reject the idea of a personal *unbeing* and declare that God does not exist. The person of faith may now look at that same power and affirm that God is real. However, that God is not a reflection of man. There is no logical reason to expect the power of the universe to display human emotions and behaviors. The ancient stories make sense as very real human beings used what they experienced and believed to explain what they could not yet define.

Belief in the power that brings about something rather than nothing as God also does not require a separate evil spirit to embody the chaos and damaging aspects of life. The same forces that produce the universe

---

3. The discovery of the Higgs boson was significant in confirming the theory and math behind this assertion.

4. Exod 3:14.

and control its functions sometimes cause local events which destroy existing bodies, including living bodies on Earth. That very process helped to produce the solar system as we now know it and the conditions which allow life. When those forces, often because we have ignored or used them in negative ways, result in death we look for a larger reason. But as I discussed in *UFT*, the world simply works the way it does. That does not mean God is both good and evil because it does not mean there is a God with human positive and negative traits at all. There are forces that have led to the majesty we witness in the universe, and sometimes those same physical forces cause events harmful to life in specific locations. It does not mean there is any devil, demon, Satan, or fallen archangel making it happen in conflict with a God who for some reason chooses to allow it for millennia while capable of stopping it at any time.

There is the power which brings both existence and the events when those same forces bring destruction.

I believe this has profound implications for being fully human. Possessing the power of conscious thought and deliberate action, humans can choose to align themselves with the power to be or elect to oppose it. As a thinking being I can examine my beliefs and actions and decide if they are aligned with existence or nonexistence. I can take actions which contribute to life on my planet, including simple acts which enhance life in small immediate ways, or I can engage in behaviors which lead to destruction of different amounts and over different periods of time. This is very much in line with Eastern practices which call for aligning human life with all that is, behaving in ways that cause as little harm as possible, and which avoid the temptation to be the power which controls life. This theology does not seek to gain the approval of the power behind all existence. It recognizes that we are already within this universe and within that power. As Richard Rohr says, "We cannot attain the presence of God. We're already totally in the presence of God. What's absent is awareness."[5]

I now see this as a possible framing of UFT. The battle is between existence and nonexistence. However, there are no magical nonbeings beyond our knowledge or power acting or manipulating us to those ends. We know the forces that exist in the universe. We know the characteristics of life on our planet. Science has revealed them. We know the nature of human beings. Science along with other human studies including history, religion, philosophy, and the arts have revealed us to ourselves. We can

---

5. Rohr, *Everything Belongs*, 27–28.

work together to identify behavior that aligns with existence, and we can avoid acts that lead to lessening of life. We are part of the universe, and we know the power that created us. We can become humans who work in ways that are aligned with the powers of being over nonbeing. The choice is ours to make, together.

E = MC² in World Religions

9/7/2019

I'M WATCHING A SCIENCE CHANNEL program on Einstein and Hawking, and my mind wants to play. That is all the explanation I have for the strangeness that follows in this essay.

M will of course be man. We start there because humans always do. Everything we create is in some way about us. That does not mean it is a negative or even a small variable. Humans are capable of great feats, both positive and negative. Everything else we are talking about may be no more than our imagination set beyond arm's length to be viewed as something separate.

Starting from my lifelong base of training, C seems logical to be Christ. It is important to note that the concept of Christ is different from the study of the life of Jesus of Nazareth, which even a brilliant atheist like Bart Ehrman can study with no belief in the Christ. The Christ is Jesus as experienced by a church which believes that Jesus, having suffered the pain of all mankind, conquered death and declared all humanity to be eternal. It is an enormously powerful idea that promises victory no matter how bleak the current period in history or individual life. It is as constant to Christianity as the speed of light to physics. For most of the church, denial of the resurrection of Jesus as the Christ is denial of the entire religion.

So, what is E? E is the Eternal God, the truth of the universe which exceeds our limits and comprehension, the divine source and significance of all things. In Christianity that Eternal transcendent looks very much like us. Of course! It is us multiplied by a factor of our ideas of a death conquering, humanity rescuing, human!

JUDAISM

What of Christianity's predecessor, Judaism? I think it would be fair to say that in the Jewish religion C is the power of the Torah and life lived in agreement with Torah. With no death conquering Christ, there is no universal emphasis on eternal life. The emphasis is on the fully human life. As I understand it, the M in Judaism is more collective. The will of the Eternal is expressed in a community of people living life according to revealed truths about the best way to live. And again, the E looks a lot like a magnified human because it is man times a powerful code of communal behavior.

BUDDHISM

C is acceptance and unity with everything that is, including suffering. In the Eastern vision of reality, the E does not look just like us. Humans do not achieve E by multiplying themselves by some power, but by realizing that we are already part of all that is. This both denies the tendency to deify ourselves and multiplies us as part of everything.

HINDUISM

Hinduism adds an almost eternal cycle of life repeated based on previous lives with the possibility of final escape into oneness with E, the nature of all things. Now the grand pattern looks more like us again because elaborate explanations of various levels of human existence, alignment with the universe, and hope of a better life or final enlightenment are created to serve as C. In both of these eastern ways of living the nature of things and how we align ourselves with reality is C squared and understood to be much greater than humanity and much larger than an individual human life which is a minuscule part of the whole. But it also adds value to all living things which is often missing in Judeo-Christian traditions focused almost solely on human life.

NATIVE/ANIMALISTIC/PAGAN BELIEFS

For me these are more natural explanations of life in the world minus elaborate constructions of religious forms to create a C. It seems to me that the indigenous cultures of the world see C as life in harmony with all that surrounds them. In Africa the result for E has long been the Eternal Now. Life is, has been, and will be as humans play their proper role as part of the community of Earth, sky, animals, and plants. The emphasis in native traditions is on walking the path with integrity in each day of life now. And that now is the product of the degree of harmony between the tribe and all that surrounds, sustains, and shares life with them.

ISLAM

I am too biased to be a fair interpreter of Islam. To me it looks very much like Judaism or Christianity translated to be Arab-centric. It does place more emphasis on Allah being far beyond our will, understanding, or manipulation. I am grateful to the young men from the mosque in Dearborn, Michigan who helped to make this distinction clear to me. However, I still see Islam as very similar to the other two Western religions with emphasis shifted to the ethnic heritage of the Prophet.

WHAT ABOUT UFT?

I want to play with that. If E is the combined power of the universal forces as studied in physics and M continues to be us, what is C squared? Perhaps it is our understanding of that universe combined with acceptance of ourselves as the universe comprehending and appreciating itself. Perhaps it includes the wisdom from all previous cultures that the universe functions well for us when we live in harmony with the forces and life forms that surround us so that our lives contribute to the Something and do not reduce any others to Nothing. I think I will allow my mind and heart to play with the idea for a while.

Space and Time

9/7/2019

EARTH SPIN: 1000 MPH
   Earth orbit speed: 67,000 mph
   Solar system travel within the galaxy: 514,000 mph
   Galaxy speed through space: 13,000,000+ mph
   I just finished watching a program on Einstein and Hawking and the nature of the universe including the interrelationship of space and time. The program included a statement that adding the fourth dimension makes picturing reality impossible for human minds used to observing everything in three dimensions.

   And this grossly oversimplified example came to mind to help see how complex things really are. Everyone past the age of toddlers first experiencing the collisions of running through their play space without watching the position of all the other children knows two people cannot occupy the same space at the same time. If two students try to sit at the exact same desk at the same time they will collide. But an hour later, the second person can occupy the same space with no problem. So why is it complicated?

   Here is just the start of understanding how the universe is more complicated than what we observe. The student desk mentioned above is not in the same place an hour later. Elementary students know that the Earth rotates causing our days and orbits the sun each year. So how fast is it moving? The earth is spinning at a rate of approximately 1000 mph. So, the shared space is actually 1000 miles away from where it was when the first person was there due to the rotation of the planet. Then the Earth is traveling around the sun at just under 70,000 mph, so we are possibly 71,000 miles from the space the first person stood.

Now we add a number less often discussed which is the speed at which the solar system moves through the Milky Way—estimated at approximately a half million miles per hour! So, our wait of an hour to go to the same spot our friend was has actually taken us to a place in the Milky Way which may be nearly 600,000 miles away from the spot we think is the same place. But observing the location from our common platform on the Earth, oblivious to any of these motions, we politely wait our turn and sit at the same desk next period with no idea we are in a totally different part of space-time than our friend with the same assigned seat was last period. And that doesn't even include the expansion rate of the universe estimated in millions of miles per hour!

Understand the multidimensional universe? We don't even realize that our desk for math class is an entirely different place in the universe than it was when our friend sat down an hour ago! Lucky for us, it works on the small scale where we live, and we can arrive at the room on time.

Is US Christianity the Religion of Paul?

9/7/2019

HAVING MOVED FROM CONSERVATIVE EVANGELICAL to progressive Christianity I see a steady stream of commentaries that Christians need to stand against Christian nationalism and other expressions of hate and discrimination by our political leaders and self-appointed spokespeople for Christianity. I want to agree with them. I want to be able to stand up and proclaim that hatred towards the other and demanding one's own rights as a Christian are contrary to the faith. But I have this troubling knowledge of the Roman Empire, the divine right of kings, the crusades, the Inquisition, and the conquest and colonization of Sub-Saharan Africa and the Americas.[1]

As I contemplate these differences in the images and behaviors attributed to the Christian faith, I see a serious difference between Jesus, the supposed center of the faith, and Paul, the biblically recorded founder of Christianity as a gentile religion. Jesus is said to have exemplified the sacrifice of one's own position, the denial of one's own rights, and the

---

1. This is a continuation of my essay, "Christianity Is Not Jesus." I must confess at the beginning that the Christians whose faith I am discussing would never accept the ideas I am exploring here in spite of my salting it generously with Bible citations. They have accepted a Bible where every word and idea is from God, perfect, and non-contradictory. Within that absolute acceptance, it makes no difference which parts were penned by Paul since everything combined into the Bible is seen as the word of God. Since Western thought does not accept truth containing both yin and yang as in Eastern thought, apparent contradictions merely represent our lack of understanding rather than anything about the nature of the source or the church's practice of it. Nevertheless, these are my thoughts.

path of taking the suffering of others on to oneself.[2] Paul, while at times speaking of himself as the greatest of sinners, is unashamed in proclaiming himself equal as an apostle to the original disciples of Jesus,[3] demands his rights as a Roman citizen,[4] and expresses a wish that those who teach a different practice of the faith from him might castrate themselves.[5]

The stories of Jesus life include a humble birth, growing up as the child of a laborer, a homeless life during the years of his adult ministry, a habit of pointing everyone to God in heaven rather than himself,[6] and submission to earthly authorities even when he knows that it will end in his own death. Critics pointed out that Jesus spent his time with people they considered evil and unworthy. Jesus reportedly agreed and said those are the people he came to seek.[7] Jesus is quoted as teaching his followers not to oppose enemies but to turn the other cheek and go the extra mile to accommodate their demands.[8] Jesus tells his disciples not to oppose others acting in his name,[9] but who are not part of their traveling group. Jesus's recorded teachings include instruction to love one's neighbor as much as yourself and that even those considered enemies are true neighbors. Jesus is quoted as saying that all the other requirements of God are found in the commands to love God and love one's neighbor.[10]

Paul boasts of having held high rank among the Pharisees,[11] his Roman citizenship, and his authority in proclaiming the proper teachings of the new religion. Paul teaches his followers to refuse to associate with people they consider sinful, especially if those same people claim also to be believers.[12] While he never directly makes the comparison, Paul recounts sufferings greater than those of Jesus short of actually dying.[13] Paul warns against others proclaiming the new faith as heretics who will

---

2. 1 Pet 2:24.
3. 2 Cor 12:11.
4. Acts 22.
5. Gal 5:12.
6. Matt 7:21.
7. Luke 19:9.
8. Matt 5:38–42.
9. Mark 9:38–9.
10. Matt 22:37–40.
11. Acts 22:3.
12. 1 Cor 5:9–11.
13. 2 Cor 11:23–27.

lead the people astray.[14] He proclaims that those who teach continued obedience to the law are still under the law and therefore not truly saved according to his teachings,[15] which he claims to have received directly from the risen Christ[16] having never associated with the living Jesus. When he is arrested for his activities, he asserts his full rights as a Roman citizen and denies the authority of local courts to decide his case.[17] The traditional explanation of this is that the process takes him to Rome to spread Christianity to the known world, but I find the contrast significant. Representatives of Rome knew the living Jesus and heard his teachings directly. There is recorded correspondence between local authorities and their superiors in Rome about the new religion and the proper response to its practitioners. This makes it difficult for me to frame Paul's insistence on receiving his rights as simply the required method of taking the message to the emperor. Even in that context there is contrast, Jesus makes no attempt to spread his word through the earthly powers of the day. If this is Paul's tactic, it is another contrast to the example of Jesus.

When I see US Christians saying that it violates their religious rights to bake a cake or issue a state marriage license for people they do not believe should marry, I wonder whether they are following Jesus or Paul. When I see one part of the church attacking others, sometimes all others, for not teaching and observing the exact same practices they do, I wonder whether their attitude comes from the example of Jesus or the teachings of Paul. It was Paul, originally a persecutor of the followers of Jesus, who became the named author of most of the early documents of the church assembled in the Bible. The teachings of how the forming church should behave, who they should accept and reject, and what specific doctrines were acceptable as recorded in the Christian Bible are written by others after the life of Jesus and most are from (or attributed to) Paul. Jesus called followers to pick up their cross and follow him home to the Father. And while I have heard teachings that Jesus's instructions on how to deal with abuse or demands from those in power contain subtle statements of defiance, taken as written they are commands to obey and do even more than one is asked. And Jesus says nothing about refusing to do anything based on the worthiness of the one making the demand. Jesus says and

14. 2 Tim 2.
15. Gal 3:10.
16. Gal 11:11–12.
17. Acts 22.

gives no example of asserting his own rights above the needs or requests of others. It was Paul who taught people to reject those who did not hold true to exact teaching and who modeled the believer demanding that their own rights be protected.

So, I conclude that US Christianity, while proclaiming the Lordship of Jesus, is actually the religion of Paul. This also means that its un-Christlike current practices are not contradictory to its nature. It is a religion like all others and evolves a greater and greater emphasis upon itself even if that obscures the example of its original God figure.

Things from Math that Do Not Exist in Nature

9/19/2019

MUCH OF THIS ESSAY COMES from reading Kaplan's *The Nothing That Is*.

I constantly get questions from people about why they need to know this or that, especially math beyond what the calculator on their phone can do for them. My usual answer is that we all need to understand solving real-life problems in logical steps leading to trustworthy conclusions, and that is the thinking required in higher math. Now two areas of math have taken my thoughts to a new level.

I did not realize before reading Kaplan's fascinating book how recent the use of zero is. Through antiquity any place value with nothing in it was simply left empty on counting boards and other systems of calculating transactions. Zero took a long time to develop. One of the reasons is that in nature there is no such thing as nothing! There is nowhere on Earth or through the telescope where there is actually nothing. There are regions of space that appear to contain nothing to the human eye, but they are filled with energy and quantum particles. The only place the nothing exists is in math in order to facilitate our calculations.

Another thing that exists only in math as an observable something is infinity. The number of stars is larger than our comprehension, and as telescopes advance, we find out there are even more than we knew. But there is a number. Growing up in a Bible-based culture, I remember grains of sand referred to as a metaphor for an infinite amount. But there is a number. It is just too large to be worth the effort to calculate. If we stand on Daytona Beach and you point North and South along the

Florida coast and say, "Surely the number of the grains of sand is infinite!" I may simply reach below the water and bring up a thimble more and say, "Plus a thousand." If there is anything that can be added to an amount, the amount is not infinite.

Buckminster Fuller rejected the idea of irrational numbers as true representations of anything in nature because he did not believe nature was irrational. His explanation was that round shapes where basic geometric calculations lead us to *pi* are based on our assumption of continuous curves. His counter claim was that all curves are made up of an enormous number of straight lines and vertices. But even if he is wrong and the curves are real, the endless nonrepeating places of *pi* exist in math. They are part of our method of understanding and working with calculations that involve curves. The curve itself is not infinite. Infinity like nothing is a construction humans use to calculate. But it does not exist outside of the mind and the scribbles we make on paper to represent it.

When I first shared this essay with a small group of friends, another type of number was added. The son of one of my friends immediately mentioned the square root of a negative number. Interestingly, we already label all of those results as imaginary!

WHY IT MATTERS

It dawns on me almost immediately how these two concepts from math relate to our greatest fears and hopes. We fear death. As Vine Deloria pointed out in *God Is Red*, even Oral Roberts told his followers that they needed to send in millions so God would not require him to die yet. Only the most desperate and hopeless of humans turns to death as a desirable choice over life. The mentally and physically healthy person wants to live. When we die, most of us cease to exist in human memory after a couple of generations. We seem to become nothing. We fear becoming nothing. As thinking human beings who have conscious awareness of our existence, we do not wish it to end. We do not want to be reduced to nothing. Contrary to the lyrics of a popular old rock song, zero may well be the loneliest number.

And so, people have turned to faith. The Christian faith promises the opposite! When required to shed our mortal being, we may continue on immortal. We may become infinite. In fact, the strict traditions of heaven and hell actually say that all humans are immortal. Some will have eternal bliss while others suffer eternal torment, but all continue into infinity. What a powerful promise and hope that those we lose have not become nothing but have merely changed form to continue on in another realm we may someday join where no person is ever reduced to nothingness. The Jewish traditions which do not have a firm teaching of immortality focus on existence as part of the community rather than only individual identity. When one is lost, the community continues. The sum is not zero.

Which leads me to ponder what a faith based on observable reality such as UFT has to say about this issue when there are no natural examples of either zero or infinity. There is nothing in nature that gives us our example of infinity. But neither is there the abyss of nothingness! In physics there is the conservation of matter and energy. Things may change form and continue in a totally new way. But they do not become nothing! There is no such thing as zero. So, are our components then infinite? To the level most of us can comprehend, they come close. Matter and energy remain as long as the universe itself exists and that appears to be a very long time and is much debated among different schools of scientific thought. But the scientific models do not say it is infinite, just a number beyond our current ability to calculate or comprehend.

We have ways of avoiding becoming nothing. We treasure the next generations of our families where our genetic material continues as long as the family line continues. Those of us who teach or preach hope that we convey something of truth that will continue on in our students after we are gone. Part of the gift of being lucky enough to publish is the hope that something of us and our thinking will exist as long as any copies of our writings are maintained and read. In UFT, I point to science and say that more than our DNA continues as all of the matter and energy currently arranged as what we know of as ourselves continues into new forms after death. And the Bible in Genesis 3 agrees saying we are dust and that we return to dust. Not that we become nothing. Although I imagine that many find simply returning to dirt and forgotten as an individual to be less than satisfying of the ego's desire to exist forever.

None of us will become nothing. There is no such thing as zero. Our store inventory or our bank balance may reach zero. But goods and money still exist, as does our account, which will quickly transition to a negative balance, requiring our work to correct it. But there is no place where there is nothing. We cannot become nothing because there is no thing which is nothing! But neither do the observations of nature give us solid ground to predict an ability to become infinite. There are very, very large numbers of years for matter and energy to continue to exist. Infinity, however, eludes us in the natural world. For that one must turn to faith in metaphysics and continued existence beyond the physical realm.

The one place we know we exist as what we comprehend as us is here for the number of years we remain, and in some ways for the number of years we are remembered. We are here together for a season and our actions tell people how much they matter while here. For me, it means that it is infinitely important that we allow no one to be treated as, or to see themselves as, a zero.

The Present as a Koan

9/20/2019

As I was working through the history and concept of zero, my mind also turned to the idea of the present. Countless Western sayings emphasize enjoying the present even within our cultural obsessions with planning for the future or clinging to the past. My studies and friends in meditation tell me that we surrender our clinging to the past or worrying about possible futures that may never happen in order to find peace in the present. Then as I was working with zero, the idea struck me that there is no present.

It is a simple concept that everything we anticipate is still in the future. But everything we experience is in the past by the time we experience it! If we are sitting face to face in pleasant conversation, the light reflected from our faces and the sounds of our voices take time, very small amounts but time nonetheless, to travel between us. What I hear you say is slightly behind real time. Even what I say leaves my voice box after my brain processes it!

If we put it on a timeline and make the past the negative numbers as the Western mind seems to do, counting backward through the years, then the future moves out across the positive numbers. And the present sits there on our nonexistent zero marking the meeting place of the two that we can never fully grasp. I am personally tempted to place the past on the right side with the positive numbers as it is more fully known and the future on the negative numbers as not yet present and in our angst-ridden times often seen as negative. But it makes no difference to the present remaining there on the precarious point of zero.

And I am presented with a paradox. The healthiest place to be is widely accepted to be the present. Yet, our senses are unable to detect, nor can our brains process, anything in the true present. All that we experience or contemplate is from the past even when we focus those thoughts on the future. For a moment I experience the teachings as a Koan. I am to dwell in a place my mind cannot go.

But with gratitude to friends who are serious practitioners of meditation, I see a deeper level. As one begins to practice meditation, thoughts cross the conscious mind. Do I need to mow the grass? Why did my boss say what she said today? And if we allow our brains to stop and focus on these we choose to reside mentally in the future or past. But that is not the path of deep mediation. The idea in meditation is to let the thought pass through, not to focus on it in any way including as an interruption to our practice. Just let it move on through. Some traditions including Christian teachings on meditation include phases of dealing with the present by lifting what is on our hearts and minds in prayer and then, turning to a text such as a Bible passage we contemplate, and finally we reach a point where we stop thinking and rest in the presence of God.[1] Eastern meditation may go more directly at the deepest point without first focusing on externals and teachings, but the goal is the same. One meditates to reach a point where the conscious mind takes a break.

This may be the only way I know where humans process being fully in the present. One is not even enjoying a favorite place, piece of music, or religious feeling. In meditation all that we know and experience is allowed to slip from our grasp leaving us simply being, being in the present. And if we are able to release everything that resides in either the positive or negative numbers and enter a state of balance on the elusive zero point, I am told that the unconscious self becomes part of all that *is*. No longer aware of time and place the practitioner is connected to all that can declare, "I am."

I have experienced moments of transcendence by intentional use of forms, in my case taken from Christian traditions. I have been surprised by it in times of solitude. My friends practice it as a regular activity that renews and calms their active lives of doing. I believe what the Dalai Lama teaches—that it is not the forms that matter. It is not the end that matters, not seeking anything including enlightenment. The power is in turning loose to simply be.

---

1. Hall, *Too Deep*.

It is a strange thing. Balancing on the zero point which represents nothing may be the only way we humans experience being part of everything.

The Observable Works of God Are the Powers of Nature

9/26/2019

LUKE 12:27
Consider how the wild flowers grow. They do not labor or spin. Yet I tell you, not even Solomon in all his splendor was dressed like one of these.

MATT 6:26
Look at the birds of the air; they do not sow or reap or store away in barns, and yet your heavenly Father feeds them.

MATT 5:44–46
But I tell you, love your enemies and pray for those who persecute you, that you may be children of your Father in heaven. He causes his sun to rise on the evil and the good, and sends rain on the righteous and the unrighteous.

ACTS 14:15–17
Friends, why are you doing this? We too are only human, like you. We are bringing you good news, telling you to turn from these worthless things to the living God, who made the heavens and the earth and the sea and everything in them. In the past, he let all nations go their own way. Yet he has not left himself without testimony: He has shown kindness by giving you rain from heaven and crops in their seasons; he provides you with plenty of food and fills your hearts with joy.

The Observable Works of God Are the Powers of Nature

HERE WE HAVE THREE REFERENCES to teachings of Jesus and one attributed to Paul guiding readers to everyday evidence of providence. I find them very interesting as I continue to contemplate whether science has shown us the very real combination of forces that brought the universe into existence and now sustain it. It is easy for those raised within church traditions to speak of God clothing the flowers, feeding the birds, and bringing sunshine and rain to both those considered righteous and unrighteous. But what do we mean when we say them?

Surely we do not entertain any fantasies of a God who flies through the field painting flowers like Jack Frost painting windows! And yet, it will sound disrespectful to some to attribute these things to anything other than the God—whose Spirit moves where it will like the wind bringing good things to life. I want to suggest that arguing about what happens would reduce us to semantics. Biology tells us about the various and complicated functions that cause the flowers to grow when, where, and how they do. We know how the seeds of new generations form, how they take root and grow, and what elements of the soil the plant uses to form the chemicals which are the makeup of the cells in each part of the plant and why those combinations appear to us as the colors we see. Some of us learned and diagrammed more of that knowledge than we cared about in school and others are fascinated by it. But very few of us really comprehend the full complexity of what is happening and even scientists are finding new information we never imagined. Flowers respond to the specific sound of bees buzzing and sweeten their nectar to attract more insects to aid in pollination.[1] Or maybe they actually like bees. We really do not know, so we assume the most obvious function.

But what I am looking at is that while science uses terms like germination, transpiration, chlorination, and other vocabulary many adults no longer care to know, the New Testament says God, and in Acts 14 identifies God as the power that "made the heavens and the earth and the sea and everything in them." I agree as I also assert that science has now identified all, or nearly all, of those forces and is working on the explanation of how they all combine to the creative power of the cosmos. Whether we refer to those processes as natural or spiritual is a divide that may have outlived its usefulness. The scientific vocabulary eliminates some of the problems of gender and association with ancient practices, while the religious reminds us of the wonder and awe of simple beauty

---

1. Donahue, "Flowers Can Hear."

from complex operations beyond most of our understanding even in one small plant.

I also believe there is a much-neglected teaching in these passages that is very universal regardless of whether one accepts other parts of UFT. The gifts of this God are for everyone—everyone—not just a particular group, nation or race, and not just those who adhere to a specific set of codified beliefs. Everyone. My deep appreciation of teachings from native cultures notes that everyone even includes living beings other than humans including both the birds and the flowers of the field. The verses are very clear that the gifts of sun and rain, nourishment and beauty, are given without preconditions or determinations of worthiness. They are given to those the religious find unacceptable right along with their faith-based neighbors. The faith of my youth would have accepted this only in the realm of physical phenomena, but not in terms of life favor, or eternal reward. Yet, here it is stated as an accurate depiction of the way God behaves towards all of us.

And it does fit very nicely with UFT. The forces that propel the water cycle and determine which days are clear with sunlight for growing and which are rainy to replenish the water supply have no human emotions or attachments to some over others. Water evaporates, condenses, and falls as precipitation and all benefit the same, at least until humans subvert the natural system and flow. Seeds and insects consumed by the birds grow according to the nature of their own life cycle and are available to all. There is no sorting of which birds deserve to eat. These passages from the Christian Bible, three of which are recorded as quotes from Jesus, proclaim that the God, the power of creation still at work in the universe, does not play favorites.

They make sense when read through the lens of understanding nature and natural processes. Those forces act without prejudice for or against any individual or group. The same passages fail to make sense if one clings to teachings that God, the power of all things, chooses some to bless and some to curse. But there they are, not just in a treatise on revisionist theology, but in the very book the faithful proclaim as the word of God. Even the more negative descriptions of grass and flowers in Isa 40 which describe them as temporary things which wither and burn says they serve as examples of "all people."[2] The poetic presentation of how God deals with the world even includes a suggestion that we might go

---

2. Isa 40:6.

to the other living things, even the earth itself, so that they might *teach us* the way the power of creation deals with all things.[3] While I have no intention of letting my old literalist training take over the reading of an ancient poem, it is there recorded by the poet.

Combined with Jesus's teaching on how heaven can be seen in a person planting seed or finding a treasure,[4] or that the joy of heaven is like a woman finding a lost coin or a shepherd finding a lost sheep,[5] we have a blueprint for living in a manner consistent with Bible teachings. We are to recognize the moments of joy when they arise from normal life events, and we are to celebrate together. The power of the universe does not discriminate in the giving of life's provisions so neither should we. I believe in these somewhat traditional teachings there is a unity with UFT and living in harmony with the powers science calls by nonreligious names.

We are here together on one small planet of rock and water hurtling through space. The rain and the sunshine keep the biosphere healthy and functioning and they are intended for everyone. Beauty is all around us to be seen by all even before we exercise our own creative efforts. The forces that make these things happen are the same ones that combined to form the universe for everyone. And there is a very good chance that everyone includes life far beyond our narrow experience. Regardless, those powers are real. Many will prefer to continue calling them by ancient and reverent names. Others express them in purely scientific terms. It is as it should be. All language is human invention for making sense of the world and communicating with others. Humans made the words, and humans pick the ones which resonate with their understanding and response to the world.

Regardless of language, if we recognize those forces as exceeding our power and full understanding, I see no reason why they should fail to invite us to the same transcendence of place and group to live together with all things in wonder. If we mimic their bringing of life to all without prejudice, we might live in wonder of the heaven that is now here not only in nature but finally in human society.

---

3. Job 12:7.
4. Matt 13.
5. Luke 15.

Free Will

10/22/2019

A LIFELONG PUZZLE FOR ME has been the idea of an all-powerful and loving God who nonetheless creates humans with free will knowing they will make the wrong choices, bringing great pain and suffering for the rest of history. The explanation that made most sense to me as a young believer was that God wanted humanity to love God, and that adoration with no choice would not be love. However, given the consequences, that belief grew more and more to sound like a selfish design of horrendous proportions. These ideas were especially troubling when combined with belief in a God who meddles in the daily affairs of humans, guiding them to right decisions and protecting them from harm if they find the right relationship with God giving the ability to discern that guidance. If God is in charge of everything and protects those who pray, it is difficult to see how the military officer on the other side has free will as to whether to shell the village that contains the praying people. I believe that UFT offers us another way to view the issue.

If God is the all-powerful, all-present combination of forces in the universe then that power is not subject to human will. We cannot change gravity or the strong or weak nuclear forces. Yet neither do they control all of our choices. When I go rock climbing there are certain safety procedures that are only ignored at the cost of increased risk of injury. But I can choose—not to double check the fastening of the harness, the placement of the rope in the belay device, the knot in the end of the rope, and so on. But I am still climbing a rock face on a planet with enough gravity to harm me if one of those areas has a critical failure. The power that controls the behavior of falling bodies is there. My free will to behave in ways that protect me from or deliver me to the negative impact of that force is also present. Whether my actions are aligned to what is or not is my choice.

I know that some scholars in neuropsychology would respond that the combination of nature and nurture limits this free will. Some would argue that the chemical and electrical processes in the brain are programmed to a level that makes my free decision an illusion. I respect their science and their work. But I am not yet convinced that everything we do is programmed by God or nature. I also find it healthier for humans to see our actions as choices for which we are responsible than preprogrammed events we are not responsible for choosing. For me it is a biological version of Flip Wilson's famous old comedy line, "The devil made me do it!"[1]

I have chosen many times to take actions which I knew put me at greater risk of harm. I have driven well above posted speed limits in full awareness of the increased possibility of any error resulting in a wreck with increased forces of inertia increasing the probability of injury. I have done it out of necessity and for the thrill. The forces of physics never changed to allow my behavior, nor did they prevent me from doing it. The powers of nature and my choices existed side by side.

I believe the confusing factor in much religious teaching is the idea of a very human-like God with opinions about our behavior. When we start attaching emotions to the power of the universe, things get messy. If that power loves humanity and arranges events in the life of believers for their own best outcome,[2] it is difficult to see how we remain free to make mistakes with disastrous outcomes. If this God also possesses the very human traits of jealousy and anger such that we face eternal punishment for making the wrong choices and has told us so, it is difficult for me to say that we are truly free to choose. Over the years I have heard and sometimes accepted some very complicated explanations for how these things coexist so that if anyone chooses wrongly, they were never in God's group predestined for good. I have also heard explanations that God's will never changes based on our choices. God simply grieves but acts justly in response to our choice of death over life. All of that becomes unneeded if we stop assigning human characteristics, positive or negative, to the power of the universe!

---

1. Elkin, "Devil Made Me," para 2.
2. Rom 8:28.

The forces taught in physics class do not have emotions. Gravity is not happier or upset if I take an exhilarating sled or skateboard ride or step off of a cliff to my destruction. Gravity simply is. I can choose activities which bring pleasure from this force, or which bring disaster. The results are what they are. They are not judgements for sin, not retribution for upsetting gravity. Neither are the enjoyable experiences rewards for pleasing gravity. The world works the way the world works, and we make choices within our understanding of those forces. Neither negates the other and it is not complicated. I am using gravity as the most widely understood force observable in daily life, but the argument holds for all of the other natural forces that combine to power our universe. Building a nuclear reactor in a location subject to earthquakes and tsunamis may be foolish and dangerous. But there is no evidence that the strong or weak nuclear forces are pleased or angered by our construction. They do not consciously operate to reward or punish us. When everything is under control, we harness energy and power cities. When disaster strikes, large areas may be made uninhabitable by humans. Both are nuclear energy doing what it does without choosing, forcing, or denying our will to manipulate it for our purposes.

The combined forces studied in pursuit of understanding the unified field created the universe. They cause it to function as it does. They act consistently according to their own nature in combination with the other forces. They do not change according to human beliefs or actions. They do not choose to reward or punish even though we may choose that language when things work well or become hazardous. We live within the cosmos the physical forces provide and we freely choose how we will respond to the world that is.

The Probability of Specific Humans

10/26/2019

A MATH PROBLEM THAT RETURNS occasionally to mind is the probability of any specific human being existing. The numbers are so large that it is easy to jump to the overused conclusion that the possibilities are infinite. But I believe there is math with very large numbers which would quantify the probability.

Perhaps the number in one generation would be the number of males times the number of females times the number of genetic combinations possible from one couple—leaving out any conjecture about the probability of those two people mating. The number of total possible DNA combinations is not infinite but is a number large enough to cause many calculators to fail to give an answer. A simpler number would be a reported sixty possible novel mutations in each person.[1] So, at 7.7 billion,[2] we would have 3,850,000,000 X 3,850,000,000 X 60 = already too large for my computer calculator to express in anything but scientific notation.

One generation back there would be four people involved and we would have two times the population of males times twice the population of females times the number of possible combinations from each couple. What number would we use for the previous generation? It seems to me that even recognizing the variables of death rates we might follow the Fibonacci sequence back towards the origin. One step back on that sequence would land us at the forty-eighth number in the sequence, $F48$.

---

1. Smith, "How Many," para. 2.

2. Seven point seven billion is both a current estimate of human population and near number forty-nine on the Fibonacci sequence.

I think, assuming none of the four grandparents are the same person, we would have (1/2 F48 X 1/2F48−1) X (1/2 F48) X (1/2F48−1) X 60.[3]

A second generation back we would be at eight ancestors split into two sexes, making 1/2 F47, 1/2 F47−1, 1/2F47−2, and 1/2F47−3 for both the males and females times sixty resulting in eight new numbers to total.[4] The next generation would have sixteen participants and we can begin to see why we either would need accurate data for world population at each generation or some trick such as the Fibonacci sequence to estimate the reduction in size for previous generations.

I now see a problem. My use of the sequence makes an assumption much like creationist theology that humanity arose from a single pair. At the same time, I am doubling the number of ancestors in each previous generation. At some point those two lines must cross. There would be a point where the number of available pairs shown in the F numbers would not support the assumption of increasing size in the ancestry pool! We would then have to start assuming that the ancestors were limited to the numbers in this ever-decreasing gene pool.

Even if I assume that humanity arose in larger numbers than one original couple, as evolution progressed in large numbers of pre-humans, the data clearly shows that the known number of human beings decreases as one moves back in time. That factor ultimately contradicts any model of an ever-expanding family tree. Using my current numbers and the Fibonacci sequence the crossover happens between F31 and F30. From this point back the number of possible mates is less than an expanding tree requires, and the math therefore turns to smaller and smaller numbers until we are back at our original number of possibilities for genetic combinations from one pair of parents, set by me at sixty in this paper based on information from Drew Smith's article, or as far as we choose to play the game.

At this point I appear to have created an absurd argument. While the number is not infinite, it also contains variables too significant to determine even with arbitrarily limited definitions. Even with the use of a laptop computer the computations involved leave me wanting a powerful processor or program to generate the numbers which would still exceed my comprehension.

3. F48 = 4807526976.
4. F47 = 2971215073.

The Probability of Specific Humans

The real point is that the number is not infinite. Even creating a problem this complex and using the largest reasonable numbers the answer will not be infinite given enough computing power. To reach infinite we must be at a point where no single extra possibility can be added to our outcome. If the answer was that the possibilities were infinite, would it not become as fantastic as multiverse theory? Would we have to include the possibility that the DNA could revert to producing an evolutionary ancestor rather than a modern human? What possible variety of results would be required for us to allow that the answer is mathematical infinity?

I enjoy the paradox when I read that equations seeking the ultimate explanations of all things become meaningless as they default to infinite thus matching long-standing definitions of God. But the real conclusion of this musing goes beyond humanity and ancient assertions of revealed truth. No matter what number I assign to the probability, we are the result of every variable in play when our parents produced us, and we exist. The combinations of human decisions and movements around the planet may exceed our understanding or ability to quantify. But each decision was a real event among available alternatives. The sum total of all of those migrations and decisions is us. But the number of possible results is not infinite. As I write this, the number of results is something just under 8 billion total outcomes alive today or an estimated 108 billion humans who have existed on Earth.[5] I might as well say that the probability of a Greg Brown is one out of all the US citizens born in August of 1956. That is a known number. The odds of Sam could be one out of all US babies his same birth year; Dale could be one out of all the people born anywhere in his birth year; for Julie, one out of the number of people currently alive, or for Jennifer one out of all the humans ever born. Feel free to move your own name to larger or smaller categories as your ego suggests. Whether we examine the life of only our own species or dare to look out into the vastness of the cosmos, the numbers may be unknowable or too large to understand. But they do not reach the realm where there is no possible plus one! When we move into particle physics, we cannot give precise numbers for an electron but must express it as a probability in spite of all the ways humanity harnessed its power in the twentieth century. Even as my mind continues to move into understanding of reality where things (quanta/particles) are not things at all by everyday definitions, there are numbers indicating their probabilities. In the world of things, we can

---

5. Smith, "How Many," para. 5.

visually observe and treat as real, nothing is infinite. In the realm of things so small that the line between things and energy waves disappears, there are numbers.

    Infinity does not exist.
    Nothing is infinite.
    Nothing does not exist.

What I Miss about Church

10/26/2019

A LOT OF MY WRITING is about why I left the practices and worldview of my youth, or in some ways how it left me. Yesterday watching the funeral of Elijah Cummings my mind turned to what I miss about being part of church regardless of any flaws.

- I miss the marker of a sabbath in my week. While I cannot claim to be overworked in my retirement, there was a regularity that came along with observing the beginning of the week as a day set aside from the general purposes of the rest of the week.

- I miss having the answers we were so sure were true for all people in all places and all times. I miss the hubris which said that I knew the answers which could solve all problems, cure all ills, and lead to a better world if we only had the skill and dedication to share them with those who had not heard.

- I miss the friendships from my youth, both the people my own age who were part of almost everything I did outside of home and school and the people my parents' age who included me in their studies and discussions. I miss the longtime pastor of my youth who was always in my corner even when times came that saw us disagree so completely that we failed to comprehend the other's view.

- I miss the peace and hope that came with belief in an eternal life shared by my friends and family meaning that no goodbye was forever and that a glorious future reunion was guaranteed. I miss the calm that came with believing Jesus was arriving at any moment to rejoin us all in a world that would no longer know pain, sorrow, or separation.

- I miss the continuity of being part of an organization my grandparents helped found and my parents helped lead. The church of my family is deeply embedded in my identity. Part of me has been missing since the day one of the many pastors who served there during my adult years invited me to leave.

- I miss the music—the old hymns played and sang too slowly, music of which we constantly made fun, music which can still transport me back to younger days and simpler times. I miss the peace and transcendence in group singing of songs from the faith tradition that formed my foundation in life.

- I miss the foundation I believed to be solid and eternal rock. As much as I love the dance of the universe and the beauty of truth that exists only in the tension of paradox, I sometimes miss the stability of ground that seemed secure, solid, and satisfying in its assurance of certainty.

- Even as I thrill in the journey of discovery and an ever-growing awareness of the unity of all things, I miss home.

Song Lyrics and Copyrights

11/12/2019

ONE OF MY MAJOR FRUSTRATIONS as I try to express my growing view of the universe in writing is the restriction on any published use of song lyrics without written permission from the copyright owner. I have lived my life to a soundtrack. When radio was the major media form, the radio was always on in my childhood home. The first car my father bought when I was old enough to understand options had a radio I paid for to make sure the music was on as we traveled around town or across country. Through the different formats to the Bluetooth headband I now wear to bed, I live in a world of music.

When I was a child of evangelical parents attending the local church where my grandparents were charter members, hymns captured the message, the hope, and the comfort of our beliefs in ways that continue in memory long after most sermons and Sunday school lessons have been forgotten. Those songs still transport me back to those years, the people who surrounded me, and the comfort of a community of certainty.

As I grew and experienced all of the normal changes of moving awkwardly from childhood to adulthood, rock music took my emotions and reassured me that they were shared by millions of other young people. When the nightly news showed us the horrors of a war that would not end fought by drafted young men barely older than myself, rock music proclaimed the madness and our anger. The music of the sixties and seventies also offered utopian counterviews of what could be.

The strength of music has never left me. When I sit in silent contemplation it is always there, playing, sometimes far in the background and sometimes overriding the thoughts or the silence I am seeking. In conversation, my mind often hears song lyrics prompted by the remarks of the other person. When I become angry, lyrics come. When I am happy, content, or thinking of those I love, music and lyrics are there in my innermost being. It is perhaps the strongest human influence on my way of thinking even after decades of formal education and the study of multiple disciplines. Whether I am trying to craft words or be still, the music of my times accompanies me.

When I sit down to write about how I see the world, I hear lyrics. When I am searching for the best expression of an idea which might be new to a reader, the work of a song writer often emerges and says, "I already said it, like this!" And I often struggle to craft any phrase which will say it better. I want to include the words that fill my head. I want to name essays with phrases from powerful music or at least include a stanza between the title and my own attempts at communication. Being used to fair use policies as an educator, I have often used the ideas and statements of others while giving them credit. When I prepared to publish *Unified Field Theology*, I found the rules I knew were not the rules for lyrics. I could not use them unless I found the writer or current owner and got their written consent. And I had to rewrite and retitle several essays even when I knew that my own words were inferior to those I was deleting.

And the system is in place because it should be. The words of these artists of language are protected because they have great value. Having created expressions of human thought and emotion which transcend the power of the prose sentence, these gifted people own their work. It is right and good that they have control over who can use their words and how. In a money-based society, it is correct that they profit when others choose to use their work rather than create their own. I cannot begrudge them control over their magnificent expressions.

And then I look back at the ancient writings of faith. The way I used to see the world said the truest use of these selections was as literal truth in every case that was not undeniably metaphor or parable. Even poetry was studied in terms of what we believed was happening in history expressed by the words. To say that a selection like the poem we call the book of Job was a poem and not a literal story was forbidden. We saw it as diminishing the value placed on holy words of God passed down to us across millennia. Here was a real man suffering beyond whatever troubles seemed ours for that day or week. And he was holding true to his faith in the face of real friends who blamed him for his own pain. He was a champion of faith with the strength to declare that even if God killed him, he would trust God. We dared not reduce him to a fictional character. Never mind that the happy ending of having a new batch of beautiful children was absurd as a literal correction of the wrong of first having one's family annihilated for the sake of a divine demonstration. It was a literal story and to call it anything less was blasphemy.

I no longer see it that way. As surely as I have looked out into the cosmos through the lenses of science, I have also lived my life strengthened and carried by the strength and beauty of poetry set to music. When I refer to ancient scripture as poetry or song, metaphor and simile, legend and mythology, there is no place in my mind and heart where those words diminish the value of the passage. They are expressions that soar above common experience or prosaic reporting. The royal songs recorded in the Psalms are songs. So are the songs of the Israelites in Exodus, in times of triumph over danger, and in worship of their God. Stories saved over all these centuries to be handed down to us today are celebrations of truth that transcends a mere event in the life of a few people long ago. They are true across time when not limited as histories of single space-time points. As surely as the lyrics of Warren Zevon or one of my many other beloved writers carry meanings that go beyond one setting at one time, the words of the ancients become free to enter the events of life in the twenty-first century when allowed to be expressions of humanity, love, pathos, and longing for meaning in a world that often seems to be only chaos.

I have struggled with the rights of poets to control words I would like to use. I have acknowledged their brilliance and their value. I intend nothing less than the same respect when I choose to open the ancient writings and let them be words of beauty and wisdom without demanding that they be history. Like so many lyrics of the late twentieth-century, they remain messages of life to me.

A Matter of Names and Perspectives

11/20/2019

IF IT GROWS IN MY backyard and blooms, I may call it a flower, insect or hummingbird food, or just natural growth. If it grows in the farmer's field across the road or the yard of my neighbor who belongs to Master Gardeners, it is a weed. If it is collected for a science class, it has a very formal sounding Latin name. We are familiar with various names for the same thing. We know that different people often have very different perspectives on the value and significance of items as well. Different people definitely have different vocabulary when looking at the same object or idea.

This is a way to view the perspective I propose in UFT. Throughout my childhood and most of my adult life God was described as omnipotent, omnipresent, and omniscient. God is the ultimate power which controls the universe. God is everywhere. And there is nothing in the universe not known to God. I now word this last trait very carefully because stating it in the positive almost immediately leads to assumptions of knowing as humans know, the awareness of things through the use of the mind, and the personification of God. The first two translate more easily. Physicists now study the forces known to control the universe from the gravity of large bodies to the strong and weak nuclear forces in the atom and quantum strangeness beyond that boundary. Science does not claim there is no possibility of discovering a new force. But reading accounts of work to look back into the conditions of the universe approaching the origin led me to the realization that I was studying efforts to explain the combination of forces that control the universe. That sounds a lot like God.

It leads me to ponder whether the realization that God is real and observable in the natural order of things leads us to new conclusions. But for some it will be seen as equivalent to saying that there is no God. In fact, many physicists including Dr. Hawking have said exactly that. There is no need for a metaphysical being or power to explain the universe. And that brings me to the opening sentences of this essay.

Fans of C. S. Lewis's magical world of Narnia may remember a conversation in *The Voyage of the Dawn Treader* when the very practical Eustace asserts that on Earth, we know that stars are huge balls of flaming gas. Ramandu, a star at rest, replies, "Even in your world, my son, that is not what a star is but only what it is made of."[1] To some this will amount to no more than wordplay. But I believe that coming from the brilliant mind of Dr. Lewis, an expert on words and their usage, it implies something deeper than a neatly constructed fiction.

In quantum physics we have learned that when attempting to study the universe in units smaller than the atom, what we expect to see determines the results we will get. If an experiment is constructed to observe subatomic units as waves, they perform as waves. If the experiment and equipment are designed to detect them as particles, they appear as particles. In ways that seem very strange to a pre-quantum worldview, what we expect to find determines the reality we will observe.

Now when I look out at the night sky with the lenses of modern science, I see a fantastic array of nuclear masses moving through space-time in keeping with the same universal forces that control what happens on Earth. I am in as much awe as I ever was. I am humbled by the vastness of the size and power of the universe I see, experience, and am. I see the classical traits of God.

When my more traditional friends and family look up at the same sky, they see the works of God. They are in awe of God's power and limitless nature. They know that stars, planets, constellations, comets, or the more distant phenomena observable by modern telescopes are not God. They know that gravity is real and powerful, but it does not make sense to them to say that gravity *is* God. They behold the enormity of the universe and believe that the things they have been taught in religion are affirmed by the glory of the world they observe.

I can express what I am saying in these terms. If we observe the grandeur of the universe through religious lenses, we will see it in

---

1. Lewis, *Voyage*, 180.

religious forms. If we observe it only with the lenses of science, we will see evidence of the properties of science much like one of us might see a flower and another a specific scientific plant form. How we search determines the results we will see, and what we see determines what we will conclude. That is acceptable to me until we start attaching teachings and judgements to those observations which declare that only certain parts of the human race have access to real truth and the rest are doomed to live in ignorance and even condemnation.

When I look out at the world, I do not believe my blooming weed is a god to be worshiped. Nor do I worship the planets, the sun or the stars. I do not propose that we form the church of gravity or nuclear energy. But when I see the totality of energy and matter, which also turns out to be energy at its most basic level, I see the omnipotent, omnipresent which includes all things so that nothing we know exists outside its realm. Now Eastern thought makes more sense to me than ever before. I am not separate from the universe. The same wonders I can observe *out there* are in me, are me. We are expressions of that totality the same as a supernova or an ant. We are part of all that is and all that is is part of us.

When my church friends walk out of an evening service and look up to see the wonders of God, that is the vocabulary they use to describe what they experience. When the scientist looks up and sees the interplay of the forces of nature, she speaks in terms from physics and equations from math. And it is OK. It is all one.

The questions remain how will we spend our time as conscious beings in this universe? How will we see ourselves, as separate from or part of the whole? How will we see others—as our equals or in some way inferior to our own group? How will we define our relationship with our planet? What is our basis for examining the meaning and significance of a life, or of all life? I discussed my reservations about the practical effects of many of the traditional answers in *UFT*.

But I want to clarify that at the base of it all, we may be discussing whether what it's made of is what it is! There is now strong evidence that what we decide it is determines what it will appear to be made of as well. When those of us who love theory and possibilities finish discussing, a question—perhaps the question—from antiquity still awaits us. How shall we live?

Connections Across Space-Time

11/27/2019

IN CHAPTER 26 OF *UNIFIED Field Theology*, I recounted a story of experiencing a spinning sensation in Ethiopia as a killer tornado passed by my home in Indiana with all of my daughters present. At first believing the sensation to be caused by dehydration, I tried to fix it by drinking water but then became convinced that I needed to come down off the cliff and focus my attention toward home. Only after the day's events were over and we returned to our hotel did we learn of the storm. As I move toward a theology which accepts rather than denies science, this story has become problematic for at least one new friend who is drawn to the ideas of UFT. Each time I speak with him he brings up this account and asks me again if I can explain it yet.

The beliefs I held at the time the events happened made the explanation simple. I belonged to a God who was an omnipresent spirit capable of giving me direction on what to do in spite of my distance from home. Such a God is simultaneously present everywhere and could therefore communicate with me while keeping the storm away from my daughters. Sadly, that view also means a God who allowed the storm to strike a trailer park killing dozens of others. This way of explaining the events is simple as long as we leave it so. In order to do that we must accept terms like omnipresent spirit with metaphysical definitions which do not require or allow physical confirmation. The matching of the time within a belief system that allows for an all-present God is the explanation. No further exploration of the means of knowing is needed or possible.

The other simple way of dealing with such things in the past is to write them off as coincidence. I was climbing a cliff in the sun. Exposure causes physical symptoms. These are known facts from human physiology. And we simply discount any connection to the events at home. They happened at the same time but there was no connection between them.

This second choice would be the easiest answer to give under UFT. We are used to seeing connections based on our beliefs and so we make them when there is no physical evidence to back our claims—no matter how many times I look at the timestamp on my photos and the news footage at home. Any significance to the timing of the two events is explained away by our knowledge of the human brain's propensity for constructing meaning for observed phenomena. When this natural trait to combine facts into stories that make sense to us is also combined with religious expectations about a God who speaks to human consciousness, the easy argument would be that once both events were known my mind created a metaphysical context and meaning for the timing of the two events. But I am not ready at this point in space-time to give up all explanations that exceed our understanding.

As I wrote the essay for the book, I saw possibilities in quantum strangeness. We know that a negative spin on one particle will be matched by a positive spin on a simultaneous particle over large distances in spite of our ignorance of anything to connect the two. I have used this to justify my lingering appreciation of the more mysterious aspects of life and my sometimes more mystical experience of them. If very small units of energy-mass can affect each other's behavior over space-time with no connection we understand, and we are made of these same small packets of energy-mass, I see room to believe that some old superstitions may be based on observations that are more than coincidence. I cannot explain how the behavior of two tiny particles in an experiment affect each other, therefore I cannot rule out that particles on one place on Earth somehow affect particles in me in another place. This also raises the possibility that particles in me affect particles in another person when I pray for them in spite of no physical knowledge of connection between the two. Hard data studies on the effectiveness of prayer are convincing that the results are not as powerful as religious traditions lead us to expect. But unexplained events do occur. It creates a possibility space which allows me to continue allowing the existence of connection between humans at a distance which we cannot explain with current scientific knowledge.

Now researchers in astrophysics are reporting that even galaxies exhibit signs of coordinated movement over distances too large to be explained by traditional science for the movement of large objects through forces such as gravity.[1] Whether these observations truly indicate connection over space-time distances of multiple lightyears remains unproven. What mechanism would allow galaxies too far away to affect each other by gravity to somehow be connected is beyond the explanations of current knowledge and theory. We have a growing number of observations supporting some such synchronization, but we do not have an explanation. For me it maintains the possibility of real phenomena which do not make sense to us as rational beings. I maintain this possibility for strange connection even though my first thought was that it is most likely coincidence based on the fact that the same forces moving one galaxy are moving the other leaving the construction of theories of connection an artifact of human thinking rather than physical reality.

What I do not return to is metaphysical explanations of a being or force from beyond the physical world causing the events we observe. I do not believe the humility of admitting our lack of current knowledge requires returning to explanations which made sense to the ancients without the scientific knowledge we now possess. Neither do I believe in writing what we do not understand off as mere coincidence causing us to quit thinking, observing, and studying. It is the unknown that draws us forward into new knowledge and greater understanding.

I know two things that happened on that day in 2005. I do not know how they can be connected, but I know I believe even now that they were. Maybe the answer lies in quantum strangeness. Perhaps there is connection between large objects our current theories do not yet explain. Perhaps I am too eager to keep the magic of my old worldview and am clinging to a construction of meaning for a mere coincidence. I cannot prove one possibility is superior or inferior to the others based on current information.

I choose to continue to be amazed by the world and to value those things which exceed our grasp. What we cannot explain tells us to remain humble. What we cannot explain invites us to wonder and draws us forward to new knowledge and greater understanding. As we gain understanding, we also gain the tools to see new phenomena which exceed our theories. I am grateful to live in a time when the mysteries are universally large and quantum small. I remain, at least in part, a mystic because I experience the inexplicable as pure joy.

---

1. Lee et al., "Mysterious Coherence."

When we understand the things that amaze us today, we will be amazed by the things we will not understand within that new knowledge. Pursuing them we will continue to evolve in understanding. I hope we will continue to grow in wisdom and wonder as well.

When the Right Answer Is the Wrong Argument

11/27/2019

I CONTINUE TO WATCH THE debate over climate change, a concept where the arguments make me wonder what happened to our ability to accept facts, if not conclusions based on facts. If you present a climate denier with a graph of average global temperatures showing a period of years with constant growth, they will likely reply that they simply do not believe it. When I open my weather app before dressing to go outside and it says the temperature is 30 degrees, I do not wear shorts. Likewise, when it says 90 degrees, I do not wear my winter coat. But switch from the weather of the moment to climate and we seem to continue behaving in opposition to the scientific evidence. I believe there are several reasons.

Upton Sinclair observed decades ago that "It is difficult to get a man to understand something, when his salary depends on his not understanding it."[1] I believe this applies to a well-educated and intelligent relative who grew up with a father in the oil business and has spent his entire life in that industry as well. He sees the benefit of his industry's products. We travel like humans of previous generations could scarcely imagine. We love cars so much we collect them. I have three of my own. We live in comfort regardless of the outside temperature. And we use oil-based products in countless other ways we never stop to contemplate. Plus, he sees the evidence about the plastics and rare earth elements in new technologies as warnings of their danger and justification of his own

---

1. Sinclair, "It Is Difficult," para. 6.

industry. To him, arguments that we must reduce the use of oil are ridiculous. I believe a great deal of the same kind of thinking affects the thinking and voting of people who live near me, especially in the area to my south, when coal is discussed. They know that working in the mines kills, sometimes suddenly and sometimes slowly through black lung. But they also know that for generations the mines have been the only dependable jobs in their area allowing people a more reasonable wage. It does not matter that energy technology has long made coal obsolete. They see any presentation on the future elimination of widespread coal use as an attack on their ability to earn a reasonable wage and provide for their families. It would be far more convincing to show the growth of new industries and the shift of employment and investing opportunities as new avenues of success.

Then there is a serious misunderstanding of physics since Einstein and its generalized meaning. The theory of relativity has been translated to a belief among many people that everything is relative, and that all views are therefore equal. My social media feed includes constant inspirational memes encouraging people to pursue their own truth and allow everyone else to do the same. Seldom is any distinction made about whether those truths involve metaphysics, philosophy, politics, or information that can be proven or disproven through simple observational data readily available to all. While I work hard to understand things I have never experienced, the old fundamentalist in me understands why people of that tradition are skeptical as more and more people publicly proclaim that the body they were born with is not who they are. They identify with the opposite sex, so the body they were born with is the error rather than their perceptions. The fact that science increasingly agrees with their claims only makes the old school religious person doubt science along with their suspicions of the LGBTQ+ person. Nobody seems to notice that a complete relativity of truth based on the person speaking would make the fundamentalist's claim of sin and bodily mutilation equal to the view of the transgendered person. Both sides actually consider their own view as true in spite of the general attitude of relativistic truth.

In the United States, it has become painfully obvious in our politics. Let a political leader state something that is clearly counter-factual, and we can observe the reactions. The person who supports them declares that they stand on the same side as the speaker and so they see the world as the leader sees it. A person from the other side pointing out clear evidence that the statement is false is brushed aside as mistaking the view caused by their observance from an opposite platform as fact rather than a contrary observation based on the relativity of their position.

If Einstein's theory really meant that no observation could be trusted as every observation is only an artifact of the observer's position, science would have collapsed in the mid twentieth century. Science accounts for the observational bias and the problem of paradigm influenced observations, but it does not deny the existence of facts.

Now to the group I am most concerned about as they truly believe their position is true and have gained influence in all levels of US government. Their influence is increasing even while their numbers in the general society are decreasing. We are faced with the political platforms endorsed by the new evangelicals. There was a time in agrarian societies, and for a time in post-agrarian societies, where Bible believers emphasized ideas like the holiness of nature as God's creation and evidence of God's creative power. Passages like Ps 65:9–13 were taken seriously as proclamations of taking care of the land and bringing from it food for the people as godly acts. And yet in the twenty-first century, those who claim to be the truest believers in the teachings of the Bible are often the most vocal critics of any effort to preserve and care for the environment. Things have changed.

Some of the change may be attributed to the societal shift of populations to the cities and suburbs and away from farmland. The person who obtains all of their sustenance from foods purchased in city groceries far removed from the process of growing and harvesting cannot be expected to have the same connection to the earth as those who work it with their own hands. Even in farming, the change to more and more industrial methods removes the worker further and further from the direct working of the soil and the enjoyment of the harvest. Some loss of attachment is easily attributed to an evolution in lifestyles and perspectives. But there is something else at work.

Lifelong evangelicals have been raised on promises of an imminent physical return of Jesus to set up a permanent kingdom on a new Earth. And they have been taught passages such as Matt 24 and Mark 13 which proclaim that a time of wars and rumors of wars will come before the end. The same passages predict famine and natural disasters as birth pains of the world yet to come. I have spent a lifetime listening to people from this worldview responding to situations of great human tragedy with a combination of concern for the afflicted and joy over another sign of the imminent return of their savior bringing a world ruled by their beliefs.

What happens when those who are concerned about global warming speak to them? Those who remember teachings that the Earth is God's creation and a gift to man to be handed down from generation to generation expect concern and a willingness to consider preventable damage to the earth as wrong. Today's evangelicals respond very differently. Some deny that the evidence can be true out of a distrust of science coupled with beliefs that all attacks on what they see as a US lifestyle given by God are evil. Others hold a far more dangerous view. While it is seldom said outside the cultish oneness of the local congregation, they believe we are reporting exactly the future they are waiting and hoping to see. We tell them that mass climate immigration will bring conflict and war and they hear Matt 24. We tell them that people will be starving, and the Earth will have become an unsafe place to live, and they hear Mark 13 as well. Instead of concern or alarm which might motivate new behaviors, they share the stories in their gatherings of the faithful and celebrate the coming end of the world.

The evangelicals of my lifetime do not believe that the end is the end. They believe that the end brings a new beginning when they will be victors over everyone they see as outside the protection of evangelical salvation. When I was young the emphasis was on reaching every people group on Earth with the gospel of salvation so that none would endure these times without hope of the new world to come. We believed that reaching every people group was a prerequisite for God to justly end the current age. The emphasis was on including everyone possible in the glory of the age to come. Among more liberal Christian traditions, the message was for the church to work to help bring about the arrival of the godly kingdom. We had formulas which told us how quickly everyone could be reached based on geometric projections of each believer reaching various numbers of more people. We sang songs of hope about the possibility of this new world arriving in our lifetime.

Now the numbers show identification with such faith, or any specific faith, in decline. The believers look at the news and current entertainment and believe that a culture war is under way which they are losing. They speak publicly of fighting this change and returning to an earlier nation based on faith.[2] Now when we try to speak to them about scientific evidence that our planet and human existence on it are in danger, they inwardly rejoice. If they cannot win the world through evangelism, laws

---

2. Dias, "Christianity Will Have Power."

against behaviors they believe are wrong, or wars against nations identified with other beliefs, then there is hope that their God is preparing to come and do it for them. The very catastrophes we use to try to justify changes in lifestyle and technology are to them promises of ultimate victory immediately after the time of disaster. And many believe that they will be magically transported to another place during the years of suffering by being *raptured* before the time of *tribulation*. When we are speaking with our neighbors, it means things as simple as continuing to value large SUVs, freely using petroleum products to sustain current lifestyles, and a growing emotional insulation from stories of suffering in other parts of the world.

When evangelicals who believe increasing chaos means acceleration of the ultimate victory of their worldview gain positions of influence with US leaders the consequences are worse. If defending the modern nation of Israel no matter how she behaves means continued instability and death in that region, their biblical interpretation tells them it is to be so before the end. If continuation of our current lifestyle means that the Earth becomes more and more unsuited for life, they anticipate the arrival of their God with a replacement. If the opposition points out that their chosen leader is becoming friendly with other world leaders long believed to be evil, that too is a sign of things moving toward a point of no return where earthly conflict and ruin will bring cosmic change by metaphysical means. Their responses to world situations are opposite of what many believe their faith teaches. And when they have the ear of those with the capacity to bring death and destruction the threat to life on Earth is real and immediate.

The oilman and the coal miner need to see other ways to earn a living capable of sustaining the kind of life they wish to have for themselves and their children. The uneducated generalizations of the word *relativity* point to a need for better education in both science and the humanities. People with religious beliefs that the destruction of our planet is a positive sign of the arrival of a new world order are more dangerous and difficult to change. The new atheists are vehement about a need to abandon religion along with all superstitions of the past in order to deal with reality as we know it. Younger theologians in more progressive circles seek to return to a message of caring for all others and the planet where we live. UFT exists in the space between the two. The forces of the universe which can be studied through science and math offer predictions of the future only to the extent that current trends in data can be extrapolated into the future. They do not promise the miraculous appearance of a new planet ruled over by God. We already have a planet ruled by the forces of nature. What we do with it and what world we leave to our children and grandchildren is up to us.

Perhaps the utopia on the other side of our increasing dystopia is a time when generations believing magic will overcome reality have reached the end of their years and passed into oblivion. Perhaps now is the time when we must somehow survive the violent death throes of their religions. If so, the coming age will be a utopia only in comparison to the chaos of today. We will still be mammals living on one watery rock circling a sun which offers us all our planet requires for our existence. We will still have to decide what to do with what is left of that planet and how to relate to each other. No matter how far our telescopes reach out into the universe there is no sign of an approaching rescue. It truly is up to us.

Something Was Conceived

12/10/2019

According to Robert Kaplan's natural history of zero, nothing is a late addition to human thought. Things have existed longer than humans and are easily observed. We still do not know of any location of an actual nothing.[1] The Greeks and Hindus are early contenders for the invention of zero for computing. And the Hindu concept is especially interesting as they saw nothing as "receptivity, a womb-like hollow ready to swell."[2] This led me back to scientific descriptions of the Big Bang.

The Big Bang by the very nature of its name indicates an explosive appearance of everything as soon as there is one small something. This cosmic seed was considered verified with the observation of a Higgs boson. To my mind these descriptions sound rather male in contrast to the more female Hindu description of nothing as womb-like. The combination causes me to consider that there is a universe because it was conceived! Something about the nature of the potential of the pre-universe supplies a seed to the waiting womb of *nothingness* and a universe pregnant with possibility emerges in an explosive moment!

Then the double meaning of words in the English language joins my mental adventure. What comes before a human sets out to make something? A thought or idea forms in the mind with sufficient power to cause the thinker to act and produce the object. With due apologies to neuroscientists who would undoubtably caution that there is a combination of physical changes and energy happening in the brain when we

1. Kaplan, *Nothing*.
2. Kaplan, *Nothing*, 59.

say thinking is happening, to the common observer nothing becomes something when it is first conceived and then produced. I will not stretch the metaphor too far partially by admitting that I am playing with a metaphor, not making a scientific observation of non-matter becoming matter. My childhood Sunday School teachers were quite thorough in pointing out that only God could do that!

But here we are. Where there appears to be nothing a tiny something appears, and this particle's arrival has been described for general understanding as being like an idea crossing a room and causing temporary concentrations of people hearing and discussing it.[3] Everything starts with something very much like a thought. My mentor, Don Pitzer, remembers a woman student gasping the first time he said in class that the universe now appears to resemble a thought more than a machine. I remember gasping the first time he said it in a class I was taking. At the time, my reaction was because it matched my fundamentalist religious beliefs in creation by the spoken thought of God. Now physics is speaking in these terms trying to explain in English what is mostly studied in equations. The universe exists because the void we call nothingness is a vessel waiting for content and that content begins as something easily conceptualized as a thought if we can avoid the anthropomorphic idea that a thought requires a human-like brain.

Many indigenous cosmologies involve male and female aspects to creation and existence as in Father Sky and Mother Earth. The Judeo-Christian creation story has typically been presented as completely dominated by the male God. However, the first verses of Genesis are not as exclusionary of the Eastern view as Western authors and speakers may make them appear. Before God speaks, the void is described as wet, possibly waiting to be filled, with God "hovering over."[4] Whether we resort to the metaphor of physical conception or follow the linguistic path of conceiving an idea, the same possibility presents itself. The universe is present because it was conceived. And it is present to such a complete extent that there is no remaining place within it that can truly be said to remain the abode of *nothing*. Small wonder that Kaplan's history shows what a very late addition to human thought the very idea of nothing is!

---

3. See TED-Ed, "Higgs Field, Explained."
4. Gen 1:1.

Anywhere humans are capable of observing, there is something rather than nothing.[5]

Now I allow myself a brief excursion over the constructionist cliff. There is a possibility that we are the gods having the thoughts that produce existence. While I do not accept that the rest of the universe did not exist until humans decided the stars were more than holes in heaven's floor, I have long been fascinated by the way things are found in reality after they are conceived in the mind. The Higgs Field and boson existed as theory before anyone produced evidence of one in the lab. Buckminster Fuller's soccer-shaped carbon molecules were considered ridiculous when he first proposed that they should exist given the nature of carbon. Then they were found to be widely present in the universe.[6] Backing away from asserting that they exist because minds created them, they at least came to exist within human paradigms and observations only after a person arrived who was able to imagine them. First, they were conceived and then they were observed.

Returning to the world of the ancients as recorded in Genesis, this is a mental exercise that a fundamentalist should only enter with great care. To the people inhabiting the story of the tower of Babel, the rest of the universe did not exist—only holes in a floor of a heaven that could be reached through great physical effort. The rest of the universe will not exist within the understanding of humans for many generations. I see no problem if we are discussing the world the way it appeared to people in the time period the text was first recorded, or as something even those authors considered a purely literary tool to explain the great variety of human language. But the literal interpreter of the Bible has a problem. Within that approach, God believes they can do it as well and takes drastic action to stop them. Within that paradigm, either the rest of the universe does not exist during the early millennia of human existence, or it is there and God as well as man is ignorant of it.

I will limit myself to the world of recognized reality. The rest of the universe did not exist for human constructions of meaning until someone was able to see beyond the imagined ceiling. Nothing as a something that is no thing still exists only in the human mind, as valuable as it is for complex computations. Radiation, space-time, and quantum particles exist throughout the regions we consider the emptiest areas of space. All

---

5. Kaplan, *Nothing*.
6. Choi, "Weird 'Buckyballs,'" para. 2.

of the rest comes to exist within the world we see, study, and seek to understand when people can conceive of the possibilities and look for evidence of that possible reality.

In the primitive sense, conception is viable language to explain how a new thing, our universe, came to be. In current usage it makes linguistic sense to say that the universe emerged when something very like a thought occurred, causing the concentration of matter and energy that exploded to form the rapidly expanding universe. In the constructivist sense, none of it existed within our understanding until we developed a sufficient background knowledge to explore further. We then developed the observational tools and skills to observe distant evidence, or to observe it as for the first time with new eyes and paradigms. Why is there something? Because something was conceived. We now live in a time where the most remarkable mental construction with no real-world observable counterpart is Nothing.

Waiting on the Light

12/13/2019

THE DARKNESS IN WINTER AFFECTS me. The dark evenings seem to last forever and living in the age of electricity does not make it less burdensome. At the same time, the activities of Christmas become more and more burdensome over the years. The season is distorted by obligations and logistics that always leave someone unhappy. While advent can be a season of anticipating the light that breaks the darkness, that is not my experience among others stumbling through the confusion. And some years ago, I started celebrating the solstice.

I endure the darkness and I wait for the natural return of the light.

I watch the apparent insanity that has overtaken the government of my country and others.

I wait for the light.

I watch self-proclaimed leaders of my lifelong faith chasing after everything but faith, hope, and love.

I wait for the light.

I watch my culture become more and more immune to the plight of anyone who is *other*, perhaps anyone beyond the self.

I wait for the light.

I watch education become ever more about financial return and less about enlightenment.

I wait for the light.

I switch to the media feed of young theologians seeking to construct more inclusive beliefs and practice and I feel the glow. I see young people standing up and demanding a healthier and more hopeful future, and I feel my own soul rise. An old friend calls and we talk at length about what may yet be done to invite people into relationship with the incredible knowledge base of our time, and I smile. But it is still dark out and I wait for the light.

I stop looking for a light that is not present and I close my eyes to both the darkness and the strain of searching something that is not yet. And there is light. So many people, in person and through their writings, have poured light out for me and into me. In spite of the questions, there is an abiding faith that the universe is good, and it lifts me. I am contacted by another looking for answers in the chaos and I share back some of what has been given to me, and I shine.

In spite of all the chaos and violence,
in defiance of all of the ignorance and forced focus on finance,
while the physical day remains short and dim,
affirming that the universe silently dependably demonstrates the
turning,
in faith, hope, and love,
I wait for
the increase of
the ever-present
light.

The Advent of Snow

12/17/2019

While waiting in the season of advent, I notice the present darkness. I notice it in its literal and descriptive forms. Yesterday while I ignored all reports of negative things I cannot change, it was still physically dark. Clouds dominated the sky, and the world was dark gray.

Then this morning enough snow arrived to cover the grass and rooftops. The difference is unmistakable. The light is almost too bright to sit by my window as I type this reflection. The temperature outside is colder. But the world seems warmer.

It dawns on me what an interesting phenomenon snow is. When the world is darkest the weather brings white reflective snow. The further one moves towards the poles, the darker the season and the greater the likelihood and amount of snow.

Some will see that as evidence of Divine design. I see it as more evidence that the universe manifests a natural balance. In the darkest months, precipitation becomes more reflective of light. It is a gift no matter how one identifies the source.

In an age of vehicles that move too rapidly for easy stopping and shoes designed for looks instead of function, it is easy to see winter precipitation as a nuisance.

Sitting in my comfortably heated house, I look out and see the natural course of seasons on Earth bringing light exactly when and where it is needed, and I am grateful.

Advent as Solidarity

12/18/2019

THE CENTRAL PART OF ADVENT for me is waiting. Some of it happens with the traditions of the season. Children wait to see if their Christmas wishes are answered with exactly the toys they want. Adults wait for time with family, and too often for the time to escape family. But many of us in wealthy nations like the United States seldom experience the deep experience of waiting.

We grow impatient waiting for our turn in a checkout line, waiting for the light at a busy intersection, waiting for our food after ordering or the waiter to come back to refill our drink. We feel the waiting if the mail is delayed, or a concert does not begin at the stroke of the designated hour. Our waiting is often measured in minutes with a securely known outcome as the reward for our inconvenience. Waiting for the slow return of the light after the solstice, we have made it a tradition in a culture influenced by Christianity to add lights on our houses and lawns. Instead of experiencing the darkness and contemplating what wisdom it might hold, we light our neighborhoods in bright colors and decorations that make us smile even as we rush past them. Those who practice the religion or traditions of Israel will light candles in memory of ancient heroes to whom no help came.

Some of us have learned to slow down and stop our rushing. Some stop simply for mental and physical rest. Some of us have learned to stop and contemplate the meaning of things beyond our present understanding. A few practice deep meditation designed to explore the unity of all things and our common connection to the cosmos by the very nature of our being. Learning to engage in such practices from positions of safety and plenty, we often experience the universal as calming, centering, and positive.

What do we know of the lives of those who wait with no sure promise of an end, who wait where life is dark regardless of time or season, who wait where hope is based on little more than the strength of the human spirit?

What is it like to wait for the end to war with its terror from unreachable phantoms in the sky, in places where children are taken for soldiers, while everything one has ever known is gradually reduced to rubble?

What is it like to wait for some sign that you are remembered in the outside world as you sit in a cell for offenses you did not commit—torn away from all that you know because of the color of your skin and being in the wrong place at the wrong time resembling the wrong person? How deep is the pain of waiting for the gift of a child to love and raise when none of your prayers are answered as the years of opportunity pass rapidly and tediously one after another? Do we understand at all what it means to wait in poverty for a chance to work, to find food, to care for your family in a land where government absorbs all assets in layers of corruption and the world makes empty promises or scolds that you should rise up and simply live lives like ours?

What is it like to live in the midst of affluence as less than equal all your life? How does the heart feel watching your children watch the same commercials as their friends knowing that Santa does not bring the same offering to conspicuous consumption to your house as to those of their classmates? How unwelcome are you when followed by security personnel every time you enter a store, with money, dressed as nicely as anyone else there, or worse, to know every time your son leaves the house that he is more likely than light-skinned young men to be shot and killed in any encounter with police? What is it like to be told that the law has changed, and all the injustice is in your own mind; you should simply get over it while you wait for a just and fair society your entire life?

The examples go on for other groups, other places, not just in distant times but in our time. The life of those who are not from the majority culture or lucky enough to be born in stable places or privileged families is one of waiting without end.

Hopefully we will never know what it is like to wait on either side of the concentration camp gates, in terror of armies occupying our cities and taking away every pretense of safety or dignity, or watching our children slowly starve for want of a world that cares and acts. We live so securely that we can choose to turn off the news and refuse to know about those who endure these pains even while we pursue our desires on schedules where the turning of a streetlight becomes a source of frustration and anger. We can look away. We can choose not to feel any of the pain. We can choose not to wrestle with the guilt of our apparent powerlessness to respond. We can choose not to let any thought of their despair remain in our thoughts to diminish our sense of balance and peace.

Before reaching this paragraph, many who live in privilege will be angry. In our age of finger pointing, they are used to all such observations equaling blame for the plight of people they have never met. Any observation that simple economics shows that the accumulation of much by the few is accompanied by the hardship of need for others is seen as a statement that the fortunate are somehow guilty for the condition of the unfortunate. We do not like to hear that we are the beneficiaries of gifts beyond our own labor and worth. None of those are the point of this essay.

Advent invites us to another practice. The darkness of the approaching winter opens a door to another possibility. Advent and winter invite both the religious and humanist alike to dwell for a time in the dark. In these weeks and months, we are invited to mentally travel into the dark that is more than the absence of the sun. We are invited to look at things we would rather not and see them through the eyes of common humanity and caring. As darkness closes in, we might contemplate the walls that enclose those in cells, hospital and nursing home rooms, or huts without food. In the darkness we can choose to participate mentally in the experience of those whose physical or mental conditions prevent them from seeing the light. We can choose to linger in the dark and see what cannot be seen and experience in some small way the world through the eyes of the *others*. We can look fully at the conditions that led the Buddha to conclude that pain is the first universal truth.

And if we lay down our defenses, if we dispense with games of blame, if we open our hearts and minds to the darkness, danger, and distress something happens. If we sit in meditation of the complexity of life by experiencing the dark we seldom tolerate, a new wholeness emerges. Dark light may yet awaken us to another side of reality.

Slowly, surely, softly we will become aware of those who surround us.

We are in the company of all humanity past and present.

We are accompanied by every creature that lives its life searching for sustenance and avoiding being food for another.

Here in the dark is wisdom concerning the unity of our life with all life.

Perhaps those who have heard the words too often will find new meaning and wonder in the proclamation,

> "The people living in darkness
> Have seen a great light;
> On those living in the land of the shadow of death
> A light has dawned."[1]

But it will only come if we are willing to wait a while in the dark—to sit with all others in the dark. We are not guilty of causing the dark we are powerless to eliminate. We may be guilty of refusing to recognize that it is as omnipresent as light. Here is a doorway to one of the great truths. Light and darkness are pervasive in the universe. Neither exists without the other. Only after we recognize the enveloping power of the dark do we truly know the miracle of the light!

> May we linger for a time in the dark.
> May we realize that we are all here and there is no *other*.
> May we dance together in the realization that light shines because of the dark.
> May we remember our oneness.
> May we become light.
> May we shine.
> But first we linger, together in the dark
> Anticipating what gifts may come.
> This is Advent.

---

1. Isa 9:2.

Advent as Practice for Democracy

12/19/2019

I AM AVOIDING MUCH OF the media. The ranting and raging by people elected to provide meaningful leadership for our country provoke unhealthy and unproductive emotional responses in me. And as I wait for the news cycle to turn, it occurs to me that the annual observance of a period of waiting is excellent practice for living peacefully in a democracy.

In a nation of very diverse views, which I value, power is bound to shift at times to those who hold views different from our own. Democracy attempts to assure us that there are limits to how far those in power may go in their acts against those who oppose them as well as promising that another election cycle will come. If we hold on, there is the possibility that every two, four, or six years the pendulum may swing those we disagree with or fear back to their former positions outside the government. An elected government is both synonym and antonym to permanent revolution. The opportunity for complete change is always with us but calls upon us not to strike out in violence to enact that change today. It requires the will and the ability to wait when our views do not hold the reins of government, even when the times seem dark.

When the current president was elected, there were huge marches in the nation's capital. The organizers and participants in those demonstrations chose to remain peaceful. But the sheer size of our population suggests another possibility. If those crowds had arrived with all of the weapons their home states allow them to legally possess, the security forces of the Capitol or the White House could be overrun by the size of the attacking force. The President and his family might be safely moved to quarters below the White House until order was restored. But there are enough people on any side of most issues to tear the Bastille down if we ever again turn to violence against our own country. Democracy insists that we hold on and keep faith that the system will allow us to bring peaceful change through the vote.

Nevertheless, there are danger signs. Many US citizens no longer believe that there is a significant difference between the choices offered in elections, that the system is unbiased, or that real change in the matters that concern them the most will ever come. Issues have been taken to levels where they are no longer presented as equal if opposite views on policy. They are instead presented as ideas and practices of good vs evil. The pro-life vs pro-choice debate has become one of seeing the other as wishing to murder babies or imprison and cause the death of women. This president has constructed prison camps on our southern borders where families are separated, people are kept in cages, and thousands of children have been officially reported as unaccounted for. How is anyone like me who has promised to never forget, supposed to respond to such a practice? Do we wait because an election cycle will bring change soon enough or because we feel powerless to bring immediate change? Those who feared our former president waited eight years.

What happens if a leader ever emerges with the skills and will to raise a force of massive resistance instead of waiting?

Such is the present darkness for which an annual observance of winter waiting prepares us. It takes strength, courage, will, and the practice of meaningful inaction to withstand both the urge to immediate action and the guilt of inaction. Those who practice Advent within the framework of religious faith do so with the assurance that they await the action of an all-powerful God. As the ovens of Germany fade into the memory of the previous century, it becomes easier to forget that God is not guaranteed to appear. For the non- or post-religious person, the task is more difficult. We wait without the hope of external intervention.

So, again, I practice the art of waiting. I allow the wheels of nature to turn. I focus on the things I control. I decide the way I treat the people in my daily encounters, the way I make myself available to those who live in prisons nobody else can see, and the way I free myself from the bonds of emotional reaction. Waiting in dark times, I also practice forgiving myself for the limitations of being human and unable to solve all things for those in pain. I wait in the hope that the power of hopeful waiting is not in vain. I see lights in the dark from friends I disagree with politically but who I also know to be good people actively working to make the world better in ways they control. At times, I recognize that their real actions exceed my own. And I am grateful for the candles they light in the dark.

The more dangerous the divides in our society become, the more I believe the practice of winter waiting contains a powerful force for good. We will hold a new election next year. Those who choose to exercise their rights and responsibilities as citizens will be allowed to choose who holds the reins of power. I believe we will reach those elections without widespread violence even as our society displays more and more violence towards itself.[1] The people will speak, and we will see who and what they choose. But the need to practice positive inaction, contemplative silence, and powerful waiting becomes greater every day. Allowing democracy to function as the agent and means of change requires it.

The wait for the light provides the opportunity to practice.
The universe provides it every year.
We decide how we respond.
Change will come.
Nothing in the universe exists forever.
The underlying energy and forces that have produced everything good remain.
The human impulses that lead us toward acts of destruction are also pervasive.
Perhaps we tip the scale by choosing anticipation of the next good.
Appalled by images of children in cages, I participate.
The light will return.
I invite you to the ancient practice of Advent.
Together we will celebrate the light.

---

1. One year later, the assurance that violence will be held at bay is less convincing as we navigate a pandemic and face the long frustration of those who say the time to wait is over.

Waiting to Be

12/20/2019

As the lead up to the solstice draws to an end and Christmas approaches, I am finishing my thoughts on the practice of Advent as a time of waiting. My first essays all deal with the benefits of learning to quietly wait for something. Sometimes we wait for the limit of the darkness and the gradual return of the light. Religious practice emphasizes waiting on the miracle of the incarnation.

Today, I want to examine the meditative experience of letting all else wait to simply be. Even as I try to word it carefully, I recognize the possibility of misreading the idea as waiting so that we might someday obtain a certain personal-emotional condition. Perhaps we expect to be happy, calm, centered, spiritual, wise, or powerful. The true meaning of this type of meditative practice is on the verb to be with no adjective. We cease our running, chasing, desiring, working, giving, thinking, and solving to simply be. We wait to be, not someday in some new more enlightened way, but to be now. While waiting seems to our Western lifestyles as inaction, it is still a verb. In this sense, we abandon the idea of any active verb, of any doing including waiting as an action.

I need to study and prepare to write a new syllabus. I wait.

I have items I want to work on for the simple pleasure of small improvements to my classic car. I wait.

I have new articles on both science and faith I wish to read. I wait.

In the twenty-first century in the United States, the list can be endless. The ego wants to be at the forefront and leads us to choose the best action to take next. We tell it to wait.

Now we choose to sit in quiet and let all thoughts and actions pass in order to simply be. Christian contemplatives express it as choosing to sit in the presence of God without asking for anything or even raising expressions of worship. Deep prayer is a time of simply being in the presence of God. The Eastern path uses different language and speaks of being part of all that is.

I have practiced both forms, and I have often missed the humor in the situation. We are. If there is an omnipresent God, we are always in the presence of that God. We are living pieces of this universe and we are always in it and surrounded by all that is. We actually cannot escape it. Only the nihilists suggest that we might escape it by choosing death. Both religious forms and physics say that all that is us at the most basic level will continue to be even if we end our time in human form. We are. It is always true. But in all of our rushing and doing, no matter how positive, we lose awareness of simple existence.

Now comes a time like Advent, a daily practice of prayer or meditation, time away from the active life and all of its noise and distractions. We simply let go—although it is counter-intuitive to the western mind and not easy at all—and be.

I do not like the dark. Many teachings of my childhood associate it with the negative side of existence. I acknowledge nonetheless that darkness like all other parts of life is a gift when we allow it to be. Darkness hides many of our distractions. There is less to catch the eye even if the imagination tries to fill the emptiness. It is easier for me in the calm and dark of winter to stop. I choose to wait, to let all my pursuits wait. The meaning is the same in spite of the order of the language.

Sitting in silence, allowing thoughts to pass through, allowing compulsions to do to pass, and allowing myself to do no external thing. I am. Dropping all adjectives of good or evil, blind or enlightened, I am.

Tomorrow I will celebrate with friends. For the coming week, I will celebrate with my family. I will continue to ponder imponderables even as we assemble and play with children's toys and eat comfort foods. I will continue to plan for future events that may or may not happen. News of happenings around the world will remind me of the joys and horrors of human existence. And I will engage them all on different levels and bless the holiday distractions from overthinking things I do not control.

But first, in the dark season of Advent, there is the invitation again to stop and let go of all else in order to be.

It is a great gift.

We are.

What God Would Not Do

12/24/2019

When I was growing up sure of the attributes of God I was taught, my non-church friends loved a sort of anti-religious koan. It went simply, "If God can do anything, can he[1] make a rock so big that even he can't move it?" At the time, I thought I was very clever to consider it equal to creating humans who were required but unable to be perfect then dying on the cross to offer us all perfection. So, I would answer, "He did and then he moved it." It was beautifully illogical and brilliant to a young mind.

Now as I reconsider the grand stories of the ancient texts, I have been contemplating if there was anything an all-mighty God couldn't or wouldn't do. The logic of making us perfect by committing fratricide or suicide escapes me now. Simultaneously, the observation that the yin is always accompanied by the yang, the good by the bad, the up by the down, the this and the that is more convincing than I ever thought it would be. Instead of an aberration caused by the failure of humanity, the combinations are part of the essential nature of the universe. In a wonderfully witty response to President Reagan's desire for the neutron bomb, Arlo Guthrie included a description of how good and bad are always paired that included, "You can't have a light without a dark to stick it in!"[2]

It takes me back to that first story in the Christian Bible of two people who have everything good including the tangible presence of God. Good is all they have. There is no bad to match the good. It now gives

---

1. I am using masculine pronouns because our discussions always depicted God as a male.
2. Guthrie, "Neutron Bomb."

me pause. How can we recognize and appreciate what is good with no knowledge of what is bad? How do we know the pleasure of great taste when we have never experienced an unpleasant taste? How would we appreciate the beauty of a kind act with no knowledge of a harmful or thoughtless action? If one requires the other, does this famous story have anything to say different from the tale of eternal guilt and blood price we have been taught so long?

We claim that God is pure love as well as completely powerful. The story begins with this all-powerful one calling the entire universe into being by merely speaking. But when it comes to humans, this God sculpts us with his own hands out of the substance of the Earth, and then with a borrowed rib. God does not stand back and command us to be animate. God breathes his very own breath into his handmade creations to give them his very own life. And places them in the garden of perfection. Those are acts of love. The story says that God warns, "You are free to eat from any tree in the garden; 17 but you must not eat from the tree of the knowledge of good and evil, for when you eat from it you will certainly die."[3]

There is one negative in the world of all good to provide the balance and the knowledge of both what is good and what is evil.[4] Except, they have never tasted it. It is still contained and as safe as Pandora's box left sealed. I read that statement from Genesis, and I fail to hear the temptation to do something that will result in eternal damnation from a bloodthirsty God. I hear the one who just created humanity with personal touch and his own breath lovingly pointing out that everything here is good, but "*when* you eat from it you will certainly die."[5] It doesn't say *if.* It says *when.* God knows it will happen. The God of the story is omniscient after all. The tree is there. The knowledge of good and evil resides in a taste of its fruit. God knows this. He tells them that *when they* eat from this tree they will certainly die. Why?

---

3. Gen 2:16–17.

4. If one accepts the interpretation that the serpent who will soon enter the story is Lucifer cast down from heaven due to his rebellion, there is already great evil on Earth and only the garden was made as perfect until he somehow invades paradise.

5. Another absurd thing we did was argue the meaning of texts right down to the English prepositions as if they matched God's original words for all time. I am going to practice one example of it here because people I would like to bring comfort to may still read in the same way.

Why would a loving God place a death trap in the midst of perfection only to condemn those he loves? I wrote about it in *UFT*. It did not make sense to me. But now a new possibility has entered my thoughts and contemplations.

Perhaps this was the one thing an omnipotent loving God could not do to his beloved little creations. Perhaps God was unwilling or unable to make humans with expiration dates. Knowing that we would have to know pain in order to know ecstasy, perhaps it was still beyond God to create humanity feeling pain including the pain of separation and death. It is required. It must exist in order for us to know and love the good, but God prefers to have his beloved live in the bliss of ignorance for as long as it lasts.

When the plot unfolds and they listen to the serpent, God shows up and finds them, clothes them, tells them what it is going to be like in a world of both joy and pain, they are banned from their garden nursery, and any promise of future deliverance from suffering is hidden in metaphor. But God is with them, not removed and waiting on a distant throne of judgement and condemnation. I can now read this ancient story as an assertion that while every light shines when it is in the darkness and every good is defined by its opposite, the power of the universe leans toward the good. I read the story as an affirmation in the face of pain that what is beautiful, life-giving, and loving is closest to the heart of the creator.

I can now love the story.

My observations of people caring for others when pain calls for help match the story. Our hope that life leans toward the good is there in the story with no denial of the reality of pain. Rather than blame for all suffering being placed on the shoulders of innocents, I see affirmation that the power of the universe kept it a different way as long as possible.

Life is filled with pleasure and pain.

But the preferential leaning of all things is to beauty, love, and life.

This is now a story of comfort.

The preference of universal power is life!

A New Year

12/31/2019

I SIT AT MY COMPUTER today in disbelief that tomorrow on the Gregorian Calendar we begin the year 2020. Growing up during the Cold War surrounded by people who believed end-time prophecies were coming true, I never expected to see a year like 2020. Many of those old friends still believe that current events signal an imminent divine reversal of human history. I no longer share that confidence.

I am pondering what the numbers and the turning of the calendar do and do not mean. New Year's Eve in the USA is devoted to parties and celebrations, resolutions for improvements in the coming year, and anticipation of change. The television is broadcasting official pleas to celebrate responsibly and make advance travel plans for arriving home safely after the consumption of significant quantities of alcohol. For most of my life, the modern age brought new technologies and advancements in knowledge every year to fuel the expectations of an immediate future worth celebrating.

But looking out at the universe, nothing changes as we flip a page or hang new calendars. We humans made them up to make sense and mark the passing of time in a world that changes very slowly. The Earth continues to spin on her axis as she dances around the sun the same way she has done, in common language, forever. The change from today to tomorrow does not include the seasonal markers of a solstice or an equinox. It is an artifact of our inherited calendar. Other calendars do not mark today as the turning of the year at all, and it causes me to ponder what it is all about.

To be sure we need markers for the passing of time, set times to reflect on our lives and improvements we desire to make, as well as social affirmations that our hope for a better future is not in vain. But our hopes that every year will be better have been disproved. Our trust in progress has brought us both amazing technologies and the capacity to destroy our lives. We are now faced with the dilemma that many things less obvious than atomic bombs may prove to be our undoing. The technologies that allow comfort and entertainment in our homes and an unprecedented ability to travel are warming the planet whether we choose to accept the science or not. Some have begun to discuss preserving the human race by escaping to other planets, a plan that would leave most people here to die and would change those who travel to become creatures of the environment of the new planetary home if one can be found.

Beyond these new understandings of the cost as well as the benefits of our technologies, the past year has also seen a decrease in our understanding of each other and an increase in violence based solely on the identity of the *other*. The US political system was successfully manipulated to put a man in the White House who encourages rejection of ideals fought for by people willing to sacrifice their lives all through my lifetime. The election of the first acknowledged black president has been followed by the ascendency of racism, sexism, and antisemitism in violent actions as well as speech. Our government has divided into two camps that act according to their party's position on each issue. Our leaders now disparage those who would dare to work for any middle ground, civility, and the common good. Even though 2020 is an election year in the United States, it is hard for me to look past tonight in hope that things will be better as the new year progresses.

However, the dark reveals the light. In the past year, I found friends who think the way I do, and my isolation has been lessened. I am working on lessons concerning methods of social change for a possible return to Haiti and in preparation for the start of a new minor at my alma mater on the history of human experiments in building healthier communities. As I work on academic lessons, I anticipate the rise of those who will not tolerate the gathering darkness.[1] I know we do not have to begin from the beginning but can learn from the brave examples of those who went before us. When I meet with people in small groups, I discover that civility continues even in discussions of differing opinions. When I listen

---

1. The outbreak of COVID-19 cancelled both of these specific plans.

to those who support different approaches than my own, I find kinship in the common human desire for the chance to raise our children and grandchildren in safety and hope.

So, tonight I will sit up and watch for the passing of the hour hand across the mark we have numbered twelve. Tomorrow, I will work to remember to write the seemingly impossible number of 2020 on dated documents. I will continue to observe what both science and the nightly news are revealing about our species, our planetary home, and our future. I will continue to contemplate what wisdom may come from our knowledge, and how we may rebuild systems required for our survival and assurance that our existence has meaning.

And I will sit in silence where truth exceeds words; I will sing songs of joy and wonder as I share life with my children and grandchildren; and I will dance. We cannot help but dance. We are after all part of a world that never stops spinning and circling a star that whirls through our pinwheel galaxy. Whether we look to the turning of a calendar page with melancholy or joy and anticipation, we are part of the dance!

May we learn to spin more gracefully and step less heavily on one another's toes!

Peace.

I Know Why Old Men Stop Talking

1/10/2020

I used to wonder why my father said so little in his later years. He never was a big talker. He went through school labeled a poor student but superior athlete. With the lack of care at the time, he lost all of his teeth by the time he was ready for high school and for a time avoided talking at all. As an adult, he was more likely to communicate with a hurting person by placing a big reassuring arm around their shoulders than by speaking much advice. But I always felt like there were many things he would like to say and just kept within himself.

The most basic explanation of why old men stop talking is that they learn not to bother when nobody is listening. Kids growing up believe they know everything. They are learning things in school that their parents never heard, and failing to be taught things their parents hold dear. Homemaking wives isolated from the workplace wonder why their husbands go on about being with other people all day while they work endless hours in isolation from other adults. Today's women who choose to, or have no choice but to, function in both worlds, have minds full of their own labor, planning, and endless lists of things to do. Neighbors drive into their garages, disappear into houses, and only emerge to return to their own agendas and pursuits.

Church never seemed to me to provide much of an outlet. Worship services and sermons are for listening, not discussing. Sunday school classes are often run as if they are for discussion but with a ready supply of already selected correct answers. Step outside those lines and people wonder if your faith is weak. Step too far outside those bounds and others are disturbed by thinking outside the usual box. Sometimes your presence is painful enough to result in an invitation to go find a place where you fit in and will be happier.

Some find outlets in traditional male gathering places and find companionship at the bar. But the people your age with careers similar enough to understand your issues have the same stories to tell and much of the comfort comes from the numbing effect of alcohol rather than the release of conversation. I have had some very interesting conversations with fellow climbers, but most sports are poorly designed for conversation. In climbing there is the quick hike to get to the crag or individual drives to meet at the local gym. Once you are there, conversation means nobody is climbing. When anyone is on the rock, attention is focused on climbing and proper belaying, not issues of the day or beliefs about the nature of life. When climbing is done, there is possibly another hike back to camp or the drive back home often in separate cars with no conversation.

I suspect those patterns can be traced far into the past. Now in the twenty-first century, new factors have become common and accepted. Televisions are on. Computers are on. Cellular phones are on. When others appear busy, it is rude to speak. Try to speak and before you can finish a sentence, a text comes in and, in many relationships, immediately becomes more important than whatever was being said. By the time the texting finishes, the original speaker has moved on to other thoughts and activities or has quit trying because of the abruptness of the interruption. My wife and I are fans of John Mellencamp, and she has one of his songs as her ringtone. Her phone lies! Every time another call comes in, it proclaims that it won't bother her anymore. But it always does. Might as well just mindlessly click through a computer game or watch meaningless television.

Then the situation compounds itself. During the silence, new essays on meaning in a post-fundamentalist world are rolling around my mind in competition with thoughts on local, national, and international events, scientific discoveries, and how our children are doing as they fight to make it in the supposedly successful US economy. When there is an opening for conversation, expressing current thoughts on any of those topics requires an entire preamble for the other person to have any context or understanding of what in the world you are saying. Before you can finish, there is a text, the end of the commercials, or some other interruption that means the thought will never be finished. If I do get out a thought on my work on meaning in the post-modern world, there is a total disconnect. My wife's energy and focus are consumed by six-day-a-week care for homebound patients and our grandchildren. Time and energy to reflect on any deeper meanings of life simply do not exist. Her world is one of immediate care, too many tasks to complete, and trying to get some rest to do it all again!

Some of us thought that social media might provide an alternative. Likeminded people could connect electronically and discuss what mattered to them. But the platform has been disappointing. Human trolls have found a form of entertainment, or even employment, in invading conversations to belittle opposing views, insult, or attempt to engage in wars of words. People are divided into groups, labeled, and dismissed. Try to talk to a person of another generation and see if dialog is possible and all too often the response is simply dismissive of your entire generation. Direct messages cause the same interruptions to personal communication as phone texts, but I have had some success in maintaining contact and conversations with friends through that medium as well as email. There might be a larger audience out there through today's technologies of podcasts and other electronic communication. But that world seems to have passed me by; my attempts to reach out to those already engaged have repeatedly led to reminders that they do it to make money and I am welcome to the conversation if I pay to play.

And typed communication has serious limitations. Statements are often misunderstood without the cues of voice tone, body language, and facial expression. Discussing different viewpoints is a minefield better left for rare face-to-face conversations. And the younger generations seem content to communicate through single pictures or videos lasting seconds and requiring no thought or interaction.

We have entered a time when belief in facts or logical conclusions seems to have disappeared into an existential maze of whatever makes sense to each person. Why speak across differences of thought and opinion if there is no understanding to be gained? People are busy, stressed out, and exhausted. The search for truth in paradox between opposing views takes too much energy. Attempting it with another person often results in a growing awareness that they are irritated by the mental energy required to even try to follow what you are discussing.

And I think many who have gained the wisdom of years simply stop talking most of the time. If I am honest, my own journey required the painful lesson that while I am talking, I am not hearing anything my mind does not already think it knows. Far less stressful to sit back and listen, let ideas roll around the mind and socialize with each other. Then, these essays step to the front and ask to be recorded in words. I have very gratefully found a small audience of people who enjoy reading them in their own times of reflection.

I think I know why old men stop talking. Perhaps there is wisdom in the ancient passage after all that invites us to "Be still and know."[1] Sometimes silence is sacred meditation.

---

1. Ps 46:10.

Gratitude

1/20/2020

If the only prayer you ever say in your entire life is thank you, it will be enough.[1]

I HAVE COME TO BELIEVE that gratitude is one of the most profound of human attitudes. It is available to any who choose to focus on the positive and be thankful regardless of their philosophy or religion. And when it is practiced, negative emotions lose much of their grip on us. It is hard to be unhappy, envious, or angry when one is actively grateful.

For those who believe that a loving God created and controls the universe, gratitude is a logical response. I believe it is even more true for Christians who believe their eternal condition is due to the voluntary self-sacrifice of Jesus Christ. But it is also a positive response for the practitioner of Eastern philosophies and religions as each moment's gifts are received. It can be found in the Native American quote widely attributed to Black Elk: "Let every step you take upon the earth be as a prayer."[2] And children who are taught basic rules of politeness know that any gift is accepted with a proper thank you to the giver.

There are also those in my country whose gods appear to be military strength and our continued lives of privilege and comfort. They credit the positive nature of our lives in the United States to the development of superior weaponry and those who have been willing to fight the native people of this continent and every foreign power deemed a threat. Even so, gratitude to those who developed and applied our military might is

---

1. Eckhart, "If the Only Prayer."
2. "Black Elk Quotes," para. 4.

in order. If the only beings deemed responsible for giving us the gifts we now enjoy are our own ancestors, then surely gratitude is owed to them.

When we are grateful for what we have, there is no need to covet what our neighbor has. We do not have to be jealous of their house, their car, their life partner, or their bank account. I may admire the beauty of their home, car, or other possessions. I may hold great respect for the relationship they have with their spouse. But, grateful for my own, I do not wish to take what is theirs or to abandon my own. We can live together in peace in appreciation of the gifts we have been given and share in the joy of our neighbors.

Quotes tend to stay in my memory, and the Meister Eckhart quote at the beginning of this essay remains a comfort to me as I journey into new views of the universe that differ from the specific dogma of my youth. We loved to argue about the core fundamentals of belief required to truly belong to God. It is strange to me that gratitude was never specifically on the list unless attached to a promise to convert to our faith. As my views evolve, this teaching comforts me. I am grateful for what I have been given. Some of it I am vain enough to believe I earned. Even there I am grateful for the opportunities life provided to work and earn for myself and my family. Surely any divine consciousness worthy of the term "parent" so often used in religion would respond to gratitude from this earthly recipient of life's gifts. I love my children without being told that they appreciate what they have been given, and my heart sings when they increase my joy by telling me that they understand and are grateful. How comforting to think that gratitude is enough—enough to gain God's presence, divine favor, or eternal life. It is enough for me that it brings simply peace of mind.

It takes a serious degree of chutzpah to offer any edit, corollary, or extension to a statement of belief which has meant so much to so many for so long. Nevertheless, I will now suggest one as humbly as I am able. What if every prayer we ever say in our lives is thank you?

This essay was triggered by a weekend marked by news of deaths, one at the end of a long life well-lived and one of a young girl taken suddenly by an accident. I have written previously about how the very pain of these losses affirms to us the great value of life and love while we are blessed to share each other's presence. So today, I choose to express gratitude for life. I am grateful for lives shared including in times of grief. I am grateful for the reminder of the preciousness of each life. I am blessed to be surrounded by others who will walk with me when life is difficult. I am honored when I am allowed to walk through the valley with others when the events of their lives call for companionship. Gratitude works when life is hard. What if every prayer we ever pray is thank you?

I offer an assertion—if every prayer you ever say in your entire life is thank you, you will live a life of joy. While my heart aches for those suffering immediate loss as I write this, I celebrate the joy of going indoor climbing with two of my grandchildren. Feeling the pain of another family's loss and wishing them consolation and strength, the joy of time with my family is affirmed and I am grateful. I am grateful for the joy we shared today, and I am grateful that there are communities of people who will gather to walk with those who have suffered loss. I watch my fourth-grade grandson top routes I can no longer climb, and my kindergarten granddaughter top out on each training wall as she starts to learn the sport and my heart sings with gratitude.

And I dare to assert that here is a path—I no longer possess the audacity to claim special knowledge of the only path—here is a path to a life of joy. Look around, reflect, and say thank you. Perhaps we say thank you for the air and strength given as one walks through natural places absorbing a power from wild things that exceeds our logical understanding. Perhaps it is joy for plaster walls, a roof, and heat with indoor parking for my car allowing me to go directly from one to the other within protection from the broader environment when I do not choose adventure. It is as simple as gratitude for the comfort of the chair I am sitting in as I type and as broad as deep appreciation of the beauty and mystery of the universe. When I look at these things and say thank you, I still feel the weight of caring for others for whom I have no magic answers, but joy remains. The very things that bring us our deepest pain are also invitations to our deepest joy when they remind us to gratefully enjoy our memories and our lives.

I invite anyone who doubts, to prove or disprove the idea by honest experiment. Even in hard times, be grateful for those who walk beside us, the things and people which brought us joy even if now taken from us, or for the simple fact that we remain and exist to choose a response. It is hard to curse in anger while expressing a sincere thank you. I am grateful for gratitude itself and it brings me the joy to continue the dance. Gratitude opens our ears to the music of life that surrounds us and invites us to live in peace.

The Location of Consciousness

1/28/2020

WHEN I WAS YOUNG, we were taught that only humans were conscious of their thoughts and actions. The idea was based on science that had not observed such behaviors in other living beings. And I suspect that science as well as general Western understandings of life were affected by the idea of humanity's unique status as created "in the image of God."[1] This capacity to think, contemplate, and create made humans copies of God, not the shape of our bodies. All other animals acted on instincts, skills for living each new generation automatically inherited either through evolution or by gift of the Creator.

Since that time, we have learned many things about animals devising solutions, making tools, grieving loss, and exhibiting other behaviors associated with thoughtful behavior. One example is juvenile gorillas seen disabling snare traps after observing the death of an infant.[2] Some of these changes in observations and conclusions are due to the work of groundbreaking scientists including Jane Goodall. I strongly suspect they are also due to a simultaneous decline in science viewing the world through religiously formed lenses. Now, research is beginning to indicate that even plants behave in communal ways—noticing, supporting and caring for the needs of their neighbors.[3]

In recent weeks, I encountered a step beyond anything I imagined as I read about scientists who seriously suggest that we correct our

---

1. Gen 1:26.
2. Than, "Gorilla Youngsters."
3. Wohlleben, *Hidden Life of Trees*.

assumptions about consciousness completely. They suggest that consciousness is a basic part of the nature of matter. In this argument, consciousness is not a divine gift or the result of complex organic forms and functions. It is basic to matter down to the level of quantum particles.[4] As strange as quantum theory is, testing such a theory boggles the mind! It is, however, an intriguing assumption. The belief that consciousness resided only in humans, and maybe other divine beings, was also an assumption. Once we realize they we have entered the realm of assumptions, the mind is free to consider not only which assumptions seem the best match to the observed world but also what the implications of each assumption might be. Recently, I held one of our rescued dogs, a very affectionate little animal who still shows signs of fear we assume are from her previous treatment. Watching her, I contemplated aloud whether our methods of buying puppies and taking them instantly from their family group might change if we knew for sure that they experienced trauma. It was not that long ago in my own country that we treated human beings with darker skin the same way we now treat animals. A broader assumption of levels of consciousness could invite us to very different treatment of all other life forms. It is not lost on me that it might lead us to beliefs and practices more common in Eastern and tribal worldviews.

In light of my conclusions in *UFT*, it takes me further in another direction as well. Dealing with death many times this year and seeking to comfort and bring strength to family members with a wide variety of beliefs, the implications of a world which contains what has long been known as God, are both practical and serious. We want to believe that somehow we continue on when our life in these bodies ends. We want to believe that it does for those we love. Those who are in the midst of loss want us to bring them some level of comfort, reassurance, and strength to go on living. I have spent some time on the issue of death and on what the end of life tells us about our actions during our days on Earth. What does it mean if consciousness does not come into existence and end simultaneously with the brain? If consciousness exists down to the level of all our physical parts, beyond our systems and organs, beyond our cells, to the very quanta that are assembled for a time as us, what happens at death? I have no idea how anyone would measure the level of consciousness of a cell, let alone a quantum of energy/matter! But if this counter-assumption is possible—and we have already seen that things beyond our

---

4. Goff, *Galileo's Error*.

previous understanding of the phenomena are not only possible, they are happening—if it is possible, what then? Does it open the door to a possibility of the consciousness we have known as ourselves continuing beyond our bodies? I find it unlikely that this would be so when all of the quanta are dispersed. But the quantum world continues to amaze us.

Perhaps it points to something like the ancient teachings of the East. The consciousness of all the innumerable quanta which we spend a lifetime trying to form into an integrated whole, may be liberated from the attempts of our egos to create and exalt our unique selves. Perhaps our consciousness is set free at death to become one with a general consciousness that pervades the universe. Some cultures have been trying to tell us so for millennia.

I do not know.

I know the universe is amazing beyond anything we understand, and we are part of it. Life enjoyed in gratitude is an amazing ride. If the life we know is all that is, it is full and a source of wonder. Even the pain of its ending points to the value of existence. I cannot prove to anyone that consciousness continues after the demise of the body. Neither can I prove that it does not. It is possible that we are transformed from our isolated bodies and truly free to join the eternal dance.

Death

1/28/2020

As I continue to explore the implications of a worldview where the power that physics describes as natural forces represent the omni-present, omni-powerful source and sustenance of all things, death continues to invade my life and thoughts. It is one thing to claim that I am content if all my thinking and conscious being are contained in this one wonderful life and remain only as I have produced records of them when death stops my brain from functioning. It is quite another matter emotionally when I am confronted with the death of a young girl simply walking in the woods at the very moment a tree falls. It takes on other dimensions when beloved relatives and acquaintances reach the end of their lives leaving us here to suffer their loss.

When I am called upon by friends or relatives to conduct memorials for those who have passed, I use texts meaningful to the family presented in ways which I find intellectually honest. As an example, I may be careful to say that a certain text or the author of that text proclaims a certain thing to be true rather than saying outright that we know it is true. A great deal of our proclamations of truth are whistling in the dark as we face permanent separation and the apparent reality that individuals last only a season and then are gone. Many of the tears we shed even as we make those proclamations speak not only to the pain of temporary loss, but also to very deep feelings that we do not know in any undeniable way that those proclamations are true.

We often participate in conversations including statements of belief that are not supported by the theologies we claim to follow. Claims are made that children who die are now the families' special angels watching over them from heaven even though nothing in traditional Christianity speaks of human beings becoming angels. Images abound in settings intended as both serious and humorous that show deceased adults occupying the tops of clouds, now having wings, and possibly playing harps. Such images are ubiquitous even though Bible passages that speak of angels describe them as an entirely different class of created being. And, of course, in spite of the fact that we have observed the tops of the clouds and know full well that there are no visible beings sitting around up there.

This week after shedding real tears over the death of another child belonging to my wife's local sisterhood of Girl Scouts, I viewed the memorial for my university's first leader. I owe this man a great deal as he oversaw the development of a small satellite campus when I began my undergraduate work to a full university today. He was largely responsible for bringing my lifelong mentor and constant companion in the journey of truth to this city and into my life. I felt a deep need for the words and ceremony of his memorial to bring meaning and consolation. He was properly eulogized for his character and contributions to our area through the university and beyond. And expected music was sang as predictable portions of Christian New Testament Scripture were read. And, especially as those scriptures were intoned, I found myself crying out that their comfort did not reach me; their promises did not convince or console me; the theology did not aid me in transcending the sadness of the loss. Watching the clergy who participated play their assigned roles, I felt they could have been priests of any real or imaginary ancient culture in a Hollywood movie pronouncing the incantations of their culture. The combined result was and is a serious body blow and a call to examine again what I believe UFT has to say in our times of deepest need.

As I have written before, and many people have said in the days that followed as a much-loved US athlete also died suddenly, I know that the grief underscores the importance the living person had in our lives. I know that the pain of endings challenges us to savor and be grateful for the living moments as they happen to the full extent that our awareness will allow. I remain grateful for the significance of individuals, and I believe expression of that gratitude is both correct and life affirming both during and after each life. But am I truly ready to accept that when human life is over the universe moves on without us as we are gradually forgotten? There is a strong pull to retreat to things I was taught as a child, or to try to return enough to find comfort in their promises against all evidence. I feel the pull both as arms of promised comfort and threatening chains of mental imprisonment reaching out when vulnerability wants reassurance.

I have read so many authors who frame the human search for meaning in the fear of death's final reality. This essay could easily follow that same path. But there is an alternative. Perhaps we fear that death's finality forces us to measure the value of the days we live. If there is no assurance of meaning in the grave, I must look at the life that has passed and ask whether its moments were well spent. It is both comforting and challenging when the answer is yes as well as it is convicting and challenging when the answer is no. When I look at the life of the person who has died, I see comparison and contrast to my own. I am both invited and taunted to take the measure of the days I have consumed and whatever quantity of time remains. It causes me to ponder whether the greatest fear is of reaching the end having failed to fully cherish, enjoy, use, and offer each of our moments back to the universe with the fullest measure of our capacity. And I hear Moses say, "Choose life!"

Expanding Universe

2/8/2020

I RECENTLY READ NEW IDEAS about why the universe is expanding faster than current theory suggests. One idea being explored involves gravitons, if they exist, having sufficient mass to account for the differences between expected and observed speeds of the expansion of the universe.[1] I would like to explore another possibility.

Most things in the universe—particles, planets, solar systems, and galaxies—spin. Objects like Earth's moon, which maintains a constant position relative to Earth resulting our labeling the side we never see as *the dark side* even though that side sometimes faces the sun, seem to be exceptions to usual motion in the universe. Why shouldn't we assume that the entire universe is also spinning? This would be very difficult to detect since we are part of the system, and everything would be moving in the same way with no unmoving reference point. Anyone who ever rode on a playground merry-go-round knows the thrill of the force causing the body to want to move outward[2] and be thrown from the spinning disc. If the universe itself is spinning, I would expect an increase in the rate of objects in it as they move to the outer extremes.

A spinning motion would also result in the universe having a higher total mass than the sum of its individual parts.[3] A higher mass is exactly what scientists have already been searching for as dark matter to explain the known expansion of the universe. The sum total of all currently

---

1. Letzter, "Photons Could Reveal," para. 9.
2. The actual inertia is to continue straight instead of turning.
3. $E = MC^2$.

known objects in the universe is not sufficient to explain the observed expansion, so assumptions are made that there must be mass we have yet to observe. However, if the universe is spinning at a high rate, the total mass would be increased along with the increase in energy related to the unobserved spin.

Studies in this area have been done by looking for variations in the cosmic microwave background.[4] Since no anomalies have been found, the odds are considered very low that the universe is spinning. However, if everything is spinning at the same rate relative to everything else, what would cause the ripples in the background? There is no known physical background external to the universe which would provide friction resulting in variations. I would also not expect any object moving in the exact same way as its existing background to change the background. So, I believe the question remains relevant.

An entirely different thought contending with these ideas about motion and energy is whether the universe is constantly changing to less matter and more energy. The largest amount of mass in the universe is found in the stars. Since the stars are constantly converting matter to energy, most observably light, it seems fair to ask if the universe is altering from plasma to light. If there is any logic in this thought, then the increase in speed is self-explanatory. Light always moves faster than anything else.

Thanks for going along for the ride. Somehow this morning I ended up on Einstein's light beam instead of a climbing wall. I'm enjoying the ride and trying to record what I seem to be seeing!

---

4. Johnson-Groh, "Does the Universe Rotate?"

What I Would Tell My Younger Self

2/12/2020

HAVING RECENTLY SEEN SEVERAL REFERENCES to what people would tell their younger selves, I thought about creating an entire book with wisdom from people I respect. So, I checked booksellers to see how many versions already exist. There were a few and they all focused on what the person would tell their younger self in order to become more successful in careers and income, with one suggesting how to make it easier as well. None of those would fit the things I believe I would now say to a younger me.

First, I would inform myself much sooner that the beliefs I was taught are not the only representations of truth. Christianity contains a wide variety of interpretations and practices today, and the ones I knew as a child are relatively new interpretations heavily flavored by US experience and ideologies. I would encourage the child to practice truth as faithfully as possible to the extent it has been revealed. I would also tell them that amazing people would come into their life from many unexpected channels and at special times and places to show them the beauty of expressions of truth from other cultures and other times. Stand true but hold absolutes loosely in anticipation of the beauty you have not yet learned.

I wasted so much time and energy arguing in favor of positions and beliefs I would later leave behind. It would have been so much wiser to listen. At a minimum, I would have learned more about the other person or group instead of only proclaiming what I thought was the one and only truth which I knew from the platform of who I thought I was. Some of the beauty of Eastern thought was still hidden from most Westerners during my childhood. What I knew of Judaism was presented by Christians either as support for our own beliefs or attacking the older tradition for refusing to accept their own prophesies as they were fulfilled according to Christian thought. Natives of my own continent were romanticized relics of an earlier age whose beliefs could not possibly save me as they had not saved them. I wonder now what difference it would have made to know the beauty of unknowing. How would the richness and variety of tradition expressed in those Jewish beliefs and texts before translation to suit the purposes of a different religion have changed my life? I wish I had learned earlier to appreciate the respect for and unity with the world which contains us long practiced by people I would not truly meet until far into adulthood. To simply be more free and less obsessed about the imminent and eternal danger of everyone who wasn't us would have been a gift allowing me to know that man's approaches to truth are far broader, deeper, and more varied than the narrow view I knew.

Second, I would tell me that no horse and chariot army was amassing somewhere above the clouds to take vengeance on all those who rejected the truth and to restore the true king to the throne. I was surrounded by people who truly believed that the restoration of the nation of Israel, the ever-growing nuclear threat, and a society with constantly declining moral standards meant that these prophetic images from ancient texts would come to pass before I became an adult. With people of faith telling me that God was preparing to bring an end to the age and school telling me to hide beneath a desk to survive a nuclear blast, an apocalyptic ending seemed plausible. It caused me anxiety for both the condemned and an earthly life I would never know. And it gave me an unjustified lack of concern for the longtime future of my planet and its life forms in spite of the fact that I was always deeply drawn to nature and often considered a tree-hugging hippie.

How absurd those images now seem. While we had abandoned any belief in a real physical location of heaven's inhabitants within this universe and consigned them to a spiritual realm, we still believed ancient tales of them walking among men, wrestling with one of the patriarchs, and even joining human battles to shed the blood of rival armies. And we believed it was still happening. Events such as the Seven Day War confirmed our assertions that God gave military victory to those he chose regardless of earthly circumstances. And now I have lived to the year 2020 and wonder why an all-powerful God would choose to appear to a world of stealth bombers, inter-continental ballistic missiles, and lasers mounted on a horse with a sword in his mouth. Sometimes we said those images were metaphors for power expressed in the only terms the author knew at the time, but at others we pictured them as about to happen exactly as described. If the events were revealed to the authors by divine will, why not show them how overwhelming technology would become? And why would an all-powerful spirit need physical armies and weapons at all? Actually, more believable is the lion of C. S. Lewis's imaginary world simply calling the stars from the sky and the closing of history with the same voice that produced them at the beginning. How different would my approach to life have been if I had understood that we have chosen, are choosing, and will choose the course of history and its end if such a day arrives without cosmic catastrophe or the demise of our star?

Third, I would tell the younger me that the arc of human existence and behavior is long and not easily changed by the work of any one man or group. Growing up I was constantly told the opposite. You can do anything. You will change the world. Such sentences sound so encouraging went you are young but become heavy burdens when believed. At church the history of faith was presented as an endless march of heroes, mostly male, who dared to trust God no matter how things appeared. They freed entire nations from slavery to empires, defeated large numbers of enemies without raising a weapon, and spread Christianity throughout the world by traveling, teaching, and leaving examples of martyrdom. At school the list of great men continued. They explored the globe and found new continents, conquered, settled, and civilized those continents. They rallied their people in times of war or negotiated solutions that prevented or postponed wars. They learned and harnessed the physical powers of the earth to do the work of men. By sharing the power of ideas, they created democracy and created and reformed a national model of education for all people. And they revolutionized human thought by translating scientific knowledge of the universe for common understanding.

When I began to learn lessons about human organizations from the history of intentional communities and doctoral studies in organizational theory, I believed I could change things. If I could demonstrate how to organize a school so that the children the regular schools said were impossible to teach succeeded instead, the system which wanted to educate all children would change. But systems are highly resistant to change. The schools were not interested in new organizational models or theories. They simply wanted the children to adapt to them or be punished for failing to fit into the existing model. Their animosity towards me for using positive methods rather than negative with the students they did not want eventually led to the end of both the school and my career in public education. As I share this negative part of my thoughts, I am thrilled to be preparing to share the information from communal societies with a new group of undergrads at my alma mater in the hopes that they may build healthier places where they work after college.

Church was no different. The only place they were looking for new methods was at megachurch conferences on growth in membership and budgets. The theme of this period in US history seems to be that something is good if it makes more money. Ideas on how our religious beliefs might lead us to function in kinder, more uplifting ways were far less than welcome by the typical male leaders of the last megachurch I attended, many of whom learned leadership in business settings. As long as the number of members—I am tempted to say customers as they did not keep traditional member lists—was increasing it did not matter if there was constant transition in who was attending. People did not need to be invited into a loving community for a lifetime as long as more people were attracted by the latest advertising, amenities, and image.

Neither did any representative of the MacArthur or any other foundation or think-tank show up at the door offering the golden ticket to pursue my work or asking me to help change the world. I was just me, a good student from a relatively small city, doing the best I could to make the world better for the people I worked with every day. My career was filled with good and powerful, rewarding work. It just did not fit the pronouncements made to youth that intellect, hard work, or a positive spirit will change the rest of the world.

Lastly for now, I would teach the younger me that all of this is good. It is healthy and productive to live well within the world that is. As I look back now on the choices I made, there were many other options. I could have pursued more money, power, or notoriety directly. And I believe I could have obtained them to a greater degree than I did with the choices I made. But I would not have met my amazing coworkers. I would not have seen the changes in so many young people who desperately needed a safe place where they could be treated with dignity and respect and where they were able to conduct themselves in ways that deserved both. I would not have experienced the many friendships with people of faith that abide regardless of what I have learned about US churches as large organizations. I would not have watched my own daughters grow up to follow careers in professions of caring. And if my focus had been on wealth or power, I would have been distracted from pursuing the truth presented in different ways by the variety of disciplines, their methods, and their vocabularies. I would not have lived a life which fills me with gratitude for accomplishments on the scale of a single life of adventure and dedication to integrity.

I would tell the younger me that it is all OK. Life does not require a rescuer from beyond the clouds or from my hometown. People live their lives and affect those around them by choosing whether to deal with them in positive or negative, altruistic or self-serving ways. And together we are, as Stephen Gaskin said, *This Season's People*. Collectively our lives become the nature of life in our times. No single one of us is supposed to rise up as the messiah. Religions tell us that prophets and saviors have already appeared if we agree with the teachings they left, or that are now presented about them. We do not have to be those larger-than-life exemplars. We are only called to be ourselves. The rest takes care of itself.

For the rest of my days, however long or short they may be, I will live life one encounter at a time and make sure that everything in my power is focused on making those encounters positive. It is enough. It is how the world becomes a better place to live. In the end, all of my advice to a younger me would be reassurance that contentment looking back over the years comes from how one walked and treated those encountered on the journey. I would encourage the younger me to relax, be kind, be grateful, and accept the opportunities that life will bring in an endless chain of surprises and small ordinary miracles. I am content.

Greed and Eternal Life

2/13/2020

ANY SERMON I HAVE EVER heard including these two ideas presented them as oppositional terms. Greed is a deadly sin. Sin leads to death, not eternal life. Greed on Earth may accumulate wealth, comforts, pleasures, and toys. Yet all are meaningless when death comes. Jesus is quoted as giving just such a sermon to a crowd of thousands.[1]

On the other hand, pursuit of eternal life is usually presented as a positive force drawing us into right relationship with God, and hopefully man as well. I have even heard arguments that the desire for something beyond what we know on Earth is evidence that there is a real something more to be desired. One of the most influential is *Surprised by Joy* written by the powerful Christian apologist, C. S. Lewis. A man whose work I have long admired and whose fiction will always be dear to me.

I want to present a different analysis. As creatures well suited to our planet for the simple reason that we are part of this planet, we usually define life as positive. There are times when tragedy arrives through our vulnerability to extreme natural events. When they do, we grieve them as abnormalities. Most of the time we celebrate the energy continuously provided by the sun and the life that springs from the soil when the sun's energy is accompanied by rain and water. We are group creatures and enjoy the company of family and friends and grieve them when they are gone. We value life. Perhaps more accurately, we value human life, or at a bare minimum a healthy mind values its own life. And we want more. What if the strong emotional pull to believe in eternal life is simply greed

---

1. Luke 12.

for more of what we treasure? In the same way that we want more wealth, more toys, more leisure, more pleasure, more knowledge, more freedom, more of more—we desire more of life itself. But the observational evidence is overwhelming that life here has a limit, a limit that seems all too brief. And we long for a life that continues beyond the body's demise.

This took me back to a source familiar to members of the large western faiths. Gen 3 begins,

> Now the serpent was more crafty than any of the wild animals the Lord God had made. He said to the woman, "Did God really say, 'You must not eat from any tree in the garden'?"
> ² The woman said to the serpent, "We may eat fruit from the trees in the garden, ³ but God did say, 'You must not eat fruit from the tree that is in the middle of the garden, and you must not touch it, or you will die.'"
> ⁴ "You will not certainly die," the serpent said to the woman. ⁵ "For God knows that when you eat from it your eyes will be opened, and you will be like God, knowing good and evil."
> ⁶ When the woman saw that the fruit of the tree was good for food and pleasing to the eye, and also desirable for gaining wisdom, she took some and ate it. She also gave some to her husband, who was with her, and he ate it. ⁷ Then the eyes of both of them were opened, and they realized they were naked; so they sewed fig leaves together and made coverings for themselves.
> ⁸ Then the man and his wife heard the sound of the Lord God as he was walking in the garden in the cool of the day, and they hid from the Lord God among the trees of the garden.

And ends,

> 21 The Lord God made garments of skin for Adam and his wife and clothed them. 22 And the Lord God said, "The man has now become like one of us, knowing good and evil. He must not be allowed to reach out his hand and take also from the tree of life and eat, and live forever." 23 So the Lord God banished him from the Garden of Eden to work the ground from which he had been taken. 24 After he drove the man out, he placed on the east side[e] of the Garden of Eden cherubim and a flaming sword flashing back and forth to guard the way to the tree of life.

The beginning is normally read and taught by Christians as the error that separated humans from close relationships with God and the perfection of Creation. The end is traditionally presented as God protecting humans from an eternal life in our now *fallen* form subject to suffering.

Under the conditions most often presented as punishments for eating from the forbidden Tree of Knowledge, to live forever would become part of the curse. Unlike the Christian New Testament, where Jesus often interprets his stories within the text, this more ancient text does not. We are left to deduce the meaning and we are not restricted to one explanation. Indeed, Jews and Christians look at the story in very different ways.

I want to consider it again as I look at greed as a possible source for our obsession with eternal life. In the story as recorded in Genesis, the real temptation offered by the serpent is not that the fruit is better than all other foods. The benefit of eating the fruit is to become like God. It is also worth noting that the warning against eating the fruit is that they will die. There is a suggestion hiding here in plain sight that humans at one time possessed the same characteristic of ancient gods, including the God of Genesis, and would have lived forever. The gods of ancient cultures varied in personalities and actions, but they had in common the ability to live forever. The desire to be like God would have included the desire to live forever as soon as the alternative of death was known. The story fails to tell us how these innocents knew what the warning meant if death did not yet exist upon the Earth. But after God kills animals to make them clothing, we can more easily presume that they knew. At this point the story continues that God removes them from the presence of the Tree of Life and places a supernatural guard to make sure they cannot obtain eternal life by accessing the fruit of that tree.[2]

So, if it is not already obvious, my examination of this same text indicates that this ancient account of the nature of humans includes a fascinating, and usually overlooked, characteristic. Already living in a setting of assumed perfection, surrounded by everything they need, and possibly capable of living forever—the humans in the story already want more. They do not desire just the fruit of a single tree; they want to be like God. Before the event that evangelical Christianity labels the fall, humans were already greedy. With everything they could possibly need, they wanted more. Before they ate the fruit, they already wanted more.[3]

---

2. An interesting side study can be done by looking up a number of scriptures in the Christian Old Testament where something of value which can be obtained is referred to as a "Tree of Life."

3. Fans of C. S. Lewis who are still within traditional Christian theologies may choose to take comfort here. If this desire exists before the fall, then it will not fit their definition of sin and might be thought of as a marker that the desire being considered is a marker of our belonging to a heavenly kingdom we have not yet seen.

We call that greed. To me, this trait combined with the presence of the serpent are indications that evil already existed in the garden and creates a serious theological problem for literalists. Evil in the garden precedes human disobedience! But that is material for another essay. For now, I am examining only greed.

I believe it exists in the story because it is a pervasive human trait. I believe it is a trait so pervasive that it was known to reflective human beings from the time of our earliest stories. To the author of this morality (or mortality) story, the human characteristic of wanting more was already so obvious that the story simply assumes that Adam and Eve would want anything they were aware of and did not yet possess. The desire for more is ubiquitous in human beings as far back as we have records of human behavior. I know of people who have traded the desire for more things, for a desire for more freedom or a more peace-filled existence. But we all want more.

Therefore, it is not surprising that we want more of life than our physical bodies can give. Loved ones pass and we want more time with them. Disease or other physical threat makes us aware of our own possible death, and we want more. It is natural to the human condition. We want more. But this traditional story of faith actually ends with a warning that eternal life is beyond our grasp!

The Jewish people, from whom we get this account, seem to have interpreted it with the ending in mind. The writings we have inherited from them are heavily focused on having more of life in this life. Further references to anything as a *Tree of Life* in the Christian Old Testament speak of things that make human existence more positive. They are not magic that can grant eternal existence. Another statement recorded in John 10:10 quotes Jesus as saying he came so that people "Might have life, and have it to the full." It is a decision of Christian theologians to attach this verse to teachings about eternal life rather than a clear focus on a fuller life now similar to the more ancient scriptures he is often recorded as quoting.

Christianity has encoded the promise of a future existence maintaining our current identity available to all those who will believe certain teachings, and possibly participate in certain ceremonies of the church. Compared across denominations and cultures, those teachings contain many inconsistencies and folk alterations. Humans who have died are pictured as angels, as sleeping until some future day of awakening, as present in a heaven beyond all suffering, as heavenly saints who can answer prayers and who specialize in categories of requests, as spirits who remain somehow close to us without visible form, or in the book of Revelation as still aware of the suffering on Earth and asking God how much longer the current age will continue. The teachings and common beliefs are not uniform. But the promise of the continuation of our current consciousness after physical life ends is widespread and highly attractive.

I propose that such beliefs are attractive not because that desire proves anything about their truth, but because it matches our common human characteristic of desiring more of what we value. We want to believe in a future that contains us because it is in our nature to want more.

However, I will also suggest that greed is an improper term for that desire. Greed is a word which carries in its meaning an indication of sin, of negative behavior or desire. Yet the very story most often used to explain the existence of sin very clearly includes humans who already wanted more before they ate the fate-filled fruit. I now see it as natural. If there is some offense in our wanting of more, it is against ourselves. Wanting a newer, faster, or luxurious car, I fail to enjoy the dependability, performance, comfort, or simple lack of debt in the car I have. It works the same with most or all possessions. I believe we would be wise to consider how true it is when applied to life. Longing for a life beyond this one, very likely causes us to miss much of the life we have.

So, I am forced to wonder whether our desire is best focused on the here and now or focused on a future beyond death for which we have traditions and teachings, but no proof.[4] I believe the ancients have much to teach us about how to live now if we can place their teachings properly in their own times and cultures without becoming too distracted by barbaric violence in their recorded histories or unenlightened prejudices in ancient times. It is part of our nature to want more.

How do we turn that desire to a force that calls for more of what is good for ourselves and others here, now, in the life we know?

---

4. The Christian answer to this is that the proof exists in the resurrection of Jesus and the church's experience of him as the risen Christ. However, it is a proof which requires acceptance of Christian suppositions and is not convincing to those who do not accept the beginning arguments.

Further Thoughts on Death

2/19/2020

I AM STARTING TO READ Brian Greene's new book, *Until the End of Time*. Like many others before him, and no doubt in the future, he begins his exploration of what we know of the universe and our search for meaning with the ever-present reality of death. Most human belief systems are in some way tied to death, our awareness of it, and our desire to endure or at least be remembered beyond a very short period of space-time.

With libraries of work by great thinkers, I begin this essay fully aware of how presumptuous I am to assume that I have something new or unique to say. Nevertheless, I wish to record my thoughts before proceeding any further into seeing what Dr. Greene offers. If it serves no other purpose, it will provide a record of intellectual honesty for any changes he provides in my thinking.

First, I think it is highly questionable when we humans assert that we are the only life forms aware of death. In my lifetime gains have been made in teaching other species to communicate with man. But we remain mostly ignorant of what mental functions do or do not occur in the brains of other beings across a divide we cannot cross due to a complete lack of meaningful communication. That is one of the reasons I am intrigued by a recent scientific suggestion that consciousness is part of nature from the quantum level up. The new idea is not that an electron would think about where it is going, how to avoid collisions in its frantic travels, or its eventual demise. Rather that there is a minute unit of consciousness present in each building block so that consciousness naturally becomes more complex as the combination of elements does the same. By the time we reach a level of complexity recognized as life, quanta are combined in

Further Thoughts on Death

numbers and uniqueness sufficient that such an assumption would lead to conclusions that consciousness would also be forming in ever increasing levels. At this time, we do not know whether consciousness is or is not pervasive in the universe. So, I do not start with an assumption of our complete uniqueness in the universe as both religion and philosophy traditionally have.

But neither do I deny the power of awareness of our eventual demise in driving our search for meaning and significance. We are born, grow, do some level of work to survive and to play our part in our cultures, produce a new generation, and then our time ends. We obsess about whether there is any meaning to the constant progression following generations of others hard to number, most totally forgotten as individuals. We want to know that we fit in some significant way, and I have written before about the comfort in realizing that we matter to each other when we celebrate a birth or mourn a death. And still, we want to know how it all fits into the enormity of the universe and the passage of time and history.

My current submission is simple. Much of our angst stems from assuming that we are separate and unique from the rest of the cosmos. Many religions depend on convincing people of exactly this, that we are something beyond our physical form which will continue after our current form disappears. We still engage in elaborate rituals and procedures to make our inanimate former self also last as long as possible. Our methods and entombments may not be as elaborate as the preparations of royal Egyptians to travel into another realm, but we place bodies in sealed containers inside sealed vaults and promise those in attendance that the person travels on to some realm beyond our physical observation. But our own discomfort with the entire process gives evidence to our doubt that such methods and teachings matter. I now assert that we are neither unique nor separate from the universe.

We are highly complex combinations of quanta the same as every other part of the universe we can observe. So are the ant and the supernova. The universe has this innate property of quanta coming together in forms as small as the atom and as large as galaxies, all of which exist for a time and return to the quantum states from which they came. We take it as a matter of fact that atoms and molecules decay over time. We use those which are convenient to measure how old something is by determining how far the return of its atoms to lower states has progressed. We know that when we manipulate chemicals to produce more complicated molecules, they are more likely to return to simpler states because their complexity is not sustainable. We know that all stars are in the process of burning themselves out and exist for periods far longer than a human life only because of their immense size. If our sun was small, it would be gone almost instantly in its continuing nuclear explosion back into quanta flung into space in forms both essential and dangerous to our existence on one of its planets. In the physical world, and in simpler forms of life, we accept it as simple reality. Like it or not, we are part of that same reality.

There is no difference at the most essential level between the stuff that forms Kilimanjaro and the building blocks that form you and me. We just happen to be combined in an amazingly intricate way guided by the DNA molecules inherited from our parents after millennia of evolution. For all of our study, there are still many aspects of our complexity that escape our basic understanding. How the combination of our quanta into molecules, cells, organs, systems, and a total functioning body results in a thinking, knowing, reflective, anxious self is complex enough to provoke the use of terms like miracle even among the who have long abandoned the concept of miracles as divine actions. We are amazing. And from the time our consciousness became aware that we are also temporary we have sought to be immortal. Our ancient texts and the preserved remains of former empires tell us it is true. However, we are combinations of quanta like every other part of the universe.

I find peace in this. What happens to us, in us, as us, is the same as every other part of the universe of which we are tiny specimens. In a process which amazes us, two cells combine and began to divide and form unique combinations which emerge after approximately ten months as a human. But the whole process is essentially the same as every other form that the complexities of the universe allow to emerge from the quanta that spring from the background Higgs field, exist for a time, and then return to that background of eternal potential. We are made of temporary stuff built from timeless background potential. For a short incredible time, it is assembled in a human form which can recognize the joy and anxiety of existence and then it goes back—just like every other complex thing in the universe, perhaps the universe itself.

I wonder what comfort we might find in knowing that, as it says in the *Desiderata*, "the universe is unfolding as it should"—including the amazing but temporary form we know as us! I wonder if we might finally find humility in realizing that the quanta that become you and I are no more, and no less, than those that form our neighbor, our enemy, and the worm that emerges from our front yard soil during a summer rain. All of our constructions of importance beyond existence as a part of this amazing universe, have told us that we matter more than everything else. We are more important than other living things. We are more important than other forms on our planet, so they must be here for our use and abuse. We are more important than the creatures and plants that were the life on Earth in the age of the dinosaur, so it is OK for us to use them extravagantly even as evidence emerges that we are destroying our planet in the process. And we dare to assume that we are more important than the person who follows another religion, another country's ideology, a political stance opposite to our own, or who commits acts that we deem unforgivable.

No, I am a temporary assembly of quanta beyond my understanding even as I celebrate my ability to think and know. Like all other complex formations of the universe, I am temporary, both built and decomposed by the normal forces of the universe. So is everyone I love. So is everyone I do not agree with or like. So was every person who ever lived and every person yet to come. Meaning? Some would find this awareness to be an implication of total lack of meaning. All things, including us, just happen and then they are gone. How can it mean anything? Why should we presume to assert that it means anything? What I am saying can drag us back to the basic existential dilemma. And history now shows that when we blindly choose meaning, then we use those choices to declare what and who also matters. That is not the response it causes in me.

We are all part of a universe that inspires awe as it always exceeds our grasp of understanding. When we called the creative force by our various names for God, we recognized that it is a gift beyond repayment that we get to enjoy the unbelievable experience of being alive. We also stretched it into dogmas that allow us to also condemn others. As I look to the combined natural forces as that creative and sustaining power long known as God, I do not back all the way into meaninglessness. I simply back away from the conclusion that our constructions of meaning elevate any of us to different from, and therefore in some way better than, others.

We will always develop social contracts that define acceptable and unacceptable behaviors for individuals and groups because it preserves life. We develop formal systems of governance, crime, and consequences because they provide an orderly system safer than individually choosing how to control our conflicting impulses and behaviors. All of this has long been known, discussed, and recorded in social contract theories of human governance. It is not new. I mention it only as reminder that the systems we form are not divine declarations that any human being is superior or inferior to another. That is not the proper function of social contracts. They provide order, not proof of inherent righteousness or sinfulness. We are all still moving reproducing piles of complex combinations of quanta.

And yet, the fact that we identify some human behaviors as good and beneficial and others as destructive raises a final point for this essay. We claim to have been seeking that better, even utopian, future of human coexistence at least as far back as we have records. It still is not here. Some choose to take from others, use others for their pleasure, even to destroy others as surely as there are people who devote their lives to caring for others. Whether we believe there is more of one than the other probably says more about our own emotional nature and ideology than it does about reality. Even efforts at objective quantification are based on our subjective decisions about what behaviors to count and what level of impact to consider significant. This I now find to point to social contract rather than eternal pronouncement from another realm. We form those contracts because complex piles of quanta that are mobile and thinking are fully capable of choosing actions we desire or disdain. Our basic physical composition is neutral. We simply are.

We amazingly are. We are built of elements as old as time itself. Those elements are part of us for a season, as they would be for any other complex universal form. Then they return to the soup of potential from which new combinations emerge. We are built of stuff that is essentially eternal. The quanta exist while the universe exists. After millennia of increasing complexity, some of the quanta exist for a time as the holy and ignominious form we call human. I continue to conclude that having reached a level of complexity that is self and other aware, it is our great pleasure to enjoy whatever years we are given. Then, laying down greed, the time comes to gratefully return the energy to its source. Whether we call it heaven as part of the god-force, nirvana as unity with all that is, or the final cloud of unknowing, does not matter so much to me. It matters to me that for this brief moment, you and I are and may bless each other when that is what we choose. I choose gratitude and blessing.

Humans as Particles

2/27/2020

SOME OF THE GREATEST ACCOMPLISHMENTS in the twentieth century involved unveiling the nature of our universe in the realm of the very small. The rapid progress from debating the existence of molecules, to the discovery of atoms, and on to categorizing the minute quanta of energy/matter from which everything else is built was an almost unthinkable success of the human mind. Knowing that something as small as a grain of salt contains a number of atoms so large that my mind has no equivalent image leaves me in awe.

When I started contemplating what new suggestions that quanta might carry consciousness would mean for understanding the human phenomena, I began by thinking of us as very large and complex on the quantum scale. Then I continued reading *Until the End of Time* and encountered again the contrast provided by looking to astronomical scales with quantities that are equally beyond common understanding.

On relative scales we are both enormous and unimaginably small, and I turn now to thinking of us in terms of the very small. Compared to the whole universe our solar system barely qualifies as an atom, leaving planets as extremely orderly electrons, and us as no more than specs on one of those tiny orbiting bits of matter. While we imagine ourselves to be of great importance and our ideas of the universe and meaning to be incredibly significant, we are so small that any study of the whole might struggle to find a place for us in the footnotes.

When I contemplate our existence on the scale of particles, the first logical response I see is one of humility. Even sacred texts that claim we are in some way made in the image of and by the divine will of God, contain statements of our apparent insignificance in comparison to the heavens.[1] So the idea is by no means new. What we have now, that we reasonably assume the ancients did not, is math to show us how amazingly small we are on cosmic scales. Far from being the center of all things, we are barely noticeable even on the scale of our own galaxy. So, first I am humbled as I seek to record my thoughts—the collected electronic impulses of one very tiny brain!

Then I begin to consider the characteristics of particles for comparison to our own existence. The first thing that fills my mind is the ephemeral nature of particles. They come and go with little notice from the larger world except in experiments at the world's great colliders. At the quantum level particles pop in and out of existence at rates so rapid that their existence barely fits our normal concept of what is real. But the experiments and the math confirm their glorious fractional moments of being. And I affirm that we have much in common. On astronomical scales the life of any of us is as short as the appearance of a particle in a physics experiment. We appear for one brief moment, and we are gone. Even when we become part of a more complex assembly of particles, atoms, molecules, organs and systems our time is brief. As beings we identify as living, we reproduce and often take comfort in the continuation of our family line in generations to come. But we now know that other species, near enough in relation to modern man to have interbred, have already lived out their entire run and disappeared from the planet. And while the numbers involved in the theories of evolution seem very large, the time occupied by any creatures similar to us has been but a cosmic moment. This too has been part of wisdom literature and is part of the drive to see ourselves as somehow immortal beyond our physical shell. In spite of all our hopes, no evidence of such continued existence has been found outside the blind acceptance of preferred religions.

We are infinitesimally small and exist for no more than a moment. But we are somehow self-aware in ways we have yet to prove in any other beings. Before I move on to explore other aspects of our existence and behavior that might be informed by looking at ourselves as particles, I pause on this seeming contradiction to our quest for meaning and find both comfort and wisdom in the poetry of William Blake. It is good,

---

1. Ps 8:3–4.

> To see a World in a Grain of Sand
> And a Heaven in a Wild Flower,
> Hold Infinity in the palm of your hand
> And Eternity in an hour.[2]

---

2. Blake, "Auguries of Innocence."

Proposing a Human Uncertainty Principle

2/27/2020

ONE OF THE MOST WIDELY discussed aspects of quantum physics is the uncertainty principle. The discovery of this principle stood our understanding of the world on its head. While we lived in the world of Newton, the world seemed predictable. Carefully measure certain aspects of an object and its future movement and properties could be predicted with accuracy. The world was predictable. Then, experiments with the smallest units of existence brought this disturbing knowledge that there are things we cannot know. The amazing math of the quantum physicist can only give us probabilities about the current or future state and location of a particle. And it is part of the nature of things, not a lack of our current methods. There are things that cannot be known and predicted with no margin of error.

So as my mind turns to thinking of humans in relation to particles, I immediately see similarities. In spite of amazing work across the social and biological sciences we are very hard to predict! While my love of history grew dramatically because of a teacher who emphasized cause and effect over the parade of dates so often used to bore young minds, I have often challenged my own students to realize just how elusive cause and effect are to identify or predict in human behavior. An example I have used multiple times is to imagine the last unexpected conflict one had with a person they did not seek to offend. Then I ask them how accurately they can describe exactly what caused the reaction they observed and why that reaction happened on that occasion when they expected a totally different response. Sometimes a combination of logical possibilities can be teased out, but I would assert that they remain in the realm of probable, not absolute, explanations. If one multiplies that complexity by the numbers involved in groups we typically study in history, the assertion that totally accurate and fully inclusive explanations of events can be formatted cleanly as cause and effect becomes very problematic.

Thinking in this way of us as physical objects, I see another large-scale example. Imagine that you observe me running. Those who know me well may tell you it is not a picture of beauty and grace. By seeing me as an object within the world of Newton, you can make predictions about my movement and future location. But the human body is not a sphere with specific patterns of seams and stitching spinning at a determined rate while traveling forward at our measured speed. I am a complicated assembly of limbs made of multiple joints controlled by a brain which may or may not record the presence of any small obstacle that might impact my motion. I might arrive smoothly at a determined finish point and yield measurements very much in keeping with what we learned from Newton and various studies in biology. However, I might trip or become dizzy. If I am running just for the pleasure of it, I may decide I am finished and stop or change direction due to the sound of an ice cream truck. The best prediction we can make is a probability of future speed and location.

We have statistics on longevity of life which can account for location of residence, genetic inheritance, diet, exercise, and other factors. We have statistics on accidental deaths as well as the prevalence and severity of disease which can be entered into our equations. But the best we are capable of when asked whether any one person will be here in ten years, one month, or tomorrow is a probability. We cannot account for every variable in the society surrounding our subject or affecting their internal response to any sudden external or internal changes.

The United States where I live is based on a system of voting for elected representatives to debate and make decisions about our governance. But the best we can do in predicting how many people will participate in voting is to sample and then publish probabilities. Likewise, we hope to predict the behaviors of the people we vote for once they take office. The current national situation seems as predictable as perhaps it has ever been because representatives are voting almost completely along party lines. And yet there are still surprises. A senator stands and announces that his own conscience prevents him from voting with his party and casts an unexpected vote in the opposite direction. Those who study our government and each participant came very close to predicting the exact vote on the impeachment of President Trump, but the best they could do was to predict a probable outcome. The same applies to how the voting public in general, specific groups, and individuals will vote in the upcoming election in spite of the fact that many on each side believe it would be an act of extreme ignorance and harm for anyone to vote for the other party!

If anyone reading this is well-versed in the differences between classical and quantum physics, you may be responding that all of these are due to our lack of critical measurements which we might somehow be able to make while quantum physics has shown us that the measurements themselves change the reality. That would make it logical to conclude that I am comparing a very complicated apple to very small oranges.

However, we have also made significant strides in understanding the study of humans. Here too it has been determined that our study changes the behavior of the person being studied.[1] Dr. Egon Guba, my mentor for dissertation research methodology, clearly asserted that objectivity in research was an illusion and advocated instead for intentionally designing the way research was conducted so that people were participants with some say in how the process would affect them rather than mere subjects (objects) to be manipulated. His position was that changes in the people being studied were an unavoidable reality. Carefully designing human research in order to include those studied as active participants was a philosophical choice over affecting them in unexamined and unintentional ways, not a choice over objectivity which a careful design might still maintain.[2] To use my crude example of running, I will run more carefully and be less likely to run after an ice cream if I know you are studying me. Or maybe, I will intentionally subvert your work and go get the ice cream due to some internal aversion to your presence or perceived intentions. A broader more scientific example may be found in examining the difference between the claimed generalizability found in quantitative studies of human behavior and the nearly total lack of exact replication in other settings. The statistics give us probabilities, not guarantees, no matter how many decimal points one chooses to use in the formulas.

1. The example from many beginning psychology classes is the Hawthorne Experiments.
2. Lincoln and Guba, *Naturalistic Inquiry*.

Proposing a Human Uncertainty Principle

Like the tiny subjects of quantum research, I find that human behavior and existence will always fall into the realm of probability rather than exact outcomes barring some extreme event which eliminates our existence completely. And in that extreme pessimistic scenario, there will be no known recorder left to examine the evidence anyway. If I pause to consider the multiple examples of totalitarian governments, I believe this human tendency to defy behavioral predictions to be a positive one—likewise in our ability to avoid becoming victims to predators of any sort. Our unpredictability makes us interesting and keeps us alive. I believe that the study of human beings will always include the principle of uncertainty. And that pleases me.

Human Particles and Thermodynamics

2/28/2020

ONE OF THE LEAST UNDERSTOOD areas of science for the uninitiated is how our universe and life on Earth are possible within the second law of thermodynamics which states that all things tend toward higher entropy. Dr. Greene gives an excellent explanation in his book of how entropy can decrease in one place due to energy input as long as the total is increasing. And it caused me to think about human activity in a new way.

Growing up as the modern period trended toward post-modern, I was always interested in and puzzled by how inventions are lauded as great life improvements at one moment and later bemoaned as the source of new problems. One of my favorite examples to use with elementary school students was the way people believed cars would lead to a better environment than the use of horses, especially in towns and cities where the horses' bodily eliminations could lead to very messy streets. Later people realized that while their feet were cleaner, their lungs were not.

I have also been fascinated by the tendency of human organizations to break down over time or in open competition with other groups. European history from the Middle Ages to the present was often taught as a wonderful evolution from a world of feudal lords to kingdoms and ultimately nations. And yet the history of that progression is filled with conflict and war causing great destruction in repeated clashes over control of both territory and people. Explorers and conquerors moved out to the continents of Africa and the Americas bringing death and destruction to civilizations that had survived for thousands of years. On a smaller scale, companies that succeed for a time later dissolve. Even the utopian communities I love to study, organized around their best information on creating more positive lives, still disappear over time.

Philosophy and religion add their questions to the mix. I love the transcendentalists of the United States. But their lofty dreams of man's power to overcome and become something greater, seem to have disappeared into a mad societal rush to accumulate as many goods as possible before one dies and leaves it all behind. Christianity taught me that we were on a quest to reach every person on Earth with the message of salvation available through Jesus Christ, thus bringing the end of the current period of suffering and inviting God to bring the kingdom to Earth. Other more mainstream and liberal Christian traditions taught that it was the faithful working to elevate the condition of all people who would create the kingdom on Earth. Now what I hear is evangelicals pointing to widespread disaster in joyful anticipation that it means Jesus will soon appear from the sky and bring a new world of perfection. Lost in the interpretation seems to be how bad the chaos has become and how severely people are suffering.

I needed some framework that would lend possible explanation to the downward spiral that now seems to result from all of man's efforts at improvement. I believe I may have found it in the second law of thermodynamics when I view our species as particles, or simply as a part of the natural world. By adding energy through human labor, and later the creation of machines, man has built comfortable and relatively safe shelter, systems of transportation, towering cities, has artificially elevated production of food, and has reached out to explore the solar system and beyond. Our addition of energy to situations that gain our focus causes an obvious appearance of decrease in entropy. But the laws of nature are not so easily overcome. All of our activity also results in an acceleration of the change of matter to energy—heat, even when our machines run by human or waterpower; light that escapes our planet; and even the release of nuclear power hopefully converted to serve our desire for light, heat, and motion.

In spite of all of our claims to be something apart and above the rest of nature, we can now observe how our activities are accelerating the increase in entropy on our planet. It makes sense to me even as I cringe to see another argument in the media about whether the warming of the planet is due to natural or human causes. We are natural beings. Our behaviors are natural causes. And as earth warms, the seas rise, threatening to overwhelm the low elevation locations of large populations, storms increase in severity even as weather patterns become less predictable, and the mass destruction of species and many of man's accomplishments themselves, possibly even the end of our existence increases, who can deny that entropy is on the rise?

It appears that human particles are especially adept at bringing about the predictions of the second law. In all of our great accomplishments, we speed the return of matter, which exists due to the energy given by the sun, back to energy which we waste. Appearing to build greater order, we actually bring a total increase in disorder. I sit in my comfortable home typing on a computer wirelessly connected to the massive global web of other connected computers and my world seems comfortable and orderly. But if I begin to run my mind backwards through time to examine what it took to create this environment, I see the harvesting of trees and other natural materials used to make the various parts of my home and belongings. I see the transportation of those materials and the industrial transformation of them into the forms I use. I see the power and machinery used to combine it all into the place where I now sit and work. I see the energy byproduct increasing entropy at every step of the process. And I see my lights and electrical appliances powered by the burning of coal along with the heat produced by the burning of natural gas. Simply sitting in a chair and recording these few thoughts, I am contributing to the conversion of sun energy collected into the Earth over millions of years back into energy, much of which is wasted through casual overuse and the inefficiency of my home. I sit in apparent order and contribute every moment to the operation of the second law and the conversion of apparent order to greater disorder.

Now we have reached a point where our contributions to the increase in our planet's entropy could destroy us, or at least life as Western society has known it. And it causes me to wonder about our status as particles tied to the laws of nature versus the hopes and dreams of all of those philosophers, believers, and scientists. Gas molecules released into a room do not appear to demonstrate any intentionality as they spread out to fill the space and enter the state of maximum entropy. The fence around my backyard does not appear to choose the process of rotting causing me to use more wood for spring repairs. Even if the energy continually escaping my house may strike my imagination as trying to bankrupt me when the bill arrives, there is no currently known evidence to confirm any intent of those quanta to escape my presence.

And I wonder not whether the increased temperature and entropy of the planet is caused by man or nature. We are natural. I wonder if our planning is an illusion. I wonder if our actions are as determined by the probabilities of thermodynamics as those of other forms of matter.

Or are we unusual particles with the power to choose our fate?

Particles that Think

2/28/2020

STARTING WITH THOUGHTS ON HUMAN consciousness, then exploring the way humans resemble particles acting in accord with the laws of nature, I am brought back to our status as a thinking life form. My inclination is to agree with scientists that say everything we call thinking, contemplating, deciding, and reflecting occurs through natural processes in our complex nervous system, mostly the brain. This is part of my change from an emphasis on eternal spiritual existence as I doubt the current existence of any *me* that is separate from my body and natural processes. I do not doubt the experiences of friends who have experimented with universal reality through Eastern approaches or hallucinogenic substances. But I believe they are just that—experiences occurring in and recorded by the human nervous system responding to a different set of focused inputs. My purpose here is to examine whether we are bound by determinism based on our physical nature or are in fact capable of making choices about our behavior and collective future.

Dr. Greene[1] offers a very detailed discussion of consciousness and human free will which is well worth reading for anyone with particular interest in this topic. He asserts that we do not have a free will separate from the laws of nature, but that in our complexity we do have an amazing array of actions to choose within the laws of nature. I will oversimplify with an obvious example. Having experiences with the freedom of movement in activities like snow skiing, I would love to experiment with the freedom of unaided flight. I can choose to get up and go out into an open

---

1. Greene, "Particles," 115.

area. I can will to fly. I can choose to run about and flap my arms or try to launch myself straight and streamlined like a rocket. I can will it. I cannot do it. The laws of physics simply do not allow the matter assembled as me to achieve unaided flight given the characteristics of the human body. I can choose whether to try approaching the experience through exercises in falling like sky-diving or bungee jumping. I could try hang-gliding or ballooning. But all of my choices are within the laws of physics. And yet, choices they remain.

I can make choices about how much I contribute to the increase in entropy by limiting my consumption and waste. My doors and windows are shut and latched while I run the furnace. I can go through the house and make sure no unneeded light bulbs are in use. I can make decisions about the balance between not wasting energy on external lighting and a felt need for extra security as my city becomes more chaotic and less safe. I can choose locally sourced food grown in Earth friendly ways. The list is long. But faced with the scale of planetary change, I am still limited by physical capacities.

I cannot reduce enough on an individual scale to balance the use of fossil fuels in the technologically advanced nations of the world, and I do not have a godlike ability to force world leaders to change course. I cannot forget hearing Buckminster Fuller declare that Earth was capable of supplying the needs of every human being if we chose to organize properly and distribute goods equitably. I also cannot forget that he said we only had twenty years left to make those decisions or face our eventual demise, and that the speech was given in the nineteen-seventies. To whatever degree he was correct, I am not physically capable of reordering the elements of the planet or the organizations of humans to counteract our destructive path. I have recently seen articles that state that individual human efforts no longer matter in stopping the overall destruction of the planet. It would seem that as a species the combined action of all of us as particles has been to expend all energy available to us and let entropy reign.

If I instead consider the entire universe, many current theories grant billions of additional years to its probable existence. However, at some point it can be predicted to no longer support human life even if we find a way to begin hopping from planet to planet. Stars burn out. Cosmic collisions, explosions and release of energy in forms and levels beyond human endurance will continue to happen. Scientists imagine different scenarios for what happens when the universe as we know it reaches its final stage in options ranging from bouncing back to another bang to simply burning out. But nothing in our current knowledge suggests that the universe, our planet as a human friendly environment, or our species will last forever. Universal is still finite—incredibly unimaginably large—but finite, nonetheless.

So here I sit. The tiny particle of the universe that is me—vibrant with the energy of imagining the immensity and finality of it all and my place in it—looks around for the choices that are mine within the laws of physics. I contemplate the presence or lack of greater meaning, and I type these essays as my gift into the mixture of particle complexity and collisions, existence and nonexistence. I offer them as a gift.

On a universal scale we are but particles and there is an invitation to humility in it. But we are also particles aware of our existence and there is wonder in it. With the capacity to be amazed by the beauty and enormity of the universe, I choose awe. Equipped with emotions—the fact that they are powered by bodily chemicals and electronic impulses not forgotten—I choose to laugh and love. I look past accounts of extreme violence towards *others* in the ancient texts,[2] certainly no more destructive than my own nation's choice to use atomic weapons, and I affirm the superiority of welcoming the stranger and caring for my neighbor. I look past theological claims of magical solutions to all our problems and find truth in Jesus teaching those who listened that our holy kingdom is here and now.

We are very tiny beings who have harnessed collective power to do great damage, and perhaps we are demonstrating that collectively we follow the laws of thermodynamics whether we are aware of what is happening or not. We are also collective beings who know the value of the herd as well as the freedom of solitude. We are not gods. We are not eternal. We cannot reverse the natural progression of the universe. But we can learn and grow in wisdom and love; we can experience awe and wonder as powerfully as we experience fear and discomfort; we can appreciate that we are *This Season's People*.[3] And we can decide what each day will be like for ourselves and every person and thing with which we interact.

One physical restriction we have never experienced directly is a Kelvin temperature of zero. In this universe, particles dance. For whatever time we have, we dance. Physics requires it.

---

2. They may never have been intended as literal history in the first place.
3. Gaskin, *This Season's People.*

This World Is a Scary Place

3/12/2020

Wondering alone through the Shawnee National Forest with no cellphone service and a vague idea of where I was last weekend, I remember thinking that I was glad the weather was still probably too cool for venomous snakes. Our family and friends have been directly affected by more natural danger in the last year than we could have imagined, resulting in both deaths and serious injuries.

Storms become severe. On calm days, trees can still topple suddenly, without warning, or in unexpected directions. And mankind has spent thousands of years adding the danger from our own inventions and devices which provide great convenience, but which can also become dangerous in one brief moment of inattention. Now the news is filled with stories and data about a pandemic which has finally arrived even though we knew for decades it would eventually happen. The stock market is tumbling as people around the world panic. In some part of my brain that defaults to silly, it reminds me of Oregon Trail, the old computer game about pioneers traveling west where most players and their virtual families died of drowning, attack, starvation, or dysentery!

It all causes me to pause and contemplate. The only way to know this fear is to exist first as a living being with conscious thought. We only fear death because we are here and we know we are here. Yes, we also know there is eventually an end to this current existence for each of us. But first we are here.

As we gain the ability to look further and further across the universe the number of possible human-life-sustaining planets has gone from an egocentric estimate of one to hundreds and then thousands. With the size of the universe, the number of stars and planets discovered, we extrapolate possibilities of how many planets probably exist at a life-sustaining distance from their stars. There is greater possibility for other life in the cosmos than ancient man believed looking up and viewing the stars as holes in heaven's floor. But as I write this in the year 2020, the number of planets we know contain thinking beings remains one. This scary planet we live on is the only place that we know hosts thinking, loving, contemplating, and frightened creatures like us.

One.

Earth.

Our scary planet has the correct temperatures, water, and atmospheric gases to support a great diversity of species including us. Setting aside the ancient accounts of our existence because a powerful supernatural being chose to put us here, we are here because all of the conditions for our existence are here. Humans exist because Earth is compatible with human existence. It is a simple but profound truth. We are where the universe provides the necessary conditions for us to exist.

Philosophers and theologians build arguments about what it all means. Explanations range from evolution over billions of years reaching a level of living complexity which allows us to exist and know we exist, to the idea that the universe exists because our minds construct it, to the ancient teachings that we are here because a loving creator put us here. But we are here. And the conditions which support life are far more ubiquitous than those which sometimes bring an unexpected end to life.

We are here. We are aware. We have the capacity for awe, wonder, and love. Our very fear of losing life points to the fact that our existence here is pleasurable and rewarding in ways that cause us to value our continued existence. We like it here and we do not want to leave early. No matter what theory one prefers for how and why we came to be, we are and we like it. We have the capacity to experience wonder and companionship, so the logical action is to enjoy them.

This world is a scary place for one underlying reason. Our existence on this planet is so positive that we do not wish to relinquish it. We only know fear of nonexistence because we know existence and all of the gifts awareness brings. Regardless of how it came to be, we are creatures of the one place in the universe proven to be hospitable to us. We can spend our time in fear of the day when our bodies fail from aging or because some unexpected event shortened our lives. Or we can turn our faces to the sun and stars, the trees and breeze, the beauty and the love which surround us and rejoice that life here is wonderful enough to be treasured by our complex minds and emotions.

Why Does Religion Emphasize Sex?

3/13/2020

TRADITION

Of course, the answer from within any of the faiths is that there are strong restrictions on sexual behavior because outside of the approved context sex is wrong. The leader of any religion that emphasizes strict rules about sexual behavior would be expected first and foremost to say that their teaching is correct because it is God's teaching. If pressed they might also give some of the answers I will discuss in the next section, but the primary assertion is that they have knowledge of what behaviors are right and wrong.

Ethical Responsibility

I believe there is also a strong possibility that what emerged through time as good for the social order and individuals within the society also became included in religion. In male-dominated societies where women and children unattached to a providing male are subject to suffering and need, it is unethical for males to engage in behaviors for pleasure which lead to fatherless children and husbandless mothers. Sacred texts from the earliest periods of the Western traditions[1] seem to approve of men having multiple sexual partners as long as they protected them within the social provisions for families. Of course, this also meant that behaviors were more acceptable for those with wealth than for other male members

---

1. I am speaking of Western religion, especially the Judeo-Christian tradition because that is my own tradition. I am leaving out Eastern and other traditions to avoid uniformed generalizations concerning other belief systems.

of the society, while the same acceptable allowance for multiple partners does not seem to have applied to wealthy or powerful women.

We only have to look at current and historical records on violent crime related to jealousy over partners to see that the social order is threatened by conflict arising from competition for the same sexual partners. If one accepts the timeline presented in the Bible and Torah for the giving of divine law, the people of Israel were traveling in search of their homeland and in frequent conflict with external enemies when Moses ascended the mountain and came down with the tablets. Internal conflict over relationship jealousies would certainly be dangerous to group unity and strength against enemies. Even in the kingdom period, King David is reported to have arranged the death in battle of the husband of a woman he desired.[2] Women belonged first to their fathers and then to their husbands. They were to be considered off limits to others the same as the taking or use of any other part of another man's property. It is a system which maintains social order and the protection of property rights which until very recent times in the West continued to include wives and children.

Likewise, those who see a certain profile of the basic family unit as foundational to social order find behaviors outside that pattern to be hazardous to society. To the extent that laws are meant to stabilize society, and that stability is seen as good, any behavior which might destabilize that pattern is seen as ethically unacceptable. More progressive believers accept that the family unit can be stably organized with same sex partners. Those who believe that only male-female relationships lead to stable families continue to find all other sexual behaviors to be harmful and therefore unethical. When this is combined with belief in traditional explanations of God given directions for life, there is little room for discussion or examination of current statistics on family stability even though it is readily available.

POWER AND CONTROL

I believe there is another, less discussed and more disturbing to believers, explanation for the pervasive emphasis on sexuality out of all possible areas of human behavior. Religions need followers. Religious leaders need explanations for why people should follow them.[3] As sexual desire of one

2. 2 Sam 11:14.
3. Tolstoy, *Kingdom*, 68–69.

form or another is naturally present in the vast majority of the population regardless of intention, it provides a large base for establishing people's need for help from religion. People who are convinced that their desires are sinful still cannot magically stop having those feelings. Also, sexual desire is powerful enough to result in sexual behavior regardless of what people have been taught about right and wrong. So religious power comes in both the need for forgiveness and in promises of divine help to control the mind and the physical self.

Of course, it does not work. Those who look to science see the evolutionary background for the desire to reproduce. But those who see such desires only as temptation to violate the rules of God have a steady supply of guilt. Religion as the provider of removal of guilt thus has a powerful hold on its clientele. Preach an occasional sermon on texts like Gal 5:19–21[4] and you have established yourself as the holder of the keys to eternal bliss rather than everlasting torment. Even those who believe in salvation by grace alone are called to live worthy of that gift. Older traditions hold that one must have received absolution from the church and be allowed to partake of the eucharist or else be damned for not being able to free themselves from these natural desires.

This is a powerful method of maintaining religious membership. An individual or a group of the faithful are insulted or harmed by some action of the church? They cannot walk away unless they free themselves from the teachings or are willing to risk eternal punishment. They stay but want to force changes in how things are done or point out error in the practices of the church or the clergy? The same passage includes discord, dissension and factions along with physical desires for good measure. The power doesn't seem to diminish even when one religious leader after another is revealed to have violated the same passage. It is just offered as proof that all humans are frail, flawed, and lost without help and guidance from the religion and the God it claims to represent. I find it especially harmful where the people condemned are refused access to the religion which claims to be the solution. We now have scientific evidence for the biological basis for same-sex attraction and opposite-sex identification. Yet much of religion continues to use ancient condemnations of these characteristics while also refusing these individuals admission to their

---

4. 19 The acts of the flesh are obvious: sexual immorality, impurity and debauchery; 20 idolatry and witchcraft; hatred, discord, jealousy, fits of rage, selfish ambition, dissensions, factions 21 and envy; drunkenness, orgies, and the like. I warn you, as I did before, that those who live like this will not inherit the kingdom of God.

circles of the forgiven. It is cruel, and it is part of this control function. The faithful are taught that they are better than others and fortunate to be among those loved by the divine. To disagree is to risk losing that status unless one is able to find a more progressive religious home or freedom from the entire body of teachings.

I believe there are people who teach the sinfulness of this basic human trait out of an honest belief in the traditional doctrines. I agree that the encouragement of stable relationships has played a strengthening role in society. I believe in ethical behavior and faithful adherence to promises made to a person's selected life partner. However, I also believe sexual guilt plays a powerful role in the control and manipulation of others whether the leaders involved realize it or not. I do not believe in a God who creates humans with both the desire and the divine command to "be fruitful and multiply,"[5] and then condemns them for having the desire to do so.

---

5. Genesis 1.

Accepting the Impossible as a Sign of Faith

3/14/2020

THIS TOPIC WAS ALREADY WAITING on my mental to-be-written list when a friend from progressive Christianity asked for responses to a sermon focused on the statement: You cannot reach God with your mind. My immediate reaction was remembering too many conversations over the years that turned to faith as the end all to discussions for which the speaker did not have an answer.

First, this idea does match mystic teachings within Christianity and other religions which emphasize experience beyond discussions of doctrine. My friends who pursue Eastern methods of meditation learn to stop holding onto thoughts in order to let active thinking flow past as one approaches a state of peace and unity with existence. A long-time Christian friend told me a few years ago that he had a sudden realization that he had spent his life studying about God, but not practicing the experience of God. Christianity has contemplative traditions emphasizing this experience of God dating back to its earliest centuries and I have written before about some of my own experiences studying and practicing methods from those traditions.

But how does one validate or reject ideas of the divine based on mystic experience alone? In the language of my former churches, how does one know whether one has opened their heart and mind to the divine or to a servant of evil dressed as an angel of light? In more general terminology, how does one explain the mystic experience with an open-minded rational person who lacks such experiences. I maintain that we return to activities of the mind. Whether we study and quote ancient texts or construct stories to explain our experience, we are using the mind. With a nod of recognition to charismatic traditions, I assert that language which makes sense to anyone else is a function of the mind. So, I have great difficulty in accepting teachings which say to ignore the mind as one attempts to properly live by faith.

History includes examples of what happens when the actions of nations are accepted through blind patriotism without application of critical thinking. In the age of conquest, European nations sailed the world searching for wealth to plunder with the written blessing of the church. Statements of manifest destiny in the US justified genocide against the aboriginal nations. Trust in the goodness of one's own country, undoubtedly accompanied by fear, allowed Europeans to sit by as millions of their neighbors were murdered by the Nazis. It has also allowed the sacrifice of untold numbers of young people who accepted the necessity and patriotism of participating and dying in wars justified by their leaders. At times this faith in political leaders is based solely on social factors. It has often also been accompanied by justifications based on the use of religious texts and interpretations. I have seen Christians become angry nearly to the point of physical violence in response to any assertion that the US founding fathers were anything less than full followers of Jesus Christ led by God in their decisions concerning the creation of the new nation. Never mind that they counted slaves as 3/5 of a person and women and children as unworthy of the full status and rights of citizenship, ideas which few would accept as proper human reasoning or divine inspiration today.

The acceptance of faith over knowledge of the mind has also led the forms of Christianity I am most familiar with to reject the discipline of science and its revelations about the world. Darwin's ideas on the evolution of species, and very weak interpretations and explanations of them by others, contradict a literal reading of creation texts, so the scientific evidence is automatically labeled inferior to faith in the literal truth of the ancient text and the God said to have inspired that text. The very real geological evidence of previous eras is written off as fake or as a test of faith placed by God to force us to choose loyalty to revealed truth. The steady state theory of the universe said that the cosmos had always been here and believers in creation rejected it. New evidence led to the theory of the Big Bang and some Christians celebrated the affirmation of an instant of creation. Then the scientific evidence of incredible periods of time contradicted young Earth interpretations of the texts and the new theory was rejected as well. Now we have reached a point where all results, especially results which indicate we should change our consumptive lifestyles, are rejected out of hand because faith rejects science.

But my earliest memories of conflict in this area came from issues I discussed in *UFT* when teaching of the religion itself seems to contain obvious contradictions. If I questioned how a God who is both loving and just could leave everyone who lived before the life of Jesus or the sharing of his teachings in ignorance, the answer was that one had to have faith that everything God does is loving and just whether our minds comprehend it or not. Question how this God could condemn all those who never accepted current doctrines because they never heard them to eternal torture and the answer is the same. All actions of God are to be accepted as good because the original assumption accepted by faith says so. Study the texts assembled as the Christian Bible too carefully and obvious contradictions appear across different books and even within a few chapters of each other. In literalist circles one is told that the required response is to accept by faith that the texts are both correct and that one's own mind, reading ability, and understanding are to be subjected to the rule of faith.

As I continue to explore the teachings of both faith and science, the acceptance of the impossible becomes more obvious. A full-scale replica of Noah's ark has been constructed near where I live, and Christians pay admission to go through it and see proof of the story. But the known species of Earth will not fit in the structure making the proof problematic. I have been told by others who visited that if you press your guide on the lack of space, a new explanation emerges. The current translation of the story says that animals of every kind were on board. So, the explanation becomes that it was not necessary to have one of every species we know. Having felines aboard, the variations in feline species developed in the very brief period of time that has elapsed between Noah's flood and now according to the numbers accepted by the faithful. The most ardent evolutionist will point out that the level of change required is not possible within the asserted time. And again, the answer is that it must be accepted by faith over reason. The same happens if one questions an ancient people building an impossible tower to heaven which God decides must be stopped before they succeed, the planet existing without rain until God orders the flood, or the travel of a massive nation of former slaves from Egypt into a conquered land of Israel leaving little or no physical

Accepting the Impossible as a Sign of Faith

trace. Recently a televised preacher claimed that people could be cured of the coronavirus by reaching out their hands to touch his image on their TV screen. The mind clearly tells us that these things are not possible as literal truths, yet the Bible literalists continue to tell us that we must turn to faith rather than thought in matters related to this just, loving, and incarnational God.

I need to pause again to say that I know there are many Christians who do not read these stories as literal truths or believe in eternal punishment for those outside the church. I am responding here to the assertions of those who continue to teach such doctrines based on faith alone. If this leap is to be made, why stop at one collection of ancient texts as superior to all others? Accepted by unthinking faith and the sincerity of people's expressed experiences with the beliefs and therefore the God behind them, why reject the beliefs of those who live lives of peace and altruism based on other religions or humanism? For that matter, why reject a new religion based on belief that all the events of the Star Wars series of movies have actually happened beyond the view of telescopes operated by scientists whose opinions we reject anyway? Without the use of reason and the mind I see no basis for distinction beyond a preference for a person's own traditions.

Pushing the idea even further, belief in some impossible things is dangerous. If the Bible says that miraculous things were done in the past in order to bring unbelievers to faith (and more recent missionary accounts also contain the same type of power displays) why not take unbelievers out to watch, announce the power of God available to those with faith, and walk into highway traffic or off of a cliff? If the televangelist truly believes that his hand can deliver healing, even through a TV set, why is he not traveling from hospital to hospital touching everyone dying of a contagious disease as a blessing to their families, an act of loving safety for the medical staff, and a proof of his religion? If the Catholic priest truly believes in transubstantiation, why stop using a single chalice to offer the saving blood of Christ to the congregation. Surely God would not transfer deadly contagions to the faithful through his own holy blood! The mind asserts that it would be foolish to take such risks. Even the fundamentalist faithful start pointing to verses about not testing God and reasoning that the faith of some person involved might not be sufficient to receive the impossible result from God.

My conclusion will cause some to label me a strong-willed cynic or an enemy to the life of faith. I do not believe that there is a God who does impossible things which can only be understood by faith. And I do not believe most of those who claim such beliefs are actually willing to fully live them. If the TV faith healer has the power to heal by touch but withholds it from those most in need, I conclude that he is following his own brain's logical warning that the predictable result of his visits will be his own death from one of the diseases. When the church (wisely in my opinion) stops using a single chalice during a pandemic or the annual outbreak of the flu, I assert that they are ethically using their minds to protect people from harm because there is at least some level of doubt that what they hold in their hands is the literal presence of God. Likewise, I have learned that certain foods which I love are damaging to my body. I do not eat them based on feelings of attraction or satisfaction detached from the logic of my mind. I have no faith in the goodness of those foods based on feelings and experience separate from the logic of my mind and the memory of later physical experience after consuming them. Acting by faith alone would be irresponsible.

When I hear people say that we cannot approach God with our minds, I hear that my seat is with the unbelievers. Given the limits of science, there are still many unknown and unexplainable things in the world. I do not believe that we know, or can know, everything. Neither do I label what I do not yet know or understand as a god simply because it exceeds my human capacities. I cannot build belief systems or ethical ways to live on what I do not know. My mind requires understanding in order to evaluate the effects and worth of beliefs and actions. My continued existence depends at least in part on my refusal to believe and act on impossible things.

I participate in activities other people find frightening or even foolhardy such as climbing up and rappelling down cliffs. But I do so with confidence in the known capacities of the equipment and the skills of my belayer. I have no intention of going to a large city mall during the pandemic and hugging every person who will let me in order to prove that there is an invisible God of love who wants people to be comforted. I believe those who tell me there is a contagion loose in my country which is invisible to the eye, but which can be seen with current technology, and I act based on the logical functioning of my mind. I do not believe the power that controls the universe calls me to search for it, approach it, or prove it without the use of my mind.

I do believe some things that church friends believe are impossible. They do not accept that life can emerge from non-life, or that new species can emerge from previous ones given sufficient time.[1] But I do not accept them by blindly or willfully choosing faith in science over religion by faith. I examine the theories. I study the time periods, probabilities, and statistics involved along with the available physical evidence. Neither do I believe that current theories are guaranteed to be accepted as true for all time. I have faith that they are our best explanations at this time based on the evidence we have.

I believe the universe is good. I believe that it is friendly to humans because we exist. I believe that humans have the capacity for good based on observation of acts of altruism and sacrifice on behalf of others, including the willingness to risk death by those who protect my life of safety and security from all manner of threats. I have faith in help from my friends and strangers in time of need based on their history of responding during previous events.

For me the life of faith and the life of the mind are inseparably linked, and I cannot approach any explanation of the ultimate which is not subject to the use of my mind. If the explanation of anything is impossible outside acceptance by blind faith, then I assert that it is simply and only impossible. One of today's many faith traditions may accept such belief as faith, but I reject it as proof of the reality of thing believed.

---

[1]. Some visit the huge land-based ark without confronting the impossibility it illustrates.

Corona Capitalism

3/14/2020

THE UNITED STATES GOVERNMENT IS finally admitting that we are vulnerable to the global coronavirus pandemic and states are taking actions to reduce public interactions. People are responding in visibly shocking ways. Told to have two weeks to one month of basic supplies at home in order to stay as isolated as possible from disease exposure, people are panic buying everything in the stores. I do not find it totally surprising. I have often joked that local weather people are paid to predict any possibility of bad winter weather in order to trigger panicked purchases of milk, bread, and eggs. This time we have reached the level where local groceries have begun to limit purchases to keep the few from buying up everything that is needed by their neighbors.

A friend who witnessed the frenzy commented that I should have a fun time writing about this human behavior. As well as he knows me, I doubt that he pictured my mind going to a recent speech by Dr. Angela Davis where she stated that while we have all benefitted from capitalism, the system must now be changed in revolutionary ways.[1] I remember a friend who attended asking me how a person could even make such a seemingly contradictory statement. My response as I type this essay is to wonder how people can be shocked and disapproving of a person with money trying to buy grocery cart loads of toilet paper but not offended by families with great wealth and power doing everything in their power to accumulate more and more of the nation's resources as their own.

---

1. Davis, Speech at the University of Southern Indiana, February 5th, 2020.

Some who challenge any criticism of our economic system will find my thoughts unfair and unfounded. But I see the difference between what is happening in the Walmart checkout line and in the homes and offices of the wealthiest in our country as one of scale rather than substance. We can see that buying up all of the toilet paper and water available at the local store is unfair to one's neighbors. But somehow, we fail to acknowledge the accumulation of astronomic amounts of wealth while the great mass of the middle class slips into poverty as yet another example of predatory hoarding. One is inescapably in our view. The other is hidden in the system.

There are serious reasons why we see these two behaviors in different ways. The self-made man is a large part of the country's mythology. The idea that anyone might have the next bright new idea or develop the next highly desired product and become wealthy is woven into the American dream. More than a few of our places of worship teach that earthly success is a sign of divine favor and thus the opposite of selfish wrongdoing. We admire those whose ideas and effort result in lives of success. We teach the motivation of access to this type of economic system as superior to the false claims of monetary equality in communist and socialist countries. And we like to believe that great monetary success could still happen for us. We could buy the winning lottery ticket and not succumb to the fate of many who won it in the past. With a little good luck of appliances, roofs, and autos not breaking down unexpectedly; with no sudden losses of property to fire or disaster; with no unexpected catastrophic illness to consume our savings we may be able to continue to live comfortably and perhaps leave something to our children. And the difference between our lives and those of the wealthiest Americans is hidden by our isolation from them, their properties, and their lifestyles.

After the Great Depression of the nineteen-thirties there seemed to be a time when we understood that everyone needs at least a reasonable cart of home supplies. An economy based on industrial production also required a marketplace with consumers able to buy the goods produced. The system allowed for the owner of the appliance factory to live a richer lifestyle than others. But the strength of unions fighting for workers to take home a livable share combined with the economic understanding of the need for spendable income in the hands of consumers meant that workers could also live a better life than most of the world for most of history. Being able to buy a home and raise a family while driving an occasional new car, we were content for others to have nicer versions of the same comforts. And there have always been those promises and mythologies that anyone might jump to the higher rungs of the ladder and live among the privileged.

Those who point out that the people at the top take far more than their share are seen as wild-eyed radicals by those who believe they also have enough. Those who have been suffering for many years from lack of enough for a reasonable life are blamed for their own condition and convinced that their only recourse is to work harder or to function outside of the conventional system by making money in ways which also risk arrest and imprisonment. The people at the bottom do not rise up and lead successful revolutions against those at the top.[2] The people in the middle with the skills to rebel have been content with their modest carts of goods. And various wars, international tensions, and crises of different forms have fueled the drive to be, and be seen as, patriotic rather than as critics of our country.

Nevertheless, the data is clear. Those at the top have been hoarding the wealth of the country to the detriment of the rest of us for some time now. Whether one supports drastic reform, moderate changes in order to provide for more of the population, or continuance of the status quo in hopes that the American dream remains true, the facts reveal that those at the top are hoarding far more than we are willing to tolerate by the scared old lady who lives next door. Those at the top have full carts; they have the store; and they have the means of production and the supply chain. They have wealth invested in ways that accumulates greater wealth whether the rest of us succeed or die. They have the power to buy control of the government and they have used it.

I do not believe we will change it. We value the traditions of our society too much to abandon them. We have seen the atrocities committed by those who claimed to champion alternative systems in the name of the people. We have no desire to become Russia, China, or Argentina. But, perhaps, just maybe, we should be less shocked by our neighbors. They are a reflection of the greed and self-interest that keeps our system running 2,000 years after Jesus of Nazareth taught that the accumulation of wealth was foolish and wrong[3] and that we should worry no more about our needs and futures than the birds of the air or the flowers of the field.[4]

May we find the wisdom of a kinder way.

2. Brinton, *Anatomy of Revolution*.
3. Luke 12.
4. Matt 6:26.

The Plague

3/17/2020

It started out as a rumor.
    Some new darkness was spreading from distant lands.
    It grew into a reality as people began to suffer and die.
    People changed their routines, avoided contact,
    hoarded supplies to hide in safety.
    But still it grew.
    Scientists sought understanding, solution, and prevention.
    Doctors and nurses cared for the ill.
    But they became victims too.
    Holy people prayed and dared to hold the hands of the dying.
    And the darkness did not care.
    It took them as easily as the others.
    Hope changed to fear and became despair.
    The dying buried the dead.
    And when the final human exhaled her last,
    Lying next to the graves of her family,
    Earth breathed a sigh of relief.
    The cure was complete.
    And life began again.[1]

---

1. This piece was written before the COVID pandemic's full effects were known and is included with great sympathy for those who have lost loved ones. Its purpose is expression of our choices for the future and the resilience of the universe with or without us.

Human Strength in a Scary World

3/21/2020

If I focus on the threats to existence on our planet, the continued existence of humans and our dominance are in some ways more amazing than we often stop to consider. Among the planet's land animals, we are just not that physically impressive. We have no exoskeletons or shells, no impressive physical strength, size, fangs, or claws. A significant number of herbivores, which have no interest in us as food, have the size and strength to easily dispatch a human who ventures too close to them or their young. Animals much smaller than us have physical weapons capable of killing a person for food or protection of territory. Even much of Earth's flora causes us real difficulty by contact or if used for food. How did we come to dominance?

There are two easy, quickly assumed, answers that hide much from consideration if merely recited. The first is religious. Humans, in the contextual language—man, is dominant because the divine power which established the order of life gave him dominance. The other is secular. We have minds and thus are automatically able to overcome the rest of life which does not. I want to look more deeply at each of these propositions.

The religious explanation does seem to be global if we allow for the diversity of descriptions of the divine and differences in teachings about our relationship with it. It can be found from the hyper-religious who see every event in life as subject to calls upon this supernatural power, to more fearful interpretations leading to constant efforts to appease the power(s) and find favor or at least avoid disaster, to even a Deist assumption that the clockmaker gave us our superior position before stepping away to allow life to play out. In the West these views have often stressed individual relationship to God, while other traditions find the relationship to be more communal in nature and dependent on the correct behaviors of the entire social group. I also note that the older beliefs of groups living in closer contact with nature often place humans as merely one of the cousins in the family of life and stress proper relationship with all things.

All of these traditions include acceptance by faith that what is has been somehow ordained by what is not observable or testable in the visible world. The tribal traditions may be furthest from this blind acceptance and emphasize visible relationships among living things in spite of the fact that a creator is also present in many of their stories of origin and meaning. For those who accept human dominance by divine fiat, there is little room for further discussion of how things came to be as they are. Although there are many active debates about current human behavior and its relationship to teachings about our intended roles as guardian and/or recipients of the planet's resources. I find it easy to see how these views would match observation of the world for the ancients comparing our strength to that of other animals. In the twenty-first century these beliefs depend on one's acceptance of the foundational texts as true. For the believer there is no room to question. But for the skeptic, there is little method to prove the underlying assumptions.

The explanation of dominance based on the mind has much to support it that can be tested in observable ways. And yet, I still think it is worthy of deeper contemplation. The same mind that can form logical plans for protection from predators and memories of the effects of ingesting various plants can imagine monsters in the dark driving one to irrational behavior or desire the effects of mild poisonings from mind-altering plants which may have benefits in broader awareness or cause disability or death. The hungry predator driven by hunger and following instinctual methods of hunting based on eons of experience as we have long been taught suffers no such distractions and might actually be seen as having the advantage of single-minded pursuit of its prey. Mere knowledge of the nocturnal hunting habits of a pride of lions will not itself guarantee the individual alone on the Savannah survival through the night. We also now have evidence that other life forms possess higher levels of memory and thinking than were considered possible when I was a child in school.

I am drawn to the collective mind of humans, especially when our collective thoughts are bent toward the mutual good. I fully grant that the human mind can lean towards greed for possession and power, destruction of others, and the horrors of war to establish the dominance of one's own people over others. These behaviors have also been observed in other mammals. But I believe the preponderance of evidence for those kinds of behaviors in humans may be skewed by histories written at the pleasure of and with a worshipful respect for conquering heroes. As we turn to studies and histories of the masses of people often taken for granted in those earlier writings, a much stronger emphasis on working for the common good may be found. It dominates the literature on intentional community which I have studied for much of the last half-century. As I write this during a pandemic which is being compared to war, stories are emerging across the US of individuals responding to the needs of health workers by sitting down to produce face masks which are in short supply. Among everyday people I find the tendency to do what is possible and supply what is needed stronger than the drive to argue politics and seek power based on attacking those who might have guaranteed adequate supplies. The tendency of the wholesome mass of citizens is to do what is in our power and meet the revealed needs of others.

I sometimes wonder how it began. Again, the traditional religious explanation is that human altruism is a reflection of the god-nature or done in obedience to divine instruction. For those who do not find meaning in the religious texts, a different kind of exploration is helpful. I think about it when I see video of primates picking bugs from the hair of other members of the group. It is possible to claim that this is, or was at the beginning, a selfish act. These bugs are a source of protein readily available where the social group sits in safety. I must consider that they are eating snacks readily available. But having once had head lice from a student along with help in removing both the insects and eggs, I know the relief from itching that occurs. And as young gorillas have now been observed destroying traps after witnessing the death of an infant, I believe it is reasonable to postulate that at some point simple behaviors transitioned from any self-centered origins to acts of caring for others.[1] Likewise procuring protein through hunting, humans are not alone as a species that has discovered the group is stronger and more effective than the individual. When one turns away from the sales-driven news which emphasizes big events like war and terror to look instead at the behavior of most people, I believe examples of caring and mutual effort

---

1. Than, "Gorilla Youngsters."

far outweigh acts of destruction. Vulnerable as we are, the species would otherwise likely have disappeared.

In the midst of the pandemic of 2020 the news and social media are filled with stories of selfish behaviors such as hoarding and price gouging. Stories of physically and emotionally reaching out to care for others are saved for final positive stories at the end of broadcasts. It creates an image that they are less common than destructive behavior that is simply not true. School personnel with their institutions closed continue to work to provide food and activities for their students, to contact students and see that they are OK, and to offer reassurance and encouragement in a stressful time. Restaurant owners forced to close are making sure their stocks of food are used to supply their own laid-off employees and local food banks. Neighbors, sewing groups, and some businesses continue sewing those protective masks to donate to local health providers. Relatives are checking on relatives. Neighbors are checking on and helping neighbors. It happens all the time and increases in times of trouble. People are scared and buying extra supplies and even firearms. But if one observes the most common behaviors, we are taking care of each other. Mr. Rogers's mother was correct. The helpers are the real and most powerful story.

Under the horrific social strains present when he took office, Abraham Lincoln called on the nation to remember the "better angels of our nature."[2] The worst war in our history followed as we battled ourselves. Great animosities continued during the reconstruction of the nation, and in many places to the current day. However, I believe President Lincoln was correct about our nature containing better angels.[3] Even those with strong negative feelings about the government or various other groups of people can be found caring for people they actually know. More than once in my life I have witnessed people expressing strong negative views of other races adjust those views significantly when they dealt with actual people from those groups. They may have seen these individuals as exceptions, but their behavior towards them was positive human to human interaction. I experienced the same in other countries speaking with individuals who had strong negative opinions of the United States. When I would point out that I am a US citizen, the response has always been, "We do not mean you! You are here with us!" Face-to-face and finding ourselves in the same groups, humans care for other human beings. One of

2. Sandburg, *Abraham Lincoln*, 39.

3. An interesting idea I will not pursue in this essay is that Lincoln spoke of angels as within our own nature, not as separate beings to be called forth to act on our behalf.

my favorite alterations of basic language is in referring to human beings as humans being.[4] Most of the time, most of us are busy as humans being human. And that is a very good thing. It is summed up in the concept of ubuntu—I am because you are. The scary parts of life are made better by the fact that we exist because we exist together. Look where the road is dark and you will find us as Ram Dass taught, *Walking Each Other Home*.

---

4. Van Halen, "Humans Being."

Is There a Fall in UFT?

3/21/2020

These thoughts were inspired in backward fashion when a friend reminded me of "Desiderata," a very positive piece of writing by another Hoosier.[1] I have loved this piece of writing for many years and often think of the assertions that we are part of the universe with a right to exist.[2] The encouragement to live out that right in peace and harmony matches very well with both the content and the spirit of my own work. And yet the author's assertion that we have as much right to exist as any other part of the cosmos, led to the question of this essay.

I want first to say that like Max Ehrmann I see our existence as positive, and my beliefs no longer contain anything like Christian doctrines of a literal fall of all mankind. I do not believe there is any act that a single person can take which brings guilt to even their immediate offspring, let alone all future generations. I do not believe that the power of the universe exhibits human responses of favoring us when we are good or leaving us in disfavor when we are wrong. This is a major part of what attracts me to the studies of physics where the combined forces of the universe simply are what they are and do what they do. In total those forces are positive for us, and we exist on a planet well suited to our continued existence. I do not believe there is any event in the past where the universe was forced to turn its back on us because we are less than part of the whole. But I live in an interesting time.

1. See Ehrmann's "Desiderata."
2. Copyrights for "Desiderata" are complicated and I am being very careful not to lift from the author's poetry. The reader is seriously encouraged to read the original in its entirety.

Friends and authors I read in ecology have warned for some time that humanity is at a tipping point where our welfare on Earth may become seriously compromised. A serious global pandemic is underway as I write this. And I just listened to the President of the United States say on television that nobody saw anything like it coming. Short of accusations of avarice, I can only assume that he spoke from ignorance caused by distrust of science. The scientific community has been warning for some time that just such an illness would appear and spread rapidly in our globalized society. Many are now using the term "Anthropocene" to describe our current environmental age because the actions of humanity are driving a large number of changes in the conditions on our planet. I find it ironic that many of the same people who reject these assertions that the size of the human population combined with the power of our technologies can change the planet have no trouble believing that one innocent couple willfully eating a piece of forbidden fruit could cause everything harmful on our planet for the rest of time. The answer, of course, is that their story has the addition of an omnipotent judge who declares the changes. As a person who sees many things through constructivist lenses, I prefer the story which calls on us to recognize our own agency and contemplate to what degree changes in our behavior might also improve life on our planet. For me the recognition of guilt or innocence is most powerful in the present tense for those who retain the power to change their behavior.

The possibility that we have the power to render the only planet currently known to be hospitable to human life unlivable raises for me the question of whether we have *fallen from grace* with the physical realities of the universe. To be sure, individuals can fall, and Wendy Northcutt has humorously published stories of people improving the gene pool by taking themselves out of it by extreme acts.[3] People who approach wild animals forgetting the lessons of our deep ancestors, often find that the animals still behave as they always have. In my own favorite sport of rock climbing, we have lost too many talented people to the well-known force of gravity combined with failures as simple as neglecting to tie a knot in the end of their rope. People who drive faster than they can safely control their vehicles find that the laws of motion and inertia behave exactly as predicted. But while such individuals may raise insurance costs for the rest of us, nobody claims that all animal lovers, climbers, or drivers are

---

3. Northcutt, *Darwin Awards*.

damned by the actions of the careless individual. But the question remains of whether we have collectively crossed some line which places us at odds with the rest of the cosmos.

I have long believed that the fear of, even aversion to, nature found among many humans considered civilized is related to our separation from the natural world and our exploitation of it. Many people fear the forest as a place of unknown dangers from plants, animals, and the simple lack of easy directions for travel. Wild animals fear us as well and we are more likely to hear the crashing noise of deer fleeing through the woods as we approach than to eat dinner surrounded by deer or other animals openly doing the same. We chose to build shelters more controlled than caves or temporary structures of wood and animal skin. With some current level of debate about which behaviors actually caused the others, we gathered together in ever larger groups to work and worship and left food production to specialists. And we became more and more separated from the rest of nature. As our populations and transportation of goods grew, food became something that came in cans or plastic wrap rather than something grown by careful tending of the soil or taken from a living animal. At some point we exceeded the beautiful words of the "Desiderata" and decided that we have more right to be here, and to be here in comfort, than other inhabitants of our planet. If there is a fall to be found in UFT, that is it.

As one who loves being away from the cities and all they entail to spend time alone or with small groups in the woods or the mountains, I must describe the loss of such experiences as a decline in our existence if not an actual fall. Part of what keeps me from a more drastic conclusion is that individuals like myself can still return to wild places, practice quiet, and be healed. The further we are from hunting or hunting season the more common it becomes to find ourselves sharing space with wild things. People climbing Colorado mountains where no hunting is allowed are finding species living there including sheep and goats bolder and bolder about sharing the same spaces and trails. There is no general inescapable fall in this small picture sense.

Still there are the changes of the Anthropocene Era. Our planet is warming and while many of us hope for friendlier technologies to gain wider use, few of us move into eco-villages and even less turn off the lights and comforts supplied through the use of carbon-based fuels. Those of us who believe in the science know that we are damaging our planet and making it a less hospitable place to live. But we choose to continue in our current comfort even though we cannot claim to be ignorant of right and wrong like Adam and Eve in the ancient story. Have we fallen so far outside the natural laws that our future is doomed?

In a speech at the University of Southern Indiana in the nineteen-seventies I heard Buckminster Fuller promise that Earth still had the capacity to care for all humans at a comfortable level. However, he also said that we had to organize to do it within twenty years or it would be too late. Twenty years came and passed with little change or notice. Few of us remember this brilliant man beyond his invention of the geodesic dome. I have also seen recent articles that state we have crossed a danger point where, fifty years after the first Earth Day, individual efforts to recycle and reuse in order to reduce one's personal carbon footprint can no longer bring the required level of healing for our damaged world. We are experiencing the first global pandemic to seriously concern the general population of first-world countries. And yet, people allowed to travel have shown that they still will. College students who should represent the generation most aware of scientific fact still flocked to Florida beaches in large numbers to socialize over spring break in spite of warnings that the virus could spread rapidly in such crowds. Perhaps we have fallen—have chosen to pursue present pleasures no matter what predictable harm we are predestined to suffer due to our own selfishness and resistance to change.

I choose hope.

Wind and solar farms are spreading across the US landscape. As shown in the current situation of temporary shutdown and by Chinese experiments with clearing the air before they hosted the Olympics, Earth is still powerfully able to heal herself if given the opportunity. People are drawn to local foods grown in healthy ways and have shown they will pay higher prices to get them. Humans care about their offspring and the continued existence of their families. Neighbors still care about neighbors if convinced that we must take a course of action in order to obtain a life-sustaining result. In spite of warnings from minds as brilliant as Stephen Hawking that humanity must prepare to move on to new planets, we know that very few would ever take those ships. For most of us, the fate of this planet is our fate and will contain the fate of our future generations.

The need for change is drastic according to the scientific data. Our separation from species facing immediate extinction is too great for many people to feel the pain which should come with the permanent departure of fellow lifeforms. I expect more damage to be done to the planet that will drastically change life as the wealthy of the world knew it in the twentieth century. The web of life will be taken to the very edge of collapse. We might see the death of unbelievable percentages of the human population. And still, I have faith in humanity. We have minds that are capable of making drastic adjustments in our behaviors and means of survival. We have hearts that do cry out as we see harm coming to others.

We are part of the universe especially fitted to life on this planet. I still believe we are capable of finding ways through the damage we have caused in order to build more sustainable lives. I have friends from farms, seminaries, and intentional communities who are actively working on the issues along with those who are professional scientists. I do not believe we have fallen beyond redemption. I do not believe the change will come through our rescue by any divine or extraterrestrial force. I choose hope, hope in humanity realizing that the time has come to focus our energy on continuing to be humans being.

Humans Being

3/24/2020

I SUSPECT THAT DISCUSSIONS OF the identity and nature of God and assertions such as mine that the combined forces studied by physics in the search for the unified theory are the omnipresent, omnipotent power behind all things will continue as long as there are people to question. However, what matters most to many of us is knowing what it means to be us. While a privileged few spend their lives studying the nature of the divine, everyone is faced daily with the small choices that guide our behavior and in sum determine our success as humans being.

What does it mean to be human? What criteria can we use to describe a life that is fully human? Again, the religious will point to the ancient texts, but we have reached a point where we can find authors who claim the texts mean just about anything we wish them to mean. My own first contemplations of what it means to be human felt like an echo of the masterful opening to *A Tale of Two Cities*. We give away all we have to help those who have less, and we rob from even the Earth; we are kind when there is no possibility of repayment, and we are cruel without cause; we rescue small animals from traffic and look the other way while fellow humans are slaughtered; we are everything our parents hoped and everything our children despise. Although I cannot find the original author, I must agree in many ways that we are well described as angels who defecate.

But I find that such descriptions fall short of my aim. I wish to explore what it is that deserves Abraham Lincoln's appeal to "the better angels of our nature."[1] And I turn first to an often-used error. Many ask what separates us from the animals. I find the question libelous to the rest of life on Earth. It is an attitude of limited usefulness left over from an age of imagining ourselves, and probably our very specific group, to be superior to all others. I want to first suggest that we would do well to remember that we are animals no matter how strenuously the creationists object. I have known many a person who would have done well to show the courage of a small bird defending her young when cowering in fear of the reactions they might get from others. I have known many leaders who would have been well served by the example of an elephant walking calmly through the world safe in its size and power rather than posturing and belittling others in an attempt to maintain their position. Even Jesus is quoted as wishing he could gather the people of Jerusalem beneath protective wings like a mother hen.[2] And I suspect that we are at our most human when we are best at being the thinking emoting animals which we are.

Having previously encountered my assertion that group identity and caring is one of our greatest strengths, the reader may find my view that many of our least human behaviors are found in trying to position ourselves, or our group, as separate from and superior to the whole somewhat predictable. It takes an all-consuming commitment to one's own group to make war on another, to commit genocide, or to destroy families which appear at our border and ask for asylum. I know arguments for just war from within Christendom as well as within other religions. I seldom find them convincing. History records acts prior to war which could have been altered leading to very different outcomes. I understand society's desire to cage the dangerous and execute the worst from amongst us. But I am very glad that I have never experienced the mental, psychological, emotional, and possibly religious effort it requires to live by guarding the cells or injecting the lethal poison and still retain one's balance as a human being. I will not debate the need to isolate the violent individual here except to say there is much that might be done differently during the developmental years of our children. I will state my strong personal opinion that if I ever choose to take another life there would be an unalterable change in my relationship to humanity. While I own and sometimes carry a firearm in these strange times, I remain

1. Sandburg, *Lincoln*.
2. Matt 23:37.

at heart a lifelong pacifist. To go a step further, I believe the percentage of people a society finds it necessary and correct to keep in prisons is probably an inverse measure of the success of that society to promote the general humanity of its citizens.

The easiest approach to what it means to be human is probably by evoking images. A person comforting a child is more human than anyone beating a child. A person risking their own safety to protect or save others represents our ideal selves. For me, a person quietly hiking in the forest is more human than those clear-cutting, although the history of humans includes clearcutting more area than we have preserved for nature and our own solitude. A person working for the good of humanity and calling us to our highest selves is more human than the person who is only interested in personal financial gain. However, I fear the current rejection of the humanities even in departments of liberal arts, unless financial benefit can be demonstrated, will diminish our collective ability to see this ideal. Humans who continue behaviors which unify, heal, and uplift us all fit my image of humans being fully human. Much of this was recorded long ago in a variety of writings with the prayer of Saint Francis representing one beautiful example as it calls for bringing love over hatred, pardon for injury, faith over doubt, hope instead of despair, light into the darkness, and joy where there is sadness. This humble pursuit of lofty ideals is difficult to reject as an exemplar of what it means to be fully human.[3]

But we are also land mammals who look to the heavens both literally and figuratively. We experience awe at the beauty and grandeur but also fear of our insignificance in comparison. We know the wonder of being alive and we struggle with the awareness that our time as individuals is short. Many cling to traditions of immortality for the faithful while others descend into nihilistic despair or choose the blind leap to existential meaning. Attempts to examine which views are more human than others can quickly become recitations of famous names from the history of philosophy or experiments in deconstructing language, neither of which provide much help to the nonacademic people who often display the finest traits of lives well lived.

I would like to explore another angle based on UFT's linkage of physics and meaning. Humans being are extremely complex arrangements of systems, organs, tissue, cells, carbon-based molecules, and

---

3. Francis of Assisi, "Prayer."

ultimately the quanta of energy-mass which compose every observable part of the universe. This causes me to consider human mortality in a similar manner. Before our time of being, our quanta were pre-existing in many forms since the emergence of the universe. For one brief season, they are being us. And after our time is finished, the quanta continue on displayed in new forms of matter and energy.[4] We want to believe that our conscious being will continue beyond the time of our physical being. We cling to hope based on religious teachings about eternal futures in spite of atheist authors pointing out that most of us hold no such illusions of eternal past existence. But I assert that we can know this much; our quanta existed before our time, during our lives exchanging constantly with new quanta from our environment, and they continue after our loved ones have been forced to say good-bye to the arrangement they have known as us. Much has been made in some circles of the urge to make sure that the arrangement of our DNA continues so that something that was us clearly continues to exist in our offspring. I confirm that urge as a true and human desire.

Perhaps this sounds like an invitation to illusions of grand immortality. My heart and mind say it calls us to humble appreciation. The very same observation of our existence as essential quanta applies to the land and sea, the soaring bird and the crawling snake, the dirt which produces our food, and the sun which supplies all of our energy. We come from the whole. We experience and ideally appreciate and enjoy a time of existence with loving awareness of our world and the lives which surround us. Then, we return to unity with the whole. As I write these words, I recall other voices from traditions of the middle and far East. We have this rapidly fleeting moment and when we experience it most fully, we become aware that we were, are, and will be part of the whole. I find great comfort in this knowledge. I also feel a call to less anxiety about my existence as different from the whole.

While I am here and aware, I choose to be a human being who is kind, living by as much wisdom as I am given. I seek to be giving while I am also consuming; a husband, parent and grandparent; student, teacher, and author, city dweller and lover of woods and rock seeking the best for those I love—categories I seek always to expand. I am grateful for the working of the universe and processes of biology that have given me existence in one of the most amazing periods of human history. And I

---

4. As I edit this essay, I am also reading *Old Path White Clouds* and find the match to the recorded teachings of the Buddha very interesting.

hope that my conclusions result from an informed mind rather than a blind existential choice. I base my conclusions on teachings from across millennia of human experience and seeking of truth with no claims of divine or superior human revelation. I fully recognize the right of others to choose different paths and sources of meaning. I recognize my deep formation in a childhood of religious definitions of the virtuous human and I continue to seek ideals which are in many ways tied to those traditions. But, as I meet and work with others who see things in different ways, I recognize that for this brief wonderful moment we are all humans being.

Falling Short of the Glory

3/30/2020

CHRISTIANS ALSO USE THE WORD *fall* in as a present-tense personal term. Old friends who encounter UFT sometimes ask me whether I still believe that I "fall short of the glory of God."[1] By this they normally want to know if I acknowledge that I am in need of the saving grace of Jesus Christ. This is interesting since the rendering of the text in question is very undecided. Many translations have footnotes indicating that the passage could either mean that the person who falls short needs to accept salvation through faith or that all are saved through the grace of the Christ. Nevertheless, it is an interesting question if we do not find the entire human race in a *fallen* condition due to the activity of a literal first man and woman. Perhaps each of us fails to live up to the intended glory individually, still resulting in all of humanity needing a savior.

Do I believe that I "fall short of the glory of God?"

My first response is to look out at the world. Last night a strong storm went just past my house and did a great deal of damage to other people's homes. My wife and I could hear the roar as we sat in the lowest level of our house. A single storm displays power beyond anything I can imagine any human ever claiming. Today as I cleaned limbs out of the yard, I saw violets and wild strawberries beginning to bloom alongside the bright yellow plants my neighbors consider weeds. In the simplest of environments, I find that nature puts on a greater display than anything I could ever claim about my appearance.

---

1. Rom 3:22–24.

I read and study across disciplines to consider the working of the universe and as I begin to believe that I have some grasp of its complexity researchers discover new phenomena through astronomy or quantum experiments. While I have no trouble believing that the combined forces of nature represent the omnipresent, omnipotent engine of the universe, I can no more comprehend them in their fullness than I can explain why the Earth's tilt is oriented toward Polaris. I fall short of understanding much of the scientific knowledge which fascinates me. And I make no claim to in any way equal any of the powers. I am an earthbound mammal and the smallest and least attractive of flying things can do what I cannot.

Of course, what is really meant is whether I live up to the level called for in response to the gifts I receive. I cannot match the generosity of either the sun or rain which give equally to all with no sign of favoritism.[2] The moon and stars put on their full display for anyone who happens to look up whether they appreciate the view or not. After a lifetime of working to develop new methods and teach all students without favoritism, I still favor the student with challenges and a deep desire to succeed over any lazy privileged ones. When I write something that I believe may have value in exploring a deeper understanding of our place in the world, I share it with friends who have shown respect for my earlier work rather than those who are likely to reject the offering. I fall short of the simple generosity of sun and rain, stars and moon.

Neither can I match the consistency of the laws of nature. Gravity always works as do the laws of motion and thermodynamics. There is no morning when we wake up to the possible terror of flying off the Earth, being unable to avoid deadly collisions with other objects, or finding that heat no longer helps water dissolve our morning coffee. Nature always works. Somedays I wake up lazy, self-absorbed, or in other ways less inclined to respond in the same way to those who expect my usual response to a shared need. I fall short of the glory of the consistency of the powers that guide the universe. As translated by born-again Christians, I sin by failing to be perfect and consistent in the use of whatever power I possess and cannot match the glory of nature or the power that rules all life.

---

2. Matt 5:45. This quote of Jesus seems to match observable science in contrast to interpretations of passages such as Deut 30 indicating that favor in the blessings of Earth will be increased for those who obey the law.

ON THE OTHER HAND

I have a friend who became lost in the desert of the SW United States hiking an area she believed she knew. Rain had changed the pattern of the dry stream beds making her expected travel markers untrustworthy. As she and her friend hiked on, the sun continued to do what the sun does, as they became hotter, sunburned, and dehydrated. When their situation became perilous to their survival, there was no help from the sun. Help came from scientists involved in the development of cell phones and helicopters. Help came from the rescue squad that answered her call, flew the helicopter, treated their dehydration and flew them to safety. I find it entirely defensible to say that on their day of need, the actions of humans exceeded the glory of the sun which always does splendidly, but only, what it does.

I have run into an alley where I was told a man was beating one of the eighth-grade girls from my school. I have run into the woods where I was told one student in a group on a hike had his father's gun. I have stood in the gap between caring adults and supervisors who did not understand their work or their success. And I have restrained both suicidal and homicidal young adults physically and by the power of calm caring in their time of crisis. All of which makes me normal as a human being, nothing more and nothing less. When Fred Rogers repeated the advice of his mother that we should look for the helpers, he knew that we would find them. They are always there. If we show a human being a problem within their ability to respond,[3] I believe we will observe their best possible response.

It turns out that our ability to respond in a variety of ways is significant to our display of the glory of the universe. We are not locked into only one way of acting when confronted with new situations. People who would never walk into highway traffic on a normal day, will do so at great risk of physical harm to rescue a child, a stray pet, or a duck with ducklings. When we see situations within our power to help, we change our normal routines and help. This ability to observe, analyze, and respond allows us to behave in ways more glorious than what is available to the

---

3. I am making a complex psychological distinction here concerning those who do not respond. I believe there is something about the situation, their capacity, and their self-image that tells them the situation is beyond them when they fail to act. Those who are willfully selfish are to my mind clear exceptions to the normal human response.

sun, wind, or rain bound by the laws which control their actions with no appearance of choice.[4]

When I was descending Quandary Peak in Colorado, weak-legged, nauseated, and finally passing out from dehydration, the clouds that appeared were unable to supply the liquid I needed in a form I could take into my body. The friend who hiked back up the mountain bringing much-needed water to the trip leader and myself was a sight more glorious in my eyes and in my memory than the snow pellets which surrounded us. Did we exceed the glory of the clouds when we gave too much of our own water away to the young people we were responsible to lead? Did our friend when he brought the water that revived us? I will not be that bold. I will, however, voice doubt that we fell below the glory.

In the end, I leave the reading of Rom 3 to any who find the text to express divine teaching. Perhaps we do all fall short but have all been raised to new levels of functioning as one translation of the text would indicate. Or if the one who became the Christ existed before the world began as the Bible also asserts, perhaps humans have all been raised to be worthy of the glory as part of the grace which makes us human. Perhaps Jesus's quoted teaching about the sun and rain in Matt 5:45 is key to understanding our place in the order of things as he exhorts listeners not to show favoritism because God does not play favorites.

I find the two opposites to be wonderfully and amazingly true! As highly as we tend to think of ourselves, we are very small creatures that fall far short of the glory we can observe in the sky or even the back yard. As small as we are, we have the gifts of mind and heart and are capable of responding in new ways when need calls for action, a change which exceeds the glory given to the galaxies and planets by the power of nature. I both fall below the glory of the skies and show a capacity for glory the stars do not possess.

What my evangelical friends do not wish to hear regardless of its accuracy is that I do not believe I am evil by nature. I do not believe humans are all evil by nature and saved only through accepting coverage by a divine act of blood sacrifice. We rise above what we often believe we are capable of being and doing by the simple glory of living as humans being!

---

4. Acknowledging those in biology and psychology who believe we are programmed for only one response which we translate to be our choice, I assert that the behavior happens nonetheless.

Growing Up with a Christian Witch

4/1/2020

As I think back on my youth, there is another factor that is probably related to how I see the world including views that at times represent a tension between apparent opposites. My mother, who was very serious about her faith as a traditional Christian, also behaved in ways which caused us to call her a witch for several years. She seemed to be attached to power in ways that extended beyond logical observation.

The most casual and easy to explain was using traditional granny cures. Years later I would buy the complete run of the *Foxfire* books and see that many of these methods, such as scratching x's on fingernails and using plant remedies, were very common from before the age of the modern drug store. But we were always amazed when her methods eliminated the hangnail, took away the sting from a bee, or informed her if we had been lying recently.

Further away from what we observed other people doing, she seemed to know when things were going to happen and enlisted us in sending messages by mind in the days before cellular phones. She would be busy cooking supper or already sitting at the table with the family and then casually turn to me and say, "Answer the phone and tell Aunt Vera I will be there in a second." The odd part is she could do it before the phone rang. But it would ring as I was walking over to its spot on the kitchen wall, and it would be the person she said was calling, usually her sister. I never could find any telltale sign from the phone that would let her know it was about to ring. At other times she would be planning supper and would realize we were out of some staple like milk or bread with Dad unreachable by phone at work. She would have my sister and I sit and *think* the message to Dad to stop and get the required item. I was too young and uniformed in experimental methods to keep a record and determine if our success rate exceeded chance or the likelihood of Dad unconsciously remembering the empty wrapper or carton. But it worked often enough to convince us that it was real even though nothing in our religious lessons said such a power should exist or be used if it did. If I asked my father how he knew to stop and buy the item, he would say that it just hit him on the way home.

She also drove a car in a different manner than anyone else I ever knew. My sister remembers her simply saying things like, "Lord, we need a parking spot," after looking with no success and quickly pulling into one. My own memories are a bit more dramatic. We would be stuck trying to get an opening to pull out into traffic. She would wait and then start checking how long we had to get where we needed to be. More than once as I sat in the front seat, I heard her say out loud, "We're late, Lord, and I'm going." Then she would step on the gas! We never got hit and I never remember seeing other cars have to take evasive action to miss us as she pulled our car into a solid line of traffic.

I also remember one of the times my parents decided it was time for a new car but had not yet found one. My dad and I were headed out to look again. Mom told him she had a dream that it was the light blue car. She said she didn't need to go along and look because she knew the right car. We went to the next dealer and there was a new light blue Plymouth station wagon for sale. Dad looked it over and tried again to see if she wanted to come see it before he bought it. She had him describe it and she said, "That is the car from my dream. Buy it." He did.

One of the strangest events I witnessed in the car with her happened on the old Highway 41 route through Vincennes. In heavy rain, the road had flooded, and we drove through it. Then she could not control the car and we were headed directly towards an oncoming semi-truck. I remember watching her turn the steering wheel back and forth and pump the brakes getting no response from either. As time seemed to go into slow motion, I heard her say, "That's all I can do, Lord!" And she took both hands off of the steering wheel and pulled both feet back to the seat away from the pedals. Our '67 Chevy Impala wagon pulled over to the side and stopped with her hands and feet off the controls as the truck went by. She simply called it the power of prayer and God's protection. To this day, I have no other rational explanation.

Eventually as an adult Sunday school teacher she decided that was inappropriate for us to call her a witch, even in jest. It also seemed to me that she was quieter about what she was doing after that. But she had a lifelong ability to do things that appeared to us as power displays. For a time, the way things worked for her seemed like an affirmation to me that her Christian beliefs were true, and God simply answered her prayers offered in full faith. Now, I only remember them as part of my training in accepting that there are things in the world that exceed our understanding and ability to explain. One of the final times came when I was doing my father's funeral. I had it typed and the pastor from their church sitting by me in case he should need to step in if emotion overcame me. As I reached a particularly emotional part of the eulogy, my voice broke. My wife was sitting near my mother in the small side room for family. She told me later, "I do not know what came out of your mom's mouth when you stumbled, but it wasn't English!" I had no knowledge of it during the service, but my voice immediately calmed, and I finished the service.

Now we still have and drive the Chrysler van that was hers when she died. It has been driven by my nephew camping with other young rock climbers in typical young male fashion, was driven by my wife as her primary vehicle for some time, and by two of our daughters after my wife got a different vehicle. All manner of aromas have been through that van! Still, every now and then, when one of us gets in to drive it somewhere a familiar perfume is evident. We just say, "Hi, Mom," and keep on driving.

Religion Abhors a Vacuum

4/4/2020

IN *UFT*, I INCLUDED AN essay playing with the idea that nothing, or what we call empty space, has gravity and attracts things to itself. It was an enjoyable mental game, but no scientist would ever agree to my absurd assertion about the physical world. Now I wish to turn it around and say it the way science teaches. Something tries to fill nothing. As my grade school teacher patiently explained in spite of many questions, the bell jar is too heavy to lift because of the pressure of the atmosphere pressing down and trying to move into the vacuum created in the lab. As a final nod to my previous mental game, I note that the two explanations describe the exact same observed effect.

In my home, I have often teased my wife about how every flat surface near her attracts stuff. No empty flat surface is safe from accumulating mail or whatever enters the room by hand. No object seems to want to stay in a cabinet if there is open space available. The living room floor is currently filled with boxes of items we no longer use set to depart at some time for donation. The back of her vehicle is constantly filled with various items for work, the grandchildren, or also on the way to donation. The same process happens naturally in the yard as well. If I clear a spot of dirt and do not immediately fill it with what we want there, weeds will not tolerate the blank canvas and will arrive in abundance. The same applies to the gravel part of our drive and every crack in the concrete. If I get the yard clean and smooth, nature will fill it with tree limbs, leaves, and trash that seems to appear from nowhere.

In a more serious vein, the atmosphere moves from areas of high pressure into areas of more empty, low pressure. Everything we know appears to have burst forth to fill what was empty of everything except potential and it keeps moving out into the emptiness. The known universe is not only expanding, but also surprising astrophysicists by accelerating its rush into the void. On a smaller more easily observable scale, nature unimpeded by humans will fill an area of Earth with both plants and animals suitable to the climate. And conscious thought appears to follow the same pattern. Where nothing is known science, philosophy, fiction, and religion will move to fill the gap. I was recently invited to consider the work of Maurice Blanchot and I was particularly drawn to his emphasis on the *neuter* and the *outside*. I believe it is a highly valuable technique to consider what, or who, is left outside of any system of belief or action. It is one of the criticisms I leveled toward the Christian teachings of my youth. As awareness of global populations increased, the literal narrative of the Christian Bible left far too many people permanently on the outside. In this essay, I am also considering the *neuter*.

Our minds do not easily tolerate the lack of thought and explanation. Practitioners of Eastern meditation know this difficulty. They must practice, ideally with guidance from a teacher, in order to let thoughts pass through without taking up residence and assuming priority. It is a skill which must be learned.

I am also thinking here about the human reaction to unexpected disaster. The perennial cry is, "Why?" Given the statistics of chance combined with the number of human beings, other life forms, and dangerous machines of our own making, there is no doubt that deaths will occur at times and in places that do not seem logical to us. The conscious mind is little comforted by this. We want an answer to fill the void. Sometimes we explain what has happened by placing blame on some person or group due to negligence or direct acts of malice. But often no one is to blame, and nobody gains anything from the loss. There is no reason, and we struggle to accept no answer as the only answer.

We make up vague explanations of it being the person's time with no idea what we mean by humans having a predetermined time. More constructively we create meaning by looking to what strength and healing we may develop as we work through pain together creating meaning from no meaning by application of our will to build something positive from negative situations. And people mix folk religion with their traditional beliefs to construct statements of comfort. I have often heard expressions including, "God needed another precious angel," or "Now our family has our own special angel watching over us." It doesn't seem to matter much whether the statements match any real theology or personal beliefs as long as they bring comfort. We prefer some comforting construction to looking into the abyss and admitting that there is none, which brings me to religion itself.

The need becomes greatest when we face not only the unexpected individual disaster, but our collective awareness that we will all die. And we are faced, ancient humans were faced, with a nothing that consciousness does not easily tolerate. Aware of ourselves as beings that think and feel, we struggle to accept the possibility that these powers come into existence merely to be snuffed out again. And yet the only direct evidence we have says that life always reaches an end. Death is not only inevitable, but also unavailable to our own senses for analysis. Many people have documented the human processing of the loss of strength and the descent toward death as well as the climb from the well of grief required after the loss of a loved one. But the moment of death and anything that might lay beyond it are beyond our ability to experience, examine, evaluate, or explain because all of those functions cease with the moment of death. If anything continues after death, it lies outside the realm of all external measurement as well and certainly was beyond any direct observation by the ancients. It is as it was a nothingness which we find as unreachable as it is unacceptable.

So, we construct meaning where science cannot provide it. A gentle breeze seems to ruffle leaves beside us in a unique way and our minds form assumptions that the one we have lost moves nearby. Allow the air to bring a momentary chill instead and we play similar games with dread. The memories embedded in the physical structure of our brains combine with other aspects of the sleeping mind and bring us realistic dreams of new visits and conversations with those who have passed and we long to believe that we have experienced a real visit in spite of all possibility of verification by another observer. We construct meanings of comfort and fear. We imagine those who have moved beyond the body traveling in a realm near but normally unobservable by us, or we may envision their essence invested in yet another physical form in cycles of consciousness moving eternally towards unity with universal consciousness.

Christianity formalizes it all and tells us there is a meaningful path to knowing what cannot be known by human effort. We are offered the assertion that there is a path, or are paths, to being in right relationship with the eternal so that the future beyond death can be known through faith that the ancient texts and the traditions of the church are true. Islam reminds us that the power of the universe[1] is beyond us and not subject to control by our acts, but still teaches that there are ways of living which align one with the will of the creator and give meaning to life with some hope of a positive afterlife. Judaism long held to the life on Earth lived according to the will of God in ways which challenge later Christian interpretation of many of their ancient texts. As mentioned above the Eastern traditions offer us a variety of patterns toward oneness with all else. Animist traditions often hold that the departed remain closer to the realm of the living and can be honored to one's benefit or offended leading to harm. My point here is not to rank, substantiate, or refute any of these systems of thought. I am considering how they are an example of *something*, conscious thought and understanding, moving to fill the gap of *nothing*, the lack of any observable reality beyond death, much as high pressure air moves into low pressure areas. My own reflections on the permanence of the quanta which are assembled for a time as us does the same while trying not to contradict anything we do know from observation and experiment.

The human mind has developed systems of thought to greater and greater complexity, sometimes in line with new observations of the universe and sometimes in order to fill the inescapable void that lies beyond each and every life. Individual imaginings and comforting sounding sayings may suffice on occasion. But religion steps in to provide authoritative answers. For the believer this is ultimately the authority of God, but at a minimum, it is the authority of one's teachers and religious leaders. To the person from outside any particular tradition, the authority of the text and tradition are assertions of meaning outside the purview of observational science which may or may not be convincing.

Religion abhors a vacuum in human understanding and provides an authoritative reference point for followers in seeking the meaning for their own lives or in explaining life to others. I will avoid criticizing here except to note that when each religion sees anywhere without its own beliefs as suffering from a lack of relief, the rush of something to fill nothing occurs. To the extent that each religion sees itself as the right thing and all others as the lack of that thing, beliefs and believers are bound to collide. Conflict is inevitable and sadly has often led to the very pain of death which religion seeks to salve. There is a strange replication at work as each group seeks to convert those seen as being on the outside and as

1. As a matter of respect, I leave out the name of this God to avoid the offense of speaking as if I know their God or their Profit as an outsider to their traditions.

the resulting conflict causes each side to need a reaffirmation of meaning in the face of lives lost.

I know this for sure. The starkness of what Blanchot called the neuter, the nearly universal aversion to the idea that all that is us can return to zero, affirms for me the beauty of what we possess here and now. Life is not made meaningless by its end but more valuable than anything else we know. Whether one turns to religion with its promises of rightness with all things, meditation for current reunion, or the naturalism of my friend who was very comfortable knowing nothing more than that his physical being would return to the soil which produced the nutrition that gave him life is not mine to tell another. I can only say that for me the contrast of *not this* to our current status as humans being affirms that being is something to be treasured and enjoyed with great gratitude.

Normal

4/4/2020

As the United States continues through the uncharted waters of mass isolation to counter the long-predicted pandemic, I have read more than one article on returning to normal. Some focus on how long it may take to get back to doing what everyone was used to before COVID-19. The ones I respect the most explore various possibilities for how normal may shift in different directions as a result of our social and economic pause. I would like to believe that there would be new respect and better treatment and compensation for those who provide our basic services—from serving our food or delivering our packages, to those who care for our children in schools, and all of those who care for us when illness strikes. My skeptical side sees people responding to fear and uncertainty by retreating further into the opposing views already dividing our country.

My own thoughts pause on the basic concept of normal, an adjective form in English that may well compare things to a standard that exists only in the mind of each thinker. It would be an interesting exercise for some enterprising investigator to try and determine if there is any global, or even national, concept of normal in the twenty-first century. I begin these thoughts with a strong suspicion that the word "normal" means the way each person sees themselves and their usual activities. This creates a problem if those who differ from us are then seen as not-normal, abnormal, or sub-normal.

I should begin by confessing that I have never been normal. I made some efforts in that direction as a child, or toward what I thought was normal. But, by high school I had given up the endeavor. And while I have often felt the sting of being considered abnormal, I have never really desired again to be whatever normal is. I grew up in the sixties when the countercultural call to escape normality ran strong. I had a body that simply would not do what I was told everyone's should from reasonably digest my food to throwing an object within a reasonable proximity to a target. And I have a mind that has always sought ideas and the wonder of the unknown over the certainty of the known. So, there is no use to pretend that I am a neutral observer in any discussion of what it means to be normal.

Where would we find this normal? Perhaps it dwells at the center of the famous bell curve. But that curve from statistics is not a measure of correctness. It only depicts the numbers of people found at certain numbers on a particular measurement. Einstein was not wrong for being at the far right of the intelligence curve, and the Dalai Lama is not bad for being at the far left of the curve for anxiety over world events. Without entering into debates about how close to the middle of the curve would still qualify as normal for any given trait, what we find in the center of the curve is the average score. While there are areas in my life where I have worked hard to move up from the left side of the curve, I have never desired to be known as average.

Part of my contention that normal may not exist comes from the publication of the book, *Cultural Literacy*,[1] several decades ago. When I read its assertion that there is no common background knowledge in my own country, I was teaching US History as an adjunct professor and decided to test the idea. I found that college freshman with a supposedly successful background of coursework in both elementary and high school could not place major events—European exploration, founding of the United States, the Civil War, or the Vietnam War in the correct order, let alone in the right time period for historical context. My skepticism was soon set aside as I explored what various people knew about other fields from math to literature and art. I had to agree with the author that with no common knowledge base, it would be very difficult to establish a common understanding of who we are. If we do not know who we are, how do we define what is normal in our culture?

As I have written elsewhere, it has occurred to me that in any setting—whether school, church, or bar—proper behavior is often equated with the way we and our particular circle of friends behave. I believe it applies to what we mean by normal and accounts for some of the

---

1 Hirsch, *Cultural Literacy*.

discrepancies I have criticized between people's stated beliefs and their observable behavior. Much of the behavior at drive-in theaters and lover's lanes by my parents' generation violated what they were taught was proper but excused as normal, nonetheless. I have observed many a lapse in behavior defended by statements of only being human. The implication was and is that while an observed behavior might not match an ideal, it was normal.

The danger in the word comes when it is applied to others. I already admitted that I have been on the wrong end of that cultural assessment enough times to know the sting of being on the outside of normal. My father was a gentle soul who was hard to provoke to anger, but he was also a tall and athletic man. Nobody accused him of being outside the proper expectations for being a male. My undiagnosed genetic issues with digestion caused me to be very thin and physically unimpressive. I liked to read and play music. As the hippy generation exploded among young people just older than me, I loved the bright colors and wild clothes. I even made some of my own on an antique sewing machine purchased at a country auction. Taught at church that people were supposed to be loving and kind, I was easily hurt and would show my emotions when others did not accept me. Even an openly gay high school classmate very recently described me in my high school days using a derogatory term that implied I was effeminate. I was in therapy in my twenties when a psychologist helped me confront the fact that I would rather be seen as who I am than fit any macho idea of what it meant to be manly. For most of my life it seemed that others used attributes I did not have or want to describe a proper male.

Normal for males required fitting other people's definitions of masculine. Females were to be and act feminine. Normal placed our expected behaviors Mars and Venus apart. And woe to those who actually were other than heterosexual. Normal was males and females attracted to each other and anything else was abnormal. And the way in which others described you had a great deal to do with it as well. I remember two wonderful old maid schoolteachers who were good friends of the family, always welcome, and hilariously funny. But I fear that if anyone had dared to describe them at the time as two old lesbians they would have been just as firmly excluded. Normal was acceptable, so whatever was different was abnormal and unacceptable unless it was left unspoken. Another friend a little older than I became known to most of us as gay early in his adult life. But under the rules of normal, his sexuality is still a topic not to be discussed with people he knew back then. To be artistic or dramatic was suspect enough. Being anything non-hetero was forbidden especially for a practicing evangelical Christian.

Normal people grew up and finished at least high school, went to work, got married, and raised children. Failing, or choosing, not to follow that pattern left one in danger of being labeled something other than normal. When I studied groups like the Harmonists and Shakers in college, I immediately wondered how many people joined these celibate societies because they felt a sense of belonging there. In a time where normal included most of the above list except completing some predetermined level of education, people who did not marry were suspect. But in these religious societies of the nineteenth century, they could be considered more than normal. Their lifestyle then became virtuous and holy. I suspect many without the expected desires for a family led by a heterosexual couple chose being seen as religious over being seen as abnormal or sinful.

Further, how different is normal for males and females in social and work settings at the turn to the twenty-first century? How many women have been told that abusive language and unwanted physical advances by men are just normal and simply the way things are? Even after all of the media attention to the #Metoo movement and the fall of a few famous men, how much have things changed for men and women in many workplaces in the United States and other countries? As some males respond that they must now live in fear of saying something taken incorrectly in an offensive way and reported to a company's human relations department, it makes me wonder how different the views of men and women are about returning to any previous definition of normal. What definition of normal would they find proper and appropriate for everyone in the future?

Then there is race. It was normal to find white people with white people and black people with black people in the USA of my youth, and it is only partially changed today. While there is now more mixing in restaurants and shopping centers, our experience of normal is still far from the same. Professional black friends have told me far too many times about the reality of trying to shop and realizing they were being followed by store security. I never had that experience even when I was a skeletal long-haired freaky young man. I was still white. Until I moved to Michigan after college, I had never had the experience of going to apply for a job and realizing I was unwelcome solely based on my race. But

I needed a job in a time when the economy was weak and answered a help-wanted ad from the Community Action Program in Benton Harbor. I was the only white in the room and for just a moment I thought I knew what it must feel like to walk into a place as the only black. Then it hit me that when I got in my car and drove over the drawbridge back to St. Joseph, I would be back among the majority culture. Even as I sat there, I had choices the others in the room did not have. I later got a job teaching in Benton Harbor and found out that my college-educated, professionally employed, black colleagues could not drive across that same drawbridge at any time approaching dark without being pulled over by the police. My normal and their normal were polar opposites.

I encountered the expectations of normal in my career as well. For a teacher to hold leadership positions in both union and on administrative committees was considered outside of normal and I was recruited into administration. A man who became a career advisor throughout my public-school years called IU over my objections and made the appointment for me to begin my doctorate. Another friend near the top of the local system insisted on my being promoted to one of the first available administrative openings because I would tell him the truth when he asked me questions—also considered abnormal. Then as the disciplinarian in a middle school people were surprised that I spent time with frequent discipline cases trying to help them adjust and change. I was just supposed to hand out consequences and move on to the next student who would never graduate. The typical athletic examples for males showed up again as a veteran educator told me that I didn't understand how things were done because I had not played enough baseball. I was supposed to realize some games are rainouts and there is nothing you can do about it. I was supposed to see the students that interrupted education, became violent in confrontations, or just irritated teachers as rainouts beyond my ability to intervene. The game was over.

When I took a semester off from that position to complete the residence requirement for my doctorate, I was failing to be normal again. When I returned the superintendent overrode my immediate supervisor's positive evaluation and threatened to fire me unless I was *perfect*—so much for normal. I had him define perfect and gave it to him in exchange for being allowed to move to the out-of-control alternative school they had created so that I could prove what I was capable of and then work toward advancement. But the alternative school turned out to be everything I wanted in education. I got to work with the not-normal students and see them succeed instead of being discarded. I had many very positive years with the staff and students at that school even though I often had to shield the staff from animosity and distrust from other educators, especially our bosses. Working with *bad kids* in a positive way while maintaining high standards was not normal and beyond the imagination of many other teachers and supervisors. When the entire system hit tight financial years and it was obvious that my school was on the elimination list, I met again with the mentor who sent me to get my doctorate. He gave me information and advice on moving to a normal administrative track and *getting mine* for myself and my family. When I asked if I could do that in a way that continued to seek what was best for teachers and students, he compared me to radical extremists. My administrative career ended because I refused to fall within the self-promoting methods that were accepted as normal.

Thanks to my secondary career in university teaching and my work with short-term missions I have also met people from many places where normal is very different from the suburban United States. I have been fortunate enough to meet people in China who have professional jobs and growing freedom to make money and enjoy material things. They are not free, however, to speak openly about their beliefs in public, express opinions, or to worship with people from other countries or in any group too large to easily assemble in someone's house. They are at one extreme of free speech while I grew up in a culture where complaining about the government is almost expected in some circles while producing angry reprisals in others.

In Africa and Haiti, I met people who do not know if they will have food from day to day. If they become ill, they recover or die often with little or no medical intervention. The ambulance in the neighborhood I visited many times on the north coast of Haiti has one vehicle with ambulance painted on one side and hearse on the other. If they take you to the hospital, they will probably transport you to be buried. People in that neighborhood remember the years of dictators but now are so separated from what happens in the capital that joking about the government does not cause anyone concern.

And I visited Pine Ridge and Wounded Knee, South Dakota where people live in horrible poverty depending on kindness from strangers to have wood to heat their homes during the harsh winters. And I learned that their poverty is completely intentional and results from official policies of my own government dating back to the first official reports about them filed by Lewis and Clark. Furthermore, their culture is a group culture which cannot be practiced in isolation leaving a bright student with few choices. They can leave and use their education to build a good life if they travel far enough away to escape those who automatically see them as *Indian*. But they will not be able to live as Lakota while alone in a distant place. Or they can stay on the reservation with little to no chance of meaningful employment or significant income no matter how well they succeed in school.

There is no normal lifestyle I see which crosses all of those cultures. Normal life in my neighborhood is far different from normal days on my city's Southside. A sound like a gunshot in my neighborhood is shocking and alarming. The same sound has been heard in their neighborhood for decades and is no longer shocking or unexpected. Even now if a group of youngsters from that neighborhood walked through mine, people would start messaging each other to be alert or might even call the police. A group of kids from my neighborhood walking through theirs would likely be confronted directly. If either group walked into the neighborhoods I visited in China, Africa, or Haiti they would be more likely to be greeted and offered hospitality. Who's normal is normal?

I know what people mean. I look forward to being able to go to the store or just get the mail without fear of a contagion that might kill me. I look forward to being able to travel where I want and can afford. I want to return to my favorite rock-climbing areas. But that is my normal. I have no idea how much it resembles and varies completely from gay neighbors on my own street.

Return to normal?

This old hippy would just as soon we forgot the word. I find it as likely to be divisive and derisive as helpful. What if we could move forward to where we can just be ourselves and live as we see fit without harming each other and quit trying to define what is normal. I lean liberal on many issues and one of my best friends is solidly conservative. I no longer believe in a literalist approach to the Bible and my neighbor across the street taught classes on seven-day creation and young Earth as long as his health allowed. After a career teaching high-school science, he continues to believe his faith-based view is also the most scientific. I could go on. But what if the new normal was accepting each other for who we are and no longer trying to judge or change each other? What if we were just happy that we lived through the first major global pandemic of the twenty-first century together?

I see just as many signs that the country will divide even further. I hear people claiming people whose lives they do not consider normal caused our current trouble by arousing the anger of God. I hear Republicans and Democrats running for office accusing each other with equal rancor. I'm not ignorant of what is happening. We could come through this having learned nothing except more fear and hate.

But hope remains. I can hope that we will find a way to be more accepting of each other and find ways to accept each other simply as we are without reference to what is normal. I can hope that when fear of the virus fades away, fear of each other goes with it. I can hope that our dreams for our own lives and those of our loved ones can extend to others as social distancing becomes unnecessary. Foolish? I warned you that I am not normal. Beyond hoping, while I wait and observe what happens in larger society, I can work to live it in my daily interactions. I can continue to practice UFT and strive to always choose the Tree of Life in how I treat each and every person I encounter day by day.

I leave normal to others. I choose faith in our better selves, hope in a kinder future, and love as both a healing and rewarding way to live. These remain.[2]

---

2. 1 Cor 13:13.

"It Is Finished?"[1]

4/10/2020

Pictures associated with Easter are coming across my social media feed. #ItIsFinished is trending on Twitter in similar fashion. My mind, body, and soul (if souls exist), all recoil. It becomes more absurd and harder for me to respond to in the old ways with each passing season. Just exactly what was finished?

The traditional answer is that the work of Jesus to pay the price for all human sin was finished, or the work of paying the price for all who would believe in him, or the price of the sin of those who would believe certain teachings, accept him in the proper manner, perform the required rituals, and belong to the correct church. The pastor of a church that used to invite me to appear as a guest preacher posted a lengthy, detailed, and nauseating description of Roman crucifixion so that people could see how horrible that price was and be compelled to accept the benefit of the sacrifice. It is that very understanding that makes me reject it more with every passing year as it becomes more difficult to decide if the death of a Jesus who was fully God is falsely or accurately described as suicide or fratricide. The Christian New Testament expresses it clearly as the sacrifice of the Son by the Father—the same Father believers accept by faith as both loving and just. As a story of the ultimate power of the universe going to the very depth of human suffering to express unity with us, it is as powerful as it is disturbing. As the required blood price for all humans because we descended from a single pair of humans who chose

---

1. John 19:30.

wrongly before they understood good and evil, it seems as barbaric as it is ancient to me.

And what was the result of finishing the payment of this price? Over 2000 years later disease is ravaging the planet. Man is abusing and poisoning our only home. Humans still suffer mental extremes that cause many to choose death—sometimes their own, sometimes the death of others. A preacher I used to be closely associated with loved to quote, "By his wounds we are healed."[2] Setting aside the fact that Jewish authors would tell us the passage has nothing to do with Jesus or the crucifixion, I don't see it. I'm watching people suffer and die. I have watched faith healers do their thing in settings that weren't set up as performance art and have not seen the healing. In earlier years, I even participated and saw some experience the effect of strongly believing they were better. But the mass of humanity is not better. Now some Christians would tell me that is because we live in an age where evil and its effects still reign. If so, the work does not appear finished to me. Others will claim that it is like payday. The work was finished but we must patiently await the day when the accounts are settled. I'm told there have been people in every generation since the birth of Christianity who believed that day was coming in their lifetime. And still they died. Many live and die believing in a resurrection and reunion with their loved ones and with Jesus Christ and that is not a small thing. Such a belief is a source of great comfort and hope to many people. But the world is not healed, and payday has not come.

The more I see of the glorification of the desecration of the very real human body of Jesus of Nazareth, the more it nauseates me. More and more I see it in light of superstitious cultures torturing women or children to death for the sake of the group because somebody declares that they are witches or possessed by evil. It reminds of truly horrible accounts of rape victims being stoned to death so that the shame brought upon the family will be finished. The Jews have been shunned, abused, tortured, and murdered for centuries over rumors and outright lies that they sacrifice animals or children when animals have not been sacrificed since the destruction of the temple in 70 AD. And yet once a year the same people who commit, condone, or ignore violence against the Jews have gathered to celebrate God sacrificing his child without feeling the revulsion. Perhaps they can do so because they excuse any act attributed to God as acceptable, and too often because they blame the Jews for the

---

2. Isa 53:5.

actions they claim their God planned and executed. In my opinion, it is an annual emotional return to the adrenaline, celebration, and release of sanctioned torture and murder. Even by the accounts of scholars who do not believe in Jesus of Nazareth as the Christ of the church, this was the brutal murder of a human being.[3]

Of course, believers are focused strongly on the resurrection. My wife and I still love the sermon refrain of, "It's Friday, but Sunday's coming!"[4] I suppose for the non-believing working class this often becomes, it's the workweek, but Saturday's coming! It is a statement of hope after endurance of what is undesirable. It is a powerful emotional tool to always look to the good that will arrive as we work through the pain that is present. Believing in the literal resurrection of Jesus is the foundation of all Christian teachings concerning our own status as eternal beyond the grave. But belief requires belief. All of the evidence that this murder was rewarded with glorification comes within the texts written by those who believed. Some of the weakest sermons I ever heard came from pastors who tried to prove that the evidence of resurrection meets current standards of proof. It just does not. You either choose to believe it or you do not. So, I see a lot of turning to emphasize the enormity of the price that was paid, the disgusting details of the death, in order to make people feel guilty if they reject the protection of the blood.

I do not believe it is finished. I do however find spring to be the perfect time to celebrate that life begins again. Give me the return of budding leaves and blooming flowers. Give me *Regalis* emerging from the soil to dry and spread wings as Gene Stratton Porter's Yellow Emperor.[5] Explain to me how the seed that falls and is buried emerges in spring as new life and I am with you. Sit with me and watch the new generations of rabbits and squirrels play behind my house and the young hawk soar overhead and we can marvel at the renewal of the web of life. It is not finished, it is renewed.

As I try to turn this essay to an ending of hope and affirmation of what is good, I am reminded that the renewal is not guaranteed. The species that are becoming extinct are not reappearing with the next birthing season. When the life of the last of their kind is finished, it is finished. And in the Anthropocene Era, it may be fair to cast us as the Roman soldiers

3. Ehrmann, *How Jesus Became God*.
4. Bramley, "It's Friday."
5. The literary symbol of hope and new beginnings she uses throughout *A Girl of the Limberlost*.

doing what we are told and not mourning what we kill. There could come a spring worse than the one Rachel Carson predicted when none of us come out of winter quarantine to rejoice in the annual renewal. Some say we have already waited so long that a current generation or one soon to be born will experience Friday without Sunday. Some of our best scientific minds have said we must prepare to emerge completely from Earth and fly away to a new home on another moon or planet. I personally am no more drawn to a story of our resurrection after the crucifixion of our planet than I am to grotesque reminders of the tortures of Rome.

I will continue to choose the Tree of Life, and the life of trees. I will continue to take hope from the return of flowers and bees. I will hope even when the evidence suggests otherwise that humans will not choose death over life as our final contribution to the universe. I will hope that we will transcend the behaviors which make us appear to be a plague upon the planet. And if we do not, I will use what I have been taught by Native Americans and sing my death song in gratitude. For dozens of springs now, I have been blessed to wonder at life's resurrection. I do not have to return to ancient rituals to affirm it. I will walk out my door and join it. I will endure the dying of fall, even if it is the final fall, trusting that the universe will do what it does, life will do what life does, and whatever new thing comes to preeminence will celebrate in our place. For now, I will feel the breeze, soak in the rain, and soar with the hawk because I do not have to cling to any blood cult to celebrate the resurrection all around me.

Life in Prism[1]

4/13/2020

BART EHRMAN'S RECENT INTERVIEW ON NPR[2] reminded me of different religious beliefs which either see the body and soul as one, or teach that the body is a temporary residence, sometimes an imprisonment, of the soul. My own evangelical upbringing included some of the latter. I remember singing along with Christian rock founder Larry Norman that we were only visiting this planet. Pain and suffering belonged to this realm inhabited by bodies of flesh. Heaven's bliss was for the soul after we left our mortal form behind, at least until Jesus returned and gave us all eternal bodies free from flaws.

At the most extreme, the body is seen as evil and in competition with the soul after salvation. Life is described by Paul as a constant battle between what we wish we would do and what we actually do[3]—a battle that has often led to seeing the body as evil and the soul as good. All pleasures of the body are then suspect as temptation to evil. This led some of the nineteenth-century utopian societies in the United States including the Harmonists and Shakers to shun all marital relations as products of sin and hinderances to realizing the perfect life of the soul. In other parts of the world, it has led to practices which actually harm the body in search of purifying the soul.

The closest my views in UFT come to this are that we are unique combinations of quanta that combine for a time as conscious humans

---

1. Word use intentional but not intended as humorous.
2. Gross, "Heaven and Hell".
3. Rom 7.

and then return to the universe to become part of other forms. This leads me to a different mental imagery than an ethereal soul lurking within a physical form. We exchange quanta many times during our lives inviting the mind away from images of an internal spiritual being that is eternally us clothed for a time in human flesh.

As photons of light are some of the best-known quanta, it invites me to see life as that point where the light passes through a prism. When bright light hits the prism, it glows. When light leaves the prism, it divides to reveal the beauty of its diversity. It matches for me the way people realize and remember all of the best qualities and talents of loved ones who are no longer with us. When we are at our best, we say that our colors shine during life's events. It is all natural and continuous. The quanta are doing what all quanta do. And the brief time of illuminating the prism as our lives seems far more positive to me than talk of imprisonment in our mortal form.

My mind stretches the image even further. The image of a polished glass prism seems too permanent and determinate. It is solid and does not appear to grow or change over time except for glowing more brightly at some times than others. Until an experimental design forces quanta to behave in certain ways, they exist in a cloud of possible forms, locations, and movement. A cloud of mist better fits my mental image of the quantum cloud of potential which surrounds and contains us. It also hints at the constant interchange that often eludes our senses.

Light striking the mist still encounters millions of prisms and displays the visible portion of its spectrum. The image I choose is made up of the mist of a waterfall which I believe also indicates the dynamic nature of the universal background in which we exist on our spinning, orbiting, weather swept planet. It is all in motion and in flux. Even though the water is constantly replaced and always new, the world seems more permanent than us. The life cycle of the rock, worn away by the water on nature's geologic schedule, is long enough to seem permanent in comparison to our time. As the mist and the light shift and change, the glowing displays come and go.

And all that composes us exists before us, submits by the laws of nature for a time to be us—transforming in shape and luminosity even as we live—and then it passes on as it was before us. The miracle included is that we are aware that we are, aware of the shining others that surround us, and aware of the background forces that form and sustain us. Reading current ideas that consciousness may be present in all quanta and increases with the complexity of their arrangement,[4] my mind wonders what consciousness unknown to us may reside in the water and the rock. Does the water enjoy the rush of the journey and the delight of joining with light to give us our existence? Does the rock notice the changing flow of water across the seasons and enjoy the show of our appearance in the mist?[5] At least at present, we have no way to detect or measure consciousness in inanimate objects, and the logical assumption of most of science is that it does not exist. However, current work in quantum physics is causing some to question the basic nature and source of consciousness. I find great joy in imagining the possibilities!

This is simply my offering of a different mental image. To my mind it captures the transience and interactive nature of our existence, the beauty of our moment in the sun, and the continuation of all that composes us in uninterrupted displays of natural wonder. The dancing visual of it brings me joy.

Shine on.

---

4. Gornitz, "Quantum Theory," and Kastrup et al., "Coming to Grips."

5. If Jesus of Nazareth had special awareness of life as it is, did he mean something more than people understood when he said that if the people were silenced the stones themselves would "cry out" in Luke 19:14?

Antisemitism and the "Old Testament"

4/17/2020

THE INTERPRETATION OF THE BIBLE that I was taught from childhood claimed that what Christian Bible's labels the Old Testament was an accurate reproduction of the Jewish holy scriptures. Ignoring the fact that the two are not the same and that Jews do not consider all of the writings equal in their significance as we were taught, this would appear to be inclusive of Jewish heritage within the writings considered holy by Christians and does not sound in any way like an antisemitic approach to the past. I now see it very differently.

Starting with the most obvious, labeling the entire Bible before the Gospels as the Old Testament (OT) dates back to Melito of Sardis in the second century. It automatically, if unconsciously, gives priority to the New Testament (NT) within the general mindset of Western society. This can be seen in a sampling of marketing appeals. People want the *new and improved* version of anything from laundry soap to motor vehicles. Apple has shown that customers will spend close to a thousand dollars every year or so simply to have the newest iPhone when their current phone is still completely functional. Even when an appeal is made to the nostalgia of returning to the old way of doing things, people want modern safe packaging of their traditional food or cure, automatic air-conditioning and heat in their rented log cabins, and Wi-Fi, or at least cellular service for continuous access to the latest information from family, entertainment, and the news. There are counterexamples, but it seems to me that they stand out as exceptions that prove the rule. If there is an old and a new option available, the new is the standard choice.

In theology the focus on old and new reaches more significant proportions. Dividing the Bible into old and new testaments (testimonies) is accompanied by a theology of old and new covenants that dates back to the early church fathers. The teachings of the OT are presented as records of God's former covenants, or agreements, with a specific group while the NT is said to present God's new way of relating to all people. The negative belief hiding in plain sight here toward the Jews is that they are still observing a way of connecting with the divine that has been replaced by a new and superior covenant. The typical expression of this presents the OT as trying to be right with God through obedience to the law, while the NT shows relationship with God to be freely available by grace through the gift of Jesus Christ. Paul's writings provide easy material for any sermon desiring to point out the futility of trying to reach God by works of the law instead of accepting the gift of salvation through Jesus. These presentations often move into blatant antisemitism by equating the following of the law with human pride and a self-righteous belief that humans are capable of being good enough to match God's holiness. In theological terms, those who continue to revere the OT are said, or implied, to cling to a manner of holiness that has been superseded by the arrival of grace through Jesus Christ. At its worst this form of teaching accuses the Jews of first-century Palestine of being so stubborn in clinging to their own self-righteous ideas that they participated in the killing of Jesus rather than hearing his message of divine love and acceptance.

A book that influenced me heavily when I was in high school was Edith Schaeffer's *Christianity Is Jewish*. In her book, she built a case for seeing the entire Bible as one continuous writing by focusing on the claims of NT scriptures such as Hebrews, believed to have been written specifically for Jews. These passages are used to lay out an interpretation of salvation through faith in God during both the time before and after Jesus. This argument claims that it was Abraham's faith in God, not his acts of obedience, that made him holy and worthy to be the father of three faith traditions. She illustrated this with a graph separating biblical characters onto two diverging lines representing those who lived by faith and those who did not. Easily added to this is the fact that Jesus of Nazareth was clearly a Jew who attended the synagogues and taught from the only scripture in existence at the time, the Jewish scripture. It satisfied me for a time and resulted in my adopting the habit of wearing a Star of David with a cross in the center, a habit which I continue to this day as a symbol of inclusivity and against antisemitism.

Other problems with this division of the Bible have become more apparent to me. Christians who read the Bible in this way still place the OT in a secondary position to the NT. This is often done by interpreting everything in the OT as pointing to Jesus and the events of the NT. When God is quoted in Genesis as telling the serpent that he will strike Eve's offspring's heel while her offspring will bruise his head, the Christian interpretation is that God announced from the beginning the day that Satan would participate in the slaying of Jesus who would defeat him by providing the sacrifice required for the forgiveness of all believers. Never mind that no such Jewish interpretation of the same Jewish text has ever existed. The pattern then continues throughout the entire OT. Characters in the history of Israel are not just who the text says they are, they are archetypes or symbols for Jesus or those who believe in him. Jewish prophesies are not read as dealing with things at the time they are said to have happened but are read instead as prophesies of Jesus of Nazareth or the Jesus of a future triumphant second coming. None of it is Jewish truth from Jewish scriptures. Instead, the overarching narrative of salvation through Jesus Christ in the NT is read into every portion of the OT. To drive home the point I wish was obvious, the OT is used to predict the NT and the supremacy of the church in ways that indicate by contrast that all who remain Jews are wrong about the meaning of their own sacred writings.

God's commands in the OT are not interpreted by the Christians of my experience as a reformed rabbi would explain the significance of the *mitzvot*. Instead of rules for living a proper life on Earth, to be lived as well as possible, and calling for making amends when possible if violated, they are presented as divine law for all time proving that everyone is guilty before God and in need of the sacrificial blood of Jesus in order to live forever in heaven.[1] The entire concept of living life in the here and now in harmony with the plans of the Creator and the order of creation is lost in the story of man's need for a divine savior. In too many instances, a single act of saying a particular prayer of acceptance into Christianity is given total dominance over the original emphasis on living as decent humans being. When the rules for life are considered in the Christian context, they are too often used as statements by God confirming one's rejection of others rather than personal guidance for each day's choices and actions.

1. An idea that scholars such as Bart Ehrman say is probably not what Jesus taught.

I am also forced to include Christian obsession with the violence of the OT accounts of the establishment of the nation and battles against invading enemies. These passages are too often used to contrast an OT God of wrath and destruction with a NT God of love and compassion even though both testaments are included in one volume referred to as the Bible which is supposedly the continuous story of a single God. The ancient descriptions of total conquest of others including women, children, and animals are unsettling to minds which have been taught that mankind is now civilized and would never commit such barbaric acts. And we maintain these mental and emotional distinctions even as our own government continues to rain bombs on other countries in the name of keeping us safe at home. Never mind that modern bombs also make no distinction between victims and often fall on the full variety of the population. We see ourselves as good people doing what must be done. Which is exactly what the OT claims that the people of Israel were doing although their battles were direct and close to home while ours are conducted far away and out of our view, frequently protecting us from the troubling knowledge of what is being done in our name. I will only mention in passing that libraries of material already exist on just war, the crusades, the age of conquest, the age of Christian empire, slavery and genocide against native people in lands claimed in the name of Christ, in addition to the denial of basic rights to women and children under the Christian teaching that males are the head of the household and all others subject to their domination. None of these ever seem to be part of the conversation when sermons or Sunday school lessons consider violence in the texts of the OT.

What is the lesson of those ancient texts? I assert that we commit a serious error in interpretation if we read them as divine sanction for total destruction of rivals. One problem is in translation with a Hebrew term meaning to give wholly over to God translated as "to destroy completely." The careful student of the OT will also find that descendants of people supposedly destroyed show up in later stories. There is also the example of the Moabites who would never have any part in Israel later followed by the much-loved story of Ruth the Moabite who becomes a member of Israel and is named in the NT as an ancestor of Jesus.

Another problem with these texts as literal accounts of real events, in spite of the efforts of Christian literalists and Israeli hardliners wishing to justify total occupation of all land within the description of ancient boundaries, is that the archaeological evidence is missing. There simply is no record in the diggings of the middle east to verify this massive immigration of people at one single time or of their total destruction of their enemies' towns. So far, I am stating the negative. I do not believe that the lesson of these ancient stories is that God orders annihilation of enemies or did so in more barbaric times—a very value-laden judgement including ignorance of our own violence.

I propose that there are two things hiding in these stories of apparent[2] total inhumanity. The first factor hiding in full sight is that these are stories of God's total power on behalf of the people. The point is not the total loss of the enemy. It is the total victory of those aligned with God. Here is the lesson which became evident as I considered some of these passages with Bible college students in Haiti. The first point of these texts for their own people was that God is completely dependable to overcome all odds. The God who can free the slaves of Egypt, guide the former slaves who know no other home through the wilderness until they are ready to be a nation, and remove all obstacles to their coming home and remaining there in safety while they remain loyal to the truth can handle any enemy faced by the faithful.

Second, and related to the first, the power of those who are aligned with truth is not to be taken lightly. I turn to this aspect based on best estimates of when the written records of the Jews from which we take the OT were written. Bible scholars tell us that the Torah was recorded in Babylon with some use of earlier material.[3] As such these writings could be reminders to the people that they belong in a different place both physically and socially. They are not to give in to a permanent condition of submission to others. At the same time, they might serve as a message to their oppressors that they should not take lightly the God that defeated Egypt and all other opponents in the past. My mind forms an image of a Jewish scribe asking a member of the dominant society how to express the idea that God completely and utterly defeated all former enemies of his people the Jews. Then, I imagine a conversation meant to be repeated assuring the captor that this past is true, and the Jewish people are not as weak as they may appear to those who have developed superior weapons because Jewish strength in battle is from beyond the human realm of power. In other words, I see purposes to these stories which are different from recording, with the accuracy demanded of the

2. Apparent in people we consider to be different from ourselves.
3. Brueggemann, *Theology*, 74.

discipline of history, actual events, or commands of God. They are myths of power and assurance of victory.

Finally confining the widely varied texts of the OT to God's old way of relating to his people robs them of power for the current reader. Seeing the story of the garden as a one-time event determining the permanent fate of humanity robs it of the power to show us ourselves living always before the choice of the two trees which is now one of the most powerful metaphors of my life.[4] Seeing the Psalms only as songs of the ancients can prevent us from relating to the psalmist who cries out so many times in fear, anger and anguish followed by affirmation of power and salvation from trouble. Seeing the stories of Abraham, Isaac, and Jacob as true history of the first generations of the people who will become the Jews prevents us from seeing ourselves in their places, lying because of fear, scheming in order to overcome negative customs or the trickery of others, or being willing to wrestle all night with the very idea of God.[5] Seeing the OT as a unified whole leading toward the single point of the life of Jesus robs us of the interplay of forces in the texts—some of which praise the power and glory of the kings and others which present the prophetic call for justice on behalf of the people.[6] The combination of texts is actually beautiful in its complexity, presenting an interplay of very opposite ideas and ideals. There is much here to enrich the pursuit of a proper life in the twenty-first century as we continue to explore the balance of the privileges of power with the call of justice for all of the people. For us to be able to inhabit the stories and gain inspiration to live our own lives with power, we must be able to see them as ours and read them in new ways. We cannot consign them to others, the Jews alone, or to a violent ancient past by considering them just the Old Testament. Reading them in that way robs them of current meaning and leads to negative, sometimes hate-filled attitudes towards the very people who created them in reverence to God and their experiences of God's power.

---

4. Brown, "Two Trees," 166–68.

5. I have used God in this essay in ways that appear to parallel the original texts. My definitions, however, have not changed. I see these ancient stories as accounts of people's experiences of, and references to, the omnipotent, omnipresent power that controls the universe. I do not believe that power ever was a human-like personage that chose favorites in any covenants old or new. Nevertheless, there is much in these ancient stories which can speak to us of human meaning if we do not separate ourselves from them by labels or beliefs that they are for a barbaric *them* and not *us*.

6. Brueggemann, *Theology*, 644–46.

A Different Reading of Genesis 3

4/19/2020

AT THE SUGGESTION OF A friend, I have recently been considering the work of Maurice Blanchot. In doing so, I worked my way through *The Disavowed Community* looking at the interplay of the ideas of Blanchot and Jean-Luc Nancy. I shared my impressions including the idea that everything we know exists against a background of nothingness[1] with a small circle of friends. One of the responses that came back was a question, concerning why it would take so long for the concept of zero to develop if everything was set against a background of nothingness.

I believe the answer in math is that zero means very little alone as a symbol of nothingness. Language can have simple words for needing food, having no children, or seeing no enemies on the horizon. The significance of zero is as a placeholder in the construction of larger numbers. I believe the current theory is that the need for this probably matched the growth of trade in larger quantities of objects or material requiring a more elegant form of expression in math.[2] The question; however, took my mind someplace further to consider when humans developed the awareness of nothing, especially the return to nothing at death. That question caused me to consider the story Christians commonly refer to as the fall in a new way.

---

1. This idea interests me in light of developing understandings of the universe at the quantum level pointing to a universe made up of quanta—that have no size and no clear definition until forced through an experiment—but out of which all other things are made.

2. Kaplan, *Nothing That Is*, 100–109, 110–11.

A Different Reading of Genesis 3

I should note at the beginning that I am well aware that any claim to have found the correct new interpretation of any of the ancient texts is to contradict millennia of church teachings, an act of hubris likely to be dismissed on the basis of its audacity. I am sharing these thoughts as another possible reading of the original, and not as a substitute for all that has gone before.

My previous views of Genesis 3 have centered on the traditional interpretation as the story of the first sin leading to the beginning of death, and I have written in other essays about my concerns with the very specific interpretations I was first taught by the church. What I am now considering is that it is also the story of the first knowledge of death, an awareness that in many ways is equivalent to the discovery of what is negative, or evil, in the universe. What if this ancient story is about mankind's first awareness of the return to nothingness?

The story is followed immediately in the current version by the killing of one son by the other—the first recorded death. If we maintain typical Western ways of reading a sequence, what comes after is normally considered an effect of what happens before and not as a cause. But I do not believe we are required to read the story in this way if we remember that it existed for a long period of time as an oral tradition before it was recorded as a written progression. If we do not return to the theology of literal translation of Scripture believed to have been given in complete accuracy through inspiration by the Spirit of God, we may consider other alternatives for the development of the account.

I want to note here that moving away from the literal interpretation is not new. The literal version has always had theological problems as I have noted before. It is difficult to see how two people innocent of any knowledge of what is good and what is evil can cause all of humanity to be guilty of having made the wrong choice, or to accept as loving and just a creator who would leave them exposed to such peril. Recent publications debating the existence of heaven and hell point to a different problem with this story as a literal account of God's first response to the commission of sin by humans. The God in this story who cares enough to make them their first clothing and teach them about what is to come says nothing about any afterlife. God does not tell them what they must do in order to spend eternity in bliss after earthly death. Neither are they told how to avoid an afterlife of eternal torment. To use this as the foundational story of sin requiring the eventual blood sacrifice of God become man and acceptance of salvation through that blood as a determiner of one's eternal fate, we are confronted immediately by the problem that the story makes no mention of any life beyond death. The story is about humanity's original encounters with God, evil, and death.

As a person who enjoys the world of the mind, I could write paragraphs about how the events all go together but might have changed order and details from the original oral tradition to the later written version. Many scribes have reordered and embellished events in order to make a stronger tale. Perhaps someone more talented in the writing of fiction than myself could do so with the ideas here and create a format which readers would enjoy. I will restrict myself to the idea that this beginning of the Christian Bible is a tale of humanity's first encounters with three factors—God, evil, and death.

Stepping away from the traditional reading of this as the story of the first two people,[3] I wish to contemplate the interplay of these factors. Humans most certainly emerged surrounded by many forms of life and would surely have encountered dead animals. I do not believe anyone can retrace events to produce an actual account of the first encounter with death by conscious and reflective human beings. We now have strong evidence that other species also experience the loss of death, suggesting humans may have emerged already aware of death. Man's first awareness of the descent back to nothingness is undoubtedly lost in the distant past. I see an account like this as a sense-making exercise that would have evolved over time to explain the nature of existence and the presence of death. And this brings me to the central thought of this essay.

While our focus has traditionally accepted God's presence in the story as a given having just created the world and the people, I believe there is another way to see the story. As human society evolved and developed shared explanations of life, current evidence suggests that the idea of a grand law-establishing God arrived later rather than earlier.[4] This suggests that the ideas of death and negative behavior came first and invites me to reconsider an alternative view of this well-known story. Perhaps as people evolved the concept of an almighty God, it was also natural to assume that almighty being as present from the beginning. That would place God in the story of our first encounters with death and evil. As a story of the emergence of death and evil, it may be an assertion

---

3. The interpretation of the early chapters of Genesis as the story of the literal first family has its own problems as their son is afraid of other people when banished, their children find others to marry, and Cain finds enough people to establish a city.

4. Whitehouse et al., "Complex Societies."

that whenever that awareness of life's ultimate challenge to meaning emerged, the comforting power of a loving God was already there as well.

When I think of the story in this way it speaks to me of comfort rather than condemnation. Rather than a story of the pre-existing God condemning humanity for being imperfect, perhaps we can approach the account as a reassurance of God's presence when things go wrong and even when death interrupts life. The God in this story is a sense-making God who explains life to the people. This God is a caring presence who teaches them to make clothing to end the embarrassment of their nakedness. It makes sense to me that as people explored the idea of an all-powerful God, they would look back to the legends explaining the emergence of human life with its pleasures and its suffering and assume that God must have always been there. In other words, humans confronted with the limits of life would seek to explain why life ends, but they would also picture any all-powerful God as having been there. One way, the traditional way, to combine the two is with God as the judge who declares death as a penalty for human failing. I now think it may also make sense to look back at the same origin story and see instead a God who is always here and who was always there when life went wrong, allowing death to exert its painful reality.

While I believe that the omni-present, omni-powerful controller of the universe is found in the combined forces of physics, I would not dissuade anyone from believing in this God who is present and cares at the time of our greatest losses. The God of Genesis who seeks out the people, who covers their shame, who explains the world to them is a God of great comfort. This is an interpretation of Old Testament texts I often see overlooked by Christian theologians seeking to build contrast between the role of God before and after Jesus. The Old Testament actually includes many stories of God befriending humans in their time of need. Israel's story of God is the story of the God who dwells among the people.

It has often been said that science and observation can tell us how and when things happen but cannot tell us why. So, from ancient times to the present, we construct stories. The great power of the universe that continues to exceed our total comprehension inhabits the ancient stories of the Torah and the Bible as a character who walks and converses with humans. As I look back at this story, I am drawn to the characterization of that universal power as a source of both understanding and comfort even when we face our hardest questions and our greatest losses.

Quantum Reality of All Things

4/20/2020

The eternal began as nothingness.
Nothingness gave birth to everything.
Every thing is composed of not things.
The energy of not things sustains everything.
Every thing returns to not things,
The source and sustenance of all things.[1]

---

1. Quanta are not things or energy until forced through an experiment designed to interpret them as one or the other.

The Blood

4/30/2020

CHRISTIAN FRIENDS CONCERNED ABOUT MY new beliefs, or possible unbelief, want to know if I am still saved. One of the strangest and to my mind archaic ways of determining this is to ask if I am washed or covered by the blood of Jesus. There is even a belief that this expression has unique powers over demons and that no person under the influence of evil forces will claim the blood.

Raised in a tradition firm on the permanence of salvation, the simple answer would be that I am. I fully accepted my nature as a sinner, my need for a savior, and the need to accept Jesus Christ as my Lord and Savior as a child. Our church took communion only on special occasions believing that weekly partaking of the sacraments weakened people's understanding of the importance and power of that came from recognizing our debt and gratitude for the blood sacrifice of Jesus. I believed and lived it all as fully as I was able.

Through most of my life, one of my greatest pleasures was leading another person to accept salvation through Jesus Christ and begin living the rest of their life as a Christian. I faithfully taught the church doctrines of the necessity of being covered by the blood in order to be forgiven for both personal and original sin. I have claimed the power of the blood in prayer when I believed I was involved in very real battles with spiritual forces of evil. I experienced the strength that faith gives in times of trouble as well as the joy of feeling connected to divine power when life was at its most positive. And I know the phenomenal assurance I felt when news arrived in Ethiopia that a deadly tornado had passed through the area of my home with all of my daughters there. I had no doubt they were either safe in this world or safe in the next because they were covered by the blood. I have lived in the joyful assurance of walking in the presence and protection of the risen Christ seated in the throne room of heaven as well as inhabiting my own being due to his willing sacrifice on the cross.

I wish I could stop there because I know the comfort it would give to people worried about my eternal destiny. The best I can offer is that my belief in the permanence of salvation was as strong as any belief I ever held. New doubts that a just and loving God would torture anyone forever for simply living as a human being add to the number of humans I believe are living in harmony with the power of the universe. New questions and examinations of the nature of the source and sustenance of the universe do not reduce my belief in the importance of living in harmony with that power. But the entire imagery of blood sacrifice now disturbs me as a continuing belief in the twenty-first century.

I wonder how many people would condone any other form of blood sacrifice today. Surely educated human beings in the year 2020 would object to the slaughtering of any animal as part of a religious ritual. I have friends who will not accept the killing of animals as a means of supplying food and who have chosen to become vegetarian or vegan. And I believe that any level of government in my country would call the sacrifice of any human by the simple name of murder. The same Christians who claim to be covered in blood by accepting Jesus look at the ancient temple practices of the Jews as law-based practice that may have pointed to the future sacrifice of Jesus but was in its own right insufficient to bring forgiveness of sins and usually consigned in some way to practices of a more barbaric antiquity. Societies believed to still practice blood sacrifice are considered evil and destructive. I have been in multiple conversations where Christians actively involved in missionary work blamed Haiti's poverty and suffering on the dedication of the country to Satan or local demons by blood sacrifice. I wish I could say that all condemnation of Jews based on conspiracy theories that they still practice blood, or even human, sacrifice had been left in the past. But they remain in some groups as powerful motivations for rejection and hatred of the Jewish people. For me, it renders Sunday morning habits of joyfully singing about being bathed in the wonderful blood of Jesus feeling like an absurd celebration of cultural traditions we would reject in any other context.

My mental image has shifted. If I am covered in blood, my mind goes quickly to other events. As a descendent and heir of Euro-Christians, I see myself covered in the blood shed by those who used military might against other cultures in the name of Jesus Christ. Raised in the faith which maintained control of Europe through much of its history, am I not beneficiary of the blood shed by the crusades? Living in comfort in the Ohio River Valley of North America, am I not a recipient of the shed blood of the Miami and other indigenous nations who lived here before men like William Henry Harrison brought the area to statehood by genocide? When I get in one of my cars and drive for the sheer pleasure of the experience, am I not enjoying the benefit of US oil wars as well as the destruction of other species by our constant pollution of the atmosphere? When I now consider an ancient metaphor, such as being covered by blood, the imagery that immediately comes to mind is the sacrifice of untold thousands of human beings and other living things in order to give me this land, this wealth, and these privileges.

But the imagery and its power persist. As an example, while the current pandemic continues, I see the son of famous evangelist Billy Graham on TV nightly inviting people to pray the prayer I use to delight in leading. But now I cringe when the original thought is that humans are evil rather than good. I hesitate at the idea that it is those who accept this specific doctrine of salvation who can be assured that the universal power is on their side eliminating their need for fear. And I am politically aware enough to suspect that people are being invited to salvation so that Franklin Graham's organizations can gain leverage to guide them to vote in the way he desires them to vote. It is a less physical kind of violence—a preying on people's fear to build power for the person claiming to care about their current and eternal condition. Maintaining the language of metaphor, politics is a bloody enterprise which worships human, not universal, power.

One of the most difficult and rewarding tasks of my journey from childhood to adult maturity has been learning to take responsibility for my beliefs, decisions, and actions. If I am short with my wife, impatient with restaurant employees, furious with other drivers, or condescending in my view of others with different beliefs, the person who experiences those emotions and engages in those behaviors is me. I cannot blame them on spirits I no longer believe exist as external realities. They are mine. If I am kind and understanding instead, I recognize a debt to those who raised me and who demonstrated life well-lived. But the current actions are mine, not those of some invisible puppeteer acting through me. And I see the power of the promise that some supernatural force can wash away all of the bad and leave only the good if I simply confess the all-important prayer and accept salvation by the blood. As appalled as I am by a belief system in the nature of all things which begins with the idea of human evil, I see the comfort and power of being promised that everything wrong can simply be rinsed away no matter how unattractive the imagery of the solvent is.

Am I covered by the blood? I accepted it long ago if salvation through Jesus Christ is real and permanent. I also see myself inheriting the blood stains of civilizations slaughtered for my present life of comfort. I no longer call on others to accept teachings of being saved by being bathed in blood. I do continue to hope, teach, and pray that we may grow more and more worthy of the blood that was shed, and continues to be shed, on our behalf. Maybe someday we will value the blood that runs through the veins of our neighbors, enemies, and fellow species as much as we now value our own sense of psychological peace and physical comfort. At Wounded Knee and Tiananmen Square I have felt the wounds of blood shed by those seeking to live in human dignity. Maybe it is time to be done with talk of the spilling of blood by God or man and transcend instead to holy preservation of the life-giving liquid that courses through the bodies of our Earthly companions.

Why I Write About Hope

5/1/2020

WE ARE NOW LIVING THROUGH a period in world history where hope stands at center stage. Why should a person who is young and healthy give up employment and social life to obey stay-at-home orders during a pandemic? They are asked to do so from the hope that the infection and death rate curves may be flattened—in less cold and statistical terms, to hope that more people may live to participate in the recovery from the current crisis. Without hope, there would be little motivation to sacrifice in the present.

My thoughts begin in a darker place. I know the pain when hope evades my consciousness. As an uncoordinated child I felt strongly the despair of never obtaining the physical and athletic skills so attached to male identity by classmates and my very athletic father. As a student I often felt that while teachers acknowledged the quality of my work, I was not among the group constantly chosen for leadership and social recognition. I experienced the deep pain for years of a body that would not properly digest food leaving me often ill and without the strength to go and do things I very much wanted to do. As a young man, I watched the one young woman who was dearest to me choose to marry another man. During a career in education, I watched hope that the larger system would take note of our innovations with expelled students and improve education for all children turn into rejection and the eventual demise of our program. As a father I experienced the rebellion of daughters who rejected the beliefs we raised them within earlier than I did. And, as I later documented in *Unified Field Theology*, I reached a place where the Christian belief systems which were the total basis for my understanding of both meaning and hope as a young man became impossible to maintain while also adhering to a lifelong commitment to follow the truth wherever it led.

All of these things are resolved by time and life experience. I discovered the sport of climbing where my tall frame and extremely low weight equaled ability rather than inability. I grew to enjoy non-competitive sports like skateboarding and skiing where the only determiner of success was the joy of the ride and managing to avoid any injury too serious to allow one to ride tomorrow. I reached years of enjoying surprising teachers by defying their expectations based on my chosen long-haired appearance. I was elected president of my high school student government. I went on to graduate college as the sole summa cum laude of my commencement year and eventually to earn my doctorate by experimenting with the ideas I chose. My physical condition was finally diagnosed and in retirement years I have a successful treatment plan that allows me to be healthy. Life took its strange turns and losing the career I thought I would follow resulted in returning to my hometown and marrying the woman I thought I lost after her own life took an unexpected and painful turn. While local officials refused to recognize the accomplishments of the teachers and students in my alternative school, officials at the state level did and awarded me not only plaques to treasure but also opportunities to work with leaders from multiple other school systems looking for ways to teach the students they did not know how to reach. Teen years passed and family relationships healed and grew. All of my daughters grew up and entered caring professions where I watch them live out the values I hold most dear. And I have found in the broad scope of human knowledge including science affirmation for values and beliefs which cause me to continually affirm that while God is not the limited character I knew as a child, the creating sustaining power of the universe is very real and active as it always has been. Situations that appeared hopeless at the moment became part of the pathway to understanding and a very real fascination and delight with paradox and the unknowable as the significance of life's events unfolded in the rearview mirror.

But I know the pain of facing situations where hope is evasive. I know the temptation to simply give up on it all and stop living a life of contemplation or even to live at all. For me there is no other life than one which includes contemplation and the search for meaning which can be shared in healing ways with others. As I write this essay, I feel strongly the paradox of recognizing that my life became an amazing journey which took me physically around the globe as well as mentally and spiritually into the universe and at the same time feeling deep pain as I watch events unfold that may well indicate that my country and my species are moving into years of collapse having pushed our consumption beyond any level that can be maintained.

I also know the manipulative power of asserting that specific beliefs are the only path to resilience when faced with pain and a lack of hope. I was thoroughly trained in the doctrines that claimed life only makes sense and has true value within a very specific set of religious beliefs and behaviors. I know the power of feeling that those beliefs work within the circle of believers amid constant mutual reassurance that everything is working the way it should if seen through the correct lenses of faith. Now I watch my country divided into opposite political camps that each claim to have the only path forward to a productive and sustainable society. When beliefs in religion or a religious commitment to political ideology are presented as the only correct path to hope and the alternatives are seen as a foolish and reckless rushing to eminent ruin, freeing the mind to consider alternatives or the truth that exists in the paradox of apparent opposites coexisting becomes almost impossible. In competitive contexts that devalue and demonize all alternatives conflict, hostility, and violence toward all opponents appear where hope and belonging are promised.

I speak of hope from the base of evidence in the universe, the beauty of paradox amidst apparently conflicting beliefs, and the joy of being human in a way that values and uplifts other humans being. Do things look hopeless? Viewed through many different lenses from belief systems to the purity of mathematics and statistical probabilities our very existence to contemplate such things is impossible. But we are here, nonetheless. The power that creates and sustains the universe produced Earth. On Earth it produced the exact conditions over the extreme periods required to produce us. The same power continues to flood our planet daily with the energy that drives the cycles which provide our sustenance and ability to live. And whether consciousness turns out to be unique to higher-level beings or present in every quantum building block of the universe we are aware, observing, and thinking beings capable of wonder and gratitude. It is true for me raised with Christian beliefs in a capitalistic democratic republic, and it is true for friends I met raised under Chinese communism which opposes any added beliefs, and Muslims I met living under a dictatorial regime in Ethiopia. The beauty of our existence is not bound by the religious, political, or social systems in which we find ourselves.

Humans can transcend if we are not bound by fear that the systems we know and have been taught to treasure are the only ones that work.

I write about hope from a position of hope that acknowledges pain. If we realize that we are all children and heirs of Earth, there is hope that more and more of us might escape the narrow pathways we were presented in our youth. The pandemic which currently interrupts all of our lives makes it abundantly clear that we no longer live in separated individual tribes unaffected by each other. A virulent new disease that emerges in one group no longer remains the tragedy of that group alone. Global economics and travel now connect every human being on Earth. We have the proof in the statistics of this disease in 2020. There are leaders and groups still demanding that everything must be done according to their beliefs, their self-interests, and their advantage over others. But there is also the possibility that the number of people who see humanity as one group bound by common fate and potentially buoyed by common hope will increase due to an expanded awareness of our common fate in a time of pain.

Diseases do not give preferential treatment based on any of our mental categories. They do show differences in vulnerability for various groups based on social and environmental factors. But, like everything in the universe, they act within the same forces which created and sustain the observable world.

I write about hope knowing that light is most obvious against an environment of darkness. It is as we sit at the edge of possible environmental and economic collapse that I am most hopeful there will also be people who see past narrow definitions and begin to work along with others to pursue a more positive future for the planet and our life on it. Those who see hope and power in pursuing the common good are the ones who will do the work which may save us all. I call to mind colleagues, friends, and former students who have the hearts and minds to pursue the work, and I choose hope.

Life After Life

5/11/2020

Refrain
I died the day they shot Kennedy,
Dr. King and Lennon too.
I died when I saw Kent State,
Jackson State and Wounded Knee.
But we're still here and we're still we.

They ask me if I still believe in eternity.
I live it every time a dear life goes away.
Do I believe in resurrection?
It's hard to count
How many times I've died.
(Refrain)
They ask me if I still hope,
For something beyond the dark,
Valley that engulfs us now.
I see the sun and stars as they rise again,
After every moonless ink blot night.
(Refrain)
They ask me if I believe in hell.
I've seen it in my city,
On dirt roads, and deep inside my soul.
I've seen it in your eyes,
When the world refused to let your good gifts grow.

(Refrain)
They ask If I know there's a heaven.
I've held her in my arms.
I've seen her in the mountains
And heard her in a thousand songs.
We find her every time,
We live as simply we.
(Refrain)

The Trinity and Unified Field Theology

5/1/2020

IN SEVERAL OF MY ESSAYS on how the forces studied in physics fulfill the ancient characteristics of God I have used the singular form of force—the force or power that created and sustains the universe. I have done this for parallel language with the use of the singular noun God even though I am well aware that science has yet to arrive at a single theory or equation that combines the weak and strong nuclear forces, electromagnetism, and gravity into one unified format.

This usage might seem to indicate a linguistic misinterpretation of current science. I believe it is consistent with the long-term use of the word God by Christians who accept the theology of the Trinity. I am not promoting that doctrine as I find it anthropomorphic and androcentric in addition to contributing more confusion than understanding in conversations with people of other beliefs. I have compared beliefs with Muslims who honestly believed the trinity was Joseph, Mary, and Jesus based on their observation of Coptic and Catholic icons.

Within the doctrine of the trinity people have long accepted that one indivisible God is revealed by various portions of the Bible as Father, ruling from heaven; Jesus, God present on Earth as fully man and fully divine; and Holy Spirit, arriving on Pentecost as the invisible comforter and defender of believers after the ascension of the risen Jesus Christ. If one adds in dozens of other names of God used in the Christian Old Testament including the more feminine, Sophia, for divine wisdom, the theology becomes even more difficult unless one simply accepts that limited human beings need multiple language forms to understand and express the many characteristics of God. My point here is very simple.

Using a single term for a complex reality observed in various ways is not new to Christianity. God as known through Jewish tradition and Allah revealed in Islam are more singular, and yet both remain highly complex and defy simple explanation.

Despite the failure of science to unify the natural forces, despite the efforts of great minds from Einstein through Hawking to many theorists working today, the natural forces work simultaneously in the universe and do not contradict each other. They do produce observable actions of physical objects and energy which are highly predictable with objects larger than quantum particles. When we speak of the power of nature determining the orbit of planets, the formation of storms, or the force needed to stop a car we do not expect to be asked to clarify which specific forces we mean. Science can clearly articulate exactly what forces are involved in most observed phenomena. But we are comfortable with common expressions that unify the way things normally behave as the power of nature.

I do not want to build a straw man by belaboring a simple point. I merely wish to provide a framework of comparison for anyone familiar with both science and Christianity who might wonder exactly what part of the natural forces I am referring to when I state that modern physics has shown that the omnipresent, omnipotent God is real and present in the observable world. I am talking about all of them.

Neither will I enter into any absurd imaginings of which force would be equivalent to each part of the trinity—an exercise I do not believe would benefit anyone. I mention it here to avoid confusion. By mentioning the trinity, I am referring to the pre-existing complexity represented by the word God as compared to the current complexity represented by various explanations for different parts of the power of nature. I am not suggesting that anyone should try to equate the strong force with God the Father, the Spirit with electromagnetic forces, or any such equivalence—although I will allow myself one observation of the evolution in human understanding over time.

Biographies of Albert Einstein recount his receipt of a compass while confined to bed during a childhood illness and being fascinated by what power could be making the needle to turn. He would pursue that curiosity to a deep level of understanding of the electromagnetic force which still can produce awe if we stop to consider the planetary and solar influences we casually refer to when we say the magnetism of Earth moves the needle. My one caveat in this discussion is that a concept

The Trinity and Unified Field Theology

like an invisible being called a spirit acting where there is no obvious physical actor makes perfect sense to me as an explanation created by a prescientific observer. Nobody in the room is moving the needle. It is sealed inside a container and not subject to any physical breeze that might be present. It seems perfectly logical to me that the ancients would conclude that there must be an invisible individual capable of producing changes in physical objects. The translation of the concept of spirits to the more recent revelation of physical forces is not simply substituting new vocabulary for the same ideas. It is a matter of the evolution of our understanding of the forces at work in the world.

One response to this evolution of thought is to assert that since no "body," no invisible "person," no God who mirrors humans, is controlling the universe the logical alternative is atheism. And here I must be careful. An educated atheist would not claim that the absence of God means the universe is out of control. But that is exactly what I was taught within Christianity. We were taught that the scientific option for understanding the universe left nothing but an image of life unfolding completely by meaningless chance. But the universe is under control. There are forces at work that are evident as far into the cosmos as we have been able to see. Confronted with the choice between belief and atheism, it matters to me that those forces are everywhere, omnipresent, omnipotent—controlling everything, and that those are precisely the ancient assertions of the attributes of God.

If confronting those forces and the otherness of the quantum world as the power we have long called God seems overly complicated, I refer anyone seriously considering the ideas to turn and look at the doctrine of the trinity. Understanding how all of the varied things we observe can be attributed to one power has never been simple. But the assurance is real. The universe is under control. The same forces that produced it sustain it today and will determine its future—and ours.

Predicting What God Will Do

5/27/2020

Deut 18:20: "But a prophet who presumes to speak in my name anything I have not commanded, or a prophet who speaks in the name of other gods, is to be put to death."

For my purposes here, I will consider anyone who claims to know what God will do as declaring themselves to be a prophet. A deep discussion of ancient Jewish practices or the evolution of the term in different religious traditions would go far beyond the scope of this essay. What concerns me here is the act of claiming to know what will happen and attributing those actions to God more than the identity or proper label of the speaker.

I am concerned about the effect of religious people making claims for God by predicting what God will do. Within the scope of UFT, the forces of nature do not speak as we typically use that term. They do however behave in very predictable ways and science often claims the ability to predict what will happen given specific sets of preliminary events. Among Christian traditions there are a variety of beliefs about how God speaks today. Some Christians believe, or claim to believe, that God speaks directly to them in prayer or through dreams and visions. A number of recent televangelists come to mind. From the time of the Reformation the most consistent view has been that God continues to speak to humanity today through the Bible—although there are various views concerning whether all parts of the Bible are true for all time or apply to all people.

Applying all passages of the Christian Bible, including promises and teachings originally given to Israel, to all people or all Christians requires acceptance of supersessionism (whether done through knowledge or ignorance). Supersessionism is problematic because of the claim that Christians have replaced the Jews and have inherited their promises and blessings. There are volumes of material both defending and critiquing this view for anyone who wishes to pursue the issue. I began this essay with the pronouncement of the law in the hopes that anyone who dares to speak for God would realize that doing so has always been considered a serious matter with the original penalty for error being death.

This essay was provoked by a social media post recently which showed people in Brazil praying as COVID-19 reached their country. The post indicated that the virus had now met its match because it had invaded the land of a praying people with the power of God to vanquish any such foe. In the days that followed, the news included the disturbing data of the devastation the disease brought to that country along with images of dozens of side-by-side graves to receive the dead. The bold assurance of victory and the images of defeat are obvious contradictions. What happened? Did God have the power to stop the disease at the borders of a land of prayer? If so, why are the people dying? A scramble begins for explanations of how the assurance of God's power and protection and the reality of the destruction can both be true. Perhaps there were not enough people praying, or there is too much sin in their country, or God has a deeper lesson to teach. Those who are solidly trained in the faith usually find some answer that satisfies them.

My concern is for the people who suffer and those outside the faith who observe the failed promises. As I discussed in the first volume of *UFT*, telling people who are in mourning that God could have intervened and chose not to do so seems cruel. It seems even more vicious to me when the logic includes reasoning that says those who are suffering lacked sufficient faith or were in some way unworthy of God's protection. For any neutral observer, the most logical explanation is that the belief in all all-powerful God guaranteed to intervene is false. Among some current atheist authors and speakers any revelation of the falsehood of beliefs would be a positive outcome. They would prefer direct logical examination of the world over anything that smells of delusion—even if it brings false hope or comfort to some—as an improvement in human understanding and reasoning.[1] But I have a lifetime of experience with the hope, comfort, and strength which come with belief in something

---

1. Dawkins, *God Delusion*.

larger than oneself. I try to be very careful to present my new views of the universe where people are ready to consider them. I also try to remain quiet where people's current beliefs give them strength to live positive lives. In the midst of this complexity, it concerns me when Christians make claims which contradict the observable facts.

Any religious belief in miracles and divine intervention requires accepting the idea that there is a power which can and sometimes does intervene in ways beyond our normal understanding of events. I have been there. I got out of a hospital bed and continued my life even though the doctors had no answers for the condition that made me ill. I remember a high school girl carried off of a mountain with a hole punched in her skull by a dislodged rock being well enough to go home in three days while we all prayed. I have experienced, observed, and read about many other events that exceeded any logical explanation those of us involved knew enough to give and we called them miracles. To remain within the religious realm which sees God as all-powerful and involved in specific human lives and activities requires the ability to believe that God's actions will sometimes appear as miracles. However, promising divine intervention and miraculous events is not the same as allowing that they are, or may be, possible. Daring to speak for God in advance and say what God will do is a matter the ancients considered serious enough to be punishable by death when the prediction was false.

As I type this, my mind recalls passages people will quote to defend their beliefs and their statements—"Where two or three are gathered…"[2] "Whatever you ask in my name…"[3] "By his wounds we are healed…"[4] "They will do even greater things…"[5] The list goes on and for those who believe each passage is literally true and applies to the church today, the proof is solid that we have the power to defy disease and prevent death. The problem is that it does not work. For over two thousand years sincere people of faith have been praying and claiming those verses and watching loved ones get sick and die. The very word "miracle" implies that the times when the prayers appear to work are rare occurrences, not normal events. I still participate in prayers for the sick and dying. I have no problem with the comfort and strength the afflicted person and their loved ones gain

2. Matt 18:20.
3. John 15:16.
4. Isa 53:5.
5. John 14:12.

from knowing that they are not alone and that others are hoping for their best outcome. The problem comes when we dare to ignore the evidence and claim that we know our prayers will overcome physical reality. When they do not, the explanations too often cause additional pain for those involved or accusations against people who have no connection to the events at all.

While I personally oppose violence, I confess an emotional temptation to agree with ancient law when people daring to speak for God turn to blame and hatred. When any of these self-appointed prophets tells a grieving nation that God is punishing them for tolerating the presence of other beliefs, the LGBTQ+ community, or anything else that person despises, I admit there is a place in me that would like to see the arrival of a group of ancients ready to do the stoning. My more rational side declares such speech to be what it is, personal hatred disguised as a message from God. Jesus of Nazareth taught his followers to love their enemies. I see these people as enemies. I cannot honestly say I love them. But I do not choose to become like them and commit violence against others who offend me. My real issue with them is the same as with the well-meaning, but incorrect, people who promise good that does not come. They make it difficult for others to find any life of faith and hope. I wish they would pay more attention to the verses in their Bible that speak to the danger of leading others away from faith.

As horrible as the pandemic of 2020 is, everything that is happening is within the laws of nature. The virus is doing what viruses do. And while we do not fully understand why it takes the life of this person while another is infected but lives, the problem is our ignorance of each person's exact physical condition and their body's interaction with the disease. It is not because of magical intervention for some and neglect of others. As the death toll in my own country passes 100,000 people, there is enough suffering without adding false hopes or condemnation from individuals daring to put words into the mouth of God.

If people wish to watch for the presence of God in it all, I wish they would turn to a passage like Psalm 46:10, "Be still and know that I am God."

At least we would stop giving people reason to lose faith and hope. We would cease inviting them to blame themselves or others when the world simply does what the world does.

For a Twelve-Year-Old Granddaughter

6/3/2020

SEVERAL YEARS AGO, I ENCOUNTERED a theory that much can be predicted about an adult and their view of the world based on what was happening when they were twelve years old. This resonated strongly with me as a person who was twelve in 1968. In that one year we experienced the murders of Martin Luther King Jr. and Robert Kennedy, Vietnam and nationwide student protests, the capture of a US ship by North Korea, the Russian invasion of Czechoslovakia, the Chicago Riots caused by police attacking protesters at the Democratic National Convention, and Apollo 8 orbiting the moon. As an adult, I am still strongly drawn to the discoveries of science on Earth and in space. And I am forever suspicious of the actions and motives of people in power and anxious about the safety of anyone who stands up and works for real change in our society.

I had not thought about it for some time until it dawned on me that my own granddaughter is twelve getting ready to turn thirteen in 2020. As a twelve-year-old she is experiencing reports of nationwide rioting, a country that has been at war her entire lifetime, and the first true pandemic with the cancellation of school and all of her activities. Closer to home she has watched her nationally competitive soccer club destroyed by the immoral, unethical, and illegal behavior of a coach who is a member of the owning family. Discipline at her elementary school became so bad that she had to homeschool for part of a year and transfer schools before selecting a quality middle school. At the same time, she has seen the US women's team in her chosen sport maintain their position as number one in the world and win the 2019 World Cup.

For a Twelve-Year-Old Granddaughter

She is a bright student who keeps track of her point requirements for *A*s in each subject without parental intervention. She plays her sport at a nationally competitive level and continues to develop additional skills even while all team events are cancelled by the pandemic. She pays attention, notices, and contemplates the world around her. And I wonder, how will everything happening in the world now effect the woman she is in a few short years?

I want her to know that people are good and that those who choose to do wrong and destroy are the exceptions which make the goodness of ordinary people noticeable. I want her to see the example of a strong woman in her mother who chooses to teach in a school with children from a lower income part of town who desperately need both the discipline and creative activities she brings to them. A woman who then comes home to provide a healthy and loving base for four children of her own. I want her to see it in her grandmother and aunts who pour heart and soul into taking care of those who cannot do it for themselves. I want her to see how women can change the world in big ways on the large public stage and also by changing one place, one home, at a time because women have been doing it for generations.

I want her to know that she is safe and that being her best in this world is safe. She already knows that when you are your best, those who are not will challenge and do their best to distract you. I want her to know that she has the strength to overcome the unfair treatment that comes from those who would have everyone do less rather than accept the challenge to also do and be better. In spite of the disease that has brought havoc to her first year of middle school, I want her to know that the world works. The sun still brings new energy every day and the rain still waters new growth. I want her to know that she is loved, admired, and respected for her positive attitude, her physical skills, her quick and conscientious mind, and for her heart.

Watching the changes in the environment, our government, and the decline in manners and civility among people from my day to hers brings me anxiety about the future. I want her to know that not only is she expected to be different, she already is and she has the power to remain a positive influence on those who come into her life. I want her to see the pain so vividly on display right now but not be discouraged or embittered by it. I want her determined to use her gifts to live the right way and to reach out to others whenever and however it is within her power and ability to do so. I want her to know that young people can change the world and to be encouraged by the number of her generation who are already standing up to demand that humanity wake up and alter direction to a healthier and more just course into the future. In a world that too often tries to tear people down, I want her to know that she is beautiful and strong—strong enough to lift up others when the world is unfair. I want her to know that national leaders do not have to be mean and petty, that having high standards for yourself does not mean hating or demeaning others, and that the situations of a point in time do not define the nature of all times.

I want her to know that she comforts and inspires me because I see in her the potential for a much better world than seems to surround us in 2020. I already see her rising above the pettiness and invitations to failure and negativity. I believe in her. I believe her generation is already showing the will power to do something better than what is currently happening. As she enters her teenage years when it may often seem like things are impossible, I want her to remember that she weathered this year and look to what is good and not be dismayed by life's difficult times.

Growing up when things are very bad is daunting. It also tells those with strong hearts that there is work to do. I want her to grow up willing and confident that she can develop the skills to join with her generation in changing the world, often one small place at a time. And when the world will not change, I want her to remember the virtue in taking care of those around her in the world that is. She has many strong examples. She has faith and a strong mind. I want her to know how many people are and will be in her corner forever as she faces whatever comes with the resolve to be the difference where difference is needed.

A Momentary Vision

6/8/2020

STILL GRIEVING THE UNSETTLING NEWS of the sudden loss of a friend, the power went out at our house for the second time in a day. For over an hour, we were left in the quiet dark with our thoughts before being interrupted by the noise of several trucks. A large bucket truck backed between our house and the next-door neighbors' and led to this momentary flash of vision.

    I went out on our back deck to watch them replace the bad transformer and take some pictures for my grandchildren as one man worked from a bucket truck and another scaled the pole. As I watched a pleasant breeze was making the temperature on the deck more enjoyable than the temperature inside the house. The trees were moving in the wind. Birds and squirrels were disturbed from their places near the human activity and in turn disturbed others as they moved tree to tree. A large rabbit ran from the yard invaded by the workers, through my fence and into the large brush pile hidden behind my yard barn specifically for her safety. A couple of workers spoke to me as they came and went. That is *all* that was happening. The scene was calm and calming but nothing extraordinary was happening. For what I want to share, it is important to emphasize that in spite of my grief it was a completely normal moment.

    But I unexpectedly saw it all as interactions of patterns of quantum energy. Some were arranged in temporary forms large enough to see with human eyes. Even the apparently empty spaces between were made of this eternal background of energy in spite of the fact that I could not see them. Everything there, including me, was a temporary assembly of various quanta of energy that would appear in these forms for a time and then transition to new realities. The trees move at a pace and live enough longer than us to seem more permanent. The ground which supports everything else changes at an even slower pace and appears more permanent still. The rabbits and birds move rapidly and seem to disappear with the changing activities of the days and seasons. And the first part of the vision struck me. My lost friend and I are like everything else, and he had changed form. Seeing our time of being human as something other than part of the whole sea of swirling energy, leads to an illusion of arriving, living, and departing. But a different perception of reality would reveal us as eddies in the quantum stream which tend to last decades, a century for the fortunate, and then move on in the flow. Sometimes, especially when a friend is suddenly taken from us, we wish we were as permanent as trees or mountains. But it is all a sea of energy and change. Their forms simply gain visible substance, exist, and disappear at a slower pace than ours. The energy is permanent as is the flow and the change from form to form.

The second part of the momentary clarity that occurred in those moments of normal activity was that the universe was observing itself and displaying understanding of the scene. I saw the men and equipment, trees, birds, squirrels, and mother rabbit and knew what each was doing. The illusion was that I was somehow separate from the same universal energy flow as everything else that was present. I am part of the universe. Everything I saw and contemplated was seen and contemplated by the universe because I was one small part of what the universe was doing in this place at that moment.

And mine were not the only eyes. The workers saw me and responded to my presence. So did the animals. While they moved from space to space none of the larger ones chose to join me on my back deck perch. They chose places of safety and hiding until the unusual activity was finished. But they knew where those places were. They became visible to my eyes for brief moments and then returned to the cover of leaves and branches. They also were the universe perceiving and responding to itself. So were countless small bugs falling from the tulip poplar over my head after consuming the juices from the tree during its blooming phase. I have no idea what they knew or thought in the air, on my arm, or brushed off as gently as I could onto the bushes below me.

But what struck me was the awareness of these temporary manifestations of the universe of each other—of the universe's awareness of itself. I am very careful with the term "omniscience" when discussing how the combined forces science examines in the search for the unified theory fit the ancient definitions of God. As soon as we say the universe, or the forces that make it work, knows all things it seems that we begin to anthropomorphize those forces. The God of the Bible acts very much like a human being as he loves, favors, gets angry, or destroys. The moment I speak of the universal forces as *knowing*, all of those things come rushing back to those trained in such beliefs. When those forces assume their momentary forms as one of us, we know that those emotions and actions are accurate. I do not know whether the birds and mammals in my backyard environment feel the same emotions or to what degree. I do not know about the tiny bugs falling from the tree, about the tree, the grass, or the ground beneath it all. But new studies say all forms of life have awareness of themselves and each other that exceeds everything I was taught as a youth. Now a few scientists are playing with a conjecture based on the lack of evidence to the contrary that consciousness may be present in very small amounts in each of the universal building blocks.

Placing everything in that simple scene in its proper place as a part of that day's manifestation of the universe at this specific place and time, the universe was aware of itself and responded to that awareness. It was a common moment. And it was a universal moment. Each living thing and physical object here was part of the universe—each and every one of us from the tiniest bug to the high voltage electrical equipment being worked on using the complicated hydraulics of the truck. And so were the humans working, observing, and participating in it all. My day of grief was interrupted by a momentary flash of awareness of a universe swirling for varying times into forms observable to human consciousness as living things, machinery, and breeze. And at least the parts of the universe we have developed the skill to study are aware of the universe that surrounds them and make choices in response to it. The universe sees and knows itself. It sees itself through eyes and understands itself through minds so common to us that we often fail to see that they also are the universe. Even plants are showing us in ways we never thought possible that they are capable of recognizing need in their neighbors and responding to it.[1]

How do I know that the universe knows and understands itself? Because I am no more separate from the universe than the wind, the trees, the birds, or the insects that accompanied my moment of refreshment

---

1. Wohlleben, *Hidden Life*.

and reassurance on a day that was hard to understand with the wisdom available through one short lifetime of seeking. But that is not the same as believing that knowledge is invested in one external supernatural being observable to me that day. The universe sees itself through countless eyes and processes the meaning of what is happening in countless ways. I saw nothing to verify the existence of one personality ruling it all with either love or judgement. The world is. It knows. It lives. And it delights in itself.

It Is the Living Who Die

6/8/2020

I KNOW THIS TITLE IS obvious to the point of nonsense. Obviously that which never lives or has already ceased living cannot die. Death comes to those who first know life. But I am talking about the pain of death for those who live. In every way that science can verify in the early twenty-first century, the person who dies feels no more pain. This perception has long brought comfort to those watching the final days of loved ones experiencing deep suffering as life ebbs away. At least the pain has ended whatever one believes through faith may also happen beyond that moment.

We who live are not so easily comforted. These thoughts come in response to the sudden unexpected loss of my former doctor. He was a person who understood the way I see the world and did not judge me for it. Sometimes he would share a slightly alternative way that the world made sense to him, but always in an open sharing of like minds. He also knew me—at my best and in the darkest days of my adult life. When I did not have the strength to overcome what life brought my way, I went to see my doctor friend. And he took care of me. Recently his office called in keeping with privacy guidelines for permission to give my address to my now retired friend because he wanted to send me a letter. I suspected it was about the copy of my book I left for him when he retired from his practice, but I did not know for sure. I watched for the mail every day. What words did my doctor friend have for me now that we no longer met face to face?

Instead, my wife at her computer started saying, "Oh no! No! No!" The message had come to her first that he was gone. It would take some time before others could fill in missing details and let me know how a person not much older than myself was suddenly gone. The information helped and made it worse. I now had a logical explanation of how his life came to an end. But with it came the knowledge that one of his lifelong friends is also in deep pain, pain that can logically be expected to stay with him in some way for the rest of his life. Knowing that another good person is in pain increases rather than diminishes my longing for an answer to suffering. We who are left among the living are the ones who feel the deep pain of death.

I'm old enough to have known it many times before as close family and other friends reached the end of their times as humans being. But having taken this winding path of pursuing truth outside the neat boundaries of my childhood, things have changed. I hope he has moved on to some eternal reward for a life well-lived. But there is no verifiable way to know that outside the assurances of religious faith. I know the energy that was him—and every particle of me seems to scream that it was very positive energy—is already moving on to reappear and reassemble in new forms according to the laws of the universe. But he is gone to me.

I should note that the loss must be unbelievably worse for his family and the friend who was with him when the accident took him. But I am openly confessing that there is a very selfish point to this pain because there is a point to be made. Like the various forms of life I describe in "A Momentary Vision" we all see things in different ways. Sometimes we are made to feel that we see the world in completely different ways from all others who surround us. People who love us and believe that there is one correct way to see and respond to the universe (and often extra-universal spirit forms) fear for our well-being and eternal future when told we do not hold the same beliefs they do about truth, religion, or life beyond life. Those who we can trust with our deep thoughts and true identity are treasures of great value. Losing them cuts very close to what Paul Tillich called the "impenetrable center."[1]

In the pain of this loss, I become keenly aware of how many friends have already ceased being among us and accessible to me. I have had many communities—those who shared my evangelistic enthusiasm as a young man, who shared the joy of speeding down a hill or mountain at the edge of control, who know the feel of moving carefully up the face of a rock surface or mountain peak, and those who study American

---

1. Tillich, *Loneliness and Solitude*, 17.

experiments in alternative communities or forms of education to name a few. Most of them are now in the past, some due to loss and others just to the changes of life and the passing of years. Rarer still are the people who have made space in their lives to share the deepest parts of my life and thoughts. They are hard to find and harder to keep.

Now as the years advance, I feel the losses of the past and the losses yet to come. I feel myself moving toward Georges Bataille's "community of those who have no community."[2] So, as Blanchot suggests, I leave my gifts here in writing to be discovered by others when they need them. They may never be known to me, but we will share this community of ideas across time and space. I leave them in gratitude for years in the company of friends who share the journey. I leave them with great encouragement of friends I never expected to meet but found thanks to the sharing in my first book. A dear friend is gone, but I am not alone. Those who remain give me strength to carry on and the things I learn in fellowship with them will be committed to the page along with musings I might otherwise share with no one in the hope that those who feel alone will find a community where none appears to exist. When life feels like dying, I will be there when I can and hope my words will be when I cannot.

2. Blanchot, *Unavowable*, 1.

Approaching the Bible

6/16/2020

2 Tim 3:16–17
"All Scripture is God-breathed and is useful for teaching, rebuking, correcting and training in righteousness, 17 so that the servant of God may be thoroughly equipped for every good work."

Defining God as the very real combination of natural forces that control the universe, questions arise about how I see the Bible. This verse provides a solid foundation to discuss the issue. I have stated before that I believe removing the restrictions caused by interpreting everything in the Bible literally frees the text to speak more clearly to today's readers as wisdom literature. Like much of the Christian Bible, scholars now question whether this passage was written by the author it is attributed to or possibly by a student of that author. I believe it provides a useful starting point for considering the present value of the ancient texts regardless.

The author clearly maintains that Scripture is from God and useful both for teaching what is right and correcting wrong thinking and practice in order to prepare people to do good work in the world. I would like to unpack the language in order to examine what it says in the context of UFT, especially since I have strong memories of its assumed meaning and uses within the faith communities of my youth.

The first phrase is critical. Before examining the uses of Scripture, it is important to know what we mean by God-breathed. What the author originally meant by the phrase may be as impossible for us to pin down as who the actual author was. But we may readily examine what it means to us. Within the literalist tradition this verse is often used as a proof-text that everything in the Bible is directly from God and therefore literally true and infallible. Realizing that the Jewish scriptures were the only scriptures at the time the passage was written provides a starting point for our examination. Accepting all of the Jewish texts as the perfect literal word of God presents several problems. First in my thinking is that the rabbinic tradition does not treat all of those writings as literal or as set law for all time. That tradition also does not give equal weight to the Torah and the writings which came later although all are considered useful. Secondly, considering the same rabbinic traditions there are often widely varied views on the interpretation of texts accompanied by a level of comfort with the truth residing somewhere in the paradox that is foreign to the literal readings of US evangelicals. We must reexamine what it means for Scripture to be *God-breathed*.

The other main text that speaks of God breathing is the creation narrative in Genesis. There, God forms man out of the earth and brings him to life by breathing into him. While I no longer believe the accounts recorded there to be literal,[1] I still believe the story is informative for the task of interpreting this phrase. The traditional interpretation translates this phrase to "inspired by God" as found in the King James Version. That interpretation leads to much of the debate about whether anything inspired by God would also be by definition perfect. Comparing the text to the creation of Adam provides an interesting way to examine whether God-breathed equals perfection. Adam was not perfect in the story or as discussed in Christian texts. Adam was alive. A more accurate reading of God breathed would then be that God gives life rather than perfection to that which is given the breath. This also matches other passages that equate breath with life. While humans live, they breathe, and the absence of breath is synonymous in general usage with death.

To push this idea even further, living things grow and change. A study of the development of the canon reveals that the Christian Bible did in fact grow and change for centuries before becoming considered finished in the various forms used today. Even after the major branches of Christianity declared the Bible complete and finished, other sects have emerged which teach continuing revelation. The Catholic Church, while not adding the papal writings to the Bible, has a tradition of considering church teaching as also infallible. There is a long tradition of practices allowing the Bible to grow.

---

1. I believe the differences in the two accounts of creation recorded directly after one another is strong evidence that they were never intended to be read literally.

I believe allowing the Bible, or at least our interpretation of it, to change as a living document may be beneficial to present usage as well. Accounts of the battles of ancient Israel including directives from God to kill noncombatants and animals are disturbing to many twenty-first century readers. The fact that these passages were never literal can be found within the ancient texts as later writings reveal that people from the groups still existed. I am more interested in how seeing them as living texts might allow better understanding in the present. If not literal histories of battles and genocide, we may find it possible to read them as assertions that God's victories are complete and that God's power is greater than any human opposition. I see hope and meaning in this interpretation while literal reading leaves only death for all of those not born into the favored people.

Ancient laws for dealing with various offenses are also more alive for current study if the understanding of the faithful and the application of the texts are allowed to grow and change. Few literalists today would risk the legal consequences of obeying the ancient proclamation not to allow a witch to live, or to stone disobedient children to death. In practical terms we already allow texts we do not choose to obey to change in meaning even among groups who hold to statements of faith that argue against any such change. Perhaps allowing Scripture to grow and change would assist us in allowing other portions such as those dealing with people often shunned by the Western church to change as well. This approach places the emphasis on the teachings of Jesus to love all people including those considered outcasts.

I believe that the writings of the Bible become far more valuable for current "teaching, rebuking, correcting, and training" when allowed to grow and change in order to speak into the culture and times where they are used. This view of God-breathed might have impacted previous uses in justifying war, conquest, genocide, slavery, separation of believers by race, and many other behaviors that have been justified using specific passages. However, it also forces me to consider an even more controversial question of whether using the texts in this way allows human discernment to take precedence over God's words.

Here I must return to definitions and the fact that I do not define God as an extra-natural super-human presence from some metaphysical realm. In UFT, God is the combination of forces that control the universe and is present within the universe rather than ruling from somewhere outside of nature. This brings me to two points. First, God-breathed would mean inspired by, and consistent with, the way the universe works. Caring for one's neighbors, the stranger in our midst, orphans, widows, prisoners, other life forms, and Earth itself is to live in harmony with the world that is. The ancient writings provide a fascinating window into the level of understanding of the natural world at the time various passages were written. Seeing understanding of the world as understanding of the ways of God also allows us to grow in wisdom as we understand more about what does and does not work in the world. Secondly, it raises an issue even more foreign to the view of God as external to the world. We are part of the universe. We are inspired by our study of it and admiration of its beauty. Along with God, we are part of the universe rather than visitors from outside of the world. When we speak love and concern for the rest of humanity and the planet, the universe is speaking. When we spew hatred and promote violence, so does the universe because we are the conscious part of the universe available to our awareness at this time. In this context, God-inspired and man-written are not opposites. I see degrees of matching what is beneficial or harmful that lead me to consider some human writings more inspired than others. And I hope for growth and change as we transcend earlier misconceptions and prejudices. But humans remain as the producers of knowledge and understanding of both the world and of proper living. We exist by the power of the universe and when we speak and act, the universe speaks and acts.

This also leaves me with a greatly expanded view of the term "all Scripture." Most of the Bible was written from inside the context of one specific group of people, the Israelites. There are portions of the Christian Bible attributed to non-Jewish authors and there is evidence that the content of many passages matches myth and wisdom literature from other cultures. But it is a text primarily from one part of the world based on oral traditions about the experiences of one specific group in one region of the planet. My genetic connection to that group is buried someplace in the distant past. And yet I find great inspiration, comfort,[2] and guidance in the teachings recorded there.

I do not, however, restrict my view of inspired teachings to only the writings found in this one source. As I have been privileged to learn more of the teachings of other cultures, my faith has expanded. As brief examples, I find Eastern practices of meditation and teachings of human

---

2. I find it interesting that this comforting value of Scripture is not included in the Timothy text at a time when many believe that believers in Jesus Christ were subject to persecution and death. It does, of course, occur in other passages.

unity with all that is to be profound. Teachings from those traditions often help me to regain calm and balance when immediate circumstances are chaotic. I find tribal beliefs in North America and elsewhere that we are related to all of life, including the life of the planet, much wiser than interpretations of the world which say the rest of life is here for our exploitation. And when two eighth-grade boys from the largest mosque in the United States pointed out to me that they saw God as beyond and not subject to our opinions of God, it brought balance to my view stated above that man is part of the universe and records sacred views as humanity's understanding of the world expands. At the time that I am writing this, physics has yet to produce the unified theory showing how all the forces of the universe form one unified field. Recent observations of phenomena on both quantum and astronomical scales reveal that there is much we do not understand. Supposedly simple occurrences like the formation of clouds, a direct hit by lightning, the unfolding of a flower, or the loss of a village in a landslide remind us that we do not yet know everything, and our own planet is not subject to our wishes and wills to determine its behavior. The combined forces at work in the world continue to exceed our understanding or control and call us to greater humility and study.

In that light, I consider new discoveries in science to be inspired and inspiring. And I continue to believe the preserved wisdom in the texts of the Bible are indeed valuable for my instruction, correction of self-aggrandizing thinking, and equipping to do good things for others. I likewise find wisdom and guidance from truth as revealed to other cultures and now widely available to those of us who are blessed to live in a time of unprecedented access to the literature and discoveries of humanity around the globe and across millennia.

Unexamined Relativism Devalues Factual Research

6/24/2020

RESEARCH HAS FOUND THAT MANY students arrive at the university level believing that truth is relative.[1] In the case of universal truths, sometimes called Truth with a capital T, politically correct writing and discussion almost demands it. Separation of church and state leads public school personnel to carefully avoid any appearance of favoring any religious belief system which inadvertently creates an impression that teachers believe all views are equal regardless of each instructor's actual belief system.

When I taught for a Wesleyan university from 1996–2015, the curriculum based on Christian beliefs included an early assignment concerning worldviews. The university wanted students with other belief systems to understand the underlying assumptions of the program. But for many students, both Christian and non-Christian, it served as an introduction to the very idea that differing worldviews exist, many of which do not see truth as relative. Both the Wesleyans in charge of the program and atheist students I taught occasionally in the program held views which were not compatible with agreeing that every other view was equal to their own. Acknowledging the existence of competing worldviews laid the groundwork for civil and meaningful graduate discussions based on information from research. The fact that many of these students were practicing teachers who had already completed one level of higher

1. Bloom, *Closing*, 25.

education unaware of the existence or significance of this issue was always troubling to me.

The issue I wish to consider here is not a return to some imagined past or a leap to some desired future where everyone believes a certain religion or set of moral absolutes. My purpose is to reflect on what unexamined relativism has done to our attitudes towards facts in considering specific issues. I would argue that where data is available, a proper understanding of the specific issue should be consistent with known facts. I fear, however, that many people in the United States have reached a point where every opinion or statement is considered of equal validity.

Due to the division between the political parties and their statements with regard to the validity of scientific research and findings, statements of facts from research are often evaluated based on which political party agrees with that position. Aligning themselves with evangelicals who have adopted negative fundamentalist and literalist responses to the findings of science since schools began teaching evolution, the Republican Party has increasingly supported a relativist view of all scientific research. As one example, research showing clear patterns of global warming and environmental impacts is rejected because members of the Democratic and Green Parties use that information to call for responses harmful to the fossil fuel industry—not because the scientific community has any serious debate about the findings.

Discussions or debates about social issues such as racism, police rights and/or actions, immigration policy, the rights of women and children, white and/or male privilege, and the proper role of government are more likely to produce statements of individual beliefs and political positions than research-based evidence. Statement of the results of a peer-reviewed study that disagrees with the views of one or more students in a university class may even result in the filing of an official complaint for violating the students' rights to safe places for maintaining their own previous opinions. I find such a situation anathema to true education.

I now see a common attitude that opposite positions on any issue should be treated as equal in order to avoid any emotional response or animosity. While others demand that the whole world honor their views, many who wish to avoid conflict have adopted positions of agreeing to disagree while each side simply continues to assume that its own view is accurate. At first encounter, the existence of strong proponents of certain views may seem to contradict my thesis. My contention is that such views are often reached due to the lack of belief in any external authority.

Unexamined Relativism Devalues Factual Research

Absent any external reference point for factual evidence, both the personality that demands its own way and those who choose paths of non-confrontation are functioning in a worldview that lacks a commitment to hard examination of evidence.

I have no problem with agreeing to disagree and tolerance or even celebration of diverse views. I need to make it clear that much of our strength resides in being a varied people willing to accept the existence of different views. I enjoy contemplation of ideas where the answer appears to lie somewhere in the paradox between opposing views. I am not arguing against the civility of allowing different views or the wisdom that may be gained from listening carefully to diverse views. Neither am I arguing against those who perceive unfairness demanding to be heard.

What concerns me is a kind of laziness which seems to have resulted from our unexamined relativism. If I can think whatever I want, and you can think whatever you want, and everything is of equal value—or if I can assert my will over yours by occupying a position of authority or by the number of people on my side—why seek out existing facts related to the issue or support further research to produce the data needed for informed views?

In recent days the President of the United States openly took a position that when it suits his purposes, the country should reduce testing for a deadly pandemic and simply not produce the results he knows will be contrary to his claims.[2] Other officials in his administration sought to convince the public that his statement was some sort of humor, but he reaffirmed that he meant what he said. On previous issues current US leaders have claimed that directly opposing statements are something labeled as alternative facts. In my own state, decisions about reopening school are being based on acceptance of the truism that *children must go to school*, while testing for the disease remains minimal and the data to know how great the risk remains in any given community is unavailable. I could just as easily state this in the opposite and say that opponents of the current leadership are making demands to keep children away from school, and by extension parents from being able to work, based on fear without data. What concerns me is the practical relativism which simply assumes that we each have our views and we do not need to do the work and collect the data in order to choose the wisest course of action.

---

2. This statement was followed within a week by the largest single-day total of reported new cases in the United States.

I have encountered the same thing in views of US History. Evangelical friends demand that all of the founding fathers be seen as people with a faith similar to their own and taught only as heroes of freedom and justice. Any effort to point out counterevidence from the written record is met with accusations of disloyalty and lack of love for country rather than respect for an accurate historical record. Now the liberal side has a radical element which is defacing or trying to destroy statues of previous presidents including the founding fathers based on their involvement in slavery without regard to the complexity of their importance to our national history and identity. Perhaps if we had a greater commitment to learning truth through research, we would have reasoned positions to discuss around those statues about both sides of our national past while searching for common ground in our desires for our future as a people. As it is, we seem content to assume our own views are superior because they are ours and scream at each other across the battle lines, or simply avoid the discussion completely. I do not know how a society functions under these conditions.

In terms of ultimate reality, I have stated my position in *UFT* that the omnipotent, omnipresent power of the universe traditionally known as God is real and observable in the natural world. The reader may correctly assume that such a view automatically predisposes me to prefer careful study of the world since careful study reveals truth about the world. I believe there are choices, beliefs, and actions which align with reality and others which do not—at least in areas subject to the rules of research. I believe it is time to move past blind acceptance of every view and encourage again the search for evidence to support varying opinions. When the research itself presents us with seemingly conflicting results we have room for disagreement, contemplation of paradox, and impetus for further research. I contend that debate without examining the evidence behind views leaves us as little more than children on a playground seeking to win arguments based on who can yell their view the loudest or the longest—or as adults who have learned topics which are simply never discussed.

As an academic, the constructivist worldview, which asserts that reality is solely the product of our mental functions, fascinates me as a field of study and served me as a powerful tool for understanding how students labeled anti-social saw the world in order to help them adopt strategies less likely to result in conflict and negative consequences. But I have no desire to drive across a bridge designed and built under the leadership of a person who assumes it will work because it does in their imagination without applying known laws of physics and rules of construction! Neither does my safety depend on whether the construction company was conservative or liberal, Christian or atheist, progressive or discriminatory in hiring—unless those views have caused them to believe that cheap (or overpriced) construction is always better, that God or chance will determine how many cars can safely cross, or that it is acceptable to hire unqualified workers or overlook poor completion of critical tasks! There are known facts about safe construction and when our lives are at stake, we care that attention has been given to the facts.

On issues like disease and public health, it remains very likely that we will disagree on the best path forward. But I want those disagreements to be informed by facts, facts beyond what political or religious leaders have told their followers to say. For a medical issue, I want medical data and research. And I want consideration of that evidence and policies affecting the public to be done in ethical open forums where misrepresentations of fact may be confronted—or misinformed opposition may be corrected. It concerns me when the present climate in my country leads people to either engage in open conflict, or politely allow for silent disagreement without feeling the need to acquire the underlying information and fairly debate its interpretation.

I believe this is the result of an unexamined acceptance of a relativist position that equates all views and opinions—or that exalts the views of certain people merely because an individual or group with power prefers them—without the effort to research, examine, and interpret factual information.

In such an environment, power wins instead of truth. Rather than doing the work to arrive at the best answers, whoever wields the most power wins, whether that is the legally recognized authority or the mob.

In spite of all that has happened, I believe in the superiority of reason.

My 2020 Declaration

7/4/2020

"When in the Course of human events, it becomes necessary for one people to dissolve the political bands which have connected them with another, and to assume among the powers of the earth, the separate and equal station to which the Laws of Nature and of Nature's God entitle them, a decent respect to the opinions of mankind requires that they should declare the causes which impel them to the separation.

We hold these truths to be self-evident, that all men are created equal, that they are endowed by their Creator with certain unalienable Rights, that among these are Life, Liberty and the pursuit of Happiness. That to secure these rights, Governments are instituted among Men, deriving their just powers from the consent of the governed, That whenever any Form of Government becomes destructive of these ends, it is the Right of the People to alter or to abolish it, and to institute new Government, laying its foundation on such principles and organizing its powers in such form, as to them shall seem most likely to effect their Safety and Happiness."[1]

When in the course of human events, it becomes necessary for people to critique the practices of society in order to assume among the powers of the earth, the universal and equal station to which the laws of nature and nature's God entitle them, a decent respect for the opinions and future of all mankind requires that they should declare the causes which impel them to action.

I hold these truths to be self-evident, that all life is equal and is endowed by the universe with certain unalienable rights, that among these are existence, self-determination, and the pursuit of enlightenment.

To secure these rights, governments and alliances are instituted among people, deriving their just powers from their benefit to all affected by their actions. That whenever any institution becomes destructive to these ends it is the responsibility of the people to alter and improve it, basing all actions on such principals and organizing in forms most likely to ensure safety and happiness to all.

1. "Declaration of Independence."

Rocks of Fire

7/21/2020

I WANT TO SHARE A perception or a way that I am now experiencing the world.

Starting with the most common view of rocks and fire, every homebuilder or person with camping skills knows that rocks are valuable for controlling fire. The pioneers of my state with their log cabins used stone for fireplaces as soon as possible in order to contain the fire and heat where they wanted without risking the destruction of their entire shelter. Training in wood skills always includes forming a fire circle free of debris and surrounded by stones whenever possible to keep campfires from spreading. Both form mental images which may bring the warmth of memories to many people.

But the rocks of the fire circle or hearth do not burn. That is why they are there. They are most likely to simply be blackened by the smoke of the things that we choose to burn.

Moving a step deeper into the imagery, photos of molten rock are common in volcanoes. None of us is surprised when we see photos or videos of this type of rock glowing, flaming, or even exploding. But those images seldom come to mind when we use stone for safety from fire or encounter rocks on the trail or by the river. These rocks are still and quiet, often cool, and considered by many to be lifeless.

I believe this perception exists because the life cycle of rocks is phenomenally larger than the life cycle of humans. We may be taught in school that sedimentary rocks become metamorphic under pressure and can transform all the way to magma under the intense environment deep inside Earth, possibly to be ejected as igneous rocks which worn down over time will complete the circle and return again to sedimentary rock. However, the time scale of this process exceeds the limits many religious people believe are true for the age of the planet as well as longer than they believe Earth will continue into the future before an apocalyptic replacement by God. Even for those of us who trust the science, the amounts of time involved exceed anything in our common experience or imagining. Rocks are just rocks, and I take great pleasure in examining them as they are—the hidden treasures in sedimentary rocks, the stripes and speckles of minerals in metamorphic stones are things of beauty in their own right. But I have begun to sense the fire in every rock as well. Somehow every stone contains all of its forms including the well-hidden glow of its potential fire.

And now I have experienced a step further. The stones are different, beautifully so, at the level observed through human eyes with or without the aid of magnification. They remain different as we move down to the molecular level that provides the variety of color and the identifying characteristics of minerals. These differences remain as we go to the atomic level as well. Then something strange happens. We now know that if we go far enough, we will reach the level of quanta where the blackened stone by the fire and the bright flaming projectile from the volcano are both temporary configurations of the quanta that form all things although long-lived compared to us.

It is both beguiling and perplexing as I begin to perceive the world in this way—to see in every common stone the potential to become part of the explosive inferno but containing the essential power of the universe in whatever state we find it. A stone is no longer just a stone, it is part of the complex quantum combinations that surround me in all the variety of observable earthly forms. There is a powerful, vibrant, light-based, humming energy to everything including the smooth stone I hold in my hand or skip across the surface of a lake.

If we finally perceive in an experiential way that we ourselves are formed of the same amazing complexity of quanta, we are now part of all the energy that surrounds us. There is no separation at the bottommost level of scientific division. There is instead one magnificent energy field taking on various forms and shapes including us as our senses observe, record, contemplate, enjoy, or label repulsive, each of the various other combinations which surround us. I personally find it both exhilarating and disorienting when this awareness breaks through my senses and my common thoughts of using a keyboard as a keyboard, moving air as a source of cool refreshment, and greenery outside my window as the growth of summer. When the moments occur that it all becomes the energy of the quanta, I am one with it all in a way that exceeds my vocabulary. I disappear. What remains is the everything, which is at its base pure energy containing the body and mind I commonly experience as my separate being.

Perceived at the base level of pure fire, pure energy, all is one as the ancients of both the East and the tribal peoples have been telling us all along. I stand and hold a stone in my hand and the concentration I feel as weight, the combinations I perceive as color and texture, the potential I now sense to become either a barrier to fire or fire itself are all combinations of the same quanta that now holds the stone in the shape of a hand. Everything is part of the same great dance of energy. To experience it is reunion. To return to the sanity of seeing things as the objects our language describes is practical and allows me to function without alarming others. It is also at a deep fundamental level an illusion.

Sympathy for the One

7/26/2020

IN 1968 THE ROLLING STONES released "Sympathy for the Devil" on the album *Beggars Banquet*. Today, it feels increasingly like evil is having its way and I am exploring sympathy of a different kind.

I wonder how lonely you were traveling the countryside even when surrounded by crowds.

How hard was it when the simplest stories and examples failed to help them see what you saw?

How difficult was it to give patient answers or more guiding questions when those who sought to know would turn the most obvious answers into riddles about things they already thought they knew?

How deeply did it wound you when they could not grasp the truth that could cure their pain?

How did you feel when your example of sacrificial living for others was met with requests to be raised to greatness in your kingdom?

How hard was it to stand between the people you freed from bondage and their God when they rebelled and begged to return to slavery?

How lonely was it to be surrounded by the comfortable ideas that come from the world people believe they know even when that world is false?

Did you doubt your sanity when confronted with the clear majority convinced that the truth was different from what you saw as clear and beautiful?

Did you feel temptation to turn, withdraw alone to bliss, and leave them to their world?

Did you feel temptation to turn to a life of comfort and rewards promised by the broad path traveled by the many?

Did you weep more than once for the pain they would not leave behind?

Did giving to so many without reciprocity leave you empty even as you were approached by crowds who knew only how to take?

Did you really know where it all would end?

How deeply did you love those few who saw and joined you on the journey in gratitude for freedom from what was and the joy of exploring what might yet be?

I write these essays watching a world that seems to prefer being fooled into believing everything is OK, a world where what each person wants determines the world they claim a right to live in, a world where the learning and insights I count as immeasurable gifts from my teachers is ridiculed and laughed at by people I thought I knew. I receive, record, and share these thoughts in a world of social media where people openly display the sides of themselves that were more often hidden in a face-to-face society. And I continue to be shocked by the beliefs and attitudes of people I have considered my closest friends and family across the decades. Sometimes as I wait for sleep, the loneliness makes me doubt my sanity. How can these things that seem so true be sane when the whole world daily proclaims an opposite reality? When comfort comes to me that truth is truth regardless of what any of us believe, my pain for others becomes almost unbearable as I watch them like the boys in Pinocchio celebrating their freedom on the road to captivity.

I write these essays hoping that somehow they reach others on a path that makes them also feel alone against the world. I write them as expressions of love for those unexpected friends who have appeared to share the journey. They are small in number, but their comfort and affirmation are as life-giving as water and oxygen. To be able to correspond and meet with them is the wealth that has come back to me in return for sharing my small insights into the nature of our lives.

And it makes me think of Jesus, of Siddhartha, of Moses, of many others of less renown who lived to share freedom and truths beyond what their neighbors already thought they knew. The most human of the stories seems to me to be that of Moses which includes his reactions of frustration and anger when the people could not, or would not, see the promised land ahead while longing for the world they knew behind them. The records of Jesus seem to present him as too perfect and god-natured to feel negative emotions during his years of ministry and yet those same records say he was tempted in every way as we are.[1] And I wonder about Siddhartha and whether his detachment was a sufficient shield against the frustration of teaching truths that cannot be expressed in words, or whether he truly possessed the ability to experience the pain as well as the joy simply as part of the unity of all things. I recently read the memoirs of Ma Jaya and was comforted by her honesty about feeling alone and possibly insane as her own journey unfolded.[2] The friends who have found me since the publication of *UFT*, tell me of the struggle to live and participate in places where sharing their own questions and journey seems forbidden because it could bring harm to others. I treasure them for their openness and friendship.

With ever-growing sympathy for the champions of the ages who have lived to share great truths with a world that favored other paths, I write my small essays as gifts and offerings to others who dare to open themselves to new and beautiful views of life that others may forever reject. I have shared in services of remembrance that it is we, the living, who must walk the lonely valley the departed already moved beyond. I write these short expressions as nourishment for all who walk paths of truth as it is revealed to them even when those paths seem darker than the road to death. I am not concerned whether they believe any limited dogma to match my views. We travel the world together as dreamers refusing to shy away from truths that others may never choose to see. One purpose of this essay is to give expression to the deep gratitude, nurture, and strength I feel from those who have come into my life to let me know that I do not travel alone.

The other purpose of this is essay is to express new awareness and sympathy for the lives and gifts of every teacher who came before us—sharing truth as it came to them whether most of those around them seemed to understand or not. I believe we owe more than we know to each and every one of them, whether of our own society and traditions or not. Their paths opened the way for our journeys of discovery. And I am grateful.

---

1. Heb 4:15.
2. Bhagavati and Houston, *How God Found Me.*

Movement in a Field

7/31/2020

A MAN ENTERS A FIELD of severely overgrown grass approximately thirty feet by a hundred feet. On one side the area is bordered by a line of old crabapple trees. On the other is a steep embankment up to a city sidewalk project which has prevented the city from grooming the area. That is the tangible reality of the event.

At the same time quanta rise up from the earth as water and minerals inside grass and trees reaching further for the sky, releasing gases, and feeding parasitic vines winding through the grass and up the tree trunks. Quanta leap from hiding in the form of countless grasshoppers and other small insects. Unseen water vapor also rises heated by the quanta descending from the sun. Heat-relieving quanta flow steadily from the west as a cool summer breeze. Other forms of radiation also flood the area from manmade TV and radio signals, electromagnetism from the high-power lines overhead, to energy from space that would kill in higher doses passing through the atmosphere and the earth continuously at levels unnoticed by humans. Quanta at the base of it all usually considered totally inactive dirt release energy through the plants and aspiration in the heat of the day all the while absorbing the vibrations of the machine and others passing nearby while forming its own record of the energy passing through the scene.

An intruder made up of a complex of quanta with internal organs and systems transferring matter for internal survival and external movement enters the area on a monstrosity of energy consumption and release. Approximately three thousand explosions per minute release quanta as heat and smoke while causing other quanta arranged as metal blades to spin at a speed of over 200 mph at the tip, separating weeks of growth from grass below and heating the ground further due to the extreme temperature of the aging engine. The complex organism above the machine guides the exploding, revolving, destruction of the machine back and forth down the field. Quanta of light enter the eyes to guide the action and identify hazards and insect companions. Vibrations of sound signal the speed of the engine and the strain of cutting loads which exceed the power of the engine's combustion causing the intruder to adjust speed and direction. Small movements of matter moving tiny arrangements labeled bone, fluid, hair, and nerves alert the operator of the machine to slight changes in slope, speed, and direction.

And somehow the movement of electric quanta within the biochemical transactions behind thought cause the intruder to become aware of something beyond a sun, air, plants, insects, and machine. The entire picture is an interacting quantum field formed from the complex interaction of every bit of matter and spark of energy present including the man. For a moment he realizes that he is part of an immensely complex vibration and interplay of quanta rising, descending, swirling, causing obvious reactions, or passing through completely imperceptible to human senses. And he is not separate. He too is a moving mixture of quanta, possibly the most complex among the observable phenomena, but quanta like all the rest interacting in the moment regardless. Even acting to destroy weeks of growth to meet the standards of local acceptability, he is part of the quantum mixture. And the awareness comforts him that he is contained in the whole when he perceives it and when he does not.

Last week I mowed the grass.

Fall as Revelation

10/14/2020

I HAVE LONG BEEN FASCINATED with fall as the season when Earth reveals the true nature of Spring as a global eruption. The rapid growth of spring, long celebrated for the joy of life returning, hides its volcanic similarities beneath the lush green of chlorophyll. And yet, minerals of the Earth are moving out toward the sky across the temperate zones. Without the heat, destructive violence, and size of volcanoes part of what is happening remains hidden from the casual observer. Perhaps only those gifted with the eyes of botanists witness the very minerals of Earth escaping the surrounding soil to reach toward the sky combining with elements of sun, air, and water as they go. In the fall, when the chlorophyll has done its job and the plants prepare for winter, the varied colors of the minerals are finally revealed. Where I live in Southern Indiana the display is often awe-inspiring in its vivid diversity. Then the apparent end brings in the barren winter.

As those varieties of leaves turn loose from their hosts to fly back earthward on the fall wind, my mind turns first to cycles. Many authors have written eloquently of the cycle of life revealed by the turning of the seasons. I am thinking of nothing less than the rock cycle normally requiring many thousands of years to complete in its obvious patterns of eruption, erosion, subduction, and transformation. In fall, that same cycle of minerals reaching for the sky and returning to join the Earth is repeated perhaps a hundredfold in a human lifetime while the larger geologic cycles exceed our time of existence far too exponentially to experience. But where we have seasons, it happens annually as we who love the show observe the rising of the green and the falling of the red, orange, yellow, green, and purple showers of the factories of life with work completed for another year.

It reminds me of the religious training of my youth about the Christian text of Revelation. This perhaps strangest book in the Bible, has been interpreted by many to predict a real time when the rising of human life will reach its climax. Scenes of great death and the falling of many are part of the text. Then, the new Earth comes into being for the emergence of the age of bliss. Perhaps it is natural for thinking animals observing the annual cycle to believe it demonstrates a long-term universal pattern as truly as it echoes the millennia long cycle of the rocks. Whether it predicts any real future is a matter of debate even among Bible scholars. Many point to its prediction of events shortly after it was written, while literalists expect a risen Christ to actually ride from the sky trailing an army to defeat all those who reject his original offer of love. I know of no scientific reason to expect any such supernatural changing of the seasons of man. I see the pattern far more clearly in the constant rising and falling of man's grand designs and empires. Groups and rulers rise to dominance for a while. Then, they reach the end of their dominance, either quietly falling away or ending in dramatic display. Both types of falls are often followed by a period of uncertainty. Then new power arises. The documentation of both history and prehistory shows this ubiquitous pattern. And one can choose to look to the fall of power as doom or the rising of new power with all the hope of renewal. It doesn't change the pattern. It happens just the same.

Of greater interest to me as I look for evidence of how the power that rules the universe acts in the observable world is that only the leaves return to the ground in fall. The brilliance of their colors and the whirling of their presence in the wind makes it easy to focus all of our attention on them. Nonetheless, the tree remains. The minerals of the Earth have combined with the elements of the sky and universal energy to build something which lasts—not forever, but far beyond the annual cycle, beyond the normal lives of humans. The Earth reaches for the sky and part of that effort endures above the surface of dirt with arms extended into the sky.

Remembering that humans are Earth,[1] I come to the efforts of our species to build toward the skies. From the small living quarters of tribal societies to the towers of great cities, we build up from the ground. We

---

1. Those who prefer evidence from the ancient text may turn to Gen 3:19.

build homes and workplaces, monuments and containers for the dead. Like leaves drawing up materials from below we build into the sky. And our constructions stand, often far beyond the lifetimes of those who conceived them, sometimes for thousands of years.

The meaning of it all takes me beyond human hopes, empires, and religions. I see the same pattern that reveals itself in the changes of fall and brings my heart to wonder. We are not separate and different from Earth. We are Earth. And the evidence in our efforts as well as other forms from trees to volcanoes is that Earth reaches toward the sky. Daily gifted with energy from the sun, there is something in the nature of the planet itself which is always reaching back toward the life-giving sky. I also find it comforting rather than defeating that when the time of each effort ends; whether tree, monument, or mountain, Earth returns to Earth and the cycle continues.

When Science Is Wrong

10/20/2020

ANY BELIEF SYSTEM BASED ON scientific observation and theories must face the possibility that any theory could be wrong. This is even more true as science has moved into theories expressed in complex equations which cannot currently be tested by direct experiment. Observations are limited by what we already know and think we understand about the world. Theories based on those observations are limited by any flaw in the observations, their interpretation, and the difficulty of explaining phenomena that exceed our previous understandings. What we believe to be true today may be shown to be false tomorrow.

During my years growing up within fundamentalism, I remember hearing the question on more than one occasion, "Why turn from the eternal truths of God to the changeable and fallible thinking of men?"[1] Presentation of scientific research by television news and general magazines added strength to the argument. The conclusions of science presented in the reports seemed to constantly reverse itself. Foods that were good for you one year were bad for you the next and vice-versa. Exercise in gym class was more effective if preceded by pressing one's hands together or pulling against each other to tire muscles before movement. Then, new studies said there was no benefit to such activities. As I write this the same debate is in progress about pre-exercise stretching after decades of insistence that it is required. It did indeed seem like human ideas constantly shifted all the way

---

1. Sexist language is intentional here. I grew up when scientific thinking was overwhelmingly presented as the thinking of males.

to opposite opinions even within science while the Bible still said each year the same things it said the previous year.

There were however, two major flaws in this comparison. The first is that popular reporting of scientific findings is very different from the actual conclusions of experimental research. Any actual research project on the benefits of a particular activity or food would report the sample size, the identified variables, the specific methods used, and—of great importance—the results expressed as probabilities of the observed effect resulting from the studied cause. In popular reporting, these parameters are often replaced with statements expressing certainty rather than probability. New studies revealed the new super food, new cancer agent, new path to permanent youth without the cautions of an actual study. The popular press does not care that those conclusions were based on one group of subjects, with variables accounted for within the researchers' knowledge and ability to a level of probability, not absolute proof. Then, fads begin with magazine articles, books, and training seminars presenting information as facts which later turn out to be non-facts. A major factor in the errors in science was our lack of sophistication in reading research and the overstated interpretations presented by nonscientists for public consumption.

The second problem with the comparison is very similar in how information from the Bible was presented and explained. Lessons in Sunday school class seldom said that a particular passage meant a certain thing to certain groups of believers based on the thinking of a particular theologian in at a specific point in history. The words which did not change from year to year, until publishing frequent new versions of the Bible became commonplace, were presented as having meant the same things to all Christians since the beginning of the church. So, once again the problem was a lack of sophistication in understanding church history and the development and change in theology and interpretation over time. Some Christians still insist on the use of only the King James Bible as if it is identical to the original language of the speakers and authors. Newer translations which point out that certain passages do not appear in the earliest manuscripts, or which point out small but significant details such as a female name being changed to a male form, are seen as liberal attacks on pure faith rather than valuable academic insights into the origin of the text, its changes over time, and the evolution of thought as to what passages meant then and might mean now. In both science and Bible study there was an inaccurate assumption of certainty and a bias in favor of ideas which matched what we already believed to be true.

But scientific findings are sometimes reversed completely by later research and deeper understanding of phenomena. I believe it is important to contemplate what this means for any worldview based on scientific ideas used to form our conclusions about the world and our place in it. It seems very fair to me to ask whether moving to beliefs based on the universe and the observable powers that control it opens us to greater error than previous religious views. Having admitted that our religious understandings were based on many changing factors and never comprised one monolithic understanding, the question becomes whether looking to scientific understanding is more or less dependable, not one of absolute superiority of an unchanging view to a changeable one.

The simple fact is that when an idea, hypothesis, or theory in science is shown to be incorrect, it is changed. Some ideas have been accepted so widely or attached to the name(s) of such respected scientists, that demonstrating any major flaw in them meets serious resistance. Scientific views about the functioning of energy and matter do not change as easily as the fluctuations of news cycles may suggest. Evidence of error in any foundational understanding must be clear, shown in repeated experiments by other scientists, and debated. But nothing in science is beyond question and revision when facts reveal that a change is in order. When science is shown to be wrong, it changes. And the question of what that means for beliefs based on science must be answered.

First, the established fact that scientific conclusions may change can lead to a humbler approach in our search for meaning. I am less likely now to proclaim that a view of human behavior which I hold is guaranteed to be true for all people in all cultures for all time. If the underlying scientific ideas may change, my conclusions based on them are even more subject to fluctuation. Within that understanding, it would require great hubris to proclaim that anyone had discovered the infallible doctrine. I am attracted to that humility over the statements of absolutes from my youth based on what the Bible was believed to say and mean at that point in the history of one small faction of Christians.

Second, it makes some Bible texts easier to understand. One I have written about before is the Tower of Babel. It makes sense within the knowledge of the world available to its author. Understanding that people in that ancient time believed there was a ceiling at the top of the sky, it is possible to understand that they could also be convinced that building a tower to reach it would be possible, and that God would want to prevent it and keep humans in the realm of humans. The story becomes an ancient explanation for the variety of people and languages set in the world as understood at the time the story was created. Now, we have been to space. Many of us have flown to heights in commercial airliners which would have seemed like traveling into space to the ancients! A static view of both the world and human understanding would make the passage nothing but nonsense. A changeable view of nature and knowledge invites us to consider such passages as they fit into the worldview of their original audiences. It is also possible to accept that it may always have been considered an explanatory myth and only became treated as factual history with the advent of US fundamentalism.

Restating the first point in a different way, the knowledge that science often proves later to have been wrong, encourages me to remember that I may be wrong. There are factors in my past that make such a conclusion unattractive. I was taught that we knew the fundamental truths that would never change. I was an "A" student who hated losing any points on an exam. If a grading scale allowed the possibility of more than 100 percent as the recorded grade, I expected myself to obtain that score. I do not like to be wrong. Nevertheless, I am much healthier realizing that I probably am wrong in many ways every day. As a mortal being living and observing the world at one brief period in human history, the drive to be perfect is a burden too large to bear. Knowing that I am probably wrong in some of my observations and conclusions allows me to record them, share them, see if they seem to hold helpful truth for others. It also allows me to be corrected and grow in knowledge and understanding if another person points out errors in my thinking!

Karl Weick introduced his explanation on the importance of doubt with Robert Graves's wonderful poem, "In Broken Images."[2] I have often been comforted by its core idea. Belief in absolute knowledge of the nature of all things causes us to doubt ourselves when the cosmos does not conform to what we believe. Awareness of uncertainty allows us to trust our senses and enjoy amazement when the same anomalies arise. I am very comfortable with and comforted by the fact that science is sometimes shown to be wrong. The world which exceeds our grasp grows ever larger and invites us to new understanding, and new wonder. I choose to live in the magic of changing knowledge and unknowing rather than in the confusion of eternal knowledge.

---

2. Weick, *Social Psychology*, 224.

Approaching the Bible as Music

11/8/2020

STATEMENTS AND SOCIAL MEDIA POSTS by Christians with opposing political views during the recent US elections caused me to pause and contemplate the complexity of the biblical texts. A widely shared graphic attempting to show the Bible as one unified whole[1] pushed my thoughts even further. Maintaining any level of belief in the Bible as a statement of literal and united truth presents real problems for the faithful. What is forbidden in one place is done in another by a hero of faith proclaimed as a man who shared the heart of God.[2] In one place a people are excluded from God's people,[3] then a member of that people is counted among the ancestors of the one Christians consider the Jewish Messiah.[4] The combinations and contradictions require a suspension of logic or comfort with an unchanging God who changes.

As I have considered these things again, it occurs to me that a powerful metaphor may be found in orchestral music. When our appreciation of music takes us beyond the single melodies and repeated lyrics of preschool favorites, we begin to discover the way the variety of instrumental voices and melody lines can combine into a united whole of great beauty. The power and grandeur of a fine piece of orchestral music arise from the interplay of very different voices rather than a reduction of everything to a single simple tune.

1. Harrison, "Bible Cross References," para. 4.
2. Matt 13:21.
3. Deut 23:3.
4. Matt 1:5.

In the music of the orchestra various voices at times seem to converse, to argue, and to compete for attention even as they form a unified expression which exceeds our capacity to communicate in simple prosaic expressions. The deep notes of the larger instruments may call forth images of storm or war, while lighter tones from other players speak of sunlight, flight, or the return of calm and tranquility. Attempting to hear it all as one simple expression can lead to experiencing the performance as a cacophony. Appreciation of the interplay of voices brings us into contact with music that invites the celebration of the combined force of diverse voices and themes.

The student of a single instrument may select specific pieces of the total to use for performance, and those pieces well played may be expressions of great beauty. But neither lofty notes of the flute nor the deep offerings of the bassoon alone bring the magic of their interplay within the context of full orchestration. The violin often invokes the human voice and may wring great emotion from its combination of notes. But it soars to even greater heights when set within the harmony and contrast provided by the full orchestra.

I now suspect the offerings of ancient Scripture are much the same. Accounts of ancient victories may thunder like timpani but lack countermelodies of resolution and compassion without the passages which speak of common humanity like the voices the strings and woodwinds. Passages of divine assurance and times of peace may comfort us in times of need but can lack the assurance of authenticity without the balance of deeper melodies and voices expressing human loneliness, sorrow, or anger. The sum exceeds the parts as surely as the human life is greater than the events of any single hour or season.

I believe this invites any who dare to present and interpret ancient scriptures to others to look toward the role of the conductor. No part of the orchestra may be ignored without damaging the beauty of the performance. Yet there are times when one section is brought to the forefront while others assume supporting roles. There are times for the music of comfort and times for the notes which call us to the difficult work of greater humanity. There are times for sharing passages of healing and assurance, and times for proclaiming writings of warning and remembrance of hard times past.

I now read these ancient writings in this way. On days when my soul resonates with promises of green pastures and caring provision, I pause and contemplate those passages. When I am keenly aware of conflict and pain in the human condition, I also appreciate accounts of previous human experience demonstrating endurance and transcendence of life's greatest difficulties. But neither can ever be read as existing in isolation from the other. Even while I contemplate one type of writing, my mind and experience remind me of the full context provided only by the interplay of the combined total with all of its complexity.

Now, as I look to growing understanding of the power behind the universe that exceeds any one tradition, I also find instruction and invitation to greater humanity in traditions beyond the writings on which I was raised. Spending time in writings from the East, new expressions as diverse as the scales and forms of oriental music add greater depth and complexity in their beauty and contrast to the preferred harmonics of the West. Together they speak to the depth and the breadth of human experience. Native rhythms speak to me of the heartbeat of the planet with which I share every substance of my physical being. And beauty shines through in ways which invite rising to stand and applaud.

What a shame it would be to try to reduce the diversity of the world's music, or the voices in a single concerto, to a single line of melody! I now believe it is an equal mistake to ask the variety of ancient writings of power, faith, hope, and anguish to morph into one single-minded song. The beauty is in the discord as well as the harmony as each calls forth the memories, appreciation, and wonder which together express the reality of humans being.

Crimson and Gold

11/13/2020

Today I passed through corridors of crimson and gold,
The news says transitions are hard won,
Equatorial friends say tomorrow will be as yesterday was,
They speak of the worlds they know,
My world sits enthroned in tapestries of crimson and gold.

Who Fears the Deep State?

10/17/2020

I JUST READ A HEADLINE about a television commentator referring to Dr. Fauci[1] as part of the medical deep state. For the first time it made me wonder about the alternative that might explain the distrust some people express for what they call the deep state. Put very simply, the opposite of deep is shallow. Could it possibly be true that those promoting this term want a shallow state? It seems absurd.

I understand the term as an accusation that there is a large group of government employees who remain in their decision-making positions regardless of election outcomes. My view of government has always labeled such people as non-partisan public servants. But as the perceived divide between people, their government, and the two major political parties grows, it is easy to cast blame on a group of people who do not answer to the voters and simply continue their work regardless of the party in power. Rather than a positive continuation of legislatively approved government services without disruption by constant replacements based on patronage, the system becomes suspect as protecting people who answer to nobody and have their own agenda that is somehow harmful to average citizens. Preference for constant replacement of workers in the various offices of government would result in those who have developed skill and understanding of the complexities and fine points of their jobs along with the effects of their actions on others being replaced by new appointees with shallow, not deep, knowledge of the job we ask them to do.

---

1. Director of the National Institute of Allergy and Infectious Diseases since 1984 and primary advisor to the administration and the US people on responding to COVID-19.

There is evidence of support for just such a system of novice employees. Today's headline may be one example. Many of the people making these claims are deniers of scientific and academic evidence. Perhaps the factual evidence produced by science is rejected for reasons beyond the evangelical backlash caused decades ago by the theory of evolution—although rejection of what contradicts their literal interpretation of the Bible is certainly part of the issue. It now occurs to me that my prejudice against many of these people may be more accurate than I want it to be. Perhaps they oppose deep thought because they do not understand it and therefore are uncomfortable with it. I have seen this in the reactions of evangelical Christians to evolution. They do not reject it after careful study and understanding of the theory currently accepted in academic circles. They describe it in ways that show they clearly do not understand the theory at all. I recall many statements that a mammal may swim until it can swim no more and never become a fish, or that an animal introduced to an environment it cannot tolerate will die rather than evolve as denials of evolutionary theory. No respectable scientist in that field would ever make such a claim.

It now occurs to me that the same may also be true in other areas such as government including civil and foreign policy. Preferring newcomers they believe will do something more in line with their own opinions, they favor those with shallow knowledge. To say it a different way, those with deep knowledge of the working of domestic and foreign policy have advanced academic training, years of experience, or both. Many of the people claiming that the deep state is the problem do not. When they criticize actions of longtime public servants or the views of academics in these areas, how often have they been insulted by statements that the problem is their own lack of deep understanding of issues and procedures? Few people like to be told that they are uniformed or that their views display ignorance. Rather than internalize the feedback that they need greater knowledge and a deeper understanding of what is happening, it is easier to turn against those presented as experts. I do not mean that they all consciously reject informed opinion based on a preference for ignorance. Many people lacking the skills needed to examine the flaws in their own views, simply conclude that those who oppose them are using academics and experience as excuses and smoke screens to hide some self-serving intent.

Being able to analyze one's own thinking and recognize errors in logic and conclusions requires the same skills that would lead to higher-quality views in the first place. Put bluntly, the same people who are not informed enough to know what is correct, are not informed enough to know if what they think is wrong. They may in fact hear it as being told they are too stupid to understand. Their self-image is kept intact by rejecting both the perceived insult and the people who say or imply it. The problem is transferred to the people on the deep side of the issue.

I also realize that there are intelligent educated people among my own friends who have adopted the language as the current terminology for government policies and practices that they do not approve. Theirs is simply a usage based on current vocabulary, although the term itself may make it easier to entice them to believe that there is some conspiracy against people who see the world the way they do. Deep can also mean hidden.

This realization that some of my associates have adopted a term due to frequent repetition which might be used to manipulate them into even more negative views of the status quo leads me to suspect the existence of yet another group. If the educated can be tilted toward more negative views by the use of a term, my own assumption is that the uniformed are even easier to deceive. It is not hard to imagine then that some using the term know exactly what they are doing and are manipulating public views of politics and the government. Many evangelicals have already done the same with science and other advanced academic knowledge. Realizing that people will reject what they do not understand more easily than accept their own ignorance of the subject matter, they have found a term with which to manipulate voters.

Recently, I also pulled up online images of the Trees of Life and of Knowledge as I worked on another project. As expected, the Tree of Life was covered with attributes known to Christians as the Fruits of the Spirit—Godly traits of people considered to be good. The Tree of Knowledge, as the one eaten from in the theology of the fall, was covered with negative and selfish human traits. Among the signs of a life lived separate from God, I also saw, "human reason,"[2] or in one slightly more subtle version, human reason apart from God. If we reject human reason as evil, then those who claim to present God's message to those who have abandoned the right and responsibility to think for themselves become the world's power brokers. Suddenly, it made sense how so many people who claim to follow Jesus of Nazareth and the teachings of the Bible can

---

2. Flurry and Macdonald, "Mystery," para. 17.

accept leaders who show few of the characteristics usually listed on the Tree of Life. Having given over their own reason, people are left accepting the word of leaders who claim to represent God. Then those leaders are free to assert that one candidate is God's chosen and the other is sinister by comparison no matter how the factual evidence may appear to their followers. Reason is not to be trusted. Faith in those accepted as God's appointed leaders reigns.

I do not accept such a worldview. I do not reject reason as evil.[3] History contains examples too numerous to list where allegiance to leaders—in small groups of people or in nations—has led to disaster and death. Within UFT's assertion that what we know as God is expressed in the combined forces of nature which control the universe, there is no such thing as escaping those forces. Precisely how those forces work within the human mind as we make what we consider to be free choices remains elusive and debated. But everything we do does occur within the natural world and within the interaction of the forces of nature. There is no empirical validation for anyone acting or producing results outside those forces regardless of the claims of various religious groups.

To hand over the use of one's reason for the blind acceptance of orders from any other person, no matter how holy they appear to be, is to abandon one's responsibility to seek what is right and true. If we do not observe and evaluate what is happening and being done, there is no limit to the evil we may accept from others or commit under their guidance. It is only in our power to observe, identify facts, and make reasonable choices that we rise above the worst that humans can do to others. When situations are complex, it is deep thinking rather than blind obedience or shallow reasoning that allows us to discern reasonable choices with desirable outcomes. I rejected Christian calls to turn off my mind and accept teachings blindly when I was very young. I still reject it. I also do not accept any interpretation that the wisdom of the East requires us to abandon our minds even though meditation often involves an emptying of self during the exercise. I do not believe that the Buddha taught his followers to walk blindly through the world ignoring the condition of their neighbors or the consequences of their own actions. The ancient call of God is recorded as "Come let us reason together," leading to the washing away of sin.[4]

---

3. A simple word search for the word "reason" in an online Bible shows how often Paul used reasoning to spread the new religion of Christianity.

4. Isa 1:18 (KJV).

If the fear is of a group of people embedded in the government, doing what they please and harming others, I will oppose them anytime evidence is produced of who they are and what they are doing wrong. If the call is to reject anything that requires deep knowledge or deep thought, then I reject the call. Answering to neither emperor, pope, nor guru, I stand accountable for my choices. And I rely on the deepest thinking I am equipped to do. I want nothing less from those who serve in leadership of either government or the church.

Weep

10/25/2020

Weep with me for the other ones.
In a land of hope and dreams, safety nets, and social programs,
Weep with me for those unknown, unseen, alone.
In a country with churches, synagogues, mosques, and civic service groups,
Weep with me for those unsought, un-prayed for, unsaved.
In a land of psychiatry for dogs and cats,
Weep with me for those descending into hell unthinkable.
In a country that has shown me every gift, opportunity, joy and pleasure,
Weep with me for those I thought I knew and failed.

RISE
Rise with me for the other ones.
In a land of hope and dreams, safety nets, and social programs,
Rise with me to search for those unknown, unseen, alone.
In a country with churches, synagogues, mosques, and civic service groups,
Rise with me to bring in those most in need.
In a land of psychiatry for dogs and cats,
Rise with me to demand access for those who cannot cure themselves.
In a country that has shown me every gift, opportunity,
joy and pleasure, Rise with me to make amends and fight again.

Just War

11/13/2020

ONE OF THE MOST LONGSTANDING beliefs across cultures has been the idea of just war. Whether based on sanction by a divine being or extreme need and self-preservation by the warring parties, humans have held that violence required justification. Individuals killing others is considered murder in most societies unless unavoidable. Extending the violence by group action has traditionally also required extreme need. The concept goes back to the ancients in both the East and West. Exceptions in Christianity are exemplified by groups like the Quakers who rejected all war. Praise of war for its own sake, even in the twentieth century, was the mark of movie villains.

When the English colonies in North America decided to revolt against English rules, they did so with the familiar words,

> When in the Course of human events, it becomes necessary for one people to dissolve the political bands which have connected them with another, and to assume among the powers of the earth, the separate and equal station to which the Laws of Nature and of Nature's God entitle them, a decent respect to the opinions of mankind requires that they should declare the causes which impel them to the separation.[1]

Obviously, they believed that an action requiring war—and which would seek the help of other nations—called for justification. Their long list of grievances against the English crown followed.

---

1. "Declaration of Independence."

When I was a public-school student, the wars in Korea and Vietnam were still presented as justified battles on behalf of the noncommunist people of those countries. Any battle against communism was considered justified by many in the sixties and seventies. But further explanations were still given in order to demonstrate that the United States was fighting for more than a preference of our system over other people's choices. With the horrors of Hitler's regime fully known, World War II required little defense and was presented as the story of the United States saving the free world. No further justification was necessary.

But the war in Vietnam drug on with little evidence of success while its images played out on television. The horror of war was broadcast to the general citizenry of the country, many of whom had growing doubts about why the United States had a vital interest requiring war in a small country on the other side of the globe. The most prominent explanation I remember was domino theory; that the communists would not stop with any one country but would continue conquering the world one piece at a time until a line was held. At the same time accounts from the war revealed that many of the people we were supposedly defending were on the side of the communists.

I believe a serious change in United States' attitudes towards war began as a reaction to my generation who grew up questioning whether this war was indeed just. We questioned whether the sacrifice of so many of our military, along with reports of even larger casualties among the Vietnamese, was justified. As a masters student I took a course on the United States since World War II that included readings in the primary documents associated with Vietnam. When I pointed out that the documents signed by the French only required a division of the country sufficient to allow French withdrawal rather than permanent separation, I heard a common phrase of the time, "America: Love it or Leave it!"[2] Even within the usually polite environment of a graduate class, there was no room for questioning or discussing our defense of the war as just. The country had begun to accept an ideology that said the sacrifices of our troops and the respect due our leaders required blind support rather than intellectual debate.

Now in the midst of the twenty-first century it appears that this transition has become complete. On the national holidays of Memorial and Veterans Day along with the ceremonies before large sporting events,

---

2. Sigman, "Brief History," para. 1.

I hear prayers of gratitude for those who served along with pleas for the safety of all who currently serve. Both seem entirely appropriate within the society which asks for and accepts their service and sacrifice. But I also hear more. There is a worshipful attitude toward the military and credit given to the military as the provider of every good thing in our society. Beyond this, the status of hero is no longer reserved for the soldier or sailor who risks or experiences great personal injury or loss in order to protect comrades in arms or further our national agenda. We are now encouraged to consider every person who joins the military as an automatic hero.

It all sounds very good. But I remember the war years of my youth. A lot of those young people just older than me did not go to war for any heroic reasons or beliefs in just war. Many went because their government gave them no other choice except prison or desertion of country. They were scared kids carted off to war by a country short on warriors. To be sure, the strength of bond between brothers in arms caused some of those young people to behave very heroically once they were in the theater of war. Others stayed in fear and died or deserted unless other fighters and the fortunes of war allowed them to merely survive their time in conflict and return home. I also remember that enlistment was given as an option rather than incarceration to more than a few who were guilty of criminal offenses at home. My definition of hero does not include accepting a shorter time in one hell to avoid a longer and less socially acceptable confinement in another.

Then there was the growing unrest at home which continues in varying forms as I write this. Guardsmen with rifles were used against students accused of throwing rocks. Reports of police causing death to citizens, often accused of very minor offenses, by the use of excessive force seemed to result in criticism of everyone in uniform. The events of 9/11 including the heroic efforts of both police and fire fighters caused a surge in patriotism and appreciation of those who serve here at home. But over the years, the news reports of excessive force also continued causing a wide range of reactions: bad things that cannot all be prevented happen in the battle to maintain law and order: black lives matter, abolish the prison system, defund the police. And the reaction is binary once again. The logic of the day seems to state that there are only two choices— resistance or blind loyalty and praise of all who serve.

Now wars that began after 9/11 have extended far beyond the original purpose of bringing retribution to the leadership behind the attack on our country. That goal was accomplished and nothing changed. Under presidents of both political parties, we have continued to drop bombs on any target suspected of including enemies to our purposes. At home neighbors are flying flags with a blue line added to the stripes of red and white[3] to show their complete support of all police. I know that when I share this essay widely many will consider me disloyal for expressing what they will interpret as less than complete support.

However, it seems to me that a significant change has occurred altering thinking which held predominance from the time of our earliest records. Rather than war requiring clear explanations of all the reasons justifying our resort to violent action, we now appear to have entered a time when any action is considered appropriate and worthy of full respect simply because we are the actors. Those who participate for any reason are considered not only justified, but glorified, just by putting on a uniform.

---

3. It doesn't seem to matter to people with patriotic intentions that adding to the country's flag is itself a violation of the code and a desecration of the flag.

Infinity Plus One

11/30/2020

INFINITY PLUS ONE EQUALS INFINITY. Infinity already includes every possible plus one and any statement exceeding it doubles back on itself.

Decades ago, my mentor and I had a conversation which we have repeated many times over the years about the mathematical improbability of our existence. The numbers of possible genetic combinations in one child from two biological parents are daunting. Then adding the improbability of those two people meeting and mating dramatically increases the size of the calculation. The numbers become astronomical without even trying to include previous generations. It has been a mental exercise which mostly led to metaphysical musing about how impossible odds become one to one as soon as we are born. Recent estimates place the odds of two people meeting and having the specific child they do at 400,000,000,000,000:1.

Confronted by those numbers another set of ideas returned to mind. During my lifetime evangelical Christians have often shared scientific facts as proof of universal design. Authors such as Lee Strobel have successfully published numerous books which use the precise nature of physical existence and the improbability of them happening by chance as proof of a creator. I have written about my response to those assertions before. The number of possible earth-like planets in the universe has grown from an assumed quantity of one to numbers more in line with the size of the universe. The odds of life, including human life, existing on this planet are very good because this planet has the right combination of matter and energy to support our existence. Miraculous would be our sudden appearance and ability to live on one of the planets without water

Infinity Plus One

or adequate energy. The improbability of everything being perfectly aligned exists only when we start with Earth as the only possibility and ask how everything could be perfect for our existence. But the question should be why humans emerged on this planet, and the answer is because it is the one that has what is needed for human life. And we have continued to adapt to the realities of the planet. There is no mystery.

I have also written about the infinity problem in the search for a single equation to express the scientific theory of everything. Quantum equations work for quantum phenomena. Equations for the physics of large objects work in that realm. However, attempts to combine the two sets of equations fall apart as they disappear into a result of infinity. Recent statements that the odds of two people meeting and having a specific child are enormous leads me to another thought. I have often mused before, that the improbability only matters if we try to predict the precise person in advance. Once they exist, they exist.

I am now considering a complete reversal of the claims that the improbability of our existence proves a designer. That designer would face the enormity of the task at hand represented by the incredible numbers our equations indicate. The odds of the universe being configured exactly as it is exceed our ability to calculate. Of course, the religious person has an answer for this. God is omnipotent. God can do it and there is no chance involved because the powerful designer made it exactly this way because he[1] chose to make it this way. Before today, I have always assumed that ends the argument. Faith accepts the answers of faith and doubt does not. I am now considering a more radical conclusion.

All of this makes sense if the omnipotent power controlling the universe is internal. Adding an external God does not yield a greater sum mathematically. The possibilities for the existence of our universe are infinite. The odds of current existence are infinity to one excluding for now multiverse theory which also does not fit the religious argument. If the power that causes the universe to be is internal, then infinite power produces infinite possibilities. If, however, we place the power in the hands of an external actor, even the Deists' watchmaker, then the power of that Creator must be infinity plus the ability to order infinite possibilities. The Creator's power must exceed the grand improbability of accomplishing what happened. Any external power would be required to equal infinity plus some amount great enough to overcome the odds. Internally, infinite

---

1. I am again using male preferential language because it is the usual language in the sources I am considering.

possibilities produce a universe of infinite possibilities. It is balanced. Externally, something greater than infinity must exist. It reminds me of the old question of whether a God who can do anything can create a rock so big that same God cannot move it. Those who answer from a position of religious instruction and accompanying faith will accept what others find impossible. But it does not prove that impossibility.

For those of us who believe in evidence and reality, I return to the beginning. Infinity plus one is still infinity by definition. I find the assertion that the omnipotent, omnipresent power behind the universe is part of the universe and is expressed in the equations of the unified theory more elegant. The equations which continue to frustrate mathematicians by defaulting to infinity suggest that the infinite lies within the universe for those of us who do not make the religious leap to belief in external realms which cannot be studied based on evidence available for direct observation and verification. The very books on my theology shelves that seek to convince me the universe was designed by an external God, lead me to assume that an internal power is far more plausible. Infinity plus one is a mathematical expression which lacks meaning.

Intolerable Dark and a Lack of Advent

12/3/2020

NORMALLY IN DECEMBER MY THOUGHTS and often my essays turn to advent and the practice of waiting in the dark. As I wrote last year's essays, I was blissfully ignorant of the pandemic and other events that would cause the darkness to seem to linger throughout 2020. Entertainment and employment were shut down by government actions and by personal decisions concerning safety. The government asked or ordered us to cover our faces. All large gatherings were discouraged or prohibited. To many people these measure also raised the ominous prospect of government interference with their freedom and their faith.

As if the threat of deadly disease were not enough, the evidence grew that our country was more politically divided than at any time since the Civil War—an extreme statement for those of us who remember the most contentious and deadly days of the Vietnam and civil rights movement years. Acknowledging a greater problem now than the ones we already survived has led to dark predictions for the country from both sides of the political aisle. Some churches have served as beacons of hope, while others have descended into pronouncements that the side they oppose is evil and likely to bring God's further judgement against the country. Neighbors have put up yard signs declaring these dire warnings and statements of judgement to each other. The year 2020 has appeared to many—realizing that wealth alone does not exempt us from disease and social upheaval—as a slow-motion disaster. And we look for the light.

This year as summer turned to fall and Halloween gave way to Thanksgiving, the ever-increasing rush toward thoughts of Christmas has accelerated noticeably. Along with personal statements on social media, retail stores have promoted putting up holiday light displays as quickly as possible. My neighborhood, already an area my family visited to see elaborate decorations when I was a child, is glowing with more frequent and extravagant displays than in any recent year. People are doing everything they can to bring light and joy to each other in spite of any political or other differences. The yard signs declaring our immediate demise are almost completely replaced by the sparkling and ostentatious displays of the season.

And it causes me to pause and consider advent anew. Perhaps this is an improper time to expect anyone to engage in the millennia old traditions of practicing a period of patient waiting in the dark. Maybe the darkness of 2020 is too large of a burden to call for the discipline of waiting for the light. Possibly advent has become an outdated practice in a time of constant declared darkness. My answer remains, as it always has been, that advent is the needed response to the darkness.

Three of my four children have contracted COVID-19 and one and her husband are still battling it along with their children. People we know have died. Normal celebrations with family have been eliminated. Neither my wife nor I have suffered a decline in employment or income, but her work in healthcare has put her in situations of unreasonable exposure. Every ache, pain, or cough is monitored for possible indication of contracting the disease. We have both been tested more than once. And still, I say that the rush to push away the darkness could call us to the need for appreciation of advent rather than its demise.

As I choose words to relay these thoughts, I intentionally avoid often used phrases like *nature knows*. We know that both the lengthening and shortening of days with the subsequent changes in weather are caused by the tilt of the planet as it orbits the sun without any true indication of or requirement for conscious thought. But those of us in the temperate zones can annually observe the benefit of seasons of both growth and rest. The dying off of leaves and seasonal plants each fall feeds the Earth with minerals needed for the rebirth of spring and next year's growing season. The cycle, to state the obvious, is natural. In the dark, the forces of nature rest and then burst forth with life again in their given season. Animals follow similar patterns of behavior. And we are, regardless of beliefs or prejudices, natural beings as well. We need seasons of rest. Many of my friends have learned the healthy practice of meditation and periods of calm and quiet during the busiest of seasons.[1] A season of such rest is as needed now as it ever was.

Nonetheless, the rush to light our segment of the planet is on as people crave relief from the strain of the year. News from our national leadership is not helping. Our president refuses to accept the outcome of the election in spite of declarations from his own party and the courts that the results are valid. Congress continues to play the game of each party trying to position the other in a negative way rather than take actions needed for the relief of many who are suffering financially and risk the opponent getting more credit. Scientists are beginning to claim that a miracle vaccine is on the way, but another year may be needed for enough doses for general protection.[2] A significant number of people will watch for sufficient evidence of safety before accepting the vaccine, further delaying general protection. And the wait still ahead seems like an eternity to people raised in the age of the microwave and the air fryer. People believe they have waited longer than can be reasonably be expected for relief. The urge to light up the world now is compelling.

Sitting here healthy and well-fed in a comfortably heated house far larger than I need, my view is undoubtedly different from those who lack basic comforts even as we all grieve those we have lost. Acknowledging that I speak from a position of privilege and comfort, I continue to believe that we need a discipline of accepting times of waiting, of accepting the dark as a time to rest without immediate satisfaction. There is health and healing in the art of stopping our constant rushing into the future. The example goes all the way back to the story of Mary the mother of Jesus quietly pondering all that she had been told as she waited not only for the birth, but also for the unfolding life events of her growing son. Before the night of the heavenly chorus, there is an entire season of quiet and waiting. Before the declaration of resurrection, there is the horror of the crucifixion and the confusing wait through the Sabbath day of rest.

Perhaps if we had more practice in the uncomfortable blessing of waiting, maybe if we had stronger traditions of experiencing life as a process which comes when the time is right regardless of our longings, possibly if we knew how to treasure and be strengthened by rest in the midst

---

1. Eastern practices have powerful systems of meditation. Ramadan takes Muslims into a month of practicing waiting by daytime fasting, and so forth. I am focusing on Christian practices here because advent is from that tradition.

2. As I edit this at the end of 2020 distribution of vaccines has begun with varying estimates of how quickly enough people will gain immunity to end the threat.

of waiting, 2020 would not have seemed quite so intolerable. Through the many dark days of this year, perhaps our own lack of practice in healthy waiting has distorted our view of how dark things really are. I believe people of faith turning now to long traditions of advent, of waiting for the arrival of the promise, will find strength and renewal to see them through the dark times still before us.

Places Too Holy

12/15/2020

THERE ARE CURRENTLY ABOUT SIXTY people trying to be the first to climb K2, the world's second highest mountain, in the winter. If a team succeeds, they will claim one of the only remaining *firsts* in mountaineering. Perhaps the most appropriate team is one made entirely of Sherpas. It is their world. But the summit belongs to no humans. K2 is sometimes called the savage mountain because she seems to intentionally attack humans who try to reach her summit. One person dies for every four human beings allowed to stand on her summit. It is not a place suited to human life in the best of weather.

The native peoples of Earth have long taught that the high places belong to the gods. The high places are holy. The heights draw our minds and spirits to awe and wonder. But they do not welcome our bodies.

We are creatures of hills, valleys, and the surface of earth's waters. In those environments we have thrived and multiplied. But the deepest places in the oceans and the highest summits of the mountains are not suited to human life. We have built machines to travel deep into the oceans. We have built machines which can fly above the highest mountains. But find a way to exit either at the extremes and humans will die immediately. The Greeks and Romans taught that the depths belong to the gods as well as the heights. But beginning with the story of Adam and Eve, humans seek to be gods.

Some team will make it. Before a human finds a way to stand on the deepest bottom of the ocean, some person will stand on the summit of K2 in the winter and return safely to the normal realm of humans. Their name will be remembered forever in the records of mountaineering. And

I believe they will remain interlopers treading places reserved for the gods.

What does my opinion matter? I have been thrilled to meet men who have survived the climb of Everest. They are remarkable people. Who am I to say that they did not belong there? I have no status in the world of mountaineering. As I write this, I remain almost completely unknown in the fields of theology and philosophy as well. But humans are observers and thinkers. Some of us also contemplate the information that comes to us and the deeper meanings and consequences of human thought and action. From that vantage point, my mind explores meaning whether in affirmation, warning, or both.

I am not concerned about K2. I firmly believe that the powers humanity names as gods lie in the combined forces of nature, and those forces are strong in an environment as extreme as K2. I will grant myself the liberty of speaking of what K2 will do, but I am not anthropomorphizing or calling K2 a god. I am speaking about the effect of the forces there. K2 will decide how high any team is allowed to climb. K2 will determine how many return to homes and loved ones. And K2 will remain.[1]

Humans have brought havoc and ruin wherever our species has come to dominance. Plastic can now be found almost everywhere on our planet. It can be found inside forms of life with no known human contact. We have altered the land, the water, and the soil wherever we live. We have sprayed chemicals deemed to work to our advantage even if they are poison to other life forms—sometimes because they are poison to other lifeforms—where we spray them and everywhere downstream and downwind. Even Everest, the tallest summit, has been littered from base camp up all the preferred routes with trash, excrement, and bodies deemed too difficult to retrieve. Thankfully, Sherpas and others are now engaged in the serious and dangerous work of trying to remove at least some of the filth we have left on Earth's highest mountain. K2 has remained less hospitable to human adaptation and intrusion. Hopefully she always will.

However, I cannot think of these brave souls, whether heroes or fools, preparing to seek the winter summit without also contemplating talk of venturing to other places outside our world. Producing more children and more damage than our planet seems capable of sustaining and remaining hospitable to us, some have begun to look longingly to the

---

1. A team of Sherpa and Nepali climbers successfully completed the winter summit of K2 in 2021. At least five other climbers died in this year's attempts.

moon, Mars, and beyond. We have already shown we can build machines capable of traveling there, and in the case of the moon, gear that will protect humans to walk on the surface and return safely home. But it is clear that they are not environments for human beings. NASA's experiments with the Kelly twins have already shown that if humans spend extended time in space our gene expression will change to match the new reality.[2] Super-terrestrial environments are the realms of the gods, the powers of nature. They are not the home of humanity. To date only the forces of nature are capable of traversing space and abiding in every environment of the universe.

Can we go there? I do not doubt that we can create vessels to take humans there and perhaps even further. To travel the lightyears to other earth-like planets seems beyond human capacity. So once did reaching the bottom of the ocean or the top of the Himalaya and the Karakoram. But men and women have won acclaim by reaching those places, although we still cannot live there. As of this writing, no government has made living in those environments a goal for research and development. We visit. We disturb the environments. Some survive and go home. Only the dead remain there.

The surface of the moon and other planets are not our homes. We evolved here to match this place and we are of this place. We are made of it. When our time is up, we return to become part of this place. We belong here at least until and unless we destroy it for human occupation. Given the history of human adaptation, invention, and achievement it is entirely possible that governments determined to place colonies beyond Earth will succeed as did the governments that placed colonies in the Americas.

But should we?

Will we ever abandon our mission to go where the gods go?

Will we ever stop trying to claim places that belong to the gods and not humanity?

Will we ever stop trying to become gods?

My own conclusion is that there are places too holy. There are depths too deep and summits too high. There are worlds beyond our world. And I am in agreement with the teachings of the ancients. The homes of the gods are entered only by invitation. To invade these realms and remain is beyond what the gods have given to us.

---

2. Leary, "After a Year," paras. 3–4.

If the lessons of summits apply, we enter the holy of holies and live when we are invited.

But we continue to covet, to plan, and to design plans to acquire what is not given to us.

There are places too high.

There are places too holy.

We are here and we are home.

What We Think We See

12/22/2020

MY MIND IS STILL FASCINATED by the conjunction of Jupiter and Saturn this week as well as the meanings various people have placed upon it. My own mind marvels at the spatial conditions allowing us to see a great meeting in the sky that never happens.

Most people with a basic knowledge of astronomy realize that the two planets never actually meet. Neither do their orbits cross. What we are seeing is the two reaching a point in their orbits which causes them to fall within a single line of vision from Earth. In some ways, this is like watching from the ground as two airplanes appear to cross paths in the sky without any real danger of collision. This however is a very rough comparison. The lines of flight for our two airplanes are askew allowing one to cross well above the other. The paths of the planets are nearly parallel. This means that the moment when we see the planets together is not even the occasion of their closest proximity! When they are beside each other in orbit, they would appear in conjunction from the angle of the Sun, not the Earth. A space traveler passing between them at that moment would not see them together, but exactly opposite one another with one invisible or appearing as a black spot against the brightness of the Sun in one direction and the other on the opposite side as a light in the dark! Conjunction from Earth is when they both reach a location on a single straight line from the observer on earth across their paths. And they are not stationary. Jupiter is traveling at 29,236 mph, Saturn is traveling at 21,675 mph, and our own orbital speed is 66,615 mph plus our rotational speed of another 1000 mph in our moment of standing still to view the display!

Then as my mind's eye pictured the paths and angles allowing us to see the beautiful conjunction, another dimension occurred to me. As my friend Doc and I were viewing the conjunction together-apart by cell phone we were trying to remember the distances involved. So, I had to look them up and compare them to the speed of light because it occurred to me that what we were viewing was not even happening simultaneously! The light we were seeing from Saturn had been traveling twice as long as the light from Jupiter. The light began its journey to our point of observation approximately forty-nine minutes ago from Jupiter, and ninety-eight minutes ago from Saturn. Said differently, the two planets we were looking at were not only separated by space, but they were also separated by time. The Saturn in our view was ninety-eight minutes earlier in time, or older, and Jupiter was forty-nine minutes past the moment we perceived from Earth. What appeared to be a single star was actually two bodies separated by 550 million miles, traveling through space at enormous speeds, both separated by us by different amounts of time as we looked up in wonder to see them sitting together in the sky.

I stood perfectly still, held my breath in order to hold my camera as motionless as possible to photograph these two giants of the solar system align. I saw it with my own eyes and experienced it with my body and mind. But none of it was true if I mean a concrete fact as my mind perceived it to be at the time. Yet there it was, and I have pictures to *prove* it.

Life

12/23/2020

Eternal Energy
Configured for
But a Moment,
Experiences
Loss and Longing
Gratitude
Love and Wonder
Persistent
Incarnation.

When Humans Choose Destruction

1/10/2021

THIS HAS BEEN A WEEK in the United States I hoped never to see. I watched in horror as an angry mob moved from a "take back our government" rally hosted by the president to attack our own capitol. The response was slow and far more subdued than against protesters in the past with darker skins in spite of their use of less destructive tactics. I really believe the much-criticized capitol police did enough to prevent extreme violence against our elected leaders, including the vice-president and maybe his family. It was an event of unprecedented seriousness for our country. But too much remains unknown to assert what the final conclusions will be after fuller investigations of both intentional and incompetent actions (as well was heroism) by those who are supposed to protect our leaders from all enemies. The data which will go into the history of the event is still being collected and many of us are waiting with some apprehension to see what larger movement may follow. For now, we are in a time of questions.

In the midst of this, I see both conservative and liberal friends posting direct pleas for divine intervention or calls upon the faithful to pray. And it causes my mind to turn to the bigger question of the role of God when human beings willingly choose destruction. Many people of faith have stories of God's miraculous intervention to stop violence. I have written before about how the very use of the word "miraculous" indicates by definition an acknowledgement of the fact that intervention is not what usually happens. It must be rare before we use the label of miracle. I have been involved in those prayers before as well as celebrations when the violence we anticipated did not happen. We joyfully gave credit to God for protecting those deserving of protection. Looking back, I also note a certain degree of personal pride in believing that I had in some way changed events on another continent.

On one particularly memorable evening we received a request to pray for a worker in a volatile country whose leader had turned against him and sent the militia to capture or, more likely, kill him. I joined in with others around the world in praying for divine protection. Then we celebrated when one group of attackers failed to find the place where he was widely known to live, and a second force dispersed as neighbors kept telling them that the people on his property were heavily armed[1] and that the soldiers would die if they went there. Efforts to seek him out then ended completely. We believed that God, or angels, had formed some sort of protective wall around him and answered our prayers. I have also read records of wind blowing a person attempting suicide back to safety. It is exactly the kind of thing a God of the Bible as interpreted by my previous tradition would do.

However, I assert in UFT that the omnipresent, omnipotent power of the universe is not an invisible superhuman waiting on our intercession and choosing who to save in the ways some interpretations of Christianity assume. If God is the power of the universe studied by physicists as the combined forces at play in the search for the unified field, there is no reason to assert that those powers change behavior in response to our entreaties. I have metaphorically asked gravity to be less as I attempted a cliff-climbing move at the edge of my ability. Gravity did not decrease, even if my confidence rose and made the move seem to become easier. Neither do I believe the witness of history bears out any claim that the power of the universe ever intercedes to stop human choices for destruction. Whether we choose peace or war, the forces of nature do what they do, and we use them to better the conditions of humanity or to bring destruction.

I especially reject literal readings of the Jewish portions of the Bible to claim that the power of the universe intervened to help people destroy other people. I do not believe that the sun stood still, or that Earth stopped rotating to make it look like it did, so that Israel's army could kill more people. I do not believe that the army of Israel attacked whole populations killing every person and animal.[2] Most of all, I do not believe the powers that control the universe told them to do so. These are

---

1. They were not.

2. A check of current commentaries shows the term is used to mean to conquer completely but does not imply complete genocide.

memories and legends of how the people of the author came to live in and control various areas, and even though they occurred in ancient and supposedly more barbaric times, they were written as national memories—not modern history.

I have met too many whose ability to believe in God was damaged by previous beliefs in divine protection. The God who defeats all enemies to protect his people was absent during the horrors of Europe between and during the world wars. Many a soldier has returned from war knowing that in their darkest hour, or that of brothers in arms, no divine power stopped the destruction brought from one group of humans against another. They have also witnessed the carnage among innocents who simply found themselves in the path of violence. The one who comes home celebrating the miracle of the bullet that struck their pocket Bible does not override the experiences of all the others. They saw the bloodshed where there was no miraculous rescue.

I am glad the man we prayed for lived and was not harmed. But I would now attribute the events that took place to forces studied in sociology and psychology. The troops sent to kill him were poorly trained and disciplined. The neighbors who conducted the whispering campaign to the passing troops knew the person they were protecting to be a good man who served their area well. The angels in that incident were as human as I am, perhaps in some honorable ways even more so. I marvel at stories of people whose efforts at self-destruction have been subverted by the forces of nature. But that is exactly what I believe the forces of nature were, natural. The wind did not spring from nowhere for the sake of the fortunate person.

The ability to produce massive nuclear destruction is a human reality. It pervades all the years of my life. In more recent years we have developed the ability to spread lies, fear, and hatred far beyond the immediate circles of humans who can hear our physical voices. With the power of the internet, we can spread positive or negative messages literally around the globe. We make them believable when the reader trusts the person whose name appears on the post even if it is at the end of a long line of people who trusted the previous person, who trusted the person, who trusted *ad nauseam* until there is no knowledge of who originally wrote the information or what they hoped to achieve by sending it. The same electricity that gives us light now allows us to transmit messages of darkness. The electricity does not change, only the sequence of keys we choose to press.

My conclusion is that the power to choose life or death, improvement for humanity or destruction, is not found in any metaphysical realm or being. It lies with us individually and collectively. When I walk down the streets of my neighborhood and remember which yards had the signs of the opposing sides in last fall's election, the response is mine. I can nurse grudges against those who put out messages that offended me. I can also see my neighbors as neighbors acknowledging that their life experiences, educations, and beliefs led them to conclusions different from mine without attaching intentions of malice to either their acts or my reactions. It was a pleasure and an honor to point out to my grandchildren as we hiked the neighborhood as part of our daily exercise that my neighbors continue greeting each other as neighbors no matter which sets of signs were on display in their yards. We choose peace.

Perhaps I should give more attention to the power of religious beliefs to bring about these positive and loving reactions to people we might otherwise reject. It was part of my religious training even in bad times when we failed to live it well toward disagreeing members of our own group. We still believed and taught that God called his people to love and care for each other. But my mind will not allow me to leave things at that level of simplicity. People, even other varieties of Christians, with different beliefs and practices were not just neighbors with differing views. They were people misled by lies and the forces of evil in the world, some of whom would eventually burn forever in hell. All people were loved by God as we sang in children's songs about all the colors of the world, but we were not to date or marry people of other faiths or different skin color. Approaching the annual celebration of Martin Luther King Jr. Day, I recall those who claimed to believe in the same God he preached who had no difficulty blaming Dr. King for the violence used against him and his followers. People reasoned that nothing bad would have happened but for the protesters daring to stand up and say that their race was equal to ours. Now there is what we say in school assemblies and often opposite things said at home over a beer or two. I do not find that religion separates the two. We do. With all of our upbringing, intentional and unintentional training from our elders, perceptions of our experiences, and trust and distrust of various people who seek to tell us what is true, we choose.

I firmly believe that what comes next is on us, not God. We will choose what actions we believe are just, or justifiable, based on our emotions as well as our attempts at rational thought. We will decide where grace is appropriate and where real actions are required. We will base our opinions on facts but also on perceived threats and emotional responses. I would like to believe that where it is needed and within our power we will choose restorative justice. I fear that what one side sees as needed justice the other will see as hateful retribution. I fear that what some will see as a need for grace to restore unity, others on both sides will see as weakness. What I do not believe is that any metaphysical power is going to appear to solve it for us. We are here. The choices are ours and those of the people we have elected. And the powers of the universe will continue on whether we choose a path to renewed unity and growth or greater destruction. The godlike power of the forces of nature is not that they can be manipulated by our rituals. It is that they will continue after us, even as they preceded our appearance, whether our choices turn out to be wise or destructive.

The Denial of Death and Pascal's Wager

1/31/2021

I REMEMBER ONE OF THE first people who told me death was not real. In reality, my religious upbringing had already told me and I will return to that later. I went to visit a walled community of spiritualists outside Anderson, Indiana. The offices were closed but a very friendly gentleman came out to see what I wanted and showed me around the grounds and the bookstore. I told him that I had learned about them when some other people drove me through the night before like some sort of childhood walk through a cemetery for thrills. He laughed and said, "Oh! People are afraid of us because they do not understand us. They think we talk with the dead." I gave some generic response and he continued, "Of course we don't talk to the dead. If they were really dead, how would they answer us? There are people still wearing their skins and people who no longer do! But they aren't dead, or we would not be able to talk with them!" At the time, I thought it was funny even though he was serious. We had an enjoyable visit.

As I now consider the lack of physical evidence that we continue in some recognizable form as *dead people*, it also occurs to me that my literalist Christian upbringing was not that different. I was clearly taught that those who died were instantly *absent from the body, present with the Lord*. While my host in Chesterfield considered those who had left the body to be near at hand, we believed heaven to be a separate metaphysical realm (and used Bible verses to warn that attempts to communicate with the dead were an evil to be avoided). We were also taught that those who died without the saving grace of Jesus were instantly in hell, and we criticized Catholic theologies which included a middle ground called purgatory. Reflecting now, it is clear that each of those doctrines denied the existence of death as an ongoing state of being. When a person was no longer present in their body, they were present someplace else.[1]

After studying with Ma Jaya of Kashi Ashram, Arlo Guthrie recorded a similar thought in the song "Gates of Heaven," reducing death to only the moment of ceasing to breathe. Now as I will explore in "Final Illusion," I see a very real possibility that death is no more than a mental construct to express the absence of something we cherish. As dark and cold are actually description for the lack of light and heat rather than independent conditions, death is simply our language for the end of animation of the body. The evidence of physics tells me that at least everything that escapes our efforts to preserve and entomb the body returns to the universal whole. Rejoining the universal dance of matter and energy, particles and waves, what is no longer us can hardly be described as dead.

Pascal's wager now takes on a UFT twist for me. I place my chips on the square of life fully and beneficially lived assuming that *God* is the combination of physical forces that created and control the universe, and which will reclaim all that is me when my time is done. If I am correct, I win by living life in full wonder and gratitude now. If I am wrong and a I continue in some identifiable form, perhaps beyond the physical realm, then I turn to the teaching of Jesus in Matt 25 about the master identifying those who belong to him by their acts of love and concern while alive. Opposite of what I have always understood Pascal's wager to imply because I applied it to a purely spiritual God, rejecting anthropomorphized descriptions of God to live well while life remains, I still collect the prize!

---

1. Oddly, there was a simultaneous teaching in both Protestant and Catholic traditions which left the dead in the grave awaiting the final resurrection when Christ returned in victory of all evil including death.

The Final Illusion

1/31/2021

THERE IS NO SUCH THING as dark. There is light in varying amounts, or there is not. We love the beauty light reveals. Even the blind can feel the warmth of sunlight on skin. We love light and our minds create a concept for its absence, and we call it dark.

There is no such thing as cold. There are varying amounts of heat. Most of us enjoy warmth. A few enjoy the more extreme heat of the desert. But as heat decreases, its absence is uncomfortable for our warm-blooded bodies and our minds create a term for the absence of heat. So, we speak about the cold. My mother used to make us laugh during our "churchiest" days by using what she claimed was an old description of feeling, "Damp cold!" We often accused her of slips in pronunciation!

But only light and heat are real.

I think now the same is likely true of death. There is life. It is a treasure of great worth. We enjoy its moments, its memories, and its surprises. We mourn it when it is absent. And perhaps it is only a concept our minds create as a shorthand for its absence causing us to speak of death. Maybe there is no such thing as death.

There is life in varying degrees and capacities. Then there is not.

But that does not have to mean that death is real any more than dark or cold.

Because life is so good and beautiful, our use of language includes a term for its absence. That does not mean that there must be any real state of being described by the word dead.

While my particles and waves vibrate in this current form, I celebrate light, heat, and life itself and I am grateful. When this time is over,

I no longer hold to the belief that I shall continue as something dead. My vibrations will rejoin the universal background of particles and waves. I believe Buddha called that oneness nirvana. "Mansions" in the "Father's house" may be too specific. But they remain comforting language for the fact that there is room for all that is—for a brief moment—me to "go home" into the whole.

I am growing in my understanding of what it means to stop believing in death—just as science has taught me to realize that dark and cold are illusions created by the absence of energy we enjoy when present. The language is opposite of those who teach us that we must learn to accept death in order to free ourselves from the suffering of trying to deny it. But I believe the meaning is much the same. We are temporary phenomena and clinging to permanence brings suffering. What if beliefs in death are a form of clinging to the idea that we can be eternal, even in a negative form?

I choose life while life remains and happily accept that I will cease to exist as me in any form including dead when my time is over.

In church language, "Death, where is thy sting? Grave, where is thy victory?"

They are illusions.

The Universe Knows

2/11/2021

YEARS AFTER I BEGAN TO explore the possibilities of life and meaning in a universe where God is real, real by the laws of physics, two symbols of Christian belief remain ubiquitous in our home. In December our home is filled with nativity scenes from around the world. Resting in the manger's hay are babies from multiple continents surrounded by the holy family, shepherds, and wisemen of every body type and skin color, including characters from favorite animated shows and children's toys. The window ledge above the kitchen sink alone holds over a dozen. As beautiful as the diversity of displays is, why does this scene remain so significant in a universe where God's presence is constant and inescapable?

The other image which can be found in every room of the house throughout the year is the cross. My office contains multiple samples from various countries and one handmade by a friend. One contains the same pattern of a cross contained within a Star of David that I have worn every day of my life since high school. The one hanging in my office was purchased in Ethiopia when I discovered it was the symbol of Tigray, the home of the last great African emperor, Haile Selassie. But how does this image of torture required as a blood price for human forgiveness according to the teachings of evangelical Christianity fit with Unified Field Theology's focus on reality?

Seeing God as the combined forces which created and control the universe leaves no room for a sinful fall requiring salvation by a godchild born to die in humanity's place. These forces are inescapable. Ignoring them has immediate, not hidden soul-damaging consequences. I can step off a cliff without my climbing gear, but gravity will function instantly. It will not sit back waiting for me to realize my error and beg for forgiveness. Ignore gravity and we fall, but not from grace. When mankind overcomes gravity to venture into space, other forces have been carefully calculated to achieve the desired results. They do not cancel gravity, defy, or anger it. A universe without an anthropomorphic God does not require what theologians usually refer to as soteriology. There is no angered God to appease, no jealous God to pacify, and no eternal judge handing down sentences to be served. And still these images are precious in our home.

I began to explain my attraction to these symbols while still firmly within the evangelical fold, not realizing at the time how drastically my path was diverging from the faith of my youth. Students have been taught for as long as science has been an academic subject that humans are Earth's apex species. Begin with evolution and we are the end of the chain, at least for now. Begin with religion and we are the crown of creation. And yet one look at the night sky with any awareness of astronomy and we know that we are barely viruses on the cosmic scale. Long ago, still clinging to concepts of a metaphysical super image of man as God, the message in these icons gained new meaning for me in the context of our desire to be known. In the texts of the Israelites God hears their cries and shows up, repeatedly. Setting aside distractions of blood-price payments, in Christianity God does it again. God shows up. God experiences human life as one of us and goes to death by ancient torture absorbing our pain while telling us that the greatest truth is that we must love. Still, I refuse to accept a belief simply because we want it, need it, desperately seek for it to be true. Our need does not make our constructions of comforts true just because we need them. Need is not evidence or proof.

Now a new awareness is beginning to intersect these ideas. Over the past several decades we have discovered that animals are aware in ways that were previously considered impossible. Young gorillas do not remove traps after observing the death of an infant by some instinctual skill. It is an act that demonstrates intelligence. It also demonstrates an awareness of the loss of life and an ability and willingness to remove the threat for others. We have discovered other things beyond our previous imagination. Trees in old growth forests care for other trees. Trees being eaten by giraffes give off scent which warns other trees which change the taste of their leaves in response. Flowers change their chemistry in response to the buzzing of bees in order to become more attractive. Our previous views said it was all autonomic response. But this does not have to be true merely because we are ignorant of other mechanisms any more than religion has to be true just because we desire its comfort.

The universe observes, questions, contemplates, fears, admires, grieves, and dances. We know that it does because we are momentary configurations of it. We know our own experiences but fail to attribute them to the whole.

Unable to communicate with other animate and inanimate forms, we previously assumed, based on our lack of evidence, that our experience is unique. This causes us to believe that consciousness begins and ends with us. And yet common speech contains idioms which point to a vague concept of awareness in other objects. Expressions like "If these walls could speak" or "What stories that guitar could tell" are taken as expressions of memories beyond our reach. I have not heard them used implying that physical objects truly observe or remember events except perhaps in fictions of paranormal events. However, I see a possibility that they indicate ideas, near perceptions, about nature that lie just beyond the trained logic of our post-enlightenment minds.

In recent years, hints like those mentioned above emerged that we are wrong about the experience and the responses of both plants and animals. The evidence is small and regarded by most as on the fringe of science. But evidence indicates that the universe contemplates itself. We are the evidence. When we see and feel, contemplate and construct meaning, the universe is doing those things as us. We may proclaim like Descartes, "*Cogito, ergo sum.*" But we exceed reality if we then imply that we are something other than brief combinations of star dust. We are the universe. We are very small pieces in our individual bodies. But we are pieces of the universe, not beings from beyond the material world. Everything we can do, the universe therefore does. We are just beginning to record how the universe perceives itself in forms other than our own.

Although previous religions taught us that we exist in some metaphysical form that extends beyond the natural universe and therefore have an objective platform or divine source of revealed knowledge that makes our observations and responses unique, we are contained within the world that is. We arise from dust and return to dust. The religions of the world do not deny it. The evidence that is us says that the elements of Earth combine in ways that experience awareness of beauty and pain, the mystery of the small and the grandeur of the transcendently immense. Without evidence to the contrary, would it not be more reasonable to assume that it is in the nature of the cosmos to wonder at itself? Some in science are now bold enough to ask whether consciousness may be contained in tiny proportions within every single particle of matter.

Here, I return to the idea that people are rarely taken in by claims that are blatantly untrue throughout. Those skilled at manipulating others know to include as much truth as possible in order to make the whole of the explanation believable. In the past, awareness of this allowed me to explore beliefs different from my own by seeking to tease out what appeared to be true among the teachings I did not accept. As my awareness of the nature of the universe grows, the old symbols which remain so dear suggest to me that a truth beyond what I understood was there all along. The universe has not changed its rules. We are growing in our understanding.

The universe knows itself and we are part of it, not separate meta-beings. The universe responds to itself and changes according to rules we understand and ones that still exceed our grasp. But what if the universe is self-aware? Observations of both subatomic particles and galaxies appearing to act in unison across immense distances indicate connection rather than randomness. If the universe is conscious of itself, then we are known. The forces of the universe do not have to put on human flesh to know us. The universe knows itself including us. That awareness would include our pain and comfort for our pain. We see it most easily when we live the way many of our religions have long told us to do. When we love each other, we experience that love exists in the universe. But perhaps we err when we assume that it only happens when it happens through us. We simply are not that universally significant. We are our own evidence for exploring the universe, but we are not the universe.

Now when I look at each of those beautiful babes in mangers, I hear, "You are not alone." It is absurd to argue otherwise. We are part of the universe and cannot escape it. We are also animated by the same powers that fuel everything that happens. When I look at those crosses, I am aware that the universe knows our pain and does in fact absorb it. Sometimes it absorbs it by the comfort of others, sometimes it is absorbed by time in nature, or by quieting our own noise to allow peace to manifest itself. For some we usually consider unfortunate, it is death itself which removes all pain as what was configured for a short time as a human reunites with the whole.

I am beginning to see that I am known because the universe knows itself. I am starting to see the image of self-correcting love and justice found in Jesus and the cross in the self-regulating nature of the entire universe. It reaches me when I am in need because it is in the very nature of all that is. Now the old promise of 1 Cor 13:12 takes on universal potential. In the present we still know in part, but we look forward to a day when we will know as fully as we are known.

Symbols of faith hold the meaning we attach to them. While God and truth were somewhere out there in the unreachable spiritual realm, the manger and the cross—the incarnation and the assumption of our suffering—reassured me that I could trust the power of the universe because it cared enough to be one of us. It was willing to experience our joys and deepest wounds. I could walk through dark times assured that I was known and that I belonged. Now, I have moved to more universal understandings. I can declare that religious warnings that rejecting the precise teachings of my youth would result in the unravelling of all basis for meaning have proven false. The universe fully knows us now while we live. All ideas of living separate from it are illusions. We are here. We belong. We are known. The meaning of the art forms in my home has grown to dimensions previously unimagined.

Universal consciousness is more than a mental or spiritual state sought by humans through ancient or new age practices. Consciousness of all is not merely a human goal. It is a description of the nature of the universe knowing itself including us. I can now add omniscient to my list of attributes of God which are pervasive in the physical realm. No external spirit is required. The universe knows and contemplates itself.

I now dare to say that I begin to know as I am known.

Death and the Circle of Life

2/12/2021

DEATH AS PART OF THE cycle of life can be found in biology texts, Disney movies, and cliches of comfort at services of remembrance. When the expression points to an ongoing process of life replaced by new life beyond the span of any one individual, it makes sense. And for those comforted by the larger picture of continued existence, it is helpful. However, the image can also carry misconceptions.

When used in reference to a single life, it seems to place death at the end. Yet circles have no end. That is the beauty of the shape that comforts us. They continue. We continue. As individuals, death would seem to be a break in the circle unless one accepts teachings of reincarnation implying rebirth as a new manifestation of the same individual. I do not. What is the circle of life and how does death fit on it?

My life has gone through several cycles already. I have gone from health to illness that seemed endless, back to apparent health, and then to acceptance of conditions that remain part of who I am as a physical being and the discovery of new anomalies that come with age. Spiritually I have gone many times from certainty; to mystery, questions, and doubt; and around to new appearances of certainty. Now, the death of one of the final remaining members of my father's family reminds me that I have traveled many times through the valley of death.

It is not the dead who experience death. The dying certainly experience the waning of strength and vitality, sometimes the lessening of awareness, and often when there is sufficient time a releasing of the desire to remain in a life that has become little more than suffering. There is, however, no valid evidence that those who die experience anything on the other side of that process. Grief and the dying of all imagined futures with that individual belong to us, the living. We are the ones who cry and attempt to comfort one another. We who continue the cycles of life know the anguish expressed by Gilbert and Sullivan that aching hearts do not die[1] but continue through the cycles of grief and reclaiming relationship with life.

I now picture death as an event that occurs many times on the circle of an individual life. Some schools of psychology tell us that it appears short of physical demise as we are forced to surrender images of our parents as perfect, of our life plans as certain, and of protecting our children from suffering. The longer we are given to live, the more times we experience the literal end of other lives. We are the ones who must cope with the finality of the separations whether we turn to the comforts of religious promises or not. At times this circle feels cruel to me as losses occur that seem out of sequence or logical explanation. It brings pain when the lost loved one is longed for decades after their time has ended. But still the circle of our own lives and the bigger cycle of the continuation of the species continue.

Recent contemplations and possible realizations also bring me a new view of this circle. While we live, we are combinations of particles and energy more complex than anything the mind can fully grasp. But we are mere combinations of the elements and forces that surround and contain us, nonetheless. Conscious thought causes us to see ourselves as separate. But I now see reason to challenge that seemingly obvious conclusion. Every moment of what we call life we are exchanging particles and energy with the environment which surrounds us. Every second we are different combinations than we were the moment before. Taught to see matter as solid, liquid, and gas my mind asserts that I am separate from this chair, this room, and the air that fills it. But every moment my body exchanges CO_2 for O_2. To remain alive, I take both liquids and solids into my body through digestion to energize and replace cells, and what was distinct plant, animal, or mineral becomes part of the combination I perceive as myself.

Beginning to see the universe as it exists at the quantum level complicates the picture further. The particles that vibrate within me are the same as those in the entire room, the space outside it, and the universe. They interchange unnoticed as I sit and try to communicate through

---

1. See "Alone and Yet Alive" in Pryce-Jones, *Gilbert and Sullivan*.

keystrokes on a machine designed to store and transmit my thoughts yet considered inanimate. The separation begins to fade into the realization that my difference from the other objects and energy that surround me is an illusion.

I have stated many times that I now find comfort in the idea that when my time of conscious existence ends all that is me will return to the source from which it came. While I do not believe those quanta will continue to be me, I do believe that they will continue and that some will become part of other living forms even as my lunch became part of me. But I am beginning to see it at another level that gives pause to my use of terms of existence and returning. Even as I sit and type this essay, I am part of the dynamics of this room. The phenomenon of conscious thought by the particles assembled as me does not prove that I exist separate from the rest until I am reunited after death. I am inescapably part of all that is now.

While the cycles of my thinking continue, I will experience joy from interactions with others and grief when relationships end. But we are not separate. We are part of a unified whole we cannot yet quantify by a single mathematical expression. We do not fully comprehend it yet, but we are fully immersed in and part of an immense whole that started from a single point in what our minds call nothing. When my time to leave the circle comes, I hope I have found some way to let those who may mourn the passing of our ability to interact know that I remain while the universe remains. Everything known as me was here from the time the universe formed. I enjoy these years when I experience the awareness of my existence. But when that awareness ends, I will remain part of the whole—same as I always was.

Matchsticks Contemplating Eternity

4/29/2021

IN THE END, WHAT ARE WE?

We live longer than many species and pass away much quicker than others. In the development of life on our planet, science tells us we are very recent arrivals. Yet, our brain capacity has enabled us to sustain very large populations and highly consumptive lifestyles—for a time.

We fight with our neighbors over the sound of pets and sticks in our yards, then we turn our minds to eternity and develop complex systems of belief to show that our lives are significant. We rescue lost and injured animals and poison the entire planet. We can build devices to take us to the moon and beyond, and we create weapons that can erase entire cities in an instant. We produce novels, concertos, and works of art in all sizes and configurations, and we spray obscene graffiti on places of worship belonging to people we do not understand.

My Sunday school teachers taught me that we are the pinnacle and the purpose of all creation. My schoolteachers taught me that we are the highest known advancement of evolution. Influenced by teachings of the native people of my country, I see us as the youngest siblings in the family of life.

We are temporary assemblies of biochemicals made entirely of the matter of this planet. In other essays I have discussed the immensity of the odds that any one of us would be the exact combination of features that we are. Somehow those combinations have become complex enough to give us the ability to think about our thinking and our being, and we seek proof that we matter—that we are more than meaningless accidents determined by chance and then erased by decomposition.

I have grown fond of a metaphor that came to me recently. We are matchsticks that dream of eternity.

Like the wood of the stick, we are composed of material derived from the matter of plants. These older lifeforms perform the amazing task of drawing in minerals and water, air and energy, and form the substance of their own bodies. We exist only by consuming them either directly or through the animals that consumed them before becoming our chosen sustenance. Our bodies are made of earth transformed by plants. It is ours for a time and when our time is done it returns to soil as surely as it came from soil.

And we have developed an ability to blaze forth and produce light. Some of us spend our lives attempting to create warmth, comfort, and safety for those around us. Others seem determined to light grand conflagrations and measure their significance by all they can destroy. But it seems to me that our collective reality tends to snuff out such destructive examples, although sometimes at a price of great pain.

Artists and scientists alike use their light to show us life in ever more amazing and beautiful ways. Like the great authors of antiquity whose light continues as thought recorded in symbols, they help us to see beyond the limits of our own sight. And we wonder about the immensity of all that is. At our best, we often become silent and simply let awe be awe.

Matchsticks are small. But the light of a single stick can reveal the reality within a large cavern. The fire of a single matchstick can begin the process of illuminating candlelight which brings an inspiring glow to the largest of cathedrals. It can also begin a blaze that consumes miles of forest destroying the homes of both humans and other species. We hold in our small beings the capacity for great beauty or immense harm. And some wait like literal matchsticks and simply mold away in the box waiting for some greater power to ignite their flame.

My mind leaps and rejoices. The beauty of newly revealed truth and the mystery of things we may never know excite every fiber of my being. The stories of the ancients and the data of the newest studies both bring light to my inner being. I am amazed by the world that surrounds us; that is us. I am comforted by the idea that the particles and energy which currently animate what I call me will continue while the universe endures. I pray that the ideas and the words I share may bring light and warmth to those who are drawn to them now and at any time in the future that someone might pick up one of my small offerings.

We are matchsticks contemplating eternity.

Bibliography

"Abraham Lincoln Quotes." https://www.historynet.com/abraham-lincoln-quotes.
Bell, Derek. *Faces at the Bottom of the Well*. New York: Basic, 2018.
Bhagavati, Ma Jaya Sati, and Jean Houston. *How God Found Me: Memoirs of an American Guru*. Sebastian, FL: Kashi, 2020.
"Black Elk Quotes." https://www.azquotes.com/author/4438-Black_Elk#google_vignette.
Blake, William. "Auguries of Innocence." http://www.public-domain-poetry.com/william-blake/auguries-of-innocence-9210.
Blanchot, Maurice. *The Unavowable Community*. Barrytown, NY: Station Hill, 1988.
Bloom, Alan. *The Closing of the American Mind*. New York: Simon & Schuster, 1987.
Bramley, Barrie. "S. M. Lockridge—It's Friday, but Sunday's Coming." *Barrie Bramley* (blog), August 3, 2018. https://medium.com/@barrie.bramley/s-m-lockridge-its-friday-but-sunday-s-coming-b2b4df2d7de3.
Brinton, Crane. *Anatomy of Revolution*. New York: Vintage, 1965.
Brown, Gregory. "The Two Trees of Genesis 2:9." In *Unified Field Theology: A Journey from Evangelical Fundamentalism to Faith in What Is*, 166–68. Eugene, OR: Wipf & Stock, 2018.
Brueggemann, Walter. *Theology of the Old Testament: Testimony, Dispute, Advocacy*. Minneapolis: Fortress, 1997.
Choi, Charles. "Weird 'Buckyballs' May Be at Root of Milky Way Mystery." https://www.space.com/29977-buckyball-molecules-milky-way-mystery.html.
Das, Ram, and Bush, Mirabai. *Walking Each Other Home: Conversations on Loving and Dying*. Louisville, CO: Sounds True, 2018.
Dawkins, Richard. *The God Delusion*. Boston: Mariner, 2008.
"Declaration of Independence: A Transcription." https://www.archives.gov/founding-docs/declaration-transcript.
Deloria, Vine. *God Is Red: A Native View of Religion*. Golden, CO: Fulcrum, 1992.
Dias, Elizabeth. "Christianity Will Have Power." *The New York Times*, August 9, 2020. https://www.nytimes.com/2020/08/09/us/evangelicals-trump-christianity.html.
Dietrich, Oliver, et al. "Cult as a Driving Force of Human History: A View From Göbekli Tepe." *Expedition* 59.3 (2017) 11–27.
Donahue, Michelle. "Flowers Can Hear Buzzing Bees—and It Makes Their Nectar Sweeter." *National Geographic*, January 15, 2019. https://www.nationalgeographic.com/science/article/flowers-can-hear-bees-and-make-their-nectar-sweeter#:~:text=Flowers%20can%20hear%20buzzing%20

bees%E2%80%94and%20it%20makes%20their%20nectar%20sweeter,-%E2%80%9CI'd%20like&text=Hadany's%20team%20looked%20at%20evening,sugar%20in%20their%20flowers'%20nectar.

Eckhart, Meister. "If the Only Prayer You Ever Say in Your Entire Life Is Thank You, It Will Be Enough." https://www.quotes.net/quote/51524.

Ehrman, Bart. *Did Jesus Exist? The Historical Argument for Jesus of Nazareth.* New York: HarperOne, 2012.

———. *How Jesus Became God: The Exaltation of a Jewish Preacher from Galilee.* New York: HarperOne, 2015.

Ehrmann, Max. "Desiderata." https://www.desiderata.com/desiderata.html.

Elkin, Eric. "The Devil Made Me Do It." https://ordinaryvoices.org/reflect/the-devil-made-me-do-it.

Flurry, Gerald, and Brad Macdonald. "The Mystery of the Two Trees: No One in Modern History Understood the Truth about the Two Trees More Deeply Than Herbert W. Armstrong." https://pcg.church/articles/1757/the-mystery-of-the-two-trees.

Francis of Assisi. "The Prayer of Saint Francis." https://www.ourcatholicprayers.com.

Garrison, C. E. "Relativism and Absolutism: Keeping College Students Involved in the Examination of Truth." *College Student Journal* 35 (2001) 517–22.

Gaskin, Stephen. *This Season's People.* Summertown, TN: The Book, 1976.

Goff, Philip. *Galileo's Error: Foundations for a New Science of Consciousness.* New York: Pantheon, 2019.

Gornitz, Thomas. "Quantum Theory and the Nature of Consciousness." *Foundations of Science* 23 (2018) 475–510. https://doi.org/10.1007/s10699-017-9536-9.

Grant, Richard. "The Whispering of the Trees." *Smithsonian Magazine*, March 2018.

Greene, Brian. "Particles and Consciousness: From Life to Mind." In *Until the End of Time: Mind, Matter, and Our Search for Meaning in an Evolving Universe,* 115–59. New York: Knopf, 2020.

Gross, Terry. "Heaven and Hell Are 'Not What Jesus Preached,' Religion Scholar Says." *NPR*, March 31, 2020. https://www.npr.org/2020/03/31/824479587/heaven-and-hell-are-not-what-jesus-preached-religion-scholar-says.

Guthrie, Arlo. "Neutron Bomb." *Precious Friend.* Recorded in 1981. Warner Bros., 1982. Compact disc.

Hall, Thelma. *Too Deep for Words: Rediscovering Lectio Divina.* New York: Paulist, 1988.

Hanh, Thich Nhat. *Old Path White Clouds.* Berkeley: Parallax, 1991.

Harrison, Chris. "Bible Cross References." https://www.chrisharrison.net/index.php/Visualizations/BibleViz.

Hawking, Stephen. "Is There a God?" In *Brief Answers to the Big Questions,* 23–38. New York: Bantam, 2018.

Hirsch, E. D. *Cultural Literacy: What Every American Needs to Know.* New York: Vintage, 1988.

"How Many Animals Were on Noah's Ark?" https://arkencounter.com/animals/how-many.

Johnson-Groh, Mara. "Does the Universe Rotate?" *Live Science,* July 7, 2019. https://www.livescience.com/65882-does-the-universe-rotate.html.

Kaplan, Robert. *The Nothing That Is: A Natural History of Zero.* Oxford: University Press, 1999.

Kastrup, Bernadino, et al. "Coming to Grips with the Implications of Quantum Mechanics." *Scientific American,* May 29, 2018. https://blogs.scientificamerican.

com/observations/coming-to-grips-with-the-implications-of-quantum-mechanics/.

Kimmerer, Robin Wall. *Braiding Sweetgrass: Indigenous Wisdom, Scientific Knowledge, and the Teachings of Plants*. Minneapolis: Milkweed, 2013.

Kraus, Lawrence, and Richard Dawkins. *A Universe from Nothing: Why There Is Something Rather Than Nothing*. New York: Free, 2013.

Leary, Kyree. "After a Year Away from Earth, Scott Kelly's "Space Genes" Set Him Apart from His Twin." *Futurism*, March 15, 2018. https://futurism.com/nasa-twin-study-kelly-preliminary.

Lee, Joon Hyeop, et al. "Mysterious Coherence in Several-megaparsec Scales between Galaxy Rotation and Neighbor Motion." *The Astrophysical Journal* 884.2 (2019) 1–16.

Letzter, Rafi. "Photons Could Reveal 'Massive Gravity,' New Theory Suggests." https://www.space.com/graviton-photon-interaction-hunting-machine.html.

Levine, Amy-Jill. *The Misunderstood Jew: The Church and the Scandal of the Jewish Jesus*. San Francisco: HarperOne, 2007.

Lewis, C. S. *The Voyage of the Dawn Treader*. New York: HarperCollins, 2001.

———. *Surprised by Joy: The Shape of My Early Life*. New York: HarperOne, 2017.

Lincoln, Yvonne, and Egon Guba. *Naturalistic Inquiry*. Newbury Park, CA: Sage, 1985.

Martindale, Wayne, and Jerry Root. *The Quotable Lewis*. Carol Stream, IL: Tyndale, 1990.

Matloff, Gregory. "Can Panpsychism Become an Observational Science?" *Journal of Consciousness Exploration & Research* 7.7 (2016) 1–16.

Northcutt, Wendy. *The Darwin Awards: Survival of the Fittest*. New York: Plume, 2004.

Parker, Theodore. "Of Justice and the Conscience." 1853. https://quoteinvestigator.com/2012/11/15/arc-of-universe/.

"Paul Tillich Quotes." https://www.brainyquote.com/quotes/paul_tillich_114353.

Porter, Gene Straton. *A Girl of the Limberlost*. New York: Grosset & Dunlap, 1909.

Pryce-Jones, John. *Gilbert and Sullivan: The Mikado*. D'Oyly Carte Opera Company. Sony Classical, October 1993. 2 compact discs.

Rohr, Richard. *Everything Belongs: The Gift of Contemplative Prayer*. New York: Crossroad, 1999.

Sandburg, Carl. *Abraham Lincoln: The Prairie Years and the War Years*. Vol. 2, *The War Years, 1861–1864*. New York: Dell, 1970.

Schaeffer, Edith. *Christianity Is Jewish*. Carol Stream, IL: Tyndale, 1977.

Schaeffer, Francis. *Escape from Reason*. London: IV, 1968.

Sigman, Michael. "A Brief History of Loving or Leaving America." *Huffington Post*, December 6, 2017. https://www.huffpost.com/entry/rick-santorum-dennis-terry_b_1377023.

Sinclair, Upton. "It Is Difficult to Get a Man to Understand Something When His Salary Depends Upon His Not Understanding It." https://quoteinvestigator.com/2017/11/30/salary.

"Slavery Today." https://www.freetheslaves.net/our-model-for-freedom/slavery-today.

Smith, Drew. "How Many Possible Combinations of DNA Are There?" *Forbes*, January 20, 2017. https://www.forbes.com/sites/quora/2017/01/20/how-many-possible-combinations-of-dna-are-there.

Strickland, Lloyd. "Answering the Biggest Question of All: Why Is There Something Rather than Nothing." *The Conversation*, November 11, 2016. https://

theconversation.com/answering-the-biggest-question-of-all-why-is-there-something-rather-than-nothing-65865.

Strobel, Lee. *The Case for a Creator: A Journalist Investigates Scientific Evidence that Points toward God*. Grand Rapids, MI: Zondervan, 2014.

TED-Ed. "The Higgs Field, Explained—Don Lincoln." *YouTube*, August 27, 2013. https://www.youtube.com/watch?v=joTKd5j3mzk&t=3s.

Than, Ker. "Gorilla Youngsters Seen Dismantling Poachers' Traps—A First." *National Geographic*, July 18, 2012. https://www.nationalgeographic.com/animals/article/120719-young-gorillas-juvenile-traps-snares-rwanda-science-fossey.

Tillich, Paul. *Loneliness and Solitude*. New York: Scribner's, 1963.

———. *The Eternal Now*. New York: Scribner's, 1963.

Tolstoy, Leo. *The Kingdom of God Is Within You*. New York: Barnes & Noble, 2005.

Van Halen, Alex. "Humans Being." Track 1 on *Twister: Music From the Motion Picture Soundtrack*. Los Angeles: Warner Records, 1996. Compact disc.

Viorst, Judith. *Necessary Losses: The Loves, Illusions, Dependencies and Impossible Expectations That All of Us Have to Give Up in Order to Grow*. New York: Fawcett Gold Medal, 1986.

Weick, Karl. *The Social Psychology of Organizing*. New York: Random House, 1979.

Whitehouse, Harvey, et al. "Complex Societies Precede Moralizing Gods throughout World History." *Nature* 568 (2019) 226–29.

Wilson, Glenn. "Nature Abhors a Vacuum: From Aristotle to Thoreau." *New American Journal*, July 14, 2019. https://www.newamericanjournal.net/2019/07/nature-abhors-a-vacuum-from-aristotle-to-thoreau.

Wohlleben, Peter. *The Hidden Life of Trees: What They Feel, How They Communicate: Discoveries from a Secret World*. Vancouver: Greystone, 2016.

www.ingramcontent.com/pod-product-compliance
Lightning Source LLC
Chambersburg PA
CBHW071224290426
44108CB00013B/1284